Are We There Yet?
Another American Journey

Julian Bishop

Published by Travellers Press

Copyright © 2023 Julian Bishop
All rights reserved.

ISBN: 978-1-7364460-4-1

To Lorna

Thank you for accompanying me on life's continuing journey

Acknowledgments

While I am passionate about researching and writing, I loathe editing. At this stage of book production, I promise myself never to write again. Lorna supposes it is a bit like childbirth.

Nonetheless, the book's quality leaps forward with each round of edits, and for that, I owe immense gratitude to my two dedicated editors.

Sarah Maguire once again displayed remarkable skill during the developmental editing stage. Her dedication, sharp insights, and courage drastically enhanced the book's structure, flow, and voice. I appreciated her pedantic wit, which eased the pain of harshly delivered feedback. I hope the final version will astound Sarah, bearing little resemblance to the one she reviewed in the summer of 2023.

Stephen Bland reprised his role as the meticulous copyeditor, providing detailed critiques line by line. Though we may debate whether a compound adjective requires a hyphen if one of its component parts is an adverb, the sheer volume of his comments has immeasurably elevated the book's quality.

Despite the above help, any remaining mistakes and errors are mine and mine alone. I will correct them in the second edition…maybe.

I want to thank Lorna and Johannes Terblanche for again helping me craft the book's title. It amazes me that I can conjure 135,000 words with relative ease but struggle to synthesize their essence into a concise title. Having discarded contemporary thinking of merely incorporating Amazon keywords in the title of one's book—apparently, the ideal title is 'Scissor Skills for Five-Year-Olds'—our collaborative brainstorming eventually alighted on a title that embodied multiple interpretations.

Contents

Prologue v
Chapter 1 – Becoming American 1
Chapter 2 – Selling An American House 22
Chapter 3 – The Southernmost Point 35
Chapter 4 – An East Coast Road Trip 67
Chapter 5 – The Big Apple 87
Chapter 6 – New York City's Boroughs 100
Chapter 7 – Philadelphia and the First State 125
Chapter 8 – The Lowcountry of South Carolina 147
Chapter 9 – Taking French Leave 161
Chapter 10 – An Italian History Lesson 193
Chapter 11 – A Reunited Italy 227
Chapter 12 – Bouncing Around Florida 257
Chapter 13 – Venice, The Florida One 295
Postscript – 2023 Updates 331

Prologue

I wrote my debut book, *High, Wide, and Handsome,* as a primer to introduce American culture to both new immigrants and foreigners with a keen interest in the USA. To my surprise, the book sold most copies to natural-born Americans who wanted to learn more about the origins of their own culture... from a Brit. I was delighted to discover these introspective Americans seemed to be okay with the history segments, too; it was as if they regretted not paying closer attention during their thirteen years of civics education.

The narrative arc of this second book begins in 2021 with us being sworn in as American citizens, and it follows our nomadic journeys through America (and Europe). *Are We There Yet?* is a travel book exploring some of America's cultural breadth. It describes a complex country with sizeable communities that defy the American stereotype.

As in the first book, I sidetrack myself easily on all manner of topics that I personally find interesting, including, this time, a whole chapter on Italy. I hope you, too, find these diversions worthy of your time.

Are We There Yet? delves into the minutiae of American culture. It addresses pardoning turkeys, living in a van, the best place to stand at a parade, how you gain entrance to a speakeasy, why Americans are so impulsive, how to behave on a dog beach, when to prepare for a hurricane, why there are so few drive-in movie theaters, and the value a stager brings to the home-buying process (plot spoiler—none). And by the end of the book, you will better understand alligators, the Amish, voting machines, Italian history and behavior, juvenile detention centers, US sports, and one hundred other pieces of American culture.

The European reception of *High, Wide, and Handsome* was also positive. I am delighted when readers tell me they now understand some aspect of American behavior that was hitherto incomprehensible. No author is happier than when someone validates the purpose of a book.

However, I regularly meet a few Europeans who delight in telling me that America is in inevitable decline and that its time as the dominant superpower is almost at an end. Taking a long-term historical timeframe, they will eventually be proven correct. You do not need to have read Edward Gibbon's fourteen-hundred-page *The History of the Decline and Fall of the Roman Empire* (and I haven't) to know that America, like all great civilizations before it, will eventually decline.

I would like to thank those gleeful Europeans for motivating me to tackle the challenging subject of the US's future in this second book. However, as another plot spoiler, I should tell you that my thesis is that the United States is still in the growth stage of its time in the sun, and I predict that, by the end of this century, America will be at least as dominant on the world stage as it is now.

Were you foolish enough to ask me why, I would give you a dozen reasons for this projection.

The first driver for my optimism is that America has massive economic, structural, and geopolitical advantages over other would-be superpower competitors. So, let's start with the economic tailwinds:

1. The USA was founded on entrepreneurialism, and almost two hundred and fifty years later, American society retains this pervasive entrepreneurial behavior at the heart of its culture. Americans of all backgrounds crave to establish and grow businesses and have a staggering desire to take risks. Compared to many other countries, there is an immense reward if you succeed and a low penalty when you fail. These encourage unsuccessful entrepreneurs to keep trying until they are successful.
2. It is easy to fund your innovation. For example, it is estimated that three hundred thousand US Angel investors are looking for the next big idea, and for those startups that survive, America has the world's most mature venture capital industry. Despite the 2023 banking crisis, the US also has a decentralized banking system of several thousand banks eager to lend money to entrepreneurs with credible business plans.
3. Large US companies have a track record of transforming themselves to avoid obsolescence. Perhaps they will diversify into a different segment of the value chain or strategically

borrow to acquire the technological advantage of an innovative competitor.

Unlike most of its potential superpower rivals, the USA will sustain a workforce to deliver continued prosperity:

4. While there have been signs of a declining natural birth rate over the past decade, the USA's one-third-of-a-billion population continues to grow through immigration. Unlike most prospective superpowers, America's population will remain youthful and adaptable, with a favorable worker-to-dependent ratio.
5. According to global ranking tables, the United States is home to nearly two-thirds of the world's top universities. This robust university system nurtures homegrown talent and draws ambitious students from around the globe. After graduation, most of these talented individuals opt to stay in the US, actively bolstering the American economy. Also, in contrast to Europe, there is a close-knit partnership between the academic and startup communities, which fosters a rapid pace of high-tech entrepreneurship.
6. While a few Asian countries work more hours, the average American works 25 percent more than their European counterpart (and has 30 percent higher productivity for each hour they work). While this may not be good for work-life balance, working longer hours produces higher real incomes, is good for the economy, and funds government investment.

Contrary to what you may hear on the Fox News channel (and believe me, I hear very little), the American system of government continues to support business.

7. The US boasts the most decentralized political system among industrialized nations. This approach fosters healthy competition between states, particularly in areas that promote economic prosperity, while simultaneously limiting the scope of centralized government. Consequently, states actively vie for businesses and residents by embracing more lenient regulations, reducing legal liabilities, and lowering tax structures.
8. The USA still has less government than any other significant OECD country. This translates into lower taxation levels and higher incentives to work.

9. The US has a more favorable regulatory environment than most other countries. Although far from perfect, regulations are less burdensome on American businesses than those imposed by the European Union or China. Starting a business in America is easy as is restructuring it through bankruptcy.
10. The presence of state-owned enterprises is minimal, and union representation, which typically focuses on the interests of those currently employed rather than job seekers, remains low. Consequently, unemployment rates are lower, and individuals—particularly the young—are likelier to secure suitable employment. This environment fosters a conducive atmosphere for innovation among established companies and provides a more favorable landscape for the emergence of new businesses.

Finally, the US has an undeniable geopolitical advantage:

11. Having only two land neighbors and maintaining enduring friendly relations with both, the United States enjoys a unique position. While America may choose to engage in conflicts in distant regions, the prospect of an enemy invading the US mainland remains remote. With South and Central America lacking significant military power, any potential aggressor would face the formidable barrier of the Pacific or Atlantic Oceans, virtually inconceivable given the unrivaled supremacy of the US Navy. Furthermore, the United States maintains military dominance, boasting an annual defense budget that surpasses the combined budgets of the following eleven countries, most of which are long-standing allies. Nations not aligned with the US tend to possess comparatively limited military capabilities. As we currently see in Ukraine, the USA can counter the geopolitical aspirations of rival powers by arming its allies.
12. America is self-sufficient in almost everything and relies on others for neither food nor energy. When the planet erupts into worldwide conflict again, I believe the US will fare better than most. In these circumstances, America's economy may decline but not as much as other putative superpowers.

The second factor supporting my prediction that the United States will maintain its status as the dominant superpower is the formidable barriers hindering its competitors—which are likely insurmountable, at least within this century. For instance, when comparing the USA to its nearest rival, it still has three times China's wealth and five times the military capabilities.

With only 5 percent of the world's population, the USA has 25 percent of its wealth and 40 percent of its military spending. Even as the BRIC+ countries have grown significantly wealthier, the US share of the world's output is the same as thirty years ago (while that of Europe has almost halved). Indeed, an investor in the US stock market would have received four times the returns of those who invested in the other G7 countries.

Now, at this point in the proceedings, I understand you will probably regret having asked the question (which, of course, you didn't).

Will all of this be easy? Will the US always get its own way? Can America prevent all attacks on its people? Will Americans be popular in the rest of the world? The answer to all of these questions is no.

Of course, I can also hear some muttered counterarguments. It may surprise you to hear that I agree with many of them:

Some US infrastructure is crumbling, and government investment has been squandered when budgets should have been balanced. US debt is now almost an average of $100,000 per citizen, compared to $20,000 just over twenty years ago. Accordingly, US government and consumer debt have rapidly become unwieldy.

America would undoubtedly benefit from more adept political leaders and robust institutions to navigate itself away from the dangerously polarized political climate we see today. It's plausible to concede that the US will continue to endure a predominance of subpar political leaders motivated by personal ambition and short-term perspectives. But bear this in mind, with only a few exceptions, the nineteenth century witnessed a string of lackluster US presidents. Despite this era of weak federal leadership, it did not impede America's ascent to becoming the world's dominant economy.

Finally—and perhaps most crucially—the escalating levels of inequality and internal tension in the United States expose profound societal divisions that threaten the nation's unity. The top 1 percent have unimaginable wealth. However, contrary to what people believe, America's poor have fared better in the last thirty years. Their real incomes (ie, after inflation) have risen by three-quarters, while those in the rest of the developed world have stagnated. Even in the US's poorest state, Mississippi, the average person has higher purchasing power earnings than their comparator in a wealthy European country such as France or the UK.

Enough of these bullet points—I promise I won't use them again.

These caveats underscore the reasons behind the book's title, *Are We There Yet?* The simple answer is, 'Not yet, kids.'

Americans' faith in their country as 'the greatest in the world' is waning, with just over half currently holding that belief. But, contrary to what some European folk think, Americans aren't fools. They know the USA doesn't rank among the top twenty countries for many vital metrics, including education, health, infant mortality, life expectancy, and mental health diagnosis, to name just five. I hope that we will take deliberate steps to improve these weaker areas.

In any case, it is positive that America is adopting a less complacent stance regarding its status as the greatest country in the world. One never achieves true greatness by resting on one's laurels.

The United States is uniquely positioned and blessed with a geography that lends itself to prosperity. It stands as a land of boundless optimism and opportunity, fostering a robust economy. The nation upholds the cherished principles of freedom, including the right to assemble, practice religion, express beliefs, and speak one's mind. With a deeply rooted and steadfast democracy, the voice of the majority prevails, while the Constitution safeguards the rights of the minority. Furthermore, America still clings to the mantle of leadership in the 'free world,' championing democracy, human rights, and justice. The nation's commitment to combat tyranny, wherever it may arise—or at the very least, where a compelling strategic advantage aligns—remains unwavering.

Everything can change, though. The technological advancements we've seen in the last twenty years have primed us for even more rapid changes in the twenty-first century. However, forecasting the direction and breadth of these changes remains a formidable challenge. One thing is clear, however—we expect a lot of change, and a flourishing society must be ready to adapt to it.

Artificial Intelligence (and other fourth industrial revolution technologies) will make the world unrecognizable in the final third of my lifetime. Microcomputers will be even more pervasive. They have already transformed how we consume information, how we communicate, and how we entertain ourselves. New devices now clean our homes, automatically order food, and keep us alive. Social media brings those with common interests together (as well as tearing our communities and relationships apart), with governments, companies, and influential people no longer controlling the flow of information. And these changes are just the beginning of this new industrial revolution.

Social change is also sweeping through the Western world. Marriage rates are declining, as is sexual activity, especially among high schoolers, with more people turning to easily accessible pornography for diversion. Most Western society has embraced casual relationships, same-sex marriage, and an increasing number of letters and symbols at the end of LGBT. I'm all for individuals deciding what they want for their lives; as King Edward VII was once reputed to have said, "You can do what you want, but don't scare the horses." However, amid these profound transformations, shouldn't we be getting happier? The rates of depression and anxiety suggest the opposite.

Inevitably, diverse communities will see the world differently in a large country with freedom of speech at its heart. However, as it did after the sixties' civil rights and hippy movements, I predict America will absorb some cultural change, come together over some future existential threat, and move forward.

Enough of all of this seriousness. Having set my default spellchecker to American English, let's get on with the journey. Chapter 1 – Scene 1 – Atlanta, Georgia.

Julian Bishop
Turin, Italy, August 2023

Julian Bishop

Are We There Yet?

Chapter 1 – Becoming American

We were sworn in as American citizens on my debut book's publication day. Not that I was busy, as the pandemic had curtailed all author bookshop signings. Like everything else, the immigration process had been affected by the global pandemic. We had almost completed the process to become American citizens a year previously, but when Covid struck, our penultimate stage was postponed. It had delayed the last two steps by ten months and deprived us of the opportunity to vote in the 2020 election.

Of course, health matters are primarily a state rather than federal responsibility, and our state (Georgia) had lenient Covid rules. However, where the Federal Government has jurisdiction— for example, immigration offices—the new president had introduced stricter rules.

The immigration facilities made me feel foreign. In the line alongside immigrants of every race, religion, color, and age, this was a valuable leveling experience. The enormous oblong waiting room, daubed in multiple soothing beige hues, was lit amply and fluorescently. Rows of gray, easy-to-clean, upholstered chairs designed for long waits accommodated us while we waited for the digital display to flash our number. The room had been hastily redesigned: the children's play area and the refreshment counter were closed, the snaky airport queuing system was dismantled, and only those with appointments were admitted.

Getting US citizenship is not speedy these days. We started with a three-year intracompany transfer visa. In 2015, we converted to a green card, which is famously not green but tan or beige. [Parenthetically, it was last green in 1964, but the old nickname has stuck.] After five years with a green card, you can apply for citizenship. We did so on our fifth green cardiversary.

Julian Bishop

There are multiple other routes to citizenship. Two-thirds of the million new green cards each year are awarded to family members of those already in America. US permanent residents can sponsor their spouses, children, or parents for a green card, while citizens can also bring in their siblings. However, this sibling visa route is not quick, with the average current wait time over a decade.

People with deep expertise receive one in six of all green cards. These might be engineers destined for Silicon Valley, college professors, people renowned in the arts, or baseball players. Incidentally, almost three-quarters of these visas are currently awarded to computer scientists and engineers born in India, which is still hemorrhaging its best engineers—of the top hundred performers in the entry exams for India's elite engineering schools, 62 percent migrated away from India.

A further one in seven is awarded to refugees and asylum seekers. Finally, as with many other countries, foreign investors who invest more than $1 million and create at least ten full-time employees will get a visa, too.

One of the least popular routes into the US is also the one that garners the most publicity. About 5 percent of green cards come from the Diversity Immigrant Visa Program, better known as the green card lottery. It is designed to broaden the pool of immigrants to the US and give everyone on the planet the chance of the American Dream. More than twenty million apply annually in October for an opportunity to come to the US.

The lottery is free to enter. However, you are not eligible if your country has provided more than 50,000 immigrants in the previous five years. At the time of writing, this means that citizens from Bangladesh, Brazil, Canada, mainland China, Colombia, Dominican Republic, Ecuador, El Salvador, Haiti, India, Jamaica, Mexico, Nigeria, Pakistan, Peru, Philippines, South Korea, United Kingdom, and Vietnam are excluded.

From the twenty million who apply each year, some 125,000 meeting the criteria are drawn randomly by computer in May of the following year. There is then a race to complete the rest of the process, with the first 55,000 who do so receiving a green card. Since 1995, about 40 percent of successful applicants have originated from Africa.

The citizenship test was the penultimate stage of our immigration process. Lorna failed the initial online practice test, but our daughters, who had a recent US education, and I— who had written a book on America— found it much more straightforward.

Are We There Yet?

A Woodrow Wilson National Fellowship Foundation survey found that only just over one-third of Americans would pass the test without revision, and accordingly, some call for an easier examination. However, I am not sure that I agree. Immigrants have a pass rate of around 95 percent because they can review the 130 questions from which the test is drawn.

To pass the actual oral test, we needed to answer six out of ten questions correctly. After performing well in later practice tests, we were all confident of passing and eager to outperform each other. Despite the challenges of taking the test with screens and masks, we all passed after only six questions.

A few weeks later, US Immigration invited us to the swearing-in ceremony. Lorna and carefree Daughter #2 had a morning ceremony, while conscientious Daughter #1 and I had an afternoon appointment. Henceforth, from this date, whenever we argue over something connected with America, my wife can say she has been an American citizen longer than me.

In non-pandemic times, these ceremonies are celebratory affairs. When we applied, I had visions of all my friends from the local court witnessing my swearing-in and celebrating with me. However, social distancing rules prohibited this.

The officials beckoned us into a second large waiting room with twenty armchairs spaced fifteen feet apart. It was much like a cavernous doctor's waiting room without the distraction of twenty-year-old *Readers Digests*. We waited in silence as they processed everyone. Then, one by one, the immigration officers took our green cards and asked us again if we had committed any crimes in the past three weeks or joined any militias.

This latter question was not as stupid a question as it sounded. Militia had been in the news after the events of 6 January at the US Capitol.

A demonstration against the confirmation of the presidential election had turned violent as almost a thousand demonstrators stormed the Capitol building, home to both the Senate and the House of Representatives. Politicians and media have since oversimplified this demonstration in line with their pre-existing opinions. What is clear a year later is that the poorly prepared Capitol police grossly underestimated the risks of this protest and were as timid as a cat facing a vacuum cleaner. In a country with several thousand demonstrations yearly, left-leaning rallies had historically caused the most violence. Ultra-progressive organizations such as Antifa regularly battled police in almost all major US cities. Authorities regarded right-leaning protests as comparatively safe. After all, these protestors usually tidied after themselves.

The work of the Capitol was postponed, and senators and representatives genuinely feared for their lives. The Capitol Police shot one protestor while three others died of medical emergencies. More than one hundred police officers were injured in battles with rioters, and one further officer also died the next day from a stroke.

The FBI and police viewed over three hundred thousand hours of video footage from the Capitol invasion and innumerable images on social media in the next few months. Police ultimately made over a thousand arrests. The University of Chicago analyzed those arrested and found they came from all but four states, hailing evenly from counties won by Trump and Biden. In addition, 62 of those detained were active or ex-military, 15 were active police officers, and 72 were women.

While some scenes—replayed endlessly on TV—were horrific, a relatively small number of militia members primarily caused the rampage. Indeed, the University of Chicago found that only 10 percent of those arrested had any links to militia or right-wing groups, with most others getting caught up in the moment.

The FBI supported this synopsis, finding scant evidence of widespread seditious conspiracy. The exceptions to this were those arrested from four relatively small organized groups: sixteen members of the Oath Keepers, a mainly police organization that believes that the government is infringing on the rights of citizens; fifteen members of the neo-fascist and male-only Proud Boys; six people from a Californian group called the 3 percenters, named after the alleged number of American colonists who fought against Britain in the revolutionary war (it was far higher); and a small number from QAnon who despised Hollywood elites and Democrats believing for some reason that they are all involved in pedophilia, Satan worshiping, and cannibalism. These relatively small contingents, brought together by dark social media corners, somehow encouraged other more peaceful demonstrators to storm the Capitol.

The scenes were shocking. One of the world's largest democracies had been attacked by a relatively small group of committed extremists, some of whom were seeking to hang Vice President Mike Pence, whose crime was that he (correctly) certified the election result.

President Trump was widely blamed for the events. During his presidency, he consistently undermined federal institutions on which society relies. Moreover, to most Americans, he had encouraged the rioters with his unproven claims that the Democrats had stolen the election from him.

Although polls from Pew Research showed that the country was briefly united around prosecuting all those involved in storming the Capitol, this unanimity lessened as the year progressed. A year later, although most Democrats continued to believe everyone involved should be charged, Republicans were much more divided on the question. Pew has also found that the so-called 'Big Lie' that the election was stolen was believed by about 65 million Americans, with 23 million (presumably gun-owning) believing that violence may be warranted.

The anti-democratic scenes were part of a global move away from democracy, which many non-governmental organizations have attempted to measure. Regimes of the World, a Swedish research institute, reported that democracy peaked two decades after the Soviet break-up when four billion people in ninety-seven countries lived in a democracy. A mere decade later, Regimes of the World calculated that only 2.3 billion of the planet now lived in democratic countries.

A more comprehensive report from the non-profit organization Freedom House has downgraded freedom scores in almost 40 percent of the 195 countries they measured, suggesting a considerable erosion of democracy worldwide. Their scoring system now has fewer than one in five global citizens living in Free countries.

This process of de-democratization is set to continue, as citizens surrender democratic rights to would-be tyrants who claim they can help people with the complexity of modern-day living.

There are, I guess, legitimate arguments against democracy. It doesn't necessarily offer political stability, it can be inefficient (as consulting people to make decisions takes time), and it isn't always fair to marginalized minorities.

Some also believe that many voters are ignorant and imply that things would be better if only knowledgeable people— notably themselves— made all the decisions. I would argue that almost all voters, including myself, are rationally ignorant. Becoming and staying informed about all political matters would take an enormous time. You would have to spend hours daily finding neutral information and correcting your biases. When doing a cost-benefit analysis, most people quickly conclude that becoming fully informed is simply not worth their time. People are, therefore, rational in choosing not to be fully informed.

According to Pew Research, most citizens in Belgium, France, Greece, Italy, Japan, South Korea, Spain, and the United States now favor significant changes to their democracies. Pessimism about the economic future was the leading predictor of dissatisfaction, followed by a decline in the reputation of media, judicial, and government institutions. Social media has made it increasingly difficult to distinguish between facts and misinformation in recent years, leading to disproportionate airtime for extreme political viewpoints, as the media highlights those with the most extreme views for clicks.

As the developing world continues to grow its share of the world economy, I anticipate that democracy will further decline in the relatively stagnating developed world. Authoritarian powers, especially China, will continue to advance their global interests, and authoritarianism will seem appealing to many political leaders compared to the messiness of democracy.

One such country that has backtracked almost entirely on democracy is Russia. In August 2020, a Russian opposition leader, Alexei Navalny, was poisoned with a nerve agent administered in his morning tea. This agent was a variant of Novichok, prohibited by numerous international chemical weapon treaties. This method of controlling activists was uncannily similar to the tea poisoning of other Russian activists, journalists, and former spies. Navalny was evacuated to Berlin and placed into a coma. Prompt treatment with the antidote atropine probably saved his life.

Investigations in the West showed that agents from the FSB, the organization that replaced the KGB, had administered the poison probably on the orders of the Russian president. As a result, some Western countries imposed limited sanctions on the FSB director and five Russian scientists.

Navalny made a remarkable recovery and, in January 2021, showed immense courage by returning to Russia. Upon his arrival at Moscow airport, he was promptly arrested for violating the terms of a previous probation that required him to report regularly. I would wager that most jurisdictions would regard 'being in a coma' as a legitimate excuse for not reporting to a probation officer. However, not in this case, where Navalny was sentenced to two and a half years at a penal colony for breaching probation conditions. A year later, he was convicted for a further nine years for contempt of court.

Russian police also investigated the alleged poisoning but could find no evidence of a crime. Moreover, a December 2020 poll in Russia found that only 15 percent of Russians believed that the authorities had tried to poison Navalny, with a majority considering that either there had been no poisoning or this was a false flag operation by Western special services.

I'm personally a big fan of democracy. I agree with Churchill: "No one pretends that democracy is perfect or all-wise. Indeed, it has been said that democracy is the worst form of government except all those other forms that have been tried from time to time."

Democracy can never provide ideological concurrence, just a viable majority that protects those in the minority. Besides, the decline in democracy severely threatens our peace and prosperity, as— for all their faults—democracies are likelier to protect human rights and the rule of law.

One week after President Trump's second impeachment— for incitement to insurrection—Joe Biden was sworn in as president. At 78, he was America's oldest president. The pandemic had also soured his celebrations. Only one thousand people, six feet apart, were present. Small flags replaced the usual two hundred thousand guests, and the dozen inauguration balls and other events were canceled or replaced by dismal Zoom celebrations.

As a symbol of a healthy democracy, the last hundred and fifty years have seen a tradition of the outgoing and incoming presidents traveling together for the inauguration. A petulant President Trump broke this tradition when he did not join President Biden for the latter's inauguration.

Before 1870, this symbol of unity was often not followed. Federalist John Adams did not join the Democratic-Republican Party (yes, they were once the same party) Thomas Jefferson for his inauguration. Once good friends, they had become bitter rivals. They reconciled later in life and died hours apart on the fiftieth anniversary of the Declaration of Independence. John Quincy Adams did not attend the inauguration of Andrew Jackson. Jackson blamed Adams for his wife's death for spreading false rumors about her character. Andrew Johnson hated Ulysses Grant and refused to participate in his successor's special day. I am sure it would have been uncomfortable for Presidents Biden and Trump to travel together as it had been for previous rivals. However, Biden did have company from Vice President Pence and former Presidents Clinton, Bush, and Obama.

The US president used to be sworn in on 4 March. However, in 1933, the twentieth amendment brought forward this date to 20 January to reduce the lame-duck period of power. There have been many notable inauguration addresses. George Washington gave the shortest speech of just 135 words for his second inauguration. That is the exact length of the previous paragraph.

I wrote about the longest inauguration speech in the previous book. It is claimed that William Henry Harrison's two-hour address, delivered in weather as cold as a polar bear's toenails, was responsible for his death one month later. However, Harrison likely died from poor-quality White House water.

In 1797, John Adams gave an average length inauguration speech of 2,308 words, but one sentence was 737 words. Fortunately for you, dear reader, I don't have an example of this sentence length. If he had had the benefit of Grammarly, it would undoubtedly have told him that this sentence may be unclear or hard to follow and requested that he consider rephrasing it.

****

We then filed into a second large room and sat again fifteen feet apart, facing a podium. My fellow inductees were diverse in age, ethnicity, and background. They had dressed differently, too. Some were casual, but most had spruced up a bit. Some were besuited, while others had taken the opportunity to display the showier parts of their wardrobe. I saw silver shoes, sparkly blue jackets, and outlandish cravats. I was relieved we had convinced nonchalant Daughter #2 to wear jeans without too many tears.

The officials had handed us an envelope in the manner of an Oscar nominee. I opened it excitedly to see what goodies were on offer and found a passport application, voting forms, lyrics to the Star-Spangled Banner, and a mini flag.

The Department of Homeland Affairs representative recited the oath of allegiance, intoning the words three at a time regardless of punctuation. Having just started narrating the audiobook for my first book, I could empathize.

I had decided to produce the audiobook myself, mainly to avoid the high cost of hiring a studio, editor, and narrator for an uncertain return. Thanks to modern technology, it was relatively easy to do. I converted my walk-in closet into a makeshift studio, using the carpet and clothes on the walls to absorb sound like padded walls.

Editing the audio of my 116,000-word book line by line to correct all the mistakes was a laborious process. It quickly made me regret some of the complex sentences.

Are We There Yet?

I also needed to educate myself on how to pronounce certain words. For example, let's take the famed Native American adventurer Sacagawea as an example. Lewis and Clark were two brave cookies—the type who would have jogged home from their vasectomies—but they were terrible spellers. They mentioned Sacagawea seventeen times in their journals and spelled her name in seven different ways.

Today, most Americans pronounce her name with a soft 'g.' However, I was persuaded by a couple of dozen articles I read that her name should probably be pronounced with a hard 'g' or maybe even a 'k,' making the meaning of her name Bird Woman rather than Boat Launcher. I then had to decide whether to perpetuate the soft 'g' that Americans are used to or use the likely more correct pronunciation. It's easy to get lost in research on pronouncing names, especially if you are looking for an excuse not to narrate a chapter.

Accents were a problem, too. I had included several quotations in the book. Should I read them in my English accent or make an approximation of their American accent? I decided to do the latter and then researched what accent they would have had. This was tricky for some people. For example, there are no voice recordings of President Jackson or Mark Twain. However, Jackson's voice was described, and a recording of Mark Twain's old neighbor impersonating Clemens's accent was recorded. Above all, however, I was mainly hampered because I still couldn't do an authentic American accent, and the voices were, therefore, only directionally accurate.

Audiobooks have come a long way since, arguably, the initial narration by phonograph inventor Thomas Edison. His earliest recorded words were, "Mary had a little lamb. Its fleece was white as snow." However, the first true audiobooks were produced in 1932 when the American Foundation for the Blind founded a studio to make vinyl recordings of classic books. Around the same time, anthropologist J P Harrington also recorded oral histories of Native Americans.

Technology development has driven the popularity of audiobooks. For decades, audiobooks had to be recorded at a studio and printed onto vinyl discs. This limited their use and appeal. However, in the early 1980s, the invention of the Sony Walkman and longer cassette tapes led book publishers to offer audiobooks. In the last decade, the digital age has led to cloud storage of recordings. As a result, a hundred thousand new audiobooks are published annually, accounting for 8 percent of all books sold. Many people, including my wife, only read via audiobook. And for this reason, a couple of jokes with her as the target were mysteriously edited from the audiobook version.

You might wonder why I invested hundreds of hours in this endeavor. The way people engage with books has evolved. Surprisingly, the percentage of adult readers in the United States has remained constant since pollsters began tracking this statistic. A solid three-quarters of adults have delved into at least one book in the past year, with a slightly higher rate among women than men. On average, an American reads fourteen books each year, although this figure is somewhat skewed, with the typical (median) American reading just five books annually.

Some people view reading by audiobook as cheating and claim that you comprehend less when listening to an audiobook. However, the academic studies on this are inconclusive. Daniel Willingham from the University of Virginia argues that "10 to 15 percent of eye movement during reading is regressive... meaning the eyes are going back and re-checking." You can't do this easily for an audiobook. Willingham conducted a 2010 study that compared students' test scores between those who had listened to a podcast lesson and those who had read the same class on paper. The podcast group scored 28 percent lower on the quiz. By contrast, in her 2016 study, Beth Rogowsky from the Bloomsburg University of Pennsylvania compared the comprehension levels of audiobook listeners and e-book readers and found no significant differences.

****

We recited the oath of allegiance, in which we had to renounce any allegiance to foreign princes. This was a straightforward declaration for me to make, given the court proceedings at that time against Prince Andrew concerning his alleged behavior with a seventeen-year-old girl.

At the end of the inauguration, the ceremonial leader told us that we were now US citizens and said we could wave our flags. There was an embarrassed smattering of applause. Daughter #1 and I self-consciously waved our government-provided mini-flag, regretting not having the foresight to carry a more substantial cloth model that others had brought.

With no family or friends allowed, it was an insipid celebration. Daughter #2 described it as seriously un-American. Covid had stripped this ceremony of all its pomp, and the new citizens could only share their moment with a bunch of strangers at a minimum distance of fifteen feet.

Are We There Yet?

Lorna felt that the insipid ceremony had voided the meaning of this occasion, while conciliatory Daughter #2 said she felt a bit American and a bit British. However, this did not describe my emotions. I was delighted that I had done it. Not only had I completed something on my year's to-do list, but we were now citizens of two great countries. I felt different. Trump had made me nervous. His scattergun approach to government policy meant that immigrants were always uncertain about their place in the US. While I still have faith in the checks and balances of US institutions, there was always a lingering doubt.

I was relieved most for the children. As a green card holder, you can theoretically be deported for any crime. It had always worried us that one of the children would do something stupid in the vein of stealing a traffic cone, so we constantly urged them first to contact an immigration lawyer if ever arrested.

Today, almost everyone in America is either an immigrant or descended from immigrants (voluntary or otherwise). The US is a large country that—post-annihilation of the indigenous population— needed people to protect its borders and grow its economic power.

Throughout America's post-colonial era, first-generation immigrants have comprised a steady 15 percent of the population, numbering some 45 million today. Contrary to what you might hear on Fox News or read in the Daily Mail, most are legal residents rather than unauthorized immigrants. Indeed, unauthorized immigrants are at their lowest levels since 2004. According to Gallup, one hundred and fifty million people from the rest of the world would move to the US if they could, more than the following four most popular destinations combined. Most of these wannabe Americans are between fifteen and twenty-nine, are well-educated, and have been enticed to America because they perceive better economic opportunities.

The remainder of this century will see most developed countries grappling with challenging demographic shifts. A strong economy generally requires a favorable demographic profile, with a birth rate above the death rate (or, if needed, supplemented by positive net migration) and a sizeable working population capable of paying for education and social programs for the young and old.

It is difficult for a country to grow economically when its population is both aging and declining. A shrinking workforce can lead to various issues, including the strain on social programs, reduced innovation, increased citizen dissatisfaction, and societal division.

The UN projects a 16 percent decline in the developed world's working-age population by 2050. If this comes to pass—and by 2032 without net immigration, it will be a certainty—a country would require a commensurate increase in productivity just to keep that country out of continuous recession.

Unfortunately, it gets worse. Working-aged citizens consume the most, so reducing their number by one-sixth will lower developed world economic demand. Secondly, as the number of workers declines, tax revenue from their income will fall along with government spending. With total private and public debt levels of developed countries already at 350 percent of GDP, there will be no borrowing one's way out of the problem.

Like many other countries, America's government debt has risen above 100 percent of GDP, the threshold at which eyebrows are raised. But, if unfunded spending continues at its current rate, it will be 200 percent by mid century if the system has not irretrievably broken by then.

When ruled over by different political parties, the US Congress and the president play this game every year where one of them threatens not to increase the maximum amount of debt that the country can issue. Everyone gets agitated that the US may default on its debt, leading the rest of the world into an economic meltdown. To date, it always ends in the same way, through a face-saving compromise where the debt is increased but less than was initially requested.

Ultimately, at some point, the investors who lend governments money will determine how much debt a society can issue without severe consequences. The debt limit game is an American game, but the same concept plays out in most corners of the world. Europe, China, the US, and scores of other countries have too much debt.

"The multitudes remained plunged in ignorance... and their leaders, seeking their votes, did not dare to undeceive them" still seems relevant about today's politicians, though Churchill wrote it in *The Gathering Storm* about the victors of World War I.

The solutions are obvious. Ultimately, some future governments will have to spend less, tax more, or do a bit of both. Unfortunately, few politicians and seemingly no electorates want this.

In researching this book, I read voraciously about demographics. I didn't think population statistics would ever turn me on... but then I came to my census.

The US's economic strength owes a lot to favorable demographics. Its historically healthy birth rate and a positive net inflow of immigrants have translated into more consumers, a larger workforce, and higher tax inflows. After the collapse of the Soviet Union, America became the third most populous country. Its on-track fertility rate and continued high immigration meant that its working-age population grew faster than any other developed country. Today, the US still has a lower senior population (16 percent) than almost any other developed country. However, in the past decade, the US population growth has slowed to less than 10 percent. More worryingly, fertility has fallen below the replacement rate to about the same rate as the UK (1.7 children per woman), a far cry from the 3.0+ levels of the fifties and sixties. This has led many to predict a less populous and more senior future for the US.

However, even the UN's low variant simulation, which models a natural fertility rate of only 1.4, predicts a significant increase in the size of the US working-age population and a rise in the US population from 330 million to a peak of 350 million by 2050. The likelier median simulations forecast the US population to continue growing well beyond this timeframe.

Some other noteworthy things are happening in American demographics. Firstly, although Americans are much wealthier than Europeans, American life expectancy is three years lower. This is because Americans have four times as many deaths per capita as Europeans between teenage and early middle age. If the US could magic away excess deaths from drugs, guns, and obesity, Americans would have a similar life expectancy to Europe.

Another noteworthy feature is that Hispanic voters recently overtook African Americans as the second-largest voting group. Although whites still account for two-thirds of the electorate, they will be in the minority later in the century.

Some progressives seem to regard white Americans as the enemy today, benefiting enormously from their ethnicity. While the median white American earns $3,000 more than the average American, other skin tones do even better. For example, median Indian-Americans earn $44,000 more, Filipino-Americans $27,000 more, and Taiwanese-Americans $25,000 more. Sri Lankan-, Japanese-, Malaysian-, Chinese-, and Pakistani-Americans also earn more than their white counterparts.

Demographics play a significant role in the prospects of superpowers, and the United States stands out favorably compared to most of its potential rivals. For decades, China, Europe, Japan, and Russia have grappled with sub-replacement fertility rates. According to UN projections, many of these contenders are expected to experience substantial population declines by the end of this century. For instance, South Korea and China are likely to see their populations halved, while Japan and Italy are expected to decrease by 40 percent. Among the principal developed countries, only the United States (with an estimated increase of 16 percent) and the United Kingdom (with a projected 4 percent increase) are poised for population growth, both of which are partly attributable to positive net migration.

China's achievements have been phenomenal since it opened its economy forty years ago. Its GDP has grown by a mind-blowing 9 percent per year to the point where China now accounts for almost one-fifth of global output. In the eighties, eighteen of twenty Chinese people survived on less than $2 per day, whereas now very few are abjectly poor. In that period, China transitioned from a mainly agricultural society to a global manufacturing hub and is now transitioning again to a service and technology economy. China has achieved this by investing heavily in its infrastructure and education system. As much of this infrastructure investment is recent, first-time visitors to China are typically in awe of how everything works. China is also the largest investor in the infrastructure of its potential allies, most of which coincidentally have significant natural resources.

China's population remained young for decades, with 90 percent of its working-age people. This helped keep inflation, borrowing, and labor costs low, which supported phenomenal economic growth. As a result, China industrialized quicker than any other country in history.

China's 'later, longer, fewer' and subsequent one-child policies may have helped propel China to its current position, but they will also condemn it to an uncertain future. However—even though two, then three, and now unlimited children per couple are permitted— China's fertility rate has stubbornly stayed at 1.18 (similar to naughty-step Italy) and well below the replacement rate. China's policy change was too little and too late. As a result, most projections have China's population halving to around 0.7-0.8 billion by the end of this century.

The intervening period will be tricky for China. Their population is aging quickly, and the number of workers has already fallen every year since 2014. By 2050, China will have one-quarter of a billion fewer workers than today. Worse still, its population will then likely have an average age of over fifty, and one-third of its people will be over 65. With basic social welfare costs set to exceed current total government revenue within the next decade, current pension obligations already unfunded to the level of their total GDP, and hundreds of millions becoming new pensioners in the next two decades, some tough decisions will need to be made.

In truth—with inflation, borrowing, and labor costs set to soar—China can do little to avoid severe economic decline. The loosening of reproductive regulations has had little effect on fertility, and the next step will probably be financial incentives for families with more than three children. Given China's low regard for individual human rights, perhaps the forced sterilization of the past will be replaced by forced insemination.

In any case, new babies take about twenty years to join the working population, so this problem cannot be solved quickly. Unquestionably, China will attempt to compete for skilled immigrants, but I fear it will struggle, as it has no modern history of absorbing large numbers of immigrants. Instead, China will probably focus on productivity gains, including installing non-human workers (robots) to do the work they no longer have humans to perform.

The age profile of China will soon look like Japan's, where almost one-third of its population is already at retirement age. Sales of adult diapers in Japan are now greater than those for infants. In the eighties, the Japanese were wealthier than the Americans. Now, they earn less than the British, the Koreans, or the Taiwanese. In 1991, Tokyo's stock market crashed, banks became insolvent, and property prices followed. These asset prices have not returned to their previous values in the three decades since. Real wages have been stagnant only due to unprecedented innovation, particularly in the senior care sector, where robots perform many routine care functions. With a profound resistance to cultural change, Japan's population will continue to shrink by a net three-quarters of a million people yearly. Its extremely high public debt will continue to put enormous pressure on healthcare and pensions.

Nevertheless, Japan has thus far muddled through its demographic decline. It remains a peaceful country with a good standard of living and long life expectancy. Will other countries be able to do the same? Unfortunately, probably not. Japan was fortunate to be able to shift labor needs to nearby countries with excess capacity. They have, therefore, avoided the worst inflation and debt levels others will likely experience.

Don't expect Russia to become the superpower, either. In almost every year since the break-up of the Soviet Union, deaths have substantially exceeded births. Furthermore, even before the invasion of Ukraine, there was substantial net emigration, as many Russians found anywhere else more attractive than their birth nation.

Russia faces severe demographic challenges, with the world's lowest fertility rate and an astonishing abortion rate of 225 abortions for every 100 births. Russian men have the shortest life expectancy among developed nations, barely reaching their sixtieth birthday, primarily due to non-natural causes such as alcoholism and self-harm.

This could be a dangerous period for the world, as declining powers in history are often more aggressive than rising ones. With a steep decline in those of service age, Russia may struggle to protect its land borders from fourteen neighboring countries and may resort to extreme methods to protect its territory.

Could Europe stage a resurgence? The European Union, while smaller in territory compared to the US, boasts a population one-third larger. Furthermore, with an economic prowess that is only about 50 percent less than that of the US, it already stands closer to superpower status economically than its rivals. However, Europe also faces demographic challenges. By mid-century, it will have roughly the same population as today but be 50 million workers lighter. Moving into the latter half of the century, the likelihood of a sustained low fertility rate will further diminish the workforce. Europe's prospects will hinge significantly on its ability to integrate immigration from Africa effectively.

Only two countries in the medium term could conceivably have the demographics to challenge the US: India and Nigeria. While these may seem like two outside bets given their economic position today, an outside chance does not mean it is impossible—after all, China's rise was once regarded as highly improbable.

India undoubtedly has the demographics to be a superpower. Its growing population will soon overtake China, the world's most populous country for hundreds of years[1]. Moreover, with two-thirds of its population below thirty-five, India has a vast working-age population, giving India a demographic window to grow when other major powers are in decline.

---

[1] One of the challenges in writing a book with elements tied to current affairs is the ever-changing nature of data. My approach has been to use the latest available data up to the end of 2022 in the book, while also highlighting, in soap opera fashion, any significant developments that transpired in 2023 in the postscript chapter.

In this specific case, during the initial writing of the book, China did indeed have the world's largest population. However, when I came to edit the book in 2023, India had surpassed it in population.

Are We There Yet?

India has the world's largest English-speaking population, the most extensive pool of engineers and science professionals, and could already be described as a technology superpower. In addition, it has significant diasporas overseas, with thirty-two million Indians as potential re-immigrants. India also has an enviable geographic position close to many Eurasian and Afro-Asian sea trade routes.

India also has considerable headwinds. It is currently hugely dependent on overseas oil for its energy needs, and the pollution from these fossil fuels is responsible for a million Indian deaths annually.

I am fortunate to have traveled to India many times, and economic development is visibly evident. With each visit, the rubbish mounds, number of cows in the streets, and quantity of beggars are all decreasing. Nevertheless, India's infrastructure is decades behind, say, China's. Its health system cannot care for its 1.4 billion people, and the poorest quartile still suffers from malnutrition. While about a third of its population receives a world-class education, another quarter is illiterate.

Furthermore, India faces significant military risks on multiple fronts. It must contend with ongoing water disputes with Bangladesh, frequent border skirmishes with China, and a fundamental ideological clash with nuclear-armed Pakistan. These disputes are likely to keep its substantial two-million-strong military engaged.

Additionally, India grapples with internal religious-based dissent that frequently escalates into violence, with separatist groups in several Indian states actively pushing for independence. Perhaps as a result, India has become less democratic, and a handful of elite families wield outsized influence within its political landscape.

India also contends with stark socio-economic disparities, marked by a significant wealth gap between the affluent and the impoverished. The lingering prevalence of the caste system continues to undervalue the talent and potential contributions of individuals from marginalized segments of society.

India's economy has grown sevenfold since 2000, making it the fifth-largest economy in the world. By 2030, India is expected to be the third-largest economy. However, even though India will likely grow a further three times between now and 2050, the US will still be over three times richer per capita. Nevertheless, it seems likely that India will become the second most powerful country in the second half of this century.

Africa is experiencing rapid growth, pivotal in propelling the global population toward a potential 10 billion by 2050. Starting from just 0.4

billion in 1975, Africa is now home to 1.4 billion people, with projections suggesting it could reach 2.2 billion by the end of this century.

Nigeria currently accounts for one-fifth of the continent and will be the superpower of Africa. Whether it can become a global superpower is much less evident.

Besides its population advantage, Nigeria enjoys robust economic growth; it has thriving call center hubs in Abuja and Kaduna, produces fifty films every week in Nollywood, and fosters a dynamic entrepreneurial environment in Yaba, Nigeria's equivalent of Silicon Valley. It may not be long, but since 1999, it has had a form of functioning democracy that has withheld five elections.

On the other hand, with oil accounting for a staggering 97 percent of its exports, Nigeria's economic prospects are heavily dependent on the oil price. Nigeria has endemic corruption and woeful infrastructure. For example, despite these energy resources, only half of Nigerian homes have mains electricity. An even larger problem, and one shared by many African countries due to European diplomats' inability to draw lines in the correct places, many Nigerian citizens define themselves by their tribe rather than nation—with the predominantly Islamic north having a long history of wanting to secede from the Christian South.

I'm sure some readers have been metaphorically yelling that these demographics are all very well, but the planet has a substantial environmental impact from having too many humans abusing the planet's limited resources. These readers will point out that humans have exceeded their carrying capacity and severely affected the planet's ecosystem, which is threatened by unprecedented deforestation, a significant loss of biodiversity, and a lower ability to capture CO_2. In addition, the demand for finite biocarbon fuel (and other natural resources) increases greenhouse gas emissions, contributing to climate change and pollution.

However, overpopulation is a complex issue with no practical and ethical solutions. The world's population has been rising since the end of the Black Death due to medical advances and improved agricultural productivity. You cannot put either of these genies back in their bottles. Better family planning and education can slow the population growth rate but can't reduce the human population to a quarter of its current size, the stated aim of American biologist Paul R. Ehrlich.

In any case, there is no (ethical) way to reduce the aging population. Population reduction through decreased birth rates is possible. However, most would agree that individuals have the fundamental human right to have children. Coercive measures from China that punished any family with more than one child or India that forcibly sterilized men are widely seen as abhorrent. Furthermore, the unintended consequences of successful birth control policies include gender imbalances, trafficking of young women, and disastrous demographics.

What's more, there is little evidence from a hundred years of the United Nations and League of Nations that the world's political leaders could agree on a solution and be trusted to implement it. As we have seen with the climate agreements, there would likely be no collective course of action.

Extraterrestrial settlement, as proposed by Elon Musk, seems extreme. Instead, I suspect we must put our faith (and investment) into innovative agriculture and behavior changes that encourage recyclable consumption.

****

In the UK, the losing political party has always dealt with electoral defeat with humility for the process and respect for the electorate. The behavior follows a predictable pattern. At 10 pm, when the polling booths close, the news channels release an exit opinion poll based on interviews conducted at a large sample of polling districts. While this has proved a little awry in a couple of elections, it is usually directionally accurate. The news anchors then interview party spokespeople, who always say the same thing. The winning team always welcomes the poll results but cautions that they want to see actual results from the votes. The more difficult interview is with the losing side. Although they look glum, they always remind the interviewer that no single actual vote has yet been counted and then refuse to answer any questions on what had gone wrong with their campaign.

As the evening progresses and constituencies announce their results, the TV presenters interview further representatives from the losing side. The outsiders blame their party leader for the wrong policies and a catastrophic campaign, while the loyalists say we have the right policies, but these policies are too ahead of their time or too tricky to explain. Everyone then says that the electorate has spoken, and they accept the people's judgment.

In the 2020 US presidential election, the losing president did not want to follow protocol by conceding. This awkward behavior made expectations for President Trump's exiting pardon list low. Surprisingly, though, the list was relatively uncontroversial.

The presidential pardon is a fascinating power within the system of checks and balances, enabling the executive branch to rectify potential injustices from the judiciary. The president possesses the authority to pardon individuals for federal crimes, except those whom Congress has impeached. It's worth noting that many crimes, such as simple murders, rapes, burglaries, and attempts to fix elections in Georgia fall under state jurisdiction and can only be pardoned by the respective state's Governor.

Technically, a presidential pardon does not erase a conviction. Within the Department of Justice, an office helps the president review each application for clemency. In most cases, the president will show forgiveness only when the convicted person has accepted responsibility and shown good conduct.

George Washington, the first president, issued the first presidential pardons. When Congress introduced a liquor tax in 1791 to pay off government debt in the days when the federal government thought these things were important, there was a protest from the liquor producers. Washington called in thirteen thousand troops to quell this protest. As a result, two leaders were hanged, and many others were tried for treason. Washington later pardoned others involved in the protests.

Pardons have often been used to unite the country after divisive events. For example, Lincoln and Johnson pardoned Confederate officials after the Civil War even though many Unionists disapproved. In 1977, Carter pardoned hundreds of thousands of Vietnam draft evaders who had fled to Canada to avoid fighting. This persuaded about half of them to return to the US.

A more recent tradition is for the president to pardon a turkey shortly before Thanksgiving. It comes from the more historical practice of the National Turkey Federation of providing the president turkeys for Thanksgiving. It was well-documented that Truman and Eisenhower ate most of their turkeys. However, when Kennedy was presented with a 55-pound bird wearing a sign, 'Good Eating, Mr. President,' JFK returned the turkey to the farm. Unfortunately, the turkey lived longer than Kennedy, who was assassinated three days later.

President Reagan first called the turkey reprieve a pardon, and his successor, George H W Bush, first described it as a presidential pardon. Since then, it has become a clichéd media event just before Thanksgiving.

Are We There Yet?

The lucky turkeys are selected from the farm of the reigning Chairperson of the National Turkey Federation. In a staggering act of sexism and racism, mainly male Broad Breasted White Turkeys are selected for potential reprieve. This turkey expert of experts reviews the behavior of their flock of birds to choose a dozen or so that will be able to handle the large crowds of journalists and well-wishers. This small group is scrutinized further, and two birds are selected to go to the White House. They spend the night before the pardon at the ultra-pet-friendly Willard InterContinental Washington Hotel. In a further act of anthropomorphism, children from the home state of the current NTF big cheese bestow names on these reprieved turkeys. The fate of these turkeys post-pardon is monitored assiduously by the press. Most seem to go on the gravy train to freedom for another couple of years.

Turkeys aside, presidents have often used their irrevocable presidential pardons to help their supporters, and there have been many controversies. For example, President Ford pardoned President Nixon before Nixon could face prosecution for his crimes, and President Clinton pardoned his half-brother, Roger, for cocaine possession.

It was rumored that President Trump would attempt to pardon himself. Legal experts argued over whether this would be constitutional. However, as it turned out, Trump did not forgive himself or any direct family members. Some believe this was because he would have to cite specific crimes that might place him and his family in legal jeopardy for non-federal crimes. Ultimately, President Trump pardoned only 237 people, amongst the lowest in the last hundred years. These were a mix of favors to political friends and more deserving cases, including, curiously, several hip-hop artists.

Another person not pardoned was Joe Exotic, the star of the fly-on-the-wall documentary *Tiger King*, who was convicted of planning his rival's murder. Apparently, a Dodge stretch limo was waiting outside his Texan prison on Trump's last day in office, waiting for his release. Exotic's legal team also brought hair, makeup, and wardrobe specialists for the inevitable post-release interviews. Unfortunately for Exotic, there is no such thing as inevitable as all these professionals went unused, and the meter just ticked on as Trump decided not to pardon him.

Unlike Joe Exotic, Lorna and I were now free Americans, able to go wherever we chose and do whatever we wished. And we wanted to do something different, and this is where the travel book starts.

Chapter 2 – Selling An American House

We lived in a city dictated by the location of my former company's office.

In a quirk of fate, I had been responsible for selecting the city of my company's new American HQ many years previously. As part of the process, I toured several cities in the eastern part of the US, compared pluses and minuses, and negotiated with local officials. Atlanta stood out among its competitors for several compelling reasons. As the ninth-largest metropolitan area in the United States, it boasted a business-friendly environment and easy access to a wide range of skills and resources. The city's relatively low cost of living, coupled with the presence of the world's busiest airport, also made it an appealing destination for relocation.

While Atlanta can be an exciting city, we lived in one of its countless featureless suburbs, where a thrilling event would be watching sloths in a sleeping contest. These neighborhoods may boast excellent schools, making them ideal for raising children, but they are about as lively as a library… on a Sunday. We enjoyed a couple of restaurants there, but generally, most food was about as enticing as that at an interpretative dance festival. As for nightlife, everything was closed by 9pm.

Life, in its grand tapestry, unfolds in distinct phases. It commences with childhood innocence, where every day is an adventure. As we discover the labyrinthine corridors of adolescence, the trials and tribulations of youth shape our character. In Act 2, with the dawn of adulthood, we step onto the path of work and, for the diligent at school, perhaps a career. In the next Act, many of us embrace the dual roles of parents and professionals. Balancing diapers and deadlines, we embark on a multi-decade journey. Then, in Act 4, as the nest empties, we savor a short stint of freedom before perhaps a taste of grandparenting. The curtain eventually falls, ushering in a final chapter of health struggles and the inevitable passage into the great unknown.

We found ourselves in Act 4 at the start of the freedom stage of our life. Meanwhile, both daughters were attending the same Georgia college ninety minutes from where we lived; they were well-integrated into their respective friend groups and had developed independent lives.

America is widely acknowledged as having the highest number of world-class universities. A coterie of analysts attempts to rank the best universities in the world. Because they disagree on what outputs are important, there is little agreement on the exact position of each college. However, all the analysts show the US to be the home of between half to three-quarters of the world's best universities.

A few years ago, I toured Chicago University and was intrigued to see that they differentiated themselves from their competitors by showcasing their forty-seven Nobel laureates. When I later checked Nobel recipients by university, I noticed that only Oxford and Cambridge gatecrashed the top ten universities for Nobel laureates. So, why does America have such strong universities?

The main reason is the high level of investment. Government and private-sector research funding is multiple times higher than in other countries. This allows universities to attract top faculty and students and provides world-class academic infrastructure (such as libraries, research facilities, and technology). This investment is critical in attracting the best international students, many of whom choose to remain in the US at the end of their formal studies.

Next, America's freedom of thought encourages the exploration of a wide range of perspectives and ideas. This diversity of backgrounds and outlooks of its students and faculty creates an intellectually challenging environment that fosters innovation and creativity.

Finally, US universities have close partnerships with the private sector. While I have listened to many a European academic debate the purpose of university, Americans intuitively understand that its primary purpose is to prepare students for the workplace. As a result, most students have a job while at college, and the class schedule is flexible to encourage this. Working one's way through college is so common that even lackadaisical Daughter #2 has a job.

American universities also actively encourage their students to be entrepreneurs. As a result, universities celebrate their dropout alumni as much as those who complete. Maybe this isn't surprising when you have

Gates, Jobs, Zuckerberg, and Dell as dropouts. However, this focus on the practical application of their studies means that not only do most students find a professional job upon graduation, but it also ensures that companies receive the skills they need for their success.

China is envious of America's dominance in further education. So, unsurprisingly, they are doing something about it. China provides special funding to 140 educational institutions, mainly in Science and Engineering. Unusually, China has given their top two universities (Peking and Tsinghua) special autonomous status to allow them to focus on competing worldwide rather than being subject to Chinese evaluation. In 2008, China spent about one-third of what America does on research and development. Today, it's four-fifths. The Chinese have also been more successful at attracting back overseas Chinese students. Two decades ago, three-quarters of overseas Chinese students never returned to China. Today, it is only one-third.

****

After enduring a year of travel restrictions, my wanderlust was burning brighter than ever. If our health held up, we potentially had a glorious thirty-five years of life ahead. Thirty-five years to savor, explore, and seize every opportunity that came our way. My longing to travel and embrace the new was intensified by the realization that life can throw unexpected curveballs—whether it's the declining health of our parents or the joyous arrival of grandchildren. The future is a mysterious realm, and none of us truly knows what it has in store. So, I told myself the time to embrace my freedom and chase my dreams was now.

Lorna was keen to move out of Atlanta but perhaps not as clear on what she wanted to do next. She did not know what she wanted from the next phase of her life. However, she was happy to go along with my plans.

We found almost no friends who thought our plan to travel was a good idea. So, out of interest in other people's attitudes to risk, I read around the academic research on the subject. Now, indubitably, risk tolerance varies considerably by person, but insurance data does reveal some indicative correlations: one study shows that risk aversion increases with wealth until you get rich (when it declines); a second reveals that risk aversion tends to increase with age; and a third demonstrates that risk aversion falls the more educated you are. All the studies show that the average woman is about 50 percent more risk-averse than the mean man, perhaps explaining why those misadventure videos so rarely feature women doing stupid things. Marriage makes you more risk-averse though this could be contaminated because risk-averse people are the ones who choose to get married. Finally, contrary to what you might think, self-employed people are substantially more risk-averse than those employed by others.

Economist Daniel Kahneman won a Nobel prize for, *intra alia*, his work on prospect theory. He and the unennobled Amos Tversky showed that humans see losses and gains asymmetrically. In other words, the pain of losing $100 is psychologically greater than the joy of gaining the same sum. When taking risks, we are generally risk averse, but, when facing the likelihood of loss, we are influenced by emotions and are likelier to take greater risks to regain what we are about to lose.

Their findings—which have since been replicated in more than fifty cultures—ran contrary to expected utility theory, which assumed that a rational human would usually select the option with the best-expected outcome. All this vital science explains a little about the pricing strategy of *Deal or No Deal* but not why anyone would watch this pointless show.

It is widely believed that Americans take greater risks than Europeans, who tend to expect the government to shield them from all sorts of dangers. You can see this, for example, in rates of bankruptcy. In the US, high bankruptcy levels are regarded as a positive sign for a healthy economy, whereas in Europe, bankruptcy tends to be seen as a failure. A European Walt Disney might have thrown in the towel when his first company went bankrupt, but it did not deter an American one from making his second company a resounding success.

You can discern contrasting attitudes toward risk by examining investment preferences. Data reveals that only a tiny fraction of Europeans opt for above-median-risk investments. In contrast, over half of US retail investors favor riskier ones. On average, Americans are more inclined to invest in start-ups, while Europeans lean toward the government bond as their preferred investment choice.

You see some of these differences in risk tolerance in regulation, where, for example, most Americans readily eat GMO foods, while Europeans consider them unproven and hence potentially dangerous.

There's evidence that the two continents are converging a little on regulation, as the United States increasingly aligns itself toward Europe's cautious approach. In the wake of unfortunate events, both continents often respond with calls for legal changes "to ensure this never happens again," sometimes without fully considering the potential negative consequences of these regulatory shifts. This level of caution is not necessarily followed in other areas of Government control, for example, sending troops into war.

****

The pandemic had forged a change in the housing market. With most working from home rather than offices, many elected to move from smaller city apartments to larger suburban homes. Others chose to move away from the colder northern regions to the warmer south, and a few were also choosing to move away from the locked-down Democratic metros to the more laissez-faire Republican ones.

With both our children settled, we decided to sell our Atlanta home and travel full-time. The market was a dream for sellers but hell for buyers. So, we had a vague plan to travel nomadically for a time before buying again in Florida when the market calmed down. We were comforted that a feature of the Florida market was that there was always a substantial number of what industry insiders euphemistically refer to as 'last-time sellers.'

I have been told multiple times that there are more American realtors than homes sold in the USA. This would be a fantastic fact if true. But unfortunately, it is a myth. Around five million homes are sold annually in America by about two million active licensed real estate agents.

The average American moves house twelve times in their lifetime, about three times more than the average European and 50 percent more than in the UK. While most Americans move house within their own district, around one-quarter of them move state in any five-year period. The primary reason for this is to change jobs, which the average American does every four years, compared to every decade for a European.

Even though Americans move more readily than their European counterparts, a downward trajectory is evident. In 1947, when the US first started to collect these statistics, one in five Americans moved in any one year. At that time, the US economy thrived, and the population skewed younger. However, as we approached the late 1990s, annual mobility declined to around 15 percent, and by 2019, the proportion of Americans moving homes had dropped to fewer than one in ten.

Millennials, despite having fewer commitments such as marriage (only half the rate of prior generations), home ownership (one-third less), and children (most don't have kids), are notably less mobile than earlier generations. This reduced mobility can be attributed to a mix of factors, including their high levels of debt and a higher probability of being in dual-income households compared to previous generations.

America's history is a tapestry woven with threads of mass internal migration. For example, Americans moved to populate the West in the nineteenth century, and, in the first part of the twentieth century, an exodus of Black Americans relocated from the South to the North for brighter opportunities. This century has seen a move away from the rustbelt of the North to the sunbelt of the South.

Today's America is also much more bifurcated. Although the USA still has the most mobile population of any Western country, two in five Americans have never left the town they were born in, and almost three in four reside near where they were raised. This is somewhat skewed by region, with those from the Midwest much likelier to stay close to home than California natives.

Patrick Carr and Maria Kefalas moved to rural Iowa for their research on mobility in their 2009 book *Hollowing Out the Middle*. Simultaneously, another team of intrepid researchers gatecrashed various high school reunions, engaging with attendees who likely welcomed the opportunity to chat with researchers when they discovered they had as much in common with their old classmates as a cat does with a pogo stick. Both sets of researchers came to similar conclusions in finding four categories of people.

Those who *stayed* typically thought that the town where they grew up was a good place to raise their children, mainly because they had multiple family members living nearby. However, these stayers were also found to be more insular and less open to other cultures and immigrants. They were also likelier to vote for Trump than Clinton.

Returners were typically people who left their hometown in their twenties but returned in their thirties, often when they started to have children. This was not a large group, but they were often the most significant source of incomers in many of these small towns. *Seekers* wanted to leave but often lacked the money or the academic grades to do so, typically using the military as their escape route. Finally, *Achievers* were those who excelled at school. Teachers spent much time with this group, encouraging them to leave town to achieve their full potential. As a University of New Hampshire demographer said, "Rural communities lose their brightest kids… They go away and don't come back."

In effect, there is a continual brain drain of talent from rural communities, leading to a widening wealth gap. Even until the seventies, hard-working Americans without a university education could earn a good salary. However, in the past fifty years, those without university degrees have seen their real income halve, while graduates have seen increased spending power.

I'm not entirely convinced that this is an exclusively American phenomenon. When I was around seven, I distinctly remember feeling that I didn't quite fit into my rural English community. It was at that age that I began yearning to reshape my identity and create a future that I had a hand in designing. I longed for a place where my past wouldn't hold me back and where I wouldn't be defined by my neighbors. Intriguingly, much like the individuals in Iowa, I've never felt the urge to return to my county of birth.

****

Most of us only buy or sell a house in our own country. As with many things, we think of our native land as 'normal' and its practices and culture as the only way something is done. Yet, substantial differences exist even between fellow anglosphere countries with similar legal systems.

For instance, in the US, most real estate deals involve two agents—one for the seller and one for the buyer. The seller covers the entire cost of both agents, typically paying 6 percent of the sale price, split evenly between them. In the UK, there is usually just one agent representing the seller, while buyers themselves directly arrange property viewings with various selling agents.

The costs of selling an American house compare unfavorably to the UK, where the seller pays only 1 to 1.5 percent. One consequence of this discrepancy in earnings is that there are many more real estate agents in the US than in the UK. Indeed, while the average US realtor sells only 2.5 houses yearly, their busier UK comparator sells 21.8 homes.

Accordingly, the age profile of the realtor in each country is different. In the UK, the average estate agent is likely in their mid-twenties and often has little training or experience. They are essentially salespeople incentivized toward selling a house as, say, a second-hand car dealer is driven to sell their lot of cars. Consequently, British realtors are the butt of many jokes in the way they are not in America. For instance, this one:

Are We There Yet?

Walking through a cemetery, two people saw a headstone with the epitaph, "Here lies Jonathan Jones, an estate agent and an honest man."

"Blimey," says one to the other. "They buried two people in here."

In the US, the average realtor is 59 years old and has much more experience. Two-thirds of these American realtors are women, and over one-fifth of them live in one state, California. Some realtors specialize as selling or buying agents, but most do both at some point in the year. The job has both hobbyists who help with one or two transactions per year and super-salespeople who make half a million or maybe more.

We interviewed a couple of selling agents, one recommended by a friend and another who sold most of the houses in our neighborhood. The first agent was very frank, with about as much sensitivity as a gynecologist with a gas mask. "You will need to replace your current bathroom… all the pictures of your children need to go… as should all modern art and anything which looks vaguely foreign… buyers don't like that type of thing… everything should be decluttered so that each room has only one feature in it." She was exceptionally thorough, but I anticipated Lorna would likely come to blows with her. We, therefore, chose the second realtor.

We would need to decorate the house. American house buyers want to buy something completely ready to move into. Therefore, all walls are repainted, carpets replaced or steam cleaned, and new kitchens and bathrooms are installed. The typical American buyer will likely be fully leveraged in their mortgage and not have money to make any improvements once they have bought the property.

Most Americans have a lot of debt. A typical American has a college loan payment, a monthly car payment, a mortgage payment, and several credit card payments. All loans are trivial to get. Indeed, it is almost impossible to buy something without it being offered on credit. Car dealers do not want you to pay with cash; they know you are likely to pay more for the car if it is translated into a more palatable per-month cost, and they get a kickback from the loan company if you lease the car rather than buy it outright. If you buy something online, you will invariably be offered some money off if you register for another credit card or store card.

The exception to this is when you make an offer on a house, where any sensible buyer would prefer a cash buyer. However, most Americans don't have that money hanging around. Therefore, the prospective buyer needs pre-approval from a mortgage company to make an offer. Despite the 2008 housing crash, these are also relatively straightforward to obtain.

The chosen realtor gave us a long list of jobs, which took us six weeks to complete. Every wall was repainted in the latest fashionable preferred hue of gray, carpets cleaned, and wooden floors repolished. Outside, decks were repainted, the yard landscaped, and the drive and garage doors jet-washed to give it greater curb appeal. Fortunately, part of the reason for the longevity of our marriage is that my wife and I have a shared approach to botching home repair projects.

We then had to declutter and remove anything personal from the house. The psychological concept is that you want the buyer to focus entirely on picturing themselves in their new home rather than wondering about the house's current occupants. Therefore, we hid all family portraits, photographs, and toiletries. Each wall could only showcase one painting. Any picture or decoration with any element of 'foreignness' was ethnically cleansed.

We filled one large basement room with superfluous furniture and other products. We then set about neutralizing the decor. White towels and dressing gowns were purchased for our four bathrooms. Finally, the house was cleaned as it had never been cleaned before. Tiles were regrouted, carpets steam-cleaned, and every ceiling fan dusted until it looked new. The kitchen work surface displayed only the aspirational coffee machine. Every other piece of kitchen equipment had been packed away in the basement. Every cupboard now held only half its usual contents, so the unsuspecting potential buyer would think there was so much storage space. Windows were cleaned—outside and in— for the first time since we had purchased the property nine years previously. We added new doormats, shiny brass door kick plates, and flowering potted plants to each entrance.

When we finished, and all signs of our personalities were suitably erased, I have to say that the house looked outstanding. I almost wanted to live there myself.

It was straightforward to live in this new environment. In truth, most of the hidden kitchen accouterments were seldom used and knick-knacks rarely glanced at. The spaciousness and simplicity of the contemporary ambiance buoyed my mood whenever I returned to the house. However, Lorna probably resented the absence of so many souvenirs of our past.

Once we had done all this work, an additional 'professional' was drafted. She was a stager. It is claimed—mainly by these middle-class charlatans—that staged homes sell multiple times faster than non-staged ones and generate 10 to 20 percent higher prices than those without staging. Their mantra is that buyers can only imagine what they see, not what it will be. In some cases, particularly where the seller has moved out, these stagers will bring in brand-new furniture to make the house look just right. In our case, however, the stager would tell us what furniture should go where and what needed to be hidden from view.

Our stager entered our home, having first viewed our curb appeal. The meeting started poorly, "I don't suppose there is much you can do with the outside." She took a look around the entrance hall and saw that there were thousands of books in the library.

"Can you get rid of these books?" she intoned.

"It's a library...," I ventured.

"Buyers don't like books."

Things had gotten off to a bad start. We went into the main living room. Although we had already substantially pared the books on the shelves here, she was unhappy.

"More books."

She walked over to the shelves and rearranged them so that some of the books were spine inward rather than the conventional spine outward, which allowed you to determine what the book was.

"Many people prefer this look."

It was at this point that I lost it.

"Not me. We are not going to do this. It's stupid. It shows a complete disrespect for books and learning. So we will not be doing this."

The remainder of the stager consultation passed quickly. The stager couldn't wait to leave our house after my directness, and we couldn't wait for her to go.

We did heed some of her advice, though. We amended the angles of some furniture, swapped out a couple of paintings, and positioned two wine glasses and an unopened bottle of chablis seductively near the deck. I doubt these small changes made any difference to the eventual sales price. No doubt, she would counter otherwise, opining—without any evidence at all—that we would have received 10 percent more if only we had denuded the house of all books or turned their covers inward.

Most houses start with an open house where the selling agent invites potential buyers and their agents to view the house when it first comes on the market. After the open house, realtors for buyers would see the house with their clients on appointment. Having produced the marketing material, the realtor for the seller would do little. They arranged meetings but were never present at the showings. Whenever a buyer was interested, we had to be out of the house with our dogs. Our dogs were well-walked for two weeks until we finally accepted an offer.

The house-buying processes are pretty different in the UK and the US. Buying a house in America is generally quicker than in the UK. Furthermore, there is much greater certainty that your offer will lead to completion.

Buying a house takes at least three months in the UK and typically much longer if you are part of a chain of buyers and sellers waiting on each other's transactions. One advantage of the American system is that there are typically no chains. Americans are generally more confident to buy a new house before they sell their own or sell their own home before they buy a new one.

Making an offer in the US is a binding contract subject to any get-out clauses. Most of these get-out clauses expire after a week when the buyer is expected to have completed their due diligence. Once the seller has accepted the offer, they cannot consider any other offers.

In contrast, a UK contract is not signed until the end of a multiple-month-long process, which leads to some peculiar British features not found in America. One is called *gazumping*, where the seller unexpectedly accepts a higher offer from another bidder. This often happens just before the contract is signed, leaving the buyer in the unenviable position of whether to increase their offer price or walk away, frustrating the buyer of their own property. In a bear market where house prices are decreasing, the opposite might happen when a buyer *gazunders* and reduces the amount they are willing to pay. These uncertainties raise the stress of buying or selling a house.

We were fortunate that our buyer was in no rush to move. Often, the buyer wants to move within ten days. We had negotiated six weeks to figure out what to take and, more challenging, what to leave.

I love the process of downsizing. More than a decade previously, the four of us had left the UK for Hong Kong with only six bags. We had a large-for-Hong-Kong but small-for-us one-thousand-square-foot apartment. Although we didn't have our stuff around us, we were never as happy as we were during that period. Furthermore, one of the six bags, filled with Daughter #2's toys, was never opened.

When we moved to the US, Lorna was deputized to pack our possessions from our UK home into one of those containers you see on freighters. Within five days, she had thrown away or donated many of the worldly goods we had collected over our lifetime.

Are We There Yet?

As part of integrating into the US culture, we accumulated stuff all over again. New electrical devices had to be bought, multiple sofas to lay on, and any number of consumer must-haves. Our Atlanta house had a 4,500 square-foot floorplan, the standard for our area but colossal by the rest of the world's standards.

The average American home is over twice the size of its British counterpart. This is not solely because there is more space. Australia, Canada, and New Zealand also have low population densities but rarely have the McMansions that are the norm in American suburbia.

Some believe that keeping up with the Joneses is critical for the popularity of large houses. However, a likelier explanation for these oversized homes is down to a combination of three main factors.

Firstly, the fifties witnessed the development of the first interstate highways and a dramatic leap in car ownership to three-quarters of US households. This increased mobility meant that land outside the city could now be used for suburban housing. As this land was close to free, families could easily afford larger plots on which to place larger homes. Secondly, keen to differentiate suburban communities from crowded city ones, local governments issued zoning requirements restricting the number of houses that could be built on each acre of land. Thirdly, why not give yourself some extra space when the land costs so little, and the additional cost of building that additional 1,000 square feet is relatively low? This explains why four out of five American homes are detached compared to only one in five in the UK.

I am a lover of installation art. One of my favorite works is *Break Down* by Michael Landy. In 2001, Landy conceived an idea to destroy all his possessions by dismembering them into their component parts or recycling them where possible. He and a team of twelve associates constructed a three-hundred-foot conveyor belt in an empty C&A store on Oxford Street and deconstructed every one of his 7,227 worldly goods. Each possession was cataloged on a spreadsheet and gradually dismantled. These ranged from his beloved Saab 900 Turbo to love letters.

The work was a commentary on consumption and consumerism. Who we are is not determined by what we have. Landy described the two weeks as the happiest time of his life. Yet, paradoxically, he also described it as like witnessing his own funeral. His mother stopped by the installation, but Landy had to throw her out when she became upset because her son was destroying irreplaceable pictures of him as a young boy. He was eliminating what she and her husband had worked so hard for.

At the end of the installation, Landy was left with only the boiler suit he wore for the dismantling process. He had no money and no other possessions. However, within five minutes, someone had given him a Paul Weller CD... and all he needed was a CD player to play it.

Our task was to downsize our possessions into a 16x8x8-foot pod, roughly equivalent to a three-room apartment. We both had clear ideas on how to achieve this. The challenge was that I saw little need for what Lorna valued, and she saw no need for me to keep my five-thousand-book library.

Like Landy, I constructed a spreadsheet that cataloged our possessions, measured each item's dimensions, and calculated the storage cost for each piece for a six-month, twelve-month, and two-year travel period. We would use this spreadsheet to determine whether we wanted to keep something. "Do you really want to pay $100 to keep that horrible table?"

Gradually, we reduced what we owned. We became regulars on the Freecycle website, and there seemingly was no shortage of Americans who wanted more possessions. We made a dozen trips to the local dump. Finally, we sold or gave sofas and fridges to our buyers.

The extended period before we moved also gave us time to say goodbye to the many friends we had cultivated in Atlanta. We would see most of them again but less regularly. Our neighbors threw a surprise party for us at a local restaurant, and we spent the last night playing pool with our immediate next-door neighbors.

Our thirty-five years of homeownership ended in a surprisingly swift one-hour signing session with the closing attorney. I couldn't help but ponder the nature of his job, which seemed like a never-ending cycle of monotony. His role was to churn out a seemingly endless stream of documents for every house sale, so numerous that he couldn't even carry them all at once. He presumably embarked on the same routine each day— preparing documents for the upcoming day's sales and meeting with buyers and sellers to put their signatures on these papers. During our session, we found ourselves signing a staggering hundred pieces of paper, not one of which we had the time or inclination to read. In hindsight, if we had attempted to peruse each document, we might still be sitting there, weeks later, buried under the paperwork.

We had things to do. We were on the move.

Are We There Yet?

Chapter 3 – The Southernmost Point

On the day we sold our Atlanta house, an East Coast gas company announced they had been the victims of a cyberattack and could no longer transport gas through their pipelines. Naturally, this caused panic among Atlanta's moms. Traffic around gas stations came to a standstill as vehicles queued for hours, and further chaos struck the forecourts as drivers tried to maneuver their cars to the appropriate positions to top up their already three-quarter-full tanks.

It had been a similar story the year before at the onset of Covid but with toilet tissue, disinfectant wipes, and groceries. Supermarket shelves were denuded of produce, leaving behind only plant-based protein, cauliflower pizza crust, and unsalted potato chips. The doomsday preppers were smug at their foresight, finally able to open their gallon cans of baked beans.

In 2020, it had taken months for the supermarkets to match demand, mainly because today's supply chain is subject to something called Just-in-Time Manufacturing in an attempt to eke out a smidgeon more margin. However, this also brings all company risks into one place because these processes remove redundancy, resilience, and spare capacity.

Panic buying is not a recent phenomenon. Throughout modern history, times of crisis have caused surging demand for certain products. For instance, during the Spanish Flu epidemic of 1918-19, demand for health products tripled; amidst German hyperinflation in the twenties, panic buying was rampant as people rushed to purchase almost anything before the price skyrocketed later in the day: and, during the 1962 Cuban Missile Crisis, Americans stocked up on record numbers of canned goods.

This pandemic wasn't responsible for the first toilet paper shortage. In December 1973, US Representative Harold Froehlich issued a press release declaring, "The US may face a shortage of toilet paper within a few months." Consequently, Americans swarmed to the supermarkets to buy toilet tissue before it ran out. They may not have known that Froehlich represented a district where the paper industry was a significant employer.

Ammunition is another perennial panic purchase during times of uncertainty. The election of President Obama and the later Sandy Hook Elementary School shootings triggered two rounds of panic buying. The gas shortage probably would have led to further bullet stockpiling, but the gunmakers still hadn't been able to reload their stocks after the post-Capitol insurrection hoarding as manufacturers struggled to produce more than their usual twelve billion rounds per year.

This may not be a popular opinion, but I regard most panic buying as logical. If something you use will be in short supply, buying some of it before it is no longer available makes sense. What isn't rational, however, is to buy twenty tins of condensed milk when you have consumed only one in the previous decade.

Moreover, there are also psychological aspects to panic buying. When there is uncertainty, hoarding allows the individual to regain some control over the crisis and relieve their anxiety. Two things also happen on social media at the time of panic buying. First, one person will demonstrate their economic virility by showing their conspicuous consumption of something in short supply. A second person will virtue signal their disdain for such selfish behavior and point out that you can easily perform your toilet rituals without bathroom tissue. Deep down, however, you know that this second person has either surreptitiously made the same purchase or, at this very moment, is taking yet another shower.

Two British universities found that the most avid panic buyers were higher-income mothers. Three-quarters of these Karens initially reported that they personally never engaged in panic buying though responses to later questions established they did so on a wide variety of products.

This gas shortage was problematic for those planning to move to Florida the next day. My truck tank was three-quarters full, and some ten thousand gas stations had signs indicating the depletion of their stocks. I wondered how far I would get with this fuel.

The background story of the cyberattack is noteworthy and merits a few paragraphs. Colonial, the pipeline company that transports oil to Virginia, North and South Carolina, and Georgia, was hacked by some apologetic Slavic whiz kids. These geeks hadn't meant to cause problems for people; they merely wanted to extort large sums of money from the pipeline owners.

Are We There Yet?

Colonial had successfully air-gapped its oil transportation systems from the internet, but its billing systems were entirely compromised. During later Congressional hearings, Colonial's CEO proudly said, "It wasn't as if the password was Colonial123." However, it subsequently transpired that an ex-employee had used a more complex password—I'm guessing c0l0n1al123—on another compromised site. Once the duplicate password had been deduced, the absence of multi-factor authentication meant it was child's play for the hackers to download 100GB of data and infect its systems with malware.

The hackers left a .txt file for Colonial, in which they threatened to upload Colonial's data onto the internet if a ransom of 75 Bitcoin was not paid. As it's not illegal for a US company to pay a ransom (provided the payee isn't on the Treasury's sanctions list), Colonial paid the ransom and received the decryption software by return email.

The brains behind the attack were an Eastern European company called Dark Side, which offers Ransomware as a Service (RAAS) to partners that break into another company's IT systems. Dark Side collects a 25 percent cut in any ransom paid, with their partners taking the rest. From Darkside's 2019 business prospectus, we know that about half the targeted companies (47 out of 99) paid an average ransom of $2 million for the decryption key.

Dark Side sees itself as a modern-day Robin Hood and regularly makes charitable donations. However, it is considered to have links with Russia because it avoids attacking sites with Russian as its default language setting.

The later Senate hearings revealed that US authorities had recovered 63.7 bitcoin from this heist a few weeks later, presumably all the bitcoin except for Dark Side's cut. Unfortunately for Colonial, the price of Bitcoin had since plummeted, leaving Colonial still $2 million out of pocket.

You may wonder why the Russians are so adept at cyber hacking. According to the International Institute for Strategic Studies and the Belfer Centre for Science and International Affairs, Russia is only a tier two cyber power along with China, Britain, Australia, France, and Israel. And the only tier-one cyber power? Yes, you've guessed it. The USA. Makes you proud.

****

Lorna set off in her car while I drove the small U-Haul truck. The U-Haul was easy to operate but less pleasurable than any other car I had ever driven. The steering wheel had a lot of give, and the brakes were slow to respond. We used different GPS apps, and I was surprised we went in different directions at the first set of traffic lights. After a few miles, my GPS suggested a slightly quicker and more unusual route that would save four minutes. So, I decided to trust the technology and take the road less traveled.

The Georgia Gods evidently disapproved of our betrayal of their state and arranged for the mother of all storms to parade their anger. For two hours, I could see the tempest chasing me from my side mirrors. The clouds grew darker to a deep shade of purple, and I glimpsed flashes of lightning hitting the ground in both mirrors and, a few seconds later, I heard the crashes of furious thunder.

The journey southward to Florida was an anxious one. With every freeway exit, my gas gauge inched closer to empty, and at each gas station, I was met with hastily written signs regretting their fuel shortages. Despite my futile attempts at the first four stations, they boldly displayed prices at a steep 30 percent premium over the regular rates. Thankfully, the fifth one had recently received an emergency delivery. This was just in time, as even in Florida, drivers were hoarding petrol, sometimes pouring it into plastic bags. As Colonial did not supply gas to Florida, this showed excessive caution.

I arrived at the first agreed meeting place about two and a half hours from our starting point. I half expected Lorna to have beaten me to the rendezvous point. Instead, when I located her cell phone position, I was surprised that she was ninety minutes behind me. She was delayed by a crash on the road I would have taken, and the bad weather had compounded her progress.

I continued my journey rather than waiting. Still in Georgia, the billboards advertised adult stores and strip clubs. I was pleased to read that they had ample room for truck parking though I suspected that my rig that day would look meager compared to the heavy-goods vehicles of the cross-country trucker. Then, in Florida, the billboards suddenly changed. They informed me that God loved me and that Jesus would return to be with us again. They also implored pregnant women to talk to them if they contemplated committing the ultimate sin.

I decided to wait for Lorna in a gas station shop just after the Florida border and people-watch my soon-to-be fellow Floridians.

Are We There Yet?

We planned to be nomads for an indefinite period, traveling as our mood dictated, freed from the constraints of homeownership. However, we still needed a registered address for credit cards and other purposes. And this was why—even though we had never been inside a Recreational Vehicle—we joined an RV membership organization.

Fourteen million American households own an RV, a sizeable component of the forty million Americans who go camping every year. I guess the perception is that most RV owners are seniors. However, Millennials are both the largest group of RV owners and the largest group wanting to buy an RV in the next five years.

Most use their RVs for about twenty days of vacation. However, as reported by the RV Industry Association, three and a half million Americans live more or less full-time in their truly mobile home. This diverse group comprises nurses, digital nomads, and retirees. While most full-time RVers choose this way of life willingly, as highlighted in the film *Nomadland*, a significant portion finds themselves in this circumstance, picking up seasonal work where they can find it.

There are two types of RVs and two types of vans. The largest is the motorized RV, which can set you back anything from $50,000 to $500,000. RVs towed by trucks share a similar price point but offer the advantage of being able to leave your home behind when you go to the supermarket or the movie theater. Both types of RVs come equipped with all the amenities you'd find in a compact home.

The campervan or converted van is the live-in vehicle of choice for the Millennial. It is smaller and more discrete. It could be a VW van manufactured explicitly as a house on wheels or a converted transit van or minivan.

The US has some eighteen thousand RV parks, and Canada has another four thousand. These will have electrical hookups, water, and sewage facilities. However, most van residents prefer boondocking, parking your vehicle for free in a remote area without facilities.

These three-and-a-half million permanent RVers or van-lifers need a postal address, and the RV Association provides mail services in Texas, South Dakota, and Florida. You are probably asking why these three states and not one of the other forty-seven. I do not know, but these three states are notable because they impose no state income tax on their residents.

It's easy to think that every country is comprised mainly of its stereotypical inhabitants. The stylish Italian is passionate about his food, culture, and lovers. The efficient German is direct, hardworking, and likes her beer. The Japanese homemaker is submissive, loyal, and reserved. The stereotype isn't always representative of those you meet. I've met Italians who can barely differentiate between red and white wine, nuanced Germans, and forceful Japanese women.

The stereotypical American is a technology-loving, gun-toting, patriotic, hardworking, home-bodied, optimistic, and charitable freedom lover. However, it is easy to find Americans who don't abide by these behaviors and choose to live on their terms rather than conform to others' expectations. Due to Americans' predominantly individualistic mindset and their acceptance of diverse lifestyles, it's straightforward to lead a life that deviates significantly from the norm. Whereas, in some other countries, the dominant culture that defines and binds a nation also restricts the size of its unconventional or maverick communities.

Befitting the world's third most populous country, minority sub-cultures can be sizeable. For instance, the only country where the Amish can flourish is America, the bushy-bearded hermit can find his peace in every sizeable US mountain range, and a few million Americans choose to roam their country in a van. Bikers, cosplayers, environmental activists, graffiti artists, hackers, hippies, hipsters, preppers, skaters, surfers, swingers, transitioners, and various religious groups are sub-cultures that live their lives by different rules. Van life is an alternative lifestyle—every bit as American as a Marine, someone on Wall Street, or a linesman.

Some of these nomads are retired, but the majority find some way of generating income as they travel the country. As in *Nomadland*, some eke out their living performing mainly manual seasonal work, while others are Generation-Z digital nomads who can perform their duties anywhere with an internet connection.

Most van lifers purchase an aged minivan or cargo van for a few thousand dollars and kit it with a rudimentary bed, storage space, and kitchen. They then add solar panels to the outer shell to power devices.

Provided they maintain a minimalist lifestyle, these van-lifers can live happily on just ten thousand dollars per person each year, which they can earn through seasonal manual work or knowledge-based tasks taking just a couple of hours a day at a nearby Starbucks. The van lifers I talk to all want to work minimally so they can enjoy life maximally.

Devotees of this lifestyle have improvised workarounds to the lifestyle's numerous challenges. For instance, they utilize America's ubiquitous public toilet facilities in preference to defecating in a bucket, transform gym chains into their personal spa with showers, and convert the great outdoors into their kitchen and dining room. They use postbox addresses or siblings' homes for their mail, and they park their vehicles overnight for free in National Forests, beach car lots, or any Walmart. The other day, I counted seven such vans at our local dog beach parking lot.

This go-with-less community has spurned the traditional nine-to-five grind and suburban McMansions, partly influenced by their parents' experiences during the Great Recession. Instead, they cherish the freedom to travel and pursue their passions. Some FIRE (financial independence, retire early), while others seek ways to cover essential expenses. What unites them all is their rejection of unnecessary consumerism.

Because I'm open to talking with anyone, I frequently encounter van lifers during my travels. I encounter them at the beach, on hiking trails, and at Aldi. They are usually eager to share their experiences, way of life, and plans with me. Many seem to view this lifestyle as a temporary adventure and plan to settle in an ideal community after a few years on the road. I find conversations with them insightful because they've taken the time to reflect deeply on their life's goals and desires.

Most are childless couples, about half of whom seem to have a dog. I have also met young couples with children in tow. Their preferred form of travel is the converted yellow school bus, or *skoolie*.

These intrepid couples, yearning for a minimalist family life on the move, invest months transforming decommissioned buses into family homes. They strip, insulate, and wire the buses before ingeniously crafting mini-kitchens, bathrooms, sleeping quarters, living spaces, and storage within every cubic inch. These revamped 'skoolies' become snug, off-grid sanctuaries that enable nomadic families to travel the open road with a taste of home comfort.

As most people prefer warm weather, van-lifers spend the winters in one of the Southern states or Central America. In the summer, they move northwards. There are some variants to this model. Rafters will spend November to April in South America and May to October in North America, while skiers will do the opposite.

The number of those living a van life has ballooned since Covid. A few decided to travel when laid off, some used van life to escape authoritarian state restrictions, and many started to travel when they were allowed to work remotely.

Our first overnight stop was the offices of this RV association, located in the small central Florida town of Bushnell. We needed to register as residents of this small town, obtain Florida driving licenses, and re-register our remaining car as Floridian rather than Georgian. We did these things in about an hour, making a small tax payment for importing our vehicle into our new state of Florida.

Our car now flaunted a brand-new Florida license plate, the number of which I still have not learned. Georgia's 'Peach Tree State' slogan had been replaced by Florida's 'Sunshine State.' We only had to pay for one license plate as Florida is one of nineteen states that does not require a tag on the front of the vehicle.

New York boldly led the way as the first state to demand license plates, but back then, resourceful drivers had to craft their own.

A short while later, in 1903, Massachusetts joined the license plate party. With about as much originality as a cover band at a karaoke night, the first state-issued tag was given to a man called Frederick Tudor. It read 1.

State slogans were an innovation from Idaho. Each license from this state simply read 'Idaho potatoes' though it has since been upgraded to 'Famous potatoes.' My favorite slogan? 'Live Free or Die;' it almost makes me want to make New Hampshire my home.

In Florida's Sumter County, responsibility for these functions fell to the appropriate-to-the-pandemic-named Randy Mask. I asked the lady at the counter if she knew the British meaning of the Tax Collector's first name. Lorna gave me that warning glare that implored me to keep as quiet as a mouse with a sore throat. The helpful lady said no. I said that it meant excessively amorous. She probably knew Randy and returned what I thought to be a knowing smile.

We never did call at our notional address in Bushnell, and with it in our back mirror, we drove south toward more coastal parts.

****

We had asked for our storage pod to be deposited in a Gulf Coast town called Venice. We had no idea where or when we would eventually settle, but having the smaller, more accessible storage in the same city seemed sensible. I selected a storage unit in an air-conditioned hangar divided into hundreds of mini-compounds, each delineated by steel wire fencing.

We emptied the U-Haul into our seven-by-ten-foot storage unit. This was back-breaking work as we piled our belongings ten feet high into the tiny cage. Unsurprisingly, Lorna soon excused herself to view a potential future apartment. As I unloaded the goods from the truck, I realized that

Are We There Yet?

most of it was essentially junk. In a future episode of *Storage Wars*, the winning bidder would be very disappointed by the haul from our U-Haul. Contrary to Lorna's expectations, progress on fitting the packages seemed to proceed more quickly without her sage spatial advice.

Americans love to rent self-storage space. Despite having houses over twice the size of other nationalities, one in ten households rent a storage unit, paying around $100 every month. They stop by these self-storage spaces only to put new things in them, and goods are only withdrawn for episodes of *Storage Wars*.

While I waited for Lorna to return, I chatted with one of the workers at the storage unit. We talked about the cult of Trumpism. When we had stayed in Florida the previous December, Trump rallies were ever-present. Even though he had lost the election the month before, there were rallies every day in multiple locations. I was surprised then and even more astonished that these rallies continued six months later. Post-Capitol insurrection, the yard signs now accepted that Trump was not president but proclaimed that the election was stolen and that Biden should be impeached.

For these zealots, it was not good enough that you did not criticize their messiah—you also had to shower him with unconditional praise. By way of example, although my debut book garnished primarily excellent customer reviews, I reflected disproportionately on the first two mildly negative reviews. They came from people who objected to my political viewpoints. While I aimed to remain politically neutral in the first book, I accepted the inevitability that some readers wouldn't enjoy it due to its differing perspectives on the world.

The first negative review was for the audiobook. The reviewer objected to my acceptance of Daughter #2's sympathy for a domestic terror group. The group in question was Black Lives Matter. On the positive side, the reviewer did rate the production as 5/5, which made the hundreds of hours of work worthwhile.

The second review (4/5 on Amazon) reads: "He's a very good writer; he is informative, funny and thorough… but he just can't help the constant snide, snarky comments about President Trump." Lorna disapproved of this review, but I was interested because I had mentioned Trump only once by name in the book and a second time by his position. Further, neither mention was hostile. The first—in the penultimate chapter 20—was a joke, and the second merely a fact that the then-current incumbent of the White House had a picture of President Andrew Jackson on the wall of his Oval

Office. My crime seemed to be that I had omitted to point out that Trump was the most wonderful person to have ever walked on the planet.

****

We drove onto our first monthly stop, Key West. Lorna had wanted something Caribbean-like for our first lengthy stop. I was pleased with this choice because Key West, the southernmost point in the lower 48 states, felt like an apt starting point for our nomadic year.

Florida is chiefly a peninsula over six hundred miles long. So, while we were already a long way south, we still had a lengthy drive to complete. The journey was punctuated with regular delays from traffic wrecks caused by inattentive drivers.

Traffic experts had assumed that the pandemic's emptier roads from fewer commuters and vacationers would reduce traffic accidents and fatalities. Unfortunately, the opposite happened.

Driving deaths—which had dropped year-on-year since the sixties due to lower speed limits, higher drinking age, and safer vehicles—rose by over a sixth during the first year of the pandemic. Other experts believe the leading cause of this increase was increased frustration and anger caused by social disengagement. Art Markman, a cognitive scientist from the University of Texas, argued that most Americans had experienced "two years of having to stop ourselves from doing things that we'd like to do. When you get angry in the car, it generates energy—and how do you dissipate that energy? Well, one way is to put your foot down more on the accelerator."

There may be other factors, too. The number of drivers testing positive for opioids doubled in Covid's first year, and those testing positive for marijuana also rose by half. Indeed, total deaths from drug overdoses hit one hundred thousand Americans for the first time in 2021, more than all traffic and gun deaths combined. Some states' progress in reducing opioid addiction that I wrote about in *High, Wide, and Handsome* was utterly annulled.

Covid-related stress levels were high, legal and illegal opioid prescriptions had increased, and addiction programs had moved online. As a result, it was easier to get drugs and more difficult to get treatment.

The one-hundred-mile US1 from Key Largo to Key West is one of the great American road trips. It is called the Overseas Highway because it runs over seas rather than being overseas. We have journeyed along its path a dozen times, savoring the expansive ocean views on both sides.

The vehicle of choice for this journey is the open-top sports car or a Harley. Expect to travel leisurely; although the maximum speed limit is 55mph, the traffic frequently moves considerably slower. The Monroe County Police Department is also as sly as a fox in a henhouse. It positions its fleet regularly over the hundred-mile journey. You only see that most of these police vehicles have no drivers in them when you have passed them at 40mph.

Our previous journey along the Overseas Highway occurred just a few months after Hurricane Irma had called in 2017. Along the route, for more than fifty miles, we encountered a striking sight—towering piles of debris flanking both sides of the road, forming a transient monument to the havoc unleashed by Irma's relentless 177mph winds, a phenomenon aptly dubbed 'Irmageddon.' The sheer force of the hurricane had compelled a staggering six and a half million Floridians to evacuate, and the aftermath cast three-quarters of the state into darkness, with power lines rendered powerless. There had been a mandatory evacuation from the Keys, and it was ten days before engineers finally deemed bridges safe enough for the return of Key West-bound traffic.

Our 2021 drive coincided with the annual hundred-mile running race from Key Largo to Key West. You can participate in this ultramarathon individually or as a six-person relay team. Brett Sanborn ran the fastest time in history at 13 hours and 20 minutes; not bad for someone running almost four consecutive marathons. He was also victorious this year but took an hour longer due to the excessive heat. Impressively, he finished nearly two and a half hours ahead of the second-placed runner. Astonishingly, the quickest relay teams run the distance in a shade over nine hours, very little of which, by the way, is in the shade.

This year's 90-degree heat had strewn runners along about fifty miles of the US1. There are no water stations along the route, and each runner must provide a support team that travels ahead, waiting by the side of the road with refreshments.

The only road to Key West offers no opportunity for shortcuts and has mile markers counting down to 0 at Key West. These mile markers are used everywhere for directions in this part of the world: "Drive to mile marker 28 and then take a left onto Kikis after the Shell Gas Station." I can only imagine how it feels after running the equivalent of a 5K to see mile marker 97.

Not everyone who runs this race does so to win it. While the annual London Marathon showcases the deeply eccentric nature of the British, there are unusual people elsewhere in the world, too. One runner thought this hundred-mile in Florida's summer heat wasn't sufficiently challenging unless simultaneously pumping heavy weights, while another man ran carrying a five-foot by four-foot American flag. I guess you have to be somewhat eccentric to compete in ultramarathons.

As an aside, did you know that most ultrarunners take two pairs of shoes? They change into a larger shoe size to accommodate their expanded feet around halfway.

****

Before World War I, the Florida Keys could only be reached by boat. Then, Henry Flagler, a big-shot from Standard Oil and a significant investor in Florida, took on a daring project—he built a railroad that connected the entire Florida East Coast to Key West. Initially ridiculed as 'Flagler's Folly' because of the immense engineering challenges, even the hurricanes of 1906, 1909, and 1910 couldn't deter the construction. When it finally opened in 1912, it earned the nickname 'the Eighth Wonder of the World.' This groundbreaking connection made Key West, already a wealthy city thanks to the wrecking industry and its strategic trade route to New Orleans, accessible to all Americans.

When Flagler's trains reached Key West, travelers had the enticing option to embark on a direct journey to Cuba, back when it was a friendly neighbor. They achieved this by hoisting some carriages onto three-hundred-foot barges to ferry them across the waters to Havana. This international route gained even greater popularity following the introduction of Prohibition in 1920.

In 1935, a category five hurricane—sometimes called 'the storm of the century'—washed away forty miles of track and killed five hundred people. The Florida East Coast Railway, bankrupted by the Great Depression, couldn't afford to rebuild. The State of Florida bought the railway for a bargain price of $640,000 and, as part of the New Deal investment, used much of it to create the Overseas Highway in 1938.

Despite now being attached to mainland USA via a series of forty-two bridges, Key West remains essentially a Caribbean Island. Famously, the final Key connected by road is closer to Havana in Cuba than Miami on the Florida mainland. President Kennedy's 1961 Bay of Pigs speech urged

Are We There Yet?

Americans not to be "complacent about Iron Curtain tanks and planes less than 90 miles from our shores." Today's fact-checkers would have pointed out that—while it is about 90 nautical miles to Cuba—the two places are 103 (statute) miles apart.

For those who want to understand the difference, a nautical mile is a fraction of the circumference of the Earth, equal to precisely one minute of latitude. So, one nautical mile is 1.1508 land-based miles. Speed on land and water is also calculated to the same conversion rate; when a boat travels at 10 knots, it's moving at 11.5 miles per hour.

While we are busting myths, it is not true that you can see Havana from Key West. If you are six feet tall (as I almost am), you can see only three miles away due to the almost spherical nature of the Earth. Even if you were as tall as a giraffe in high heels, you wouldn't see much further. To see one hundred miles away, Pythagoras's theorem informs us that you would need to be at a height of 6,660 feet (1,878 meters). This is almost two and half times higher than the world's tallest building at the time of writing, Burj Khalifa in Dubai.

Until the economic boycott of Cuba in 1960, you could also take a car ferry from Key West to Havana. The four-hour ferry left Key West in the late morning and arrived in Havana in time for dinner and dancing. It then returned the following day to Florida. Assuming relations between Cuba and the USA continue to improve, I suspect a boat service will return in my lifetime.

One person did not need the ferry for the journey. In 2013, Diana Nyad was the first to swim from Cuba to Key West without the aid of a shark cage. Her mother had told her when she was a girl that Cuba was almost close enough to swim to. Strong currents, asthma attacks, venomous jellyfish injuries, and storms thwarted her first four attempts. Finally, at sixty-four—thirty-five years after her first attempt—she made a successful fifty-three-hour swim from Havana to Key West.

Key West has offered other endeavors for the keen open-water swimmer. Anna Fugina used to swim as a therapy to recover from a severe car accident. In 1977, she swam twelve and a half miles around Key West in under thirteen hours, mainly against the tide. Fugina studied tide tables the following year and improved her time to eight hours. As a result, she inadvertently started an annual competition for open-water swimmers and still competes on landmark birthdays.

Julian Bishop

We were as snug as a bug in a rug with a heated blanket in our cozy apartment in the southern heart of New Town. Our short-term home included a pair of bicycles, and we pedaled everywhere under the cloudless azure sky and the sun's fiery embrace.

The first thing that you notice is Key West's unusual wildlife. Strolling along its charming streets, you'll find an unexpected sight—chickens freely roaming about. At first, Dog #2 couldn't contain her excitement when she spotted some unattended, tantalizing, non-flying snacks. With the zeal of a caffeine-fueled tourist chasing the last piece of key lime pie, she tugged at her leash, determined to get a closer look. Another evening, as the sun dipped below the horizon, Dog #1's curiosity led him to a brood of bantams nuzzled in the soft grass. With a sudden burst of energy, he lunged toward them, causing a ruckus that disrupted their peaceful slumber and our neighbors' tranquility. Alas, there was no grand feast for Dog #1 on that occasion, as I managed to restrain his adventurous spirit just in the nick of time.

The chickens originated from Cuba and other Caribbean islands as part of the cockfighting industry. When cockfighting was outlawed in Key West, the chickens were left to fend for themselves. They have fared pretty well due to a lack of wild mammal predators on the island; however, if a chicken is foolish enough to leave the tree-lined streets, it is not uncommon to see a hawk swoop down and bring home its own bargain bucket.

Cockfighting was banned in England and Wales in 1835, and you might think this practice has been illegal in the USA for a similar length of time. You would be wrong. Cockfighting was proscribed in Key West in the seventies, and the last state to prohibit it was Louisiana in 2008. It is now a felony in the mainland USA to attend a cockfight, and Federal Law supposedly also banned it in its territories in 2019, but it is reckoned that Puerto Rico still has two hundred thousand fighting birds.

I enjoy the company of these chickens and appreciate the distraction their presence brings. Many chickens descend from Red Jungle Fowl and are bright reds, yellows, blues, and greens. As I write this paragraph from Key West's excellent library, I see four fowls with fashionable flowing feathers foraging for food. They peck into people's private patios and bound down the bustling boulevards. It's poultry in motion.

Not everyone enjoys the chickens. Sleeping late in Key West is challenging, as the cockerels will wake you just before dawn arrives. Chicken feces are everywhere. Angry residents are not allowed to kill the wild chickens but are permitted to trap them. A local wildlife center will then re-house these captured birds. In an example of not counting your chickens, there is no estimate on the number of feral fowl in Key West. However, the local wildlife center takes in around two thousand every year.

Why did the chicken cross the road? The original 1847 punchline still has not made anybody laugh, and frankly, the chickens want to live in a world where they can cross the road without their motives being questioned. In Key West, it is because the chicken is free-range. It is commonplace to see a car or bicycle come to an abrupt halt as a family group of chickens decides that the other side looks a little bit more appealing.

I know some readers may have been disappointed by the lack of a punchline. How about this chicken joke:

What do you get when you cross a chicken with a fox? A fox.

Chickens aren't the only animals given free range. Wherever you walk in Key West, small lizards—skinks, anoles, and race runners, to name just three—dart out of their sun traps at the sound of your footsteps. Lizards up to six feet in length are pervasive here, too. Green iguanas first appeared in Key West in the sixties though there are conflicting stories about how they got here. Some say they stowed away amongst food shipments from South America, while others believe they were unwanted pets. This exotic but non-native iguana is now a resident of most Key West neighborhoods, and these orange and yellow prehistoric dinosaurs occupy every habitat. The country club pool we swam in would regularly have a dozen sunbathing iguanas jostling for space with the human sun hedonists. At first, the Keys' community welcomed these dinosaurs; it was similar to *Jurassic Park* but without the danger. However, they soon came into conflict with humans in bothersome ways, as they burrowed into sewage lines and would occasionally appear from your toilet. If you are afraid of spiders, think about how you would react to a lizard about your size unexpectedly emanating from beneath your nether region.

In 2010, there was a cold snap over much of Southern Florida. Temperatures fell to the 30s (low degrees Celsius), highly unusual in Florida. Residents reported iguanas dropping from trees onto the ground or perhaps onto an unfortunate passerby. As a result, there was a considerable thinning of Florida's iguana population. However, not in Key West, whose lowest-ever recorded temperature is 42°F (6°C).

Invasive lizards are at record levels in the Keys, and the authorities are determined to eliminate iguanas. The Florida Wildlife Commission urges people to hunt and kill iguanas on their property or public land. How should we kill them, I hear you ask. I am no expert in this, but Chuck Meier, the author of the best-selling iguana cookbook, says, "Shoot them in the top of the head or right behind the eye above that little ear plate. If the iguana is facing you, hit it in the chest."

Because, contrary to what you may believe, not every Floridian is a crack shot, the municipal government is also employing contractors to eradicate these six-foot monsters. In Key West, these professionals have removed three thousand iguanas in the Key West cemetery over the past two years. In a great double-sided business model, these professionals make money from local governments and selling these iguanas. The young iguanas are typically sold as pets outside Florida, while the older ones end up as pet food or perhaps specialist sausage for human consumption. The professionals prefer the old-fashioned method of pole and lasso but must shoot them when in the mangrove and other water areas.

Keeping an iguana as a pet in Key West is no longer allowed. If you have an existing pet, you can 'grandfather' it, but it must be chipped. You are also no longer permitted to take it for a walk.

Another invasive species is the *aedes aegypti mosquito.* These little buggers are the party crashers of the insect world, transmitting dengue, Zika, and yellow fever to the fiesta. While in the Keys, Oxitec, a British pharmaceutical company, decided to play matchmaker by releasing over one hundred thousand genetically modified male mosquitoes that will mate with the female invasive species. The female offspring of these encounters will not survive.

Some environmental groups described the plan as a Jurassic Park experiment and warned that once you release these mutant mosquitoes into the environment, you will never be able to recall them. Yet, despite these portents, the project was approved via referendum.

Yet another annoying invasive species is tourists. We first visited Key West as a stop for a large cruise ship many decades ago. The twenty-five-thousand-person town was overwhelmed by thousands of cruisers walking along the same street. As I recall, Lorna and I escaped the madness and went snorkeling at a nearby beach.

However, the residents are fighting back. The big political issue when we were there was whether to accept 75 percent of the investment from the State of Florida to improve the Key West Cruise Pier. A few months earlier, residents of Key West voted in favor of three referenda that would limit the size and frequency of cruise boats. According to these plebiscites, ships carrying over 1,500 passengers and crew will be prohibited, and preference will be given to cruise lines with excellent health and environmental records.

The local government leaders needed to balance heeding the wishes of their electorate with repairing a dilapidated pier. Not taking state funds would likely lead to a 1 percent increase in sales tax. As we were leaving Key West, the island's leaders had agreed to rebuild only a smaller pier (which would only accommodate smaller and fewer liners) with the State's money. The next move was with the Republican Florida Governor, who, one month after our visit, imposed statewide seaport legislation that overruled outcomes of the Key West referenda.

Although June was officially out-of-season, Key West hit record accommodation bookings, and every hotel and rental was booked. The Comfort Inn, a cheaper motel similar to a Premier Inn, was offering its rooms at a staggering $700 a night. Many Americans had convinced themselves that the virus had subsided, and they wanted to play.

****

Our days gradually formed a familiar pattern. Lorna would work in the morning, and I would get out of her hair by playing tennis or pickleball and, after exercise, go to the library to write.

The gentler pickleball scene was more vibrant than that for tennis. Part tennis and part ping-pong, pickleball requires a court about half the size of a tennis court. It can be played on the concrete part of the front drives in Florida and, more professionally, on public pickleball courts.

Being similar to an ex-pat community, Key West was an easy place to make friends. You had to make friends as fast as a cheetah on roller skates because you or the other person might be moving somewhere else shortly. After so long of socializing distantly, it was a joy to talk to people again. I enjoyed the diverse mix of military veterans, nomads, LGTBQ+ individuals, retirees, conchs of all types, and recent transplants as I played pickleball.

I like to think of the following people as a representative sample of the people who call Key West their home:

Natalie, the manager of a vegetarian café I frequented, shouted at some tourists chasing chickens. 'Stupid Americans,' or words to that effect, she yelled. When I asked whether she was American, she affirmed but told me she often had little affinity with her nationality. Furthermore, she said she was a saltwater conch—pronounced with two hard 'k' sounds—someone who was born and raised in Key West. Otherwise, you are a foreigner. There is a halfway house. If you have lived in Key West for over seven years, you have become a freshwater conch.

Missy and Judith wished that Key West was more like it used to be and echoed the thoughts of many other conchs I met. They lamented that it used to be a unique place in America, but now it resembled many others. Big companies had bought all the waterfront property, and locals were being priced out of their homes. They supported the Key West mayor, who wanted to keep out the large cruise ships and were exasperated with Florida's Governor.

Ed was also a conch but one with a more positive attitude. His twenty-four-year-old son had come out as gay earlier that summer. Ed told me that, deep down, he had always known it. While momentarily disappointed about the probable lack of grandchildren, he was happy that his son could live authentically.

Derek was a third-generation conch and former high-school football coach in town. He had little in the way of formal tennis coaching but was obviously sporty. However, he resisted my advice, telling me his former teaching friends would bar him from playing in their socials if he got good.

Jay was a confident investment banker and as cool as a cucumber at an iceberg convention. He moved to the Keys for nine months after Covid struck and traveled everywhere by Vespa. He worked remotely but somehow managed to play pickleball every morning.

Rod was an itinerant software engineer and had been here for a year. He wanted to get out before the summer hit and thought he might walk the Appalachian or Pacific Crest Trail. He did not want to take the vaccine but said he was looking at all the CDC data. Ideally, he would love to travel to Europe but conceded that this was not likely without him taking a vaccine.

John had arrived in Key West nine months previously and completed his realtor license. He had a couple of buyer clients but, as a thirty-year-old outsider, struggled to attract any sellers.

Andrew and Lisa lived in Hell's Kitchen in New York in non-pandemic times. They longed to return to New York City and were distraught that so many of their favorite restaurants had closed.

Are We There Yet?

Chris and Madison, a young couple in their twenties, had an unconventional journey. They made a move as bold as a sledgehammer at a clock mender, selling their rural Georgia home and investing the proceeds in Bitcoin. They slept in the bed of their truck at night with their dog and had a vague plan to travel along the Florida coast until they found where they wanted to be. They believed they could buy a house with cash if they did well enough with Bitcoin. In their unique way, they were living their American Dream, doing precisely what they desired.

Another John, a military veteran turned trailing spouse, faithfully followed his wife across the United States. He liked Key West more than most places because many people had military backgrounds.

Larry was a semi-retired freshwater conch who managed vacation rentals for friends. He was a shy gay man with exquisite taste. He had chosen Key West for its relaxed lifestyle.

Mike had retired from an engineering career to Key West a few years ago. His mother-in-law, who lived in an adjacent apartment, had recently passed. He played tennis twice daily and socialized with friends the rest of the time.

Apologies to all the others I met but neglected to record at the time. These individuals had a handful of things in common. They all liked the Caribbean lifestyle, were tolerant of what anyone else did with their lives, and were politically unaffiliated.

Lorna preferred to fish rather than to play tennis. When we became Florida residents, the first thing she did was purchase a Florida fishing license. She fished off piers, sea walls, and old bridges. Bridges were my favorite because the overhead powerlines dangle floats and tackle from a hundred misadventured casts. Lorna loves eating her catch unless it is a catfish or shark. In Key West, she caught grouper, jacks, mackerel, mahi-mahi, pompano, sheepshead, snapper, and yellowtail. As a vegetarian, I was as happy as a clam at high tide to sit alongside her in my travel chair, admiring the tapestry of turquoise blues where the lighter shallows meet the deeper azures of the ocean and then the darker blues of the cloudless sky. I loved the echoes of the water lapping against the pilings, the splosh of fish jumping, and the cries of the seabirds overhead.

Incidentally, I learned what square groupers were when in Key West. They are bales of cocaine, often disposed of by drug smugglers from boats, that regularly wash ashore on the Keys. Unfortunately, the Keys are not an especially good place for a criminal. There is only one road in and the same road out, so it's child's play for law enforcement to put in place roadblocks to stop the fugitive from justice.

****

My rental house bike had a big basket on the front that accommodated my tennis racket, borrowed pickleball bat, and laptop bag. I liked it very much, as it allowed me to blend in as a local. It wasn't the transport of choice in Key West, however. Instead, the cool kids' ride was either a chopper bike or a retro scooter.

British readers of a certain age will recall the Raleigh Chopper from the seventies. It was based on an American low-to-ground motorbike with high handlebars and a frame that had been chopped up to look different from other models.

In seventies Britain, every groovy kid had one… except me. These flamboyantly colored style machines had high-rise handlebars, different-sized wheels with chunky tires, a comfortable motorcycle seat with a high sissy bar that could be used to give a ride to a mate, and a gear lever resembling an automatic American car. I did not have one because it represented a week's earnings for my dad. However, this bike single-handedly saved Raleigh when it sold one and a half million bikes in the seventies. Unfortunately, it lost popularity as the more image-conscious eighties took over, and the BMX replaced it.

It didn't matter that Choppers were tough to ride; the bike wobbled at higher speeds, and most of your mates had frequent accidents. Neither did it deter you that the build quality was famously poor, and most gear levers seem to lose their knob converting it into a metal spike where you need it least. However, the chopper could perform awesome skids and was the bike of choice for wheelies, some of them intentional.

You can buy a chopper in reasonable condition today on eBay for about a thousand pounds. However, the place to see them in the wild is Key West. They have hundreds if not a thousand. They look similar to the original model but have been slightly modified to take a cup holder and Bluetooth speakers.

In contrast to the ungainly chopper, the stylish lines and sleek design of a green Vespa scooter are a wonder of Italian culture. The Vespa is fun to ride, and you look great while zipping in and out of traffic. It's ideal for a small island such as Key West, with its hundred-mile gas tank perfect for ten or more journeys.

Are We There Yet?

The purchase I wanted to make was a Piaggio Vespa Primavera 50 scooter. I pictured myself on its light-green iconic frame, speeding along Smathers Beach. I say speeding, but its 50-cc engine restricted the top speed to only 30mph, more than enough for Key West's gentle roads.

Transport in Key West doesn't convey your status but rather your lifestyle. Here, extra kudos can be gained if you show how little you need in the way of material goods.

Most people need a home, and Key West, despite being known for its unique style of homes, showcases a delightful blend of architectural influences, including Spanish Colonial, Victorian, American Craftsman, and Art Deco. Yet, a common thread among most Key West residences is the presence of white picket fences, balconies, patios, and balustrades with various intricate designs. While some houses sport the classic white, others flaunt a palette of lighter hues.

Global warming is a grave concern for Key West's residents. Its highest point, fittingly the cemetery, is only eighteen feet above sea level. Most homes stand at a considerably lower altitude. According to the National Oceanic and Atmospheric Administration, sea levels in Key West will rise by between one and seven feet this century. Therefore, the Local government has passed a regulation that any significant house improvement in many parts of the island has to include the elevation of that property. Almost five thousand homes must be jacked up at least one and a half feet above the projected flood levels. For a two thousand square feet ranch home, it will cost you more than a quarter of a million dollars to raise your brick home—something to consider when purchasing a property in Florida.

Although May in Key West certainly brought the heat, the island's continuous breezes kept the humidity from becoming overwhelming, making the temperature almost tolerable. I relished the warm sun on my face as I cycled back home. However, as the week progressed toward garbage day, the scent of refuse emanating from the trash bins became less enjoyable. The intense heat here speeds up the decomposition of organic matter, turning it into simpler gas molecules. Bacteria feast on decaying meat proteins, while microbes liquefy the cell structure of vegetables, leading to pools of fermenting liquid at the can's bottom. The predominant odors include hydrogen sulfide, reminiscent of rotten eggs, and the pungent methanethiol that carries a cabbage-like aroma. Some of these lingering scents persist even after the garbage has been collected, which is why many Floridians opt for professional monthly cleansing of their large garbage containers.

****

My hair was growing longer. At my last cut, I asked a Tennessee-based stylist the innocent question of whether she was planning to get a Covid vaccination.

"This vaccine is a cruel trick by sociologists to poison us," she told me. "These sociologists are ruining this country, telling us what to do. It is up to us good-minded Christians to fight back. These sociologists will not know what has hit them."

In as confused a tone as I could muster, I asked, "Do you mean socialists?"

"Yes, that's right, socialists. Not sociologists."

"That's an honest mistake," I said. "Most sociologists are likely to be socialists."

In later research, I may have been unkind to a minority of sociologists. A 2006 survey of American sociology professors found that only 26 percent of these academics described themselves as Marxist, with a further 50 percent adherent to other forms of socialism. Although both groups share an attachment to systems thinking, many sociologists do not want to put their faith in any one form of government to control complex matters.

I visited the local Key West barber. It had been almost twenty-five years since my hair had been cut in the country (or, more latterly, state) of my residence, and I didn't wish to break the streak. Although we officially lived in Florida, we didn't really live here, so I convinced myself I was in a foreign land. After over a year of subdued business, the barber owner beamed with excitement at his packed salon and continually paused my cut to post photos on Instagram that proudly demonstrated that his business was again booming.

The barber asked me how I styled my hair. I told him that—to be honest—I brushed my hair roughly every three months, probably heresy to a hairdresser. He told me I would fit right in here in Key West, as everyone was lazy. He was very much a conch, moving away briefly only once to Miami for hairdressing school. He had hated this nearby city and was relieved when he returned home.

Are We There Yet?

In pre-Covid times, Key West was a tolerant place where people got on with their own lives and let others live the life they wanted. However, fear of contracting the virus had nibbled away at some of this tolerance.

Key West stands out for its unique blend of communities, where various groups seamlessly intertwine. While it's not uncommon in America to have distinct sub-communities within a single place, Key West is exceptional because these communities often engage with each other and share in each other's company. Here, you'll find LGTBQ+ communities, military and veterans, conchs of both types, Cuban escapees who still occasionally arrive by raft, retirees, and snowbirds all mingling harmoniously. This remarkable synergy might be attributed to the individuals who bridge these diverse groups or perhaps the prevailing 'More Caribbean than Floridian' culture.

Key West has a rich history of hosting the US military, with the Navy establishing a base in 1823, followed by the Marine Corps a year later, and the Army in 1831. Nestled along the coast with its natural deep water port, Key West emerged as an impeccable strategic outpost to protect US interests from the looming menace of Caribbean pirates. In those days, the Caribbean waters were treacherous, with American vessels frequently falling victim to pirate raids, leaving crews brutally dispatched and unceremoniously cast adrift in the unforgiving sea.

In 1860, the US declared illegal slave ships as a form of piracy and increased the size of the US Navy in Key West. A few years later, the Navy blockaded the Gulf and captured 199 ships laden with supplies for Confederate troops. Some historians believe this action may have shortened the Civil War by two years.

During World War II, the then-defunct navy base was revived as a home for destroyers, submarines, and seaplanes to counter the German U-boat threat. Since this time, serving military and veterans have been a mainstay of the population here.

We toured President Truman's Little White House, a property where he spent 175 days during his presidency after his doctor ordered him to take a warm-weather vacation. The eleven working vacations were popular with White House staff who had to accompany him to enable the efficient running of the country.

The Little White House is located in a former navy base renamed the Truman Annex on President Truman's death in 1973. A year later, when the Navy again reduced its presence in Key West, this area was closed, and the Little White House and the surrounding white houses were shuttered for a dozen years. A private developer restored these historic houses, which once billeted senior naval officials, to their original design. As a result, they now represent prime real estate in a town full of prime real estate.

When Truman was president, the house had a view over the docks. However, as the navy ships grew, the waters had to be dredged to accommodate them. They used this silt to fill the old dock, and then they built more houses on top of it, which blocked the house's view of the sea. Although the house is primarily associated with President Truman, six other presidents (Taft, FDR, Eisenhower, Kennedy, Carter, and Clinton) have either stayed or hosted events there.

In 1982, US customs agents installed a post just north of Key West to control the movement of drugs and people into the US. This roadblock caused long delays and aggravated residents. In a curious historical incident, Key West momentarily seceded from the USA and declared itself the independent Conch Republic. The Key West mayor proclaimed himself Prime Minister of the new micronation, declared war on the United States, and then promptly surrendered. This rebellion lasted sixty seconds. He then (unsuccessfully) applied for one billion dollars in foreign aid in the next minute. To this day, Key West residents celebrate 23 April as Conch Independence Day.

It was the first time since the Civil War that any part of the US had seceded, even if it were in jest. As with many other political unions worldwide, provisions were never made on how a country could be disbanded. As with other matters without legislation, it falls to the US Supreme Court to interpret existing law. The Supreme Court has historically held that states have no unilateral right to secede, with the Civil War providing sufficient legal precedent prohibiting secession.

Theoretically, at least, there could be a path to secession. This would involve widespread public support within the state, lengthy negotiations with the federal government (which resolved the division of assets and liabilities), and resolution of all anticipated potential disputes. Secession would necessarily involve consent from Congress and the majority of other states. All of this is about as likely as a mime in a heavy metal band waterskiing with a house cat. The political reality is the states are united until some future conflict.

Despite the difficulties in seceding legally, about a third of Americans would like their state to secede from the Union, with Republicans in the South and West Coast Democrats driving this interest.

Are We There Yet?

In the seventies, the military's repeated withdrawal and subsequent return to Key West forced the city to investigate other industries. As Key West is a Caribbean island, tourism was an obvious option.

Local politicians repositioned the town toward tourism and were the first to court the pink dollar openly. About 30 percent of Key West residents now self-identify as LGBTQ+. Not surprisingly, Key West was the first US city to have an openly gay mayor in 1983 (which may not sound long ago, but it was some twelve years before Boy George officially came out as gay). Key West is very much in this group's debt, as it is estimated that two-thirds of the three thousand wooden houses in Key West Old Town have been refurbished by someone from the LGBTQ+ community.

In the eighties, Key West was greatly affected by AIDS. On Higgs Beach, there's a memorial made of Zimbabwean granite to honor the 1,240 Key West residents who died from AIDS during that time, a significant number considering the city's population was fewer than 25,000.

Larry, the shy gay man mentioned earlier, invited us to see a drag queen show. These are common in Key West, and on any day, there will be a handful of such shows for the tourists' entertainment. Surprisingly, it was our Midwestern-born friend's first drag show, and he was mortified and embarrassed at the humor. Every joke was filled with innuendo.

Miss Bouvee, who liked her men like her coffee—strong, hot, and ready to keep her awake all night—sang well and worked hard with her audience. To those who looked uncomfortable (and Larry was undoubtedly the most awkward man in the room), she would say, "Don't worry; I won't bite... unless you ask nicely," or to the most heterosexual man in the room, she would say, "I may not be a baker, but I've got the buns that'll make you rise."

I'm sure you get the idea. Having survived the humor of the seventies British comedians and working in a holiday camp in the eighties, I was accustomed to this type of entertainment.

****

Covid had hit Key West hard when Monroe County roadblocked the overseas highway in March 2020 to keep the virus out of their paradise. However, with just over a hundred infections, four deaths, and ample vacant hospital beds, local businesses pushed to re-open. They filed lawsuits against the county, which removed the roadblock on 1 June. The roadblock had turned away some nineteen thousand vehicles and dissuaded thousands more.

The city then doubled down on mask adherence. Businesses that did not enforce regulations were temporarily closed by the city. With three out of every five jobs here related to tourism, unemployment rose from 2 percent to 20 percent as tourists stayed home. According to the *Citizen* newspaper, one hundred and fifty businesses had closed by the summer of 2020, and lines of people snaked for blocks around the temporary food banks in the Catholic Church. By August, these food banks were serving half of the population. Key West was accustomed to temporary hurricane shutdowns, but this prolonged lockdown was the worst in living memory.

You could still feel a palpable tension between the Covid concerned and businesses. Banners adorned the main tourist streets, urging people to wear masks. A few days after our arrival, the CDC announced that vaccinated people no longer needed to wear masks inside or out. However, many people continued to wear masks, as there was no way of telling whether a mask wearer was vaccinated or a die-hard (sic) Republican.

Attitude to risk is personal. In Florida, helmets for motorbike and scooter riders are optional. In practice, almost nobody wears one. However, it was commonplace to see a moped rider helmetless but double-masked. The risk of contracting this virus at 30mph in the wind must be negligible, certainly less than the risk of serious head injury. Either people are poor at assessing risk, or mask-wearing on a moped is used as a signal to one's tribe.

This runs true for cycling helmets, too. The only helmeted cyclists in Key West are those from the Navy compound, who must wear one while on base. I've seen Californians yelling at their fellow citizens who won't helmet up as they have. But nobody pays much attention either way in laid-back Florida.

****

Key West isn't the last island in the archipelago; there's a group called the Outer Keys that round out the set, but they're only reachable by boat. As part of our ongoing mission to discover every US national park, we had our sights set on Dry Tortugas Key. Back in 1513, the Spanish adventurer Ponce de Leon dubbed the seven islands located sixty-eight miles from

Are We There Yet?

Key West the Dry Tortugas, signifying the presence of turtles but the absence of freshwater.

One consequence of Key West's recent popularity was that we could not buy tickets to this national park by plane or boat even a month in advance. Thankfully, another stalwart of Key West's tourist industry—Duval Street, a party street similar in intent to those in New Orleans or Memphis—came to our rescue. We learned that some people, undoubtedly over-fortified by the previous evening's libations, do not present themselves for their 7:30 am reservation. Those at the dock on standby could buy any unclaimed seats.

Amidst the post-War of 1812 jitters over potential enemy attacks, the United States embarked on a grand plan to fortify its East Coast. Fort Jefferson, situated on the largest Dry Tortugas Island, stands as the most ambitious of these forts and remains the largest brick masonry structure in the Western Hemisphere. This colossal fortress, often hailed as the 'Gibraltar of the West,' boasts an awe-inspiring irregular hexagonal design. Its mighty walls, a whopping fifty feet high and eight feet thick, are an astounding testament to craftsmanship, comprised of an astounding sixteen million individual bricks. The plan was to have this fortress armed to the teeth by a formidable garrison of 1,500 soldiers, with 450 cannons aimed at the sea, standing guard against any maritime threat.

An 1825 assessment was that the site was unsuitable for a naval station, as the Dry Tortugas had no fresh water or possibility of cultivating fresh food. All supplies would need to be brought to the island by boat, not the three-hour journey by today's diesel engines but by sailing boats that took a day or more to reach the island. Two decades later, the Navy changed its view. The US Government needed to protect itself from piracy, and this was the best location from which to do this.

The construction of the fortress spanned over thirty grueling years. Workers considered it a fate more dreadful than death itself—enduring harsh labor in stifling heat, with meager rations and scarce fresh water, all the while plagued by merciless mosquito attacks. From 1847 until the Civil War, the heaviest lifting was carried out by enslaved people. When the 1863 Emancipation Proclamation freed this workforce, Lincoln replaced it with Confederate soldiers convicted of the then-capital offense of desertion.

Fort Jefferson was a pretty effective prison. Its most famous resident was Samuel Mudd, a doctor convicted of harboring Lincoln's assassin, John Wilkes Booth, when he was merely treating his broken leg. Seventy miles from the nearest land and shackled with a ball and chain day and night, escape was unlikely. Mudd did try to escape with several others on the fort supply boat but was discovered and left in a dungeon for three months. One of his co-escapees, George St Leger Grenfell, a serial mercenary who had served in Africa, South America, Crimea, India, and, as a Confederate colonel, later escaped successfully from the island with four others. The sixty-year-old slid down the fort's walls and fled in a fishing boat in a horrendous gale to rejoin the Civil War.

Life was tough in this fort. Malaria was endemic, scurvy common, and an 1867 yellow fever epidemic infected most island residents. While the prisoners may have had panoramas of crystal-clear waters and pristine corals to die for, these vistas were as welcome as a clown at a comedy club during the intolerable summer months.

Incidentally, you might think air conditioning—omnipresent elsewhere—would have resolved this issue of sweltering conditions in American prisons today. Unfortunately, fourteen (mainly Southern) states do not offer air conditioning as standard. Florida, for example, has air conditioning in only two out of every five state jails. This could be easily rectified, but few politicians want to be seen as soft on crime. Elsewhere, none of humid Louisiana's seven male prisons provide air conditioning where prisoners sleep. This lack of cooling in the cooler may contribute toward the shortage of about one-quarter of their full complement of correctional officers.

You may think this would be a good time for a joke about air conditioning. However, I'm not a fan.

Dr. Mudd worked tirelessly to treat the infected prisoners and was eventually pardoned by President Andrew Johnson in 1869. He returned to his farm and medical practice in Maryland and became active in democratic politics. Mudd died at forty-nine of pneumonia and was buried in the same church where he met John Wilkes Booth.

We shall never know whether Mudd was involved in the assassination conspiracy. However, we know he delayed reporting the treatment for twenty-four hours and lied when he said he had not met Booth previously. Numerous descendants of Dr. Mudd have made earnest efforts to vindicate their forebearer's reputation, believing it had been unjustly muddied. Presidents Carter and Reagan contributed to this cause, expressing their belief that Mudd was, in fact, clean.

Are We There Yet?

As the Confederate workforce at Dry Tortugas thinned out, construction slowed. Ultimately, the fortress was never completed, and the Army finally abandoned it in 1874.

Almost all of today's sixty-thousand visitors are day-trippers, most served by the daily ferry and a few by seaplane or fishing boat. Some people camp, a few for up to fourteen days, though they must be fully self-sufficient, as the island has no water, food, electricity, or bathing facilities. The ferry ride takes just under three hours each way, and the sun blistered down on us when we took it. On both journeys, pods of dolphins sliced through our wake with effortless ease. Their playful energy was palpable as they leaped and dove in perfect unison.

Many centuries ago, ancient mariners taking this same route had known that citrus fruit prevents scurvy. However, it was believed that acidity—rather than the then-unknown vitamin C—was the preventative cure for a long time. Consequently, to these sailors, the more acidic limes were better for avoiding scurvy than sweeter lemons or oranges. But, unfortunately, these limes of the ancient mariners had only half the Vitamin C of their citrus fruit cousins and were less effective at warding off scurvy.

Had they known it, British sailors would have replaced their vast vats of lime juice with similar quantities of orange juice, and the Yankee epithet for British people would be orangies and not limeys. There would also have been much less scurvy in the British Navy.

Scurvy is a pretty distressing disease. After a month of no Vitamin C, most people will have gum disease, bruising, and skin bleeding. Then, after about two months, they will start to die. In the age of sail, ships expected to lose around half of their seaman from the disease on long voyages. Remarkably, it wasn't until 1795 that the Royal Navy routinely fed its sailors with fresh fruit and vegetables.

The British penchant for limes over oranges likely led to the creation of one of America's favorite desserts, Key Lime Pie. One origin story is that ancient Florida Keys fishermen, nicknamed hookers by locals, made the pie from ingredients they carried on their boat. This is why some people used to call it Hookers' Pie, although a better name might have been the rind of the ancient mariner. A second origin story is that Florida's first multi-millionaire asked his cook to create a pie from key limes in the late nineteenth century.

The first time the recipe seems to have been recorded was in 1931 when a New York condensed milk producer substituted key limes for lemons in its famous Magic Lemon Cream Pie. Another tidbit persuades me that

Key Lime Pie was probably invented in New York because it was not included in a 1927 Key West recipe book but did appear in a later 1933 version. Whatever its origin story, I do enjoy Key Lime Pie, especially the one they sell at Publix.

Another lover of Key Lime Pie was one of the world's most eminent twentieth-century writers. Ernest Hemingway had a life full of adventure before he committed suicide at sixty-one. At eighteen, during World War I, he volunteered as an ambulance driver for the Italian Army. When hit by a mortar shell, Hemingway became the first American wounded in that Great War. He spent the subsequent six months in a Milan Red Cross Hospital and fell in love with his nurse, Agnes von Kurowsky, about whom he later wrote *Farewell to Arms*.

These experiences made him addicted to war. Fortunately, there was much of it about at that time. As a journalist, he covered both the Greek army's retreat from Constantinople in 1922 and the Spanish Civil War in 1937-38. Then, in World War II, he entered it before his compatriots and was both a journalist and spy in the Sino-Japanese War of 1941. He flew on RAF bombing missions and was one of only half a dozen journalists on the D-day beaches in 1944. Famously, he was the first American to enter Paris later that year, where he liberated the Traveler's Club, Café de la Paix, and the Ritz Hotel Bar.

After the war, he became an African adventurer and couldn't shake the desire to experience that adrenaline rush. Handsome in his youth, he was the celebrity of his time and lived life to the full. He deep-sea fished, boxed, and fought bulls to excess. Unfortunately, these risky passions caused nine serious concussions, which may have led to his brain demise later in life.

Hemingway had a charmed life. He survived two airplane crashes on consecutive days, with premature obituaries both appearing in the press. In addition, he also suffered four serious car accidents and inadvertently shot himself when hunting sharks.

After his first marriage at twenty-two, Hemingway wed four times and had only seven months as an unmarried man. As you can imagine, he won no awards for the Husband of the Year, and in these modern times, his behavior would have had him continually canceled.

Hemingway wrote nine novels, four non-fiction books, one hundred short stories, and four hundred press articles. He won the 1953 Pulitzer Prize for *The Old Man and the Sea* and the 1954 Nobel Prize for Literature for his body of work. Famously, he would write drunk and edit sober. By the way, if you are going to write while inebriated, this is definitely the right way around.

Hemingway had significant mental health issues and endured electric shock treatment to try to cure his condition. When these did not work, he attempted suicide on multiple occasions. Ultimately, in 1961, he eventually killed himself—as his father had done before him.

With a reasonable understanding of his life and works, we visited Hemingway's Key West home that his wealthy second wife, journalist Pauline Pfeiffer, had bought. They lived here in the thirties before divorcing, after which he moved to Cuba with a new wife, Martha Gellhorn, another writer and journalist.

The house itself has more than a vague smell of cat piss. This is because it is still the home to several dozen feline descendants of the many cats he and Pfeiffer had in the thirties. To this day, half of these cats have six or more toes on their front paws rather than the typical five.

According to your preferred source, the first polydactyl cat may have been named Snowball or Snow White. It was given to Hemingway by a sea captain with whom Hemingway got drunk at a local bar. Hemingway started the tradition of naming the feline descendants of this original conch cat after celebrities, and now the museum's caretakers vote on new names. If you drop in now, you might meet attention-seeking Rita Hayworth, the precocious Shirley Temple, or the reclusive Howard Hughes. Each female cat is allowed one litter before they are spayed. When the cats die, they find their final resting place in the backyard cat cemetery, adorned with simple gravestones bearing the names of these beloved felines.

Unfortunately, you can no longer see the famed Joe Di Maggio boxing ring. It was replaced by a swimming pool in 1938, designed by Hemingway himself. A penny is embedded at the end of the pool to commemorate his faux-anger. "Pauline, you've spent all but my last penny, so you might as well have that."

If you are in Key West, I would recommend this as a place to visit unless, that is, you are allergic to cats. Of course, you will see where Hemingway wrote, his living quarters, and the pool. For most people, however, the main attractions are the six-toed cats.

****

As our month in Key West ended, we reflected on why we had been so happy here. Key West, being a Caribbean island, offers perfect weather.

Moreover, it's quirky and independent, with most stores being independent rather than part of a chain. Key West even boasts a Poet Laureate, a unique feature we thought was absent from Bushnell. Lastly, bicycles rule the road as the primary mode of transportation, gracefully weaving around the wild animals that also share Key West as their home.

Even though it was our first stop, Lorna and I talked about moving to Key West full-time. To put this into context, though—except for Berlin—Lorna has never visited a place to which she didn't want to move. Sanity prevailed as it had done on previous occasions. Although Key West is a wonderful American Caribbean Island joined by road to the lower forty-eight, it is a four-hour drive to Miami. Who wants to make an eight-hour round trip to buy a pickleball bat or see a baseball game?

With that decided, we took the only road out of Key West to our next destination.

Are We There Yet?

Chapter 4 – An East Coast Road Trip

It wasn't until Ford's Model T that the road trip became an American icon.

More than three-quarters of American vacations are now road trips. Travelers are increasingly eschewing trips involving airports as the security lines lengthen, the add-on costs increase, and the seat space shrinks... or, perhaps, it is just that Americans are becoming wider. Americans love the flexibility to fling what they want into their huge vehicles, stop where they choose, and return when they have had enough. In theory, they also love the sense of adventure.

Modern culture immortalizes road trips. My favorite movies include *Thelma and Louise*, *Easy Rider*, and *Rain Man*, whereas Lorna would undoubtedly choose *National Lampoon's Vacation*. Many of America's best writers—including Steinbeck, Kerouac, and Wolfe—have also written about the freedom and self-discovery a road trip offers.

We had a few weeks until our next destination, so I did what I liked doing best: planning a road trip that filled the gap. I plotted a route that took us to four National Parks and two sets of old friends.

The first stop was Biscayne, a predominantly water-based National Park south of Miami. In the forties, environmentalists proposed that Biscayne Bay should be part of a much larger Everglades National Park, encompassing most of Southern Florida.

Unfortunately, National Park status was given only to a smaller Everglades area, essentially the slow-moving river that flows from Lake Okeechobee to the Gulf of Mexico. Its hydrology filters and purifies the water, enabling a range of habitats—including marshes, swamps, and forests—that provide a home to alligators, crocodiles, manatees, and panthers. While you can hike or bike its 1.5 million acres, it is best known for its ten thousand islands and mangrove tunnels, which are only accessible by airboat or kayak.

In the sixties, President Johnson approved federal protection for the underwater wonderland of Biscayne Bay, and by the start of the eighties, it had become its own national park.

With just one day allocated for Biscayne National Park, I scheduled a boat tour encompassing snorkeling, kayaking, and visiting an outlying island's beach. To accommodate the tour's early start time, we had to set out well before sunrise for the lengthy drive along the Overseas Highway.

We dropped our dogs off at a doggy daycare just as the sun was rising. The dog custodian had a spacious yard and other dogs to play with. I do not believe either dog noticed us leaving.

We drove a couple of miles to the coast for our tour departure. On the way, a weather app alert warned there may be rain later. When we arrived at the meeting point, we were greeted by the glum faces of our fellow passengers; somebody had told them that the trip was potentially in jeopardy. Whether we would go would be decided by the boat's captain, and everyone was awaiting his arrival.

When the captain arrived, it was evident he wanted a day off. So, our tour of this particular national park would have to wait another year. However, as crying over spilled milk cleans no carpets (and we had already paid the admission), we visited the Deering Estate, the 1920s home of Charles Deering, a Chicago industrialist and committed environmentalist who bought and developed a property overlooking the now national park.

Once a familiar backdrop in the iconic series *Miami Vice* and now a cherished spot for weddings, the lawn overlooking Biscayne Bay is lined with palm trees and, on the day we were there, hosted a grand marquee for several hundred wedding guests. Should you be interested in such an extravagant celebration of your love, the booking fee alone—without any food, drink, tent, accommodation, or staffing—will set you back some twenty thousand dollars. I felt sad that the happy couple might have some inclement weather for their perfect day but noticed that, at least, the couple's celebrant wasn't angling for a day off from his official duties.

Two stories about the house made this visit a tolerable diversion for us thwarted travelers. The first was that a concealed wine cellar was only discovered when Hurricane Andrew hit it in 1992. The entrance to this hidden chamber was cleverly disguised to safeguard his valuable wine and art collections and keep them safe from theft and natural disasters. This worked extraordinarily well as nobody knew about the cellar for sixty-five years.

The second story relates to Charles's younger half-brother, James, who built a competing villa and gardens thirteen miles further along the coast in Coconut Grove. Uncomfortable around people, James was a life-long bachelor. Nevertheless, he strongly desired to produce a better house overlooking the bay than his brother's 'plain Jane' estate. So, using Villa Rezzonico in Vicenza as a model, James employed 10 percent of the working population of Miami to build the 34-room Villa Vizcaya.

James Deering hired celebrated designer Paul Chalfin to decorate his summer house. Nicknamed the Hearst Castle of the East, Chalfin decorated Villa Vizcaya with gay abandon with the finest European antiques and furnishings. When one set of antiquities was sunk with the Titanic in 1912, James merely bought a new selection. When James died in 1925, the estate passed to his older brother, who now had two estates on the same coastline.

We think of today's billionaires as a modern-day phenomenon. In truth, since the Gilded Age at the end of the nineteenth century, when the USA became the world's most prosperous, America has had ample numbers of wealthy people with more money than they could possibly spend.

We traipsed back to our dogs, who looked at us as if to say we thought you would be longer. This early finish meant we could drive further north than originally planned. Unfortunately, unlike the comparable drive on Florida's West Coast, the I-95 is a slog with little of interest to view along the way.

National Public Radio was broadcasting an article celebrating Juneteenth, a combination of June and 19th. On 19 June 1865, Gordon Granger, a general from the Union army, rode into Galveston, Texas, and liberated all the enslaved people there. In Texas, this date has been celebrated as a state holiday ever since by the African-American Community.

The big news from two days earlier was that Juneteenth had been declared the eleventh federal holiday, which means that most federal employees didn't have to work that day. However, it doesn't necessarily mean it is a public holiday for the rest of the US. Most private companies give their employees about eight of the eleven federal holidays. Which ones they choose are decided by the company. There are some holidays that more or less every company gives: New Year's Day, Memorial Day, Independence Day, Labor Day, Thanksgiving, and Christmas Day.

In a former lifetime, when I formed an American subsidiary of a company, I found that it was for me to decide which federal holidays the new subsidiary would give as paid time off. I chose the above holidays, plus Christmas Eve and the day after Thanksgiving.

Relatively few private-sector employees take time off on three federal holidays. Only around one in ten private companies award a day off for Veterans Day, one in six for Columbus Day, and one in five for Presidents' Day. The challenge for supporters of Juneteenth is how they convert this federal employee holiday into something enjoyed by all.

The campaign to have Juneteenth as a federal holiday had run for some time. As recently as 2020, a reputable magazine suggested it would take a very long time to get approval for this holiday. One year later, the House of Representatives voted for the holiday with a vast majority, and the Senate ratified this with their own one hundred to zero vote. A day later, the president signed the bill into law. Perhaps it demonstrates that you can attempt, Sisyphus-like, to push a rock up a hill without progressing. Or you can wait until the public dialogue supports action and make rapid progress.

Juneteenth fell on a Saturday in 2021, so the public holiday was the previous day. Unfortunately, this was only one day after the bill came into law. Very hurriedly, non-essential federal employees were told the following day was a holiday. Mail was not delivered, immigration ceremonies were canceled, and federal courts closed.

****

The day after the first federal Juneteenth, I surprised Lorna by driving to see our daughters in their Georgia college town. Daughter #1 had kindly agreed to have Cat #1 in her plush student apartment; unfortunately, things were not going well. Having just returned from her 4 am shift as a barmaid, Daughter #1 found that the cat had peed on her bed. We hastily washed her sheets and left the cat to get reacquainted with her former dog siblings.

As Daughter #2 joined us at the latest in-demand restaurant, I couldn't help but recall a blog I had recently read. It claimed that Athens (Georgia) was home to unbelievable food. If that were true, then it's somewhat puzzling that my daughters consistently chose dining establishments that offer such ordinary fare.

However, the more plausible explanation is that the aforementioned blog might have been nothing more than a marketing puff piece, skillfully masking that there's not much clamor in Athens for high-class eateries. After all, the university reigns supreme in this sizable town, with its forty-thousand students and fifteen-thousand faculty and staff comprising nearly half the population.

According to Google, Athens boasts sixty restaurants, but that number is dwarfed by its eighty downtown bars and a further twenty music venues. It is quite clear where its priorities lie. Still, it's worth noting that this quaint college town has gifted the world with two legendary bands of my generation: the B-52s and REM.

With the disappointing food digested and out of our system, we continued northward the next day to stay with old friends in Charlotte, North Carolina. They had known us before we had children, and only distance prevented us from spending more time with them.

American homes such as theirs are becoming increasingly connected to the internet. Doorbells film every visitor and passerby, new fridges automatically order food when you run low, and treadmills give the impression that you are running through an Italian town. My favorite toy of our friends was the voice-activated garbage can. It opened when you said, "Open the can." Unfortunately, this only worked when you talked in an American accent. When I used my God-given accent, it remained closed. The lid magically only opened when I approximated my friend's over-the-top redneck accent, and I could deposit my detritus inside the container. You still had to empty the bag insert, however. In my estimation, humankind will only make real progress when this garbage magically transports itself out of the house without waiting until it is overfull.

****

We were confident that Shenandoah National Park would not be closed because around one and a half million frequent it annually. We stayed at one of the park lodges, more or less in the middle of Skyline Drive, a road that stretched over a hundred miles along the ridge of the Blue Ridge Mountains. Our cabin had magnificent views over the western forested valleys and distant peaks of Virginia. From this and other Shenandoah views, you were simultaneously awed, humbled, and inspired as you took in Virginia's vastness.

National Park food is similar in all thirty parks we have been to. It is healthier than the average American fare, yet still mainly designed for hikers who have just completed a twenty-mile hike. But, of course, most Americans have completed no such walks in National Parks. For example, the average visitor to the Grand Canyon's South Rim spends only four hours there, with many merely toddling from their vehicle to glance over some scenic overlook and post a selfie on Instagram.

With 267 hikes to choose from, Lorna and I embarked on a couple of shorter walks that led us to captivating waterfalls. We also tackled the hike to Old Rag, just one of numerous Shenandoah trails offering breathtaking 360-degree panoramic views from the summit, showcasing a world of peaks, meadows, and endless forests.

Lorna had less interest in a longer walk, so I ventured out on a solo hike along the slightly more challenging path to Rapidan Camp, which served as the summer home of President Herbert Hoover, the first US president hailing from west of the Mississippi River. Born in Iowa, this California resident had been president for only a few months when the 1929 stock market crashed and ushered in the Great Depression. That same year, he bought 164 acres of land a hundred miles from DC and asked the Marine Corps to build the camp during their training. His wife, Lou Henry Hoover, oversaw the construction of thirteen wood buildings, hiking trails, trout pools, and a mini-golf course. For its construction, Hoover fastidiously paid $114,000 (the equivalent of $1.9 million today).

These Marines guarded Camp Hoover during its time as a presidential retreat, and they spent much of their time in a losing battle to rid the environs of the abundant copperhead snakes, whose descendants still sunbathe on its decks today.

A daily national park bus tour usually takes you almost all the way there. However, with Covid temporarily shuttering this service, I had to hike on one of the Skyline trails. My route followed the Appalachian Trail for the first part of the journey and was chiefly downhill. It was undoubtedly a pretty walk, with plenty of crystal-clear streams to traverse, small cascades to listen to, pine trees to scent, and birds and butterflies to marvel at. I met not a soul on the trail.

With its nine-hundred-foot change in elevation, the three-and-a-bit mile hike took a surprising amount of time. Then, suddenly, I neared the camp road with its stone bridge over the River Rapidan.

Hoover and his wife loved the camp; it became their summer White House. The Press quickly nicknamed the Hoovers' summer cabin residence, the Brown House. The president spent most of his free time fishing and the first lady horse-riding. An airplane would drop mail and newspapers daily into the valley compound. If his aides or others wanted to see him, they would have to take a similar hike to the one I had walked.

The UK's first Labour prime minister, Ramsay MacDonald, visited the camp for a week in 1929 with his daughter. Allegedly, while sitting at opposite ends of a tree trunk, the Republican Hoover and MacDonald discussed how they would achieve world peace by dismantling the world's navies. This led to the largely ineffective 1930 Treaty for the Limitation and Reduction of Naval Armament. What happened later in the thirties suggests that their world peace plans were unsuccessful.

The two leaders disagreed on British World War I debt. MacDonald refused to accept Hoover's offer of canceling the American loans in exchange for Bermuda, Trinidad, and British Honduras.

In addition to political guests, Camp Hoover received visits from many celebrities. American Aviator Charles Lindbergh, future British Prime Minister Winston Churchill, automotive heir Edsel Ford, and inventor-extraordinaire (but by then aged) Thomas Edison were amongst those who stayed at the camp. At the end of his one-term presidency, Hoover donated the land and the buildings to what would later become Shenandoah National Park.

I had a long chat with the ranger stationed at this retreat. A college student in her early twenties, she was an intern still thinking through what to do with her life. I asked how many people she saw on an average day. As all honest answers should begin, she said, "It depends." However, on that day, I was the first person.

I asked if she ever got lonely. She said she would see people most days. Another ranger would check in on her every few days, and she had a two-way radio for emergencies. In any case, she told me that she liked solitude, as it gave her a chance to complete her college work in peace.

The ranger accommodation was one of the buildings in the compound. The ranger said it had a small kitchen, a desk, and a bed. She felt very safe there; it wasn't as if she needed to lock the door.

We talked a little about the genesis of the camp. Like me, she had read the many informational signs around the center. However, she didn't have the historical background—or possibly interest—to contextualize them. The ranger was sociable but also diffident. She lacked the outer self-confidence of my similar-aged daughters, but I doubted whether either would have the will to live by themselves miles from others for weeks at a time.

The ranger had warned me of a copperhead snake that liked to sunbathe on the front deck of the main building. I had forgotten this counsel when it came time for me to leave. As I turned the corner at a pace, I stepped over this serpent, fortunate not to touch it. It scared the bejeezus out of me.

There have been eight new national parks created thus far this century. This is a marvelous addition to the public spaces available to all. However, it is not straightforward to create a new national park. When a government announces a new one, it must then plan to remove human habitation from the park boundaries. This was especially contentious for this park in the 1930s.

In the case of Shenandoah, figuring out who owned a thousand tracts of land on the proposed national park and who merely occupied their farm holdings (and hence were ineligible for compensation) was challenging. Many homesteaders refused to sell at any price and were also against the compromise of living there until their death.

The Commonwealth of Virginia slowly acquired the land, primarily through eminent domain, roughly equivalent to compulsory purchase in the UK and other places. Once Virginia acquired the land, they donated it to the federal government for the new national park. This happened slowly for this park, so the government had to resort to underhand tactics to remove the recalcitrant farmers. They hired a social worker to write a report on the Shenandoah communities that might accelerate their departure. Her exaggerated report of pervasive poverty and widespread inbreeding gave the government the cover to evict the remaining residents forcibly, burning their cabins as they left so the residents could not return.

We had enjoyed our two nights at Shenandoah, but, with 262 trails left unhiked, we drove on to our next national park. This was America's newest and sixty-third national park, New River Gorge. It had been upgraded from a national river only the previous year as part of the Covid-19 stimulus package. You may ask what national parks have to do with pandemics—this national park was in West Virginia, one of whose senators President Biden relied on to pass the $2.3 trillion coronavirus stimulus bill.

The New River is spectacularly poorly named. At around three hundred million years old, it is apparently the third oldest river in the world. However, to the first colonist that came across it, it was new to him. Incidentally, if you were wondering how you age a river, you do so by averaging the age of the two mountain ranges it dissects.

Are We There Yet?

You may further ask how one dates a mountain range. You do this through carbon dating its rocks or—more jocularly—by asking nicely and not pointing out its tectonic faults.

The owners of restaurants and campgrounds in Fayetteville seemed excited by this upgrade and anticipated a 20 percent uptick in customers coming to this part of West Virginia. This town was devoted to coal in the nineteenth century. However, in the late twentieth century, when extracting this mineral from the ground became uneconomic, Fayetteville transformed itself into a tourist town. Today, almost every resident is employed in the tourism industry.

We stayed in some Amish Cabins hastily constructed in a forest near the bridge. They were cute two-story affairs. We slept on mattresses on the upper floor while the dogs, defeated by the wooden ladder, slept downstairs. The cooking facilities were limited, and the TV—unthinkable in an actual Amish household—was unworkable, but we enjoyed our retreat from society.

When it was built with federal funding in 1977, the New River Gorge Bridge was both the longest and highest bridge in the world. This single-spanned steel arch bridge reduced the journey time from forty-five minutes to forty-five seconds between two towns on either side of the gorge. While the bridge is no longer the highest or longest—one in Shanghai has surpassed it—the bridge and the Appalachian Forest are remarkable backdrops to almost every part of the park.

The bridge's height makes it popular with thrill-seekers. On the third Saturday of October, the bridge is handed over to these daredevils for Bridge Day. This is the only day you can walk across the bridge. However, the more adventurous jump off the bridge with parachutes or rappel down the bridge on ropes. Pre-pandemic, some four hundred base jumpers and three hundred rappellers did their stuff in front of eighty thousand spectators. They land, usually safely, almost one thousand feet below. I say usually safely; these Bridge Days have also seen the deaths of four risk-takers.

We found an isolated spot for fishing by the side of the river. Canoes would glide past us downriver every thirty minutes or so. They were as quiet as mice wearing noise-canceling headphones, so we would often not notice them until they almost tangled with Lorna's line. The less occasional phalanx of much noisier rafts with their helmeted thrill-seekers would also drift past us, anticipating the fifty-three miles of grade three and four rapids further downstream. It was this activity that drew most people to this park.

Every hour on the other side of the river, a train sounded its klaxon on the tracks built for nineteenth-century miners. We never saw the train, as it was hidden behind trees, but we could hear every squeak, puff, and chug. Of course, these days, the passengers were tourists rather than miners, and the cargo cameras and polystyrene cups of Pepsi rather than picks and coal. Other than those distractions, there were few sounds besides those of the native birds and insects.

****

America possesses a significant geopolitical advantage due to its abundant natural resources. The US and Canada have between them $110 trillion of natural resources, with both countries also having vast areas of fertile plains for agriculture, abundant fresh water, and plentiful oil and coal reserves.

Although the US is once again a net energy exporter, it isn't yet energy independent. Despite being the world's number one oil and natural gas producer, the US finds it more efficient to import rather than mine and refine some forms of petro-carbons. However, assuming fracking and renewable technology continue, the US should be able to be entirely self-sufficient if required.

The US isn't entirely mineral self-sufficient, though. It is entirely dependent on imports for twenty-one mineral commodities, such as asbestos, strontium, and cesium, and partially reliant on sixty-nine others. Fewer than 10 percent of America's minerals are recycled because digging them out of the ground is cheaper than repurposing them. Continued shocks to the global supply chain may change this dynamic.

However, the bulk of natural resources is held in BRICS+ countries. While China has only one-fifth of North America's natural resources, its savvy infrastructure investment overseas is a long-term play to ensure self-determination. Taking the two most essential components of batteries by way of example, China is responsible for processing at least two-thirds of the world's lithium and three-quarters of its nickel. Not surprisingly, therefore, China is the largest provider of American mineral commodity imports, presenting a considerable risk in the event of a conflict.

Are We There Yet?

In most parts of the US, there are strict leash laws. As a result, dogs generally only get the freedom to roam in designated dog parks. In West Virginia, however, dogs can roam as they wish. This turned out to be not very far. Dog #2 took sporadic trips to the water's edge to quench her throat but tended to stay close to the underemployed fisherman. Dog #1, however, would investigate the nearby undergrowth and have to be called back to home base occasionally.

Lorna was determined to catch fish for her dinner. Given past experience, I was not buying the barbecue equipment until the fish had been caught. Lorna was not born to be a fisherman, as she has the patience of a sales director at a start-up. She would try one fishing spot, then another. She would change from nightcrawlers (earthworms to you and me) to artificial lures and then back again.

Cursing her ill fortune, we hiked to a beauty spot that overlooked the gorge and the bridge. We had thought the Old Rag views in Shenandoah to be magnificent, but this seemingly infinite panorama was even more awe-inspiring. It suddenly became apparent why this bitty national park had been awarded full national park status. The horizon stretched endlessly, revealing a patchwork of forests and distant peaks. Two focal points improved this symphony of colors and textures. First was the looping river and deep canyons hundreds of feet below us, and second was the immense bridge that crossed the gorge.

My fear of heights kept me firmly in the middle of the craggy endpoint. However, Dog #2 was fearless in her viewing habits, pulling on her leash to the very limits of its extension so that she could place her paws on the final rock of the mountaintop. I swapped leashes with Lorna so that I was responsible for the more muscular but also more circumspect canine.

Lorna tried fishing again in a nearby recreational lake area. It was a hive of boating activity, and I enjoyed swimming in its cool waters while Lorna attempted to catch dinner. Unfortunately, Lorna is to fishing what King Herod was to the babysitting industry. Having failed a second time to catch anything, we found ourselves again on the main drag of Fayetteville, West Virginia.

Fayetteville is named after the French Revolutionary War hero, the Marquis de Lafayette. He was a wealthy orphan whose male ancestors had perished in France's omnipresent conflicts of that time. At nineteen, he chartered a ship—which he presumptuously called La Victoire—and set sail to fight for the colonists against the British. He said that he had dreamed of glory since childhood, which, in his case, was the year before.

Julian Bishop

The Marquis de Lafayette was injured in the Battle of Brandywine, where you think his nationality might have given him an advantage. However, he fought bravely and was mentioned in dispatches by Washington. In his second battle, the Battle of Monmouth, he made the best of a disastrous mistake by his opposite number, General Lee. These two incidents made him a French poster child for the revolutionaries.

Four months before the signing of the Treaty of Paris that recognized America as independent, North Carolina named a town after him. In the decades after, as residents from this town moved further west, they created a further thirteen Fayettevilles, including this one in West Virginia.

The Marquis is present in modern-day culture, too. For example, he is prominently featured in *Hamilton, The Musical,* and *The Aristocats* basset hound is named Lafayette.

Fayetteville, West Virginia, is a small town of fewer than three thousand people. It is the type of town with a yoga studio, a store that sells crystals, and a proud gallery of many public murals. You could see that this community was starting to rejuvenate on the ascension of the nearby national park.

After three days in New River Gorge, we drove through West Virginia toward Ohio. As befits the state with the highest deer collision rate (see the previous book), there were ungulates everywhere. Try as they might, West Virginia's careless drivers didn't seem to be able to make a meaningful dent in its antelope population, even if its deer population made considerable dents in their own vehicles.

As we drove, it was impossible not to admire the United States' remarkable landscape diversity. Spanning from the Atlantic to the Pacific, and from the Arctic Circle to the Tropic of Cancer, this vast country encompasses a wide range of climates. Consequently, it showcases diverse vegetation, including lush rainforests, expansive grasslands, and arid cacti-studded deserts.

Geological processes have played the pivotal role in shaping this diverse terrain. The majestic Rockies, for instance, owe their existence to tectonic activity, while the arid deserts of Arizona are remnants of a pre-Cambrian ocean. Countless canyons, etched by wind and rain over millions of years, testify to erosion's relentless power. Meanwhile, the coastal wetlands of the Southeastern region starkly contrast with the sprawling expanses of the Great Plains.

In a surprising twist, the often-overlooked state of Oklahoma emerges as a hidden gem in this mosaic. It proudly boasts a remarkable diversity of landscapes, encompassing mountains, tranquil cypress swamps, vibrant tallgrass prairies, and lush hardwood forests. Notably, it stands as one of only four states that can lay claim to ten distinct ecoregions, offering their highest density per square mile in the entire United States.

Human activity, too, has left an indelible mark on these landscapes. As we crossed into Ohio, a new transformation awaited. Despite the region's modest affluence, every residence boasted sprawling lawns, each meticulously maintained with its own ride-on mower. The grassy expanse was carefully striped, sometimes even double-striped, a testament to the unspoken norms of this society.

As we drove further into Eastern Ohio, the norm turned to farming communities, yielding golden wheat, corn, and tobacco stretching as far as the eye can see. Quaint red barns and white farmhouses dotted the countryside, while grain silos, such as the ones in *Witness*, adorned every landscape. This countryside is reminiscent of the Peter Weir film because it was shot just over the Pennsylvania border. Amish communities and their beautifully maintained farms are widespread in this part of America.

Sharing the road with Amish buggies enabled us to examine the landscape more carefully. One of the most striking aspects of Amish influence was their agricultural practices, which have shaped the landscape into a picturesque tableau of rural America frozen in time. Horse-drawn plows and reapers replaced the roar of tractors, and an absence of power lines, streetlights, billboards, and modern machinery in the fields added to its pastoral charm.

****

Our destination that day was the rural Central Ohio community of American Boss #1 and her husband, the Judge. We had been friends for decades, and because we had children of a similar age, we had vacationed together several times. Like us, their daughters had recently left home, and they were adjusting to a new phase in their lives.

I have a long-standing interest in criminal justice. More than thirty years ago and for about a decade, I was appointed by the UK Home Office to check on the welfare of those detained in South London police stations. After relocating to the US, my focus had shifted slightly, and I became a volunteer *guardian ad litem*, advocating for children in foster care.

Aware of this interest, the Judge arranged for me to tour a juvenile detention center in Central Ohio. The facility proudly bore his name, forming a significant part of his legacy in the community where he had lived almost his entire life. His mission was to inspire troubled youth to become responsible and productive citizens.

The facility's Superintendent, a former police officer who suffered severe neck injuries in a work-related road accident that prevented him from traveling in a patrol car, transitioned from running the police dispatch unit to volunteering for outreach community work after realizing his passion for it.

The Judge's predecessor had phoned this disabled police officer every month to ask him to consider being Deputy Superintendent for the juvenile facility. In a demonstration that persistence does pay, he was finally successful in the sixth month.

Later promoted to Superintendent, this highly affable and committed ex-police officer was proud that he had moved the system from punishment to rehabilitation and from a consequence-based system to one that rewarded good behaviors. He and his team of custodians seemed to have created a culture where any staff members could test new ideas to see if they worked.

The thirty-bed facility looked brand new but was, in fact, twenty years old. The maximum-security detention center was hi-tech, with each door controlled via video security. Notably, it bore no resemblance to Brixton's police detention rooms, for it was exceptionally well-resourced, with each feature hard-won by the Superintendent and others. The center had an indoor gymnasium, an outside area with a basketball court, and a library packed with books donated by the local community.

The facility had two corridors of cells for boys and another designated for girls, reflecting the distribution of their typical intake. These cells, while clean, were quite basic in their furnishings. Each held a simple block bed with a mattress and sheets, along with essential amenities such as a toilet and a drinking water dispenser. The stark, minimalist furniture, mostly in white or stainless steel, was illuminated by artificial lighting, occasionally complemented by slender tempered glass windows.

The Superintendent said some other jurisdictions euphemistically called these cells 'rooms,' but his county's authorities were adamant that they were cells because these juvenile detainees were accused of serious criminal offenses. Everything at this detention center seemed deliberate, calculated, and purposeful.

The center serves as a last-resort detention facility for children who pose a risk to themselves or their community, with pre-trial detention being permitted only if they are a danger to others or at risk of not appearing in court. In practice, the inmates I saw were mature teenagers awaiting trial for typically non-bailable felony crimes or convicted juveniles who had repeatedly broken their parole terms.

Most children were only in the center for a matter of weeks before being released into the custody of another carer. The Superintendent told me many did not want to leave, and I believed him. The staff posts inspirational quotes on almost every detention center wall. For instance, "Show me your friends, and I will predict your future."

The Superintendent gave me the resident's guidebook, which each new arrival must read in their first two hours. There's a written test on its contents—if a resident fails this test, a corrections officer will help them understand it until they pass it.

Every new resident starts at Level 1 and earns privileges to the next level after seven days without violating the thirty-seven rules. These stringent rules include addressing all staff by Sir or Ma'am, always keeping the guidebook with them, and treating others with respect.

If a resident chooses to violate these rules, they will initially be given refocus time. This apparently is not intended as a punishment but rather a period that allows them to process their thoughts, feelings, and behaviors. If the offending resident recognizes their poor behavior and develops strategies toward not repeating it, they will return to regular programming. If not—or if there is a severe breach of the rules—they will be relegated to the next lowest level.

The center also has twenty defined exemplars of good behavior—for instance, clean cell, self-control, or good citizenship. When children displayed these behaviors, they earned rewards, for example, three hours of family visitation or informal card-playing time.

A new detainee had to attend mandatory group sessions: drug and alcohol (most had found their way here partly through substance abuse), anger management, art therapy, and resilience training. You would receive a rule violation if you chose not to attend these sessions.

Though it was the summer break, the kids who hadn't passed their classes were attending summer school to catch up on what they had missed. The facility had excellent teaching resources, with a teacher supervising as the students diligently worked on their assignments. The classroom was as quiet as a mouse on tiptoes in a library.

The Judge told me the Superintendent's staff wrote a report for each child. Before he pronounced sentence on any detained juvenile, he said he always took time to read their statement in detail. In his experience, they knew each child pretty well.

I had spent many weeks at a suburban Atlanta County Juvenile Court, waiting for my assigned foster children's cases to be heard. Most of the three-quarters of a million American kids in care are placed there due to their parents' actions, with nearly two-thirds of them there because of their parents' problems with drugs or alcohol.

Approximately one-third of these children can be placed with relatives, while the younger four hundred thousand kids are typically found foster homes. The older ones, who are less in demand among foster parents, often end up in group homes.

I've learned much about America from this voluntary work and have had the privilege of seeing sides of America that would otherwise be unknown to me. If you want to give something back to your community, I would wholeheartedly recommend fostering or becoming a volunteer *guardian ad litem*.

The Superintendent told me that staffing was his primary challenge but not for the same reason as every other business that summer. He told me he looked for one thing in any hire; he wanted people who instinctively cared for these troubled children. Everything else could be taught.

I asked the Superintendent whether he could prove that all of this worked. He said that they had difficulties with metrics. They would like to measure the long-term effectiveness of this type of detention center versus another facility with comparable demographics. However, the sealed records for juveniles usually made it impossible to measure long-term success. The things they could measure were, therefore, short-term and mainly input-based. For example, violence and other conflicts compared to other detention facilities. His facility crushed these metrics.

Perhaps surprisingly, as the home of woke, America is pretty conservative in its punishment policy. For example, corporal punishment at school—banned in UK state schools two years after I left compulsory education—is still legal in public schools in nineteen US states and permitted in private schools in forty-eight states.

Famously, the US has the world's highest incarceration rate, with relatively few Americans arguing for less incarceration. However, some pressure groups lobby against the imprisonment of any juveniles, arguing that recidivism at detention centers is higher than for those not detained. Of course, this is another example of comparing apples with oranges.

Are We There Yet?

Those detained are almost always repeat offenders committing higher-level offenses.

Many generalities are written about the criminal justice system in America. As a casual observer, you might conclude that all Democrats are so soft on crime that their cities have all become lawless anarchies. Similarly, you could pigeonhole all Republicans as wanting to incarcerate anyone who has transgressed any law and separate them from society. While a few cities are worryingly lawless, and a minority of Republicans lack compassion, almost all Americans are somewhere in the middle.

What I saw in Central Ohio differed from what I saw in the news. It was a community genuinely trying to resolve the shared community problem of errant juveniles. All residents here were children of someone within their rural community, and the juvenile justice system here was expending considerable resources to give young people a chance to transform their lives.

On a previous visit many years before to this part of Ohio, the Judge had arranged for me to tour the sister Adult County Jail. This felt different from the Juvenile Center and was administered by a Marine. Compared to the prisons I've seen in Britain and read about in the American South, this adult facility was modern, almost like a very basic hotel, with each single-person cell equipped with a TV and bathroom. The jail had one—disturbingly large—wing reserved for serious sex offenders and a large (seldom-used) education area.

With fewer than 0.2 million people in federal prisons (and 1.9 million in state prisons or local jails), the American prison system is predominantly delivered by the states and their counties. Therefore, it's for local communities to choose the incarceration system they think appropriate, and despite the certainties of a few at the fringes, it is a delicate balancing act between providing rehabilitation opportunities and protecting their community. This (very much Republican) part of Central Ohio was putting its resources into trying to break the intergenerational cycle of crime by showing troubled juveniles an alternative pathway.

****

Later that day, our friends invited us to be part of one of the hundred and forty floats in Ohio's Blue Tip Parade. At one point, the Ohio Match Co. was the world's largest firestick company, producing three hundred million matches every day, and was headquartered in the town until it downsized in the eighties. Its matches had distinctive blue tips, and these azure-colored heads gave the parade its name even though the match company had long left the town.

American boss #1 and her husband, The Judge, were driving in the parade as part of the never-ending electioneering process in America. They had borrowed their younger daughter's Jeep Wrangler and decorated it with a dozen American flags and awnings. The Judge's name was emblazoned on both sides of the vehicle to ensure name recognition for the next election, some five years away.

All paraders had to assemble an hour before the starting klaxon, so we socialized with the other participants.

There were palpable nerves amongst the town's many youth organizations. Gymnasts worried if their handstands would receive perfect scores, the robotics team repowered their batteries, and Girl Scouts were concerned lest their cookies should melt. Martial arts enthusiasts channeled their inner energies, soccer players played keepie-uppie, and young girls in tight jodhpurs and navy shadbellies pampered their ponies. Marching bands tinkered with their instruments, twirlers twiddled their batons, and the Scottish band squeezed out the soothing sound of bagpipes. Country Line dancers ensured they were aligned from the right, and Jazzercise decided they would wing it. Owners of commercial companies made sure that their branding was visible to potential customers; they wanted the maximum Return on Investment from their $50 entry fee. Horses and dogs defecated before their big moment, church groups said one final prayer, and classic car owners gave their pride and joy one last buff.

The many political candidates just talked but obviously not to people of the opposite faith. I spent the most time with this group, and—given the recent inarticulacy at the top of American politics—I was surprised by how knowledgeable they were about their community's challenges.

The sky was deep blue and cloudless, and there was no chance of anyone raining on our parade. The parade kicked off when the Grand Marshalls lit the eighteen-foot-tall blue-tipped match from their vantage point in a cherry-picker basket. Its ignition formally started the five-day Blue Tip Festival.

The crowd was ten rows deep in most places, and the front rows were generally reserved for children. The town's twenty-thousand community had all turned out after the previous year's Covid cancelation. Some were smartly dressed, while others were I'll-just-come-in-my-sweatpants people. The bearded, blue-collared worker, the dreadlocked hippie, and the flamboyantly dressed members of the LBTQ+ community provided the diversity at this parade.

American Boss #1 had purchased seven buckets of candy to throw to the children on the two-and-a-half-mile parade route. She had also bought dog biscuits for any canine spectators. The marshals instructed us to throw our candy onto the sidewalk, not the road.

A range of parenting styles were in evidence. A 'wait for the candy to come to you' group received conspicuously less candy than those who didn't seem to mind that their children were scavenging for candy on a busy road. Children of all upbringings chanted "Candy" or "Me, please!"

Unfortunately, the good people of Wadsworth would not form much of a baseball team. Almost none of them could catch the flying candy, which would bounce off their hands (or heads) back onto the road. Other kids would then dart into the street to retrieve the prized teeth rotter. As the parade progressed, I became skilled at projecting the candy directly into the child's bag or box. From the other side of the car, I noticed that most of Lorna's largesse generally found storm drains. Later in the parade, I changed my throwing strategy, directing my aim toward adults instead of children. These adults had the critical advantage that they might vote in the next election.

American Boss #1 had the most challenging job; she had to direct the Jeep away from any wandering child who had just run into the road to retrieve candy from the poorer-throwing Girl Scouts in front of us.

The Judge waved to the crowd, who shouted his name as we passed. Occasionally, he would call back, "I'll see you later this week," to some random long-haired juvenile.

Our entry did not trouble the All-American Judges Association of Pageantry. This esteemed body was obviously not constituted of his types of judges. A Ford Model A won the best classic car, followed by two Studebakers from four decades apart. Best overall was, surprisingly, not won by a plumber. The Wadsworth High School Marching Band again took home this honor.

After the parade, we repaired to a local Mexican eatery with some new friends. The food tasted as if Ohioans had cooked it, that is to say, much better than in Mexico.

While in Ohio, we dropped in at yet another national park, one so anonymous that we hadn't been aware of its existence even though we had visited American Boss #1 many times. Between the World Wars, local civic leaders acquired land in the Cuyahoga Valley and began to push for federal protection and investment. In 1974, President Ford established Cuyahoga Valley as a National Park. Designated seemingly not for its natural beauty but rather to restore wetlands and protect the area from urban sprawl, we took a pleasant enough walk along a canal rather than the more popular scenic railway. Compared to most other National Parks, this was a disappointment. One for the completionists, of which, undeniably, I am one.

After four perfect days with our friends, we said goodbye and started the six-hour journey to New York City through Ohio and Pennsylvania. In New Jersey, we foolishly stopped for gas on the turnpike. I wish I had remembered from *High, Wide, and Handsome* that New Jersey was the other state that did not permit you to pump your own gas.

While taking the dogs for a bathroom break, I saw Lorna gesticulating wildly like a mime with laryngitis. While she could have been attempting to escape from an invisible box, I thought it more likelier that she was subtly seeking guidance about whether she needed to tip the attendant. I recalled that the gas pump operator in Oregon had looked at us strangely when we had tried to tip him and shook my head. Later, I was relieved to find online that 94 percent of New Jerseyans said they never tipped. They also lamented that they couldn't be trusted to pour their own gasoline.

Are We There Yet?

Chapter 5 – The Big Apple

We had no choice other than to drive to Midtown Manhattan, the first part of our month in NYC. Unfortunately, we had too much luggage and two dogs, and the latter were not permitted on public transportation unless carried in a bag.

Driving in New York City is not a journey for the faint-hearted. The constant cacophony of car horns and the relentless hustle and bustle of the city can be overwhelming. I vividly remember the first time I found myself amid this urban chaos; it was a scorching summer afternoon, and I was navigating through a labyrinth of intersections. As I approached an exceptionally crowded crossing, I hesitated momentarily, unsure of the right of way. In that split second of indecision, the traffic lights changed, and I unintentionally blocked cross traffic from moving forward. The chorus of car horns that erupted around me was deafening. It felt like every driver in the city had their finger on the horn, and I had unwittingly become the epicenter of their frustration.

That day, I learned first-hand the art of driving in the city, one which required nerves of steel and an intimate understanding of the unspoken rules of the road. While the city has implemented hefty fines for unnecessary honking, the car horn remains a necessary mode of communication—both a weapon of annoyance and a lifeline for survival. I can still recall the incredulous glares and impatient gestures from other drivers, and it's an experience I have no desire to repeat.

It could be worse; fewer than half the households in New York City own a car, but this is heavily skewed by borough. For example, where public transport is best (Manhattan), only 22 percent own a car, while, where it is worst (Staten Island), only 17 percent don't have one.

Besides the cars and buses, other forms of transport navigate New York City's roads. Sure enough, as in every other major city, cyclists and skateboarders abound; however, you also see young men on kids' electric scooters, weaving in and out of traffic. This includes an army of food delivery specialists bringing sustenance to the income-rich, time-poor New Yorkers. As in Key West, many wore masks, but almost none sported helmets.

Parking in NYC is prohibitively expensive, around $75 per day where we were staying. Therefore, we agreed to park our vehicle at a friend's New Jersey house to save a couple of thousand dollars. Lorna selected me to drive back the way we had come to park at their house. After a second drive through New York City's chaotic streets, I could see why families might choose the relative haven of suburban peace over the bustle and noise of The Big Apple.

I took the train back into the city. The screech of the brakes echoed off the platform while the sunlight reflected off the train's silver exterior, and as I ascended the impossibly high egresses, a powerful blast of cold air hit me. This commuter experience was luxurious compared to the one I had endured in Southeast England for two decades. The plush, cushioned seats allowed the passengers to relax a little before arriving at the hullabaloo of Penn Station. I surveyed the New Jersey suburban landscape with its residential neighborhoods and neatly manicured lawns through the large picture windows as the train glided along the tracks toward one of the many city bridges. As we approached the bridge over the Hudson, the Western Manhattan skyline towered into view. Other passengers saw these vistas daily and preferred to work on their laptops, read books, or engage in muffled conversations with their neighbors. But I was enthralled.

When the pandemic hit, car registrations jumped by over a third as New Yorkers either fled the city or disdained public transport and the company of others. However, with few places to go, traffic passing through the city's tunnels or over its bridges halved, and the average speed doubled to an almost rapid 2.7 miles per hour.

Of course, America's most international city was the first to be hit hard by Covid. The first case was diagnosed in March 2020, and by April, Covid deaths exceeded five hundred people per day.

By the time we were there, in June and July 2021, New Yorkers seemed equally divided between mask-wearers and those who went cloth-free. After our experience of the republican states of Florida, Georgia, North Carolina, West Virginia, and Ohio, it was a shock to see so many covering up.

Are We There Yet?

The city had recently reopened to tourists and had just launched a campaign to regain the sixty million-plus visitors it used to host. I loved New York and thought this might be a once-in-a-lifetime opportunity to see the city relatively tourist-free.

Unfortunately, all forty-one Broadway theaters were still dark, as procuring and training the talent required to put on a Broadway show demanded substantial time and preparation. The allure of the theater in New York City is undeniable; annually, more patrons fill its seats than the combined attendance of all the city's sports teams. Pre-pandemic, the Big Apple's theaters generated an impressive two billion dollars of annual revenue. Over the previous quarter-century, theatergoer numbers had more than doubled, while ticket prices, even adjusted for inflation, had surged by nearly 70 percent.

Theatre is, however, not a wise investment, with 80 percent of producers not recouping their investments—a lack of return that has been remarkably consistent since the sixties. This is because the upfront costs of a theater production are high; a standard production might have a capitalization of $4 million, while a musical has perhaps four times this setup cost. The running costs are substantial, too. Though you may hear that the big-name actor only earns a low weekly minimum salary of $2,000, this star typically takes home 5 or even 10 percent of the weekly gross. That represents a decent paycheck for the star launching a play in its first three-month run. Unlike movies, these productions can't easily be scaled globally, and their audience is limited to the numbers that can fit into an auditorium. The only way to make money, therefore, is through longevity.

Aside from Andrew Lloyd Webber and his ilk, the theater landlords are the principal part of the value chain that makes money. They charge around $20,000 weekly for the theater, plus about 6 percent of the box office gross. In 2019, one anonymous theater owner told Variety, "All we do is open the door in the morning, and there's a line of suckers—well, I should say, producers—begging to get in. This business has never been better."

Unfortunately for this theatre owner, schadenfreude called. The pandemic has been catastrophic for theater owners, and it's unclear when this will change. Theatergoers are reluctant to sit inside a cramped building for three hours alongside people they don't know. Furthermore, with two-thirds of tickets typically sold to tourists, Broadway won't be genuinely back until tourism returns to its pre-pandemic norms.

Incidentally, you may have heard of the term Off-Broadway. This has nothing to do with the theater's proximity to the diagonal street of the same name. A Broadway show plays in a theater with more than 500 seats; an Off-Broadway show is one with between 100 and 499; and an Off-Off-Broadway fewer than 100.

Another New York institution facing challenges was its restaurant scene. Before the pandemic, the city boasted an impressive forty thousand eateries, and the quality of its cuisine could (almost) rival that of Hong Kong. In both cities, it's common to find apartments with compact kitchens and no dedicated dining spaces, often leading people to choose restaurants for socializing over home gatherings. What sets New York apart is its diverse and independent restaurant landscape, showcasing a global array of cuisines that mirror the city's rich immigrant population. With fierce competition, even in less touristy areas, a subpar restaurant in the Big Apple is unlikely to thrive.

By the end of 2021, the pandemic had forced the closure of five thousand restaurants, and thousands more were hanging on. While the city authorities had permitted restaurants to put outside tables where the street's parking spaces used to be, New York is a cold place in winter. The critical question for many New Yorkers was, "Will these restaurants come back?"

****

Neither Dog #1 nor Dog #2 enjoyed NYC. Dogs can't use public transportation unless carried in a bag. So, we could only take them to parks that Dog #2, who's less active, could reach. Unfortunately, most nearby green spaces did not welcome dogs. However, in both NYC locations, we eventually found dog parks—poorly maintained miserable places designated as dog parks only because they couldn't be built on.

Dog #1 was trained well and preferred to do his bathroom business in a natural setting. Too often, he had to suffer the indignity of going to the bathroom on the street. The other change for Dog #1 was the street noise. The usually taciturn Dog #1 heard the emergency vehicle sirens so often that he could imitate their sounds with unerring accuracy.

I met many New Yorkers with new Covid canines at these miserable dog parks. In the early stages of the pandemic, the dog shelters had quickly become denuded of second-hand mutts. There were no dogs going cheap… they all just went woof woof. Therefore, isolated New Yorkers were forced to spend thousands on a brand-new pup to relieve their loneliness. As a result of this increased puppy purchase, the Journal of American Veterinary Medical Association estimates that 45 percent of American households now have a dog, seven percentage points up from 2019.

These enforced homeworkers had never expected such isolating work conditions. Had they read the twentieth-century futurists, they might, however, have expected to work fewer hours.

In 1930, the economist John Maynard Keynes predicted that improved technology would lead to humans working only fifteen hours per week. By 1960, that poorest of predictors—a Senate subcommittee—projected that Americans would work only fourteen hours per week by 2000.

What has actually happened since 1950 is that Americans have both increased their working hours and quintupled their productivity, and the combination of these two factors has made America and Americans economically wealthy.

What I believe both Keynes and the Senate subcommittee underestimated was the role of culture.

Hard work is deeply ingrained in American culture. Immigrants didn't settle for a fifteen-hour work week to subsist. Instead, they embraced working hard to improve their families' economic standing. This drive was further amplified by the influence of religion, which emphasized work as a means of drawing them closer to God. As a result, generations of offspring from these immigrants have diligently instilled this Protestant Work Ethic in their children from a young age.

This culture is so pervasive that it has fed into American society's systems: capitalism, entrepreneurship and innovation, ambition and education, self-reliance and individualism, and the US tax code, to name just a few.

Many Americans work long hours to improve their social status, which strongly correlates with income. Working harder buys a bigger house, a newer car, more Botox, or the opportunity to send their children to an Ivy college. The American may also work harder to avoid being laid off, with the potential loss of expensive employer healthcare a potent motivator.

Most Americans are willing to put in long hours to get the job done. The average US employee works 1,800 hours per year, substantially higher than in France (1,500) or Germany (1,400) and somewhat higher than the UK (1,700 hours).

Part of this is because Americans take shorter vacations. In much of Western Europe, workers will take a month or so vacation in the summer to top up their suntan, whereas an American worker will take three days of vacation time to receive open heart surgery.

Moreover, Americans have higher workplace productivity than Europeans, a result of increased investment in training, greater labor market flexibility, wider adoption of productivity-enhancing technologies, and a more competitive work environment. On average, Americans are 20 percent more productive each hour, delivering $15 higher output in goods and services per hour compared to their European counterparts.

This greater work ethic, multiplied by the higher productivity levels, is why Americans have greater purchasing power than Europeans. A blue-collar worker in Moscow must work 18 minutes to buy a one-kilogram loaf of bread, compared to 12 minutes in London and only 8 minutes in Washington, DC.

When a nation reduces its working hours without a corresponding boost in productivity, its citizens will find themselves with less money to enjoy life's pleasures. Additionally, the government will face funding constraints on its essential activities due to reduced revenue.

Unlike in European countries, there are relatively few government regulations in the American workplace, particularly on working hours. This means that employers can require longer work hours without facing legal consequences. In contrast, France has chosen to prioritize workers' health by restricting working hours and making it illegal to send work emails out of hours.

In the US (and elsewhere), technological advances have made it easier for workers to stay connected to work outside regular business hours, leading to longer workdays and a blurring of the line between work and personal time.

You may think this hard work sounds ghastly. Isn't it more civilized to have a balanced life where you spend quality time reading books or socializing with your family and friends? Of course, you are right.

Unexpectedly, some of America's Generation Z seems to be moving in this direction, seemingly valuing work-life balance to prioritize their mental health. This is one of several behaviors that differentiates them from previous generations, but whether this pattern of wanting to work less will stick is unclear.

For instance, with just fifteen hours of work per week, you would require an exceptionally high hourly wage to fully embrace the unmatched opportunities that NYC offers, given its sky-high costs of rent, entertainment, and taxes.

Are We There Yet?

In the sitcom *Friends*, Monica paid only $200 for her rent-controlled two-bedroom apartment in West Village, inherited from her grandmother. This monthly rent was an exceptional deal.

NYC introduced rent controls in the twenties as evictions rose after new constructions fell during World War I. After WW2, when sudden demand caused a severe housing shortage, more rent controls were introduced as soldiers sought apartments for their families after demobilization.

In New York, there are two main types of subsidized apartments. The more well-known one is *rent-controlled*, but it is pretty rare. To be eligible for rent-controlled apartments, the building must have been constructed before 1947, and the tenant or their family member must have lived there since before 1971. Consequently, there are fewer than twenty thousand rent-controlled apartments in NYC. To obtain one, you'd need to have lived with a family member in such an apartment for at least two years and, after their passing, claim your right to continue living there. The average rent-controlled apartment is just under $1,000 per month, making Monica's apartment look an absolute steal.

Almost half of NYC apartments are the second type, *rent-stabilized*. These flats were either built between 1947 and 1974 or constructed before 1947 and leased after 1971. City authorities calculate a maximum base rent biennially for each of the 2.1 million rent-controlled units. The landlord can only increase these rents by 7.5 percent every two years until the maximum is reached. The average rent-stabilized apartment is $1,400 per month compared to the $1,900 unregulated unit. This may sound as if the renter is getting a good deal, but you are often comparing old decaying apples to new juicy oranges.

The market rent for Monica's apartment would be around $7,000 a month today, perhaps affordable for daytime soap actor Joey and transposter Chandler but well beyond the salary of chef Monica. The puzzling question is how masseuse Phoebe could afford to live in the trendy West Village.

From an economic perspective, rent control benefits tenants in the short term by protecting them from significant rent increases. However, it decreases overall affordability and fuels gentrification in the longer term. Economists have also observed that it leads to a reduction in the supply of rental housing, a decay of the housing stock, and encourages small families to live in large apartments, and vice versa.

In the 1920s, New York City was the world's largest city and cultural center of the Jazz Age; it was during this time that its nickname, 'Big Apple,' was coined. This term originally referred to the prize at horse racing events, and a journalist started using it to describe New York as the ultimate prize on the planet, saying, "There's only one Big Apple, and that's New York."

With the occasional sideways step, the Big Apple continues to grow in economic and political importance. Even today, it provides headquarters to over 10 percent of the world's largest companies and is home to the United Nations, the IMF, and the World Bank.

Of course, US companies constitute a staggering 83 percent of the planet's largest five hundred companies. There are many reasons for this success, but one of the most overlooked is their astonishing ability to pivot into new industries, different parts of the value chain, or new types of customers. For instance, Amazon began life by selling books, Netflix delivered DVDs to your mailbox, Twitter once promoted podcasts, and Western Union used to send telegrams. Now, each of them has found different ways to generate revenue.

However, the American government finds it more challenging to pivot. In a 2011 article in *Foreign Policy Magazine*, then-US Secretary of State Hillary Clinton announced a strategic shift for the country. The US would redirect its diplomatic, economic, and strategic resources from the Middle East and Europe toward Asia in the coming decade. She outlined plans to strengthen treaties with Asian allies to establish a trading community called the Trans-Pacific Partnership.

This hasn't been what has happened. The same article began with an assumption that America would shortly withdraw from Iraq and Afghanistan, but the latter took more than a decade to complete. Historically, the primary strategic interest of the United States in the Middle East has been centered around oil. Some argued that with the US becoming a net oil exporter, the Gulf region was less strategically important. While this argument holds some truth, it was difficult to envisage America disengaging from this region, potentially leaving it to other world powers.

Emergencies elsewhere—from ISIS in Syria, a nuclear Iran, and the Russian invasion of Ukraine—have further derailed the well-signposted US pivot. While I am not sure you can label it a comprehensive strategy, US policy now seems to be to avoid the future 'forever wars' that have dogged its foreign policy for half a century.

Are We There Yet?

It's my impression that Americans of most political backgrounds have become fatigued with the US's involvement in unwinnable overseas wars. Given that the world is just too chaotic to police, it's probable that a new generation of isolationist politicians will eventually emerge, embroiling themselves only in the most strategically essential conflicts.

Incidentally, the Trans-Pacific Partnership was agreed upon by twelve Pacific countries but never ratified by the US. Despite the passage of almost a quarter of a century, it isn't clear that America's Asian century has yet materialized.

****

With its eighteenth-century grid system, Manhattan Island is uncomplicated to traverse; avenues run vertically from First to Twelfth, and streets horizontally up to 220th. Traffic flows east to west along odd-numbered streets and vice versa for even-numbered ones. In a further example of coherent forethought, odd-numbered street addresses are always on the north side of the road.

One person who found the city easy to navigate was Thomas Fitzpatrick. In 1956, as part of a bet and while drunk, he stole a small plane from New Jersey and landed it on one of these narrow Manhattan streets in front of the bar where he had been drinking. Then, incredibly, he repeated the same feat two years later when another man didn't believe he'd done it the first time.

However, there are three main exceptions to this rational system. First, all the roads below Houston Street in Lower Manhattan have names rather than numbers. Second, you may come across some additional avenues in a few places; for example, 6.5th Avenue, also known as Vanderbilt Avenue. Third, one diagonal street, Broadway, runs from the southeast of Manhattan to the northwest.

New York City is best known for its towering skylines. The traditional one is of lower Manhattan, but Midtown, Brooklyn, and even Jersey City also make splendid vistas. No matter how often you have been to New York, these panoramas always take your breath away.

One way to appreciate these views is to go out of Manhattan to view them from afar, while another is to go high. One that does both is the walk across Brooklyn Bridge, which gives excellent views of Brooklyn one way and views of Midtown and Lower Manhattan in the other direction. When in New York, I always take this hike.

On most visits to New York, I also find myself on the High Line. This abandoned elevated freight railway in the west of Manhattan was converted into a one-and-a-half-mile public footpath thirty feet above ground about a decade ago. Its southernmost point is near the Whitney Museum of American Art, and its northernmost is the anemic but ultra-pricey Hudson Yards. The High Line's defining feature is the remarkable view over the Meatpacking District, whose products the former railway once took to the docks.

The architects of this elevated footpath have created a serene and tranquil escape for the bustling city streets below. This urban oasis is loaded with seasonal flora and supplemented with contemporary public art installations, which provide an extra layer of visual stimulation and create communal areas for people to congregate.

With six-and-a-half thousand high-rise buildings in the city, building rules are necessary. To prevent these giants from blocking natural light onto the streets below, the 1916 Zoning Resolution restricted both the size of the base floor print and the maximum height of each skyscraper. You will see the effect of this regulation in the older New York skyscrapers, which typically have setbacks, often in step form, where the top of the building is much narrower than its base.

New York City's planning authority substantially revamped its zoning rules in the sixties by introducing the Floor Area Ratio (FAR) concept. Depending on the ratio in that part of town, a maximum total floor area is allocated to each new building. For example, the FAR might be 10 in the city's most congested areas. This FAR would enable the builder to construct a building ten stories high, covering the whole of its lot, or up to twenty stories if only half of the base footprint was covered.

However, a loophole enabled owners of New York lots to purchase unused clear air above adjacent smaller buildings. This is why you often see supertall buildings next to standard-size ones. The two Trump buildings, for example, take advantage of the adjacent unused airspace, enabling the construction of the former president's fifty-eight and seventy-two-story buildings.

In the most recent decade, we have seen the rise of residential skyscrapers for billionaires. These supertalls congregate around the southern part of Central Park and are super-slender, attractively so to my eye. These new builds utilize two loopholes: the purchase of nearby air rights and the deliberate unfilling of many floors. About one-quarter of the total space is reserved for mechanical works, which doesn't contribute to usable floor space.

Essentially, these skyscrapers are stacks of apartments, each offering 360-degree views of New York. At the time of writing, you could purchase an 8,000-square-foot penthouse at 432 Park Avenue for $169 million, which amounts to over $20,000 per square foot. This six-bedroom, nine-bathroom apartment provides stunning views of all of NYC, and its annual property tax bill is comparable to what many Americans might pay to purchase a house. Despite doubling in value since its construction five years ago, this apartment has never been lived in.

****

I first noticed a sticker that read 'Birds Aren't Real' on a New York lamppost. I was puzzled by this statement, especially because a pigeon was cooing beneath it. So, I typed 'Birds Aren't Real' into a search engine and discovered a political movement (apparently from the seventies) that believed the US Government had 'genocided' twelve billion birds in 1959 and replaced them with surveillance drones that still watch our every action. The movement was unsuccessful in preventing the extinction of real birds and claimed that every bird we could now see was a robotic replica. I didn't think much more about it, except that some people will believe anything.

As is the norm for something new, I later began to see 'Birds Aren't Real' everywhere I looked. The slogan was emblazoned on a few young people's clothing, the subject of an occasional billboard, and multiple internet ads. I dug a bit deeper and found a different type of movement.

Peter McIndoe, a college dropout from Ohio, created the slogan on a whim in 2017. He had been home-schooled by his parents and taught many things he now understood as conspiracy theories. Wanting to protest misinformation and combat lunacy with absurdity, he adopted the persona of the chief proponent of 'Birds Aren't Real.'

He attracted some genuine believers and a more significant number who were in on the joke. McIndoe had little sympathy for those who were duped: "If anyone believes birds aren't real, we're the last of their concerns because there's probably no conspiracy they won't believe."

The movement website welds countless conspiracy theory themes into one seamless pile of unbelievability. As with other movements, there are doubters. These skeptics pose challenging questions: 'What are eggs?

What is bird poop? And I have a pet bird; what should I do?' All these questions are answered with aplomb and humor. Incidentally, if you do have a pet bird, it means you have a highly advanced government surveillance drone, which watches your every move and reports data back to the Pentagon… The best advice is not to talk about any confidential matters around them.

I love that someone has tried to thwart this American tendency to believe in conspiracy theories, even if—as in this case—it is futile.

****

In the eighties and nineties, New Yorkers had a global reputation for being rude and impatient, only second perhaps to Parisians. I don't think that's true anymore… at least for New Yorkers. Some attribute this change to the 9/11 atrocities, while others see it as a result of a new generation choosing to behave differently.

New York faced setbacks in the last century, becoming synonymous with crime in the late eighties and nineties. However, the city fought back with policy initiatives, resulting in a much safer environment. Today, it doesn't even rank in the top 100 most dangerous cities in the US, as measured by crimes per resident.

In a kinder gesture, many New Yorkers leave bagged food for people experiencing homelessness on top of fire hydrants and near subway entrances. Elsewhere, a recent five-cent recycling charge for each can or bottle has led to entrepreneurial homeless individuals returning sackfuls of recyclables, effectively contributing to society by acting as outsourced refuse workers.

It may sound obvious, but homelessness in the US primarily correlates with housing availability. Some see the mass of homelessness on America's West Coast and falsely deduce that these homeless people choose to live in generous, liberal states with warm weather. However, many cold places in republican strongholds also have high homeless populations. It turns out that those cities with the most restrictive building programs have the highest proportion of homelessness, and conversely, cities with less NIMBYism have the lowest.

The fact is that America has about two-thirds as much housing construction as it did two decades ago, as affluent people put pressure on city planners to protect their neighborhoods. Not surprisingly, this lower level of house building is the leading cause of homelessness.

Are We There Yet?

Julian Bishop

Chapter 6 – New York City's Boroughs

I had been to New York City numerous times before, so this time, I focused on experiencing activities that locals enjoy rather than frequenting the typical tourist spots I had already explored.

Although New York City has five boroughs, most tourists experience only one: Manhattan. Even then, they typically only see a small part of Manhattan.

Manhattan is the wealthiest and most densely populated borough—it is the part of the city that doesn't sleep. Brooklyn has the largest population and, although gentrifying very rapidly, also has a high disparity in wealth. Queens is the largest by land area and is ethnically diverse. The Bronx is the poorest borough and has historically been the first home for many new immigrants to the US. Lastly, Staten Island doesn't feel like New York City at all.

New York is diverse in many ways, particularly in the breadth of first-generation immigrants. New York's three million immigrants come from every corner of the planet, comprise almost half its workforce, and speak eight hundred languages. Not surprisingly, New York has the largest Jewish population outside of Israel, the largest Chinese population outside Asia, and the largest Puerto Rican population outside Puerto Rico.

What sets New York apart from any other city is that you often feel you are visiting another country without leaving your own city. This diversity leads to the enormous variety in the art, entertainment, and food world.

The five boroughs formed into a single, eight-million-person metropolis in 1898, instantly surpassing London as the world's most populous city. New York County, essentially Manhattan, is the most densely populated county in the United States, while the other NYC counties rank as the second, third, fourth, and thirteenth most crowded.

Are We There Yet?

Although Manhattan is densely populated, it was almost twice as dense in 1910. Tourists often consider Manhattan as the part of New York City below Central Park. However, the borough stretches ten miles above the park's northern boundaries to Inwood Park and the Bronx River. Therefore, I took the time to delve into many of northern Manhattan's neighborhoods on several separate trips.

At the northern tip of Manhattan Island is the Inwood Park neighborhood. So I decided to delve into Inwood Hill Park, one of NYC's 1,700 parks, and spent a couple of hours observing competitive softball matches on its ten softball fields.

Softball is like baseball, except the fields are smaller, the mounds are non-existent, and the distances between bases are shorter. Furthermore, the softball is one-quarter bigger and heavier; it is pitched underarm in a whirligig action at slower speeds to a broader softball bat, making it easier to hit.

This enclave is now decidedly Dominican, with Dominicans comprising almost three-quarters of its population. Spanish is the primary language spoken here. I say 'spoken,' but a more accurate description would be 'shouted.' Every umpire call was disputed raucously by both sides, and the sound of these arguments was so deafening that you couldn't hear the blaring Latin music that accompanied each game. Swings and misses were ridiculed by the opposing side, and insults, which I would never understand, greeted each fielding error.

Most of the players here were older... some older than me. Nobody could claim they weren't taking the game seriously; they sported uniforms sponsored by local businesses, limbered up as they would in the big leagues, and were refereed by professional umpires.

The hitting seemed powerful, but the fielding was littered with errors as these older men struggled to dive onto the ball or move quickly in the outfield. However, the joy of these old-timers as they scored was life-affirming. It was unclear whether it was the pleasure of scoring for one's team or merely the satisfaction of completing the 260-foot run around the diamond. At the game's end, the two sides greeted each other as if they were long-lost best friends.

Elsewhere in the park, families were picnicking, barbecuing, or simply watching their children play. Single people—or those looking for entertainment apart from their spouse—played chess, dominoes, or card games I was unfamiliar with. I seemed to be the only person passing through this neighborhood.

While the park has manufactured attractions such as soccer pitches, American football fields, running paths, tennis courts, and children's playgrounds, most of the park remains natural. The woods and hills here are likely similar to how they would have been three hundred years ago and include caves and the last salt marsh in Manhattan. Waterfowl abound here: mallards and Canadian Geese, of course, but also egrets, herons, moorhens, coots, and cormorants. I even spied a Bald Eagle soaring high overhead. Who would have thought you could see an eagle in New York City?

It is said that Peter Minuit from the Dutch West India Company purchased Manhattan Island here in 1626 from the Lenape tribe for a basket of goods worth 60 guilders ($24), just over a thousand dollars in today's money. According to legend, the two parties agreed on the transaction beneath a liriodendron tree, which had since fallen during a 1933 storm. A boulder with a plaque has now replaced the site of this fantastic deal.

The secluded, leafy forest within Inwood Hill Park was surprisingly vast, with ten miles of winding hiking trails. It was easy to get lost, and I did. However, just when I began to despair of finding my way back to civilization, a passing runner who knew the route would speed past me.

The Hudson River bounds Inwood to the west and the Harlem River to the north. Henry Hudson Bridge makes a splendid backdrop across the marsh, and over the river, you could see towering blocks of tiny apartments in the Bronx, the only borough of New York City not based on an island.

Although separated by only a river, the income disparity between Manhattan and the Bronx is sizable. The former is the wealthiest county in New York, while the latter is the state's poorest. Many in the Bronx live in poverty, and the average income would be even lower if it weren't for its northern suburban areas.

The residential areas of Inwood Park seemed to be bifurcated by the still diagonalizing Broadway. As a result, the more affluent streets with attractive Art Deco buildings were to the west of this street, while to the east of Broadway, residents could enjoy the lowest rents in all of Manhattan, often in relatively low-rise apartments.

Some vestiges of the former dominant Irish community in Inwood Park still lingered. For instance, the park boasted a Gaelic football field, and the commercial area featured a couple of Irish pubs. Nevertheless, today's Inwood Park residents had a different profile; half were born outside the

US, and the non-Hispanic white population had dwindled to just 15 percent.

Further south than Inwood Park, I visited Washington Heights on another day, an area made famous by the Lin-Manuel Miranda musical *In the Heights*. We had seen the movie earlier that week and enjoyed it immensely. Unfortunately, the film performed poorly at the box office. The inferior Spielberg competitor, *West Side Story,* filmed simultaneously literally in the next street, won both awards and box office returns.

Having seen the movie, I expected Washington Heights to be Hispanic—after all, part of it is called Little Dominican Republic. Dominican restaurants were abundant here, as were further eateries from Ecuador, Mexico, and other Latin domains. Nonetheless, Spanish was the only language you heard on the streets. When I bought some water at a corner store, the owner spoke to me in Spanish, and I automatically responded in Spanish... at least the version of Spanish/Italian that I kept for those occasions.

One theme of *In the Heights* is how some Dominican businesses had to relocate to the Bronx in the early 2000s due to rising Manhattan rental prices. While I didn't expect to see choreographed people singing and dancing in the streets, I also didn't anticipate the extent of white gentrification that had transformed so much of the city. Like the rest of Manhattan, the housing stock here was built to last, so you'd also find thirty-year-olds skateboarding, yoga salons, and coffee shops everywhere you looked. Gradually, these urban professionals were reshaping the area's culture.

Although Covid laws had supposedly barred landlords from evicting tenants for yet another month, there were many indications of economic hardship on the Heights's sidewalks. All the family possessions of some former residents were there for all the world to see. Chairs were piled onto sofas, and black plastic bags of clothes were balanced on top. There were bookcases, too, but rarely any books to accompany them.

I caught the slow bus back to our temporary Midtown hotel apartment. It took longer than the subway, but you could observe more. I also find that those who ride the bus are somehow more representative of their community.

A cute eight-year-old girl in a wheelchair wore her LGBTQ+ mask with pride. Her disability meant she had her own space on the bus, but the driver had a lot of work to do to accommodate her. He lowered the ramp onto the street, folded three seats against the bus wall, helped the mother and daughter onto the bus, and secured the wheelchair with restraints. In the end, though, the girl had the best view on the bus.

On another day, we took a Sunday morning walking tour in Harlem before most residents were awake. Lower Manhattan is almost fully gentrified, with one-bedroom apartments starting from $1 million and a monthly service charge of a thousand dollars. Along with its northern neighbor, Washington Heights, the latest gentrification target is Harlem. Realtors initially focused on the southern part of Harlem—which they renamed SoHa to annoy locals—just north of Central Park. Once this area became gentrified, Spanish Harlem and the previously overwhelmingly Black neighborhood of Harlem became the next targets for realtors.

Named Haarlem by the Dutch, the British removed an 'A' from the name of this then-farm village. As New York became wealthier, this northern area of Manhattan Island provided weekend residences for downtown residents in the days when the ten-mile journey might take several hours by horseback or carriage.

Harlem was predominantly Jewish and Italian until the early twentieth century when three factors combined to transform the area's ethnic composition. Initially, many African Americans were displaced when Penn Station was built. Subsequently, Black veterans returning from World War I chose to settle in Harlem. Finally, during the Great Migration, 1.6 million African Americans sought refuge from Jim Crow laws by relocating to Northern cities, with Harlem emerging as a favored destination.

The 1920s was an exciting time in Harlem as it became the center for Jazz music and the Jazz Age generally. The Harlem Renaissance promoted a range of Black creators: Duke Ellington, Louis Armstrong, Paul Robeson, and Bessie Smith for music; Langston Hughes for writing; and Marcus Garvey for activism. Harlem also became the fashionable place for the hipster white people of their time to hang out. The Cotton Club was in Harlem, and the neighborhood was peppered with speakeasies. By 1930, 70 percent of Harlem's population was African American, and for almost the next fifty years, it was the most populous Black city globally.

The Great Depression put an end to Harlem's prosperity. The thirties saw multiple Harlem riots, discouraging wealthy whites from patronizing the area. Most of the remaining white Americans left the neighborhood, along with the middle-class African Americans. By 1950, Harlem was 98.2 percent Black, and impoverished.

Are We There Yet?

NYC's neighborhoods continue to transform themselves every few generations. Harlem's well-built stock of townhouses makes an attractive investment for wealthy financiers and internet start-up workers. From the late-1990s, rich people of all races began buying houses in the area. It is now estimated that only 40 percent of residents are Black.

****

Joel Garreau coined the term 'edge city' to denote new urban areas that have developed in the suburbs of America's largest cities. Once green pastures three decades ago, these emerging cities now feature gleaming glass office towers, boast the best shopping complexes, and are always situated close to major highway interchanges. While many people live in these new urban areas, the population swells in the morning and dwindles in the late afternoon.

The US now has more than two hundred significant edge cities. These areas offer more space, are generally more affordable, and typically have lower crime rates. Their 'parent' cities often find it challenging to compete with their offspring for jobs and residents, leading to a degradation of their tax base and further urban deterioration. Los Angeles, Washington DC, Atlanta, and even New York City each have a dozen or more edge cities.

New York City also contains 'mini-cities' within its boundaries. We had never been to Roosevelt Island, a 147-acre island located in the East River between Manhattan and Queens. In the nineteenth century, the island housed a penitentiary, workhouses, and a hospital for the incurables. It remained largely uninhabited until the seventies when it became home to the technology campus of Cornell University. Connected to other parts of NYC by cable car, ferry, bridge, and subway, there is no better view of the midtown skyline from this 'other island.' Unfortunately, the island with fewer skyscrapers had been hit hard by the pandemic, with half of its stores and restaurants closed or unleased. Nevertheless, we enjoyed a pleasant walk around this mini-city.

Hudson Yards is another relatively new business and residential area. Formerly a train storage yard in western Manhattan, its charmless glass skyscrapers lack the appeal of other Manhattan districts. This upmarket area features a two-hundred-million-dollar art installation called the Vessel, a 155-foot-tall structure comprised of 154 interconnected copper staircases. While this art exhibit offers terrific city views and is highly Instagram-friendly, it left me feeling empty and $10 poorer.

On the other side of Manhattan, I stopped by StuyTown, an earlier purpose-built community. To give it its proper name, Stuyvesant Town-Peter Cooper Village was named after the nineteenth-century industrialist and last Director-General of the Dutch colony of New Amsterdam, on whose farmland the complex now sits. Its 110 skyscrapers on 80 acres of Lower East Manhattan land house 58,000 people in 29,000 apartments.

StuyTown's history is noteworthy. Originally a slum area called the Gas House District, a prominent New York financial institution used eminent domain to remove twelve thousand residents at the end of World War II. MetLife was determined to attract wealthier renters for their new properties. Their President, Frederick Ecker, once famously said, "Negroes and Whites do not mix," and StuyTown initially refused to accept Black families until 1951. This historical legacy still affects StuyTown today, as it remains as white as a cucumber at a mayonnaise festival.

With an excellent gift for timing, MetLife sold StuyTown to Tishman Speyer and Blackrock in 2006 for $5.4 billion. In 2011, Tishman Speyer defaulted on its mortgage payments; it had lost 60 percent of its value.

Almost all StuyTown residents are both renters and middle-income, defined in New York City as individuals earning up to $128,000. Therefore, a two-bedroom apartment has a monthly rent-stabilized payment of around $3,200, considered affordable for New York.

I can attest that StuyTown is a pleasant place to live. It is ideally located, offers ample outdoor space and multiple gyms, hosts a farmers' market, and falls within the zoning area of one of the best public high schools in the US. If I were to live in New York City, I would undoubtedly consider residing there. However, it's not a tourist destination.

We did indulge in some more mainstream Manhattan tourist activities, too.

We took escorted walking tours of several Manhattan neighborhoods, with the food tour of the former trendy area, Greenwich Village, the most enjoyable. It showcased the diverse flavors formed by its rich immigrant history. Within a couple of tree-lined brownstone blocks, we sampled a mosaic of culinary delights, including a quintessential slice of New York's finest pizza, delicacies from India, French pastries, and meats and cheeses from a traditional Italian deli.

Further north, Central Park is often called Manhattan's lung, measuring about six miles by one mile. But it is only New York City's fifth-largest park. Residents can enjoy snow sports in winter, such as skating in the park. In the summer, however, the park is at its most glorious.

Cyclists, runners, and in-line skaters circumnavigate while lovers walk hand-in-hand, picnic on a tablecloth, or frolic unashamedly in a meadow. Owners walk their dogs, or is it the other way around? In our case, it was both. Dog #1 walked us by pulling us via his leash. In turn, we dragged Dog #2 on hers.

Teams of young(ish) people play sports of many different types. Similar to Inwood Hill Park, my favorite spot was the baseball area. We had a great time watching the mixed softball teams—where at least three of the ten players had to be women—play their early-evening games. When one of the women hit the ball deep into the outfield, the other women on both sides would playfully scream, "That's right, girl. You hit like a girl."

We explored Lower Manhattan, as well. The financial district was as empty as a coffee shop during a Wi-Fi outage, with most Wall Street workers still not back in their offices. On a Friday at 5 pm, we found ourselves as the sole passengers in a subway carriage. In normal times, this would have been unthinkable, as commuters would pack these trains.

Later, we visited a rooftop bar in TriBeCa and quickly realized we were the oldest and least extravagantly dressed partygoers by several decades and price points. Perched high above the city streets, this stylish outdoor space provided breathtaking views of the Manhattan skyline. While sipping cocktails crafted by Manhattan's finest mixologists, we observed the trendier guests socializing noisily on plush, contemporary furniture. Fortunately, our humility levels remained high enough to spare the Hudson River from our selfie attempts.

****

We frequented the Bronx three times: the first time to visit the Bronx's Little Italy, the second to watch a Yankees baseball game, and the third to see some museums.

I haven't sampled all of New York City's Italian food, obviously, but that of Arthur Avenue seemed authentic to this Italophile. Admittedly, Arthur Avenue may not be straightforward to reach by public transport, but the Bronx's most famous Italian district dates to the mid nineteenth century. Named after forgotten US President Chester Arthur, Robert De Niro's *A Bronx Tale* is set in this neighborhood.

Julian Bishop

The Bronx is the best borough to understand what New York would have been like for early-twentieth-century immigrants. We embarked on a long bus ride, not necessarily in distance but in duration. The noise on the bus was deafening, with competing conversations in half a dozen languages making it impossible to understand what your neighbor was saying. These languages reflected the vibrant tapestry from which the community was woven. If you had to guess the country you were being transported through, you might have suggested somewhere in South America, except that there were no goats or chickens on the bus.

In this fast-paced urban environment, the bus revealed a strong sense of camaraderie thriving in the Bronx. Passengers on the bus looked out for one another. The driver helped two veterans in wheelchairs get on and off the bus, elderly Asian ladies received assistance from fellow travelers when boarding and disembarking, and unaccompanied children were guided to their stops by concerned passengers who noticed they were out alone at night.

Outside the secure confines of the bus, all manner of life was on display. You caught glimpses of colorful murals adorning walls, vibrant street vendors selling their wares, and bustling markets brimming with fresh produce. At one chaotic junction, for an unknown reason, NYPD police officers occupied every corner while their vehicles obstructed the middle of the road. Because of this turmoil, the bus had to weave through the cityscape slowly, creating a thrilling sense of motion.

We visited the same subway station in the Bronx on consecutive days. On the first day, we turned left upon exiting the subway station and joined tens of thousands of others to attend a Yankees baseball game. The crowd was primarily White as is often the case at baseball games. On the next day, we turned right to explore some Bronx art galleries and didn't encounter a single White person. Remarkably, we observed that almost no one was wearing masks on the first day, whereas everyone we encountered was masked up on the second.

The demographic composition of Bronx immigrants has evolved. In the early part of the twentieth century, the majority were Jewish or Irish. By the sixties, it had transitioned to include Puerto Rican and African American communities. A new shift is occurring, with Dominicans surpassing Puerto Ricans and recent African immigrants outnumbering African Americans.

Are We There Yet?

We explored parts of Queens, which is often considered the most ethnically diverse area on the planet, home to immigrants from over a hundred countries. Approximately half of Queens's residents were born outside the US, and the borough is relatively evenly divided among the four main ethnic groups.

One reason for this incredible diversity is that Queens is home to two of New York's three airports. Unfortunately, despite their significance, these airports are among the worst in the developed world, and neither of them is seamlessly connected to the city's subway system.

We delved into the Queens' neighborhood of Astoria, named after the once-wealthiest American who invested $500 in the area but never visited it. Our first stop was Welling Court, a part of Astoria recently celebrated for its street art. Residents apparently offered their blank walls for artists to beautify, and a hundred representations certainly breathed life and color into this otherwise ordinary suburb.

We were quickly immersed in this open-air gallery showcasing the community's creativity and diversity. Some murals depicted daily life in Astoria, capturing the essence of the neighborhood and its people, while others delved into social issues. With each wave of the spray can, these murals contributed to the ever-evolving narrative of Astoria.

Lorna and I strolled through Astoria Park along the banks of the East River, passing under the Robert F. Kennedy and Hell Gate Bridges that transport cars and trains into the Bronx. On a sunnier day, after visiting Astoria's excellent Museum of the Moving Image, I retraced these steps to enjoy one of NYC's sixty free swimming pools. Astoria Park's Art Deco Olympic-sized pool offers magnificent views of the park, Manhattan, and the bridges.

Astoria lays claim to many sub-communities. As in other neighborhoods, signs are in both English and the most common language of that district. We continued walking to the Greek area of Astoria. In the sixties, Greeks began immigrating to this area, followed by Greek Cypriots in the seventies. The top ten restaurants here were all Greek, so we dined outside at Taverna Kyclades, a Greek seafood restaurant. We may have ordered too much food, but Lorna was delighted with her mountain of sardines, and I thoroughly enjoyed my stuffed vine leaves. The baklava that accompanied the very reasonable check was to die for, probably literally.

You've undoubtedly seen this charming neighborhood in many films, TV shows, and video games. *GoodFellas* and *Cosby* were filmed here, but for youngsters, it will be most familiar from *Grand Theft Auto*. It is becoming a little less Greek. With its relatively affordable low-rise housing, Astoria has caught the attention of new diasporas: Ecuadorians, Arabs, and Turks.

One neighboring area I could not access was Rikers Island, New York City's notorious jail. In the nineties, it was reckoned to be the world's largest penal colony, holding as many as twenty-two thousand inmates. Rikers technically comprised eight separate facilities. However, during the city's 'broken windows' initiative, the prison added a ninth facility, an eight-hundred-room barge—unimaginatively called 'The Boat'—to keep pace with the increasing number of involuntary guests.

Accessible only by an almost-mile-long bridge—the inaptly named 'Bridge of Hope'—the jail has a long-standing reputation for brutality. Detainees and professional visitors report that gang members run the complex as they would in a Central American prison. As a result, lawlessness is rampant, with thirty-eight (reported) serious assaults per day. Stabbings and slashings are as common here as an email in your inbox from LinkedIn imploring you to reactivate your Premium Service. In 2021, fifteen inmates died, mostly from suicide, overdoses, or violence.

Roughly 85 percent of Rikers' inmates are awaiting trial, with the only convicted individuals being some juveniles and those serving sentences under one year. Over the last decade, the jail's population has dramatically decreased to between five and six thousand, primarily due to significant changes in New York bail laws and some Covid compassion.

Despite such a significant reduction in inmates, more corrections officers than detainees, and a twice-the-national-average annual cost of $200,000 per incarcerated person, you might think that conditions in Rikers have improved. Unfortunately, the opposite has happened.

The latest challenge for the corrections system is staff absenteeism. The eight thousand prison officers have a daily absence rate of over 25 percent. The staff are demoralized, feel unsupported, and claim they no longer have the tools to perform their duties effectively.

The one thing that everyone agrees on is that Rikers should close. Despite this consensus, the new mayor will face a significant challenge to replace it by 2027 with smaller facilities in each borough except Staten Island. Then, maybe, as with so many other NYC neighborhoods before it, Rikers Island might transform into a wealthy community. If you think this impossible, Welfare Island once housed the city's jail. Now, that same piece of land is known as Roosevelt Island.

Incidentally, while writing about the new mayor's challenges, this is probably the time to address a bungled US election.

While we were in New York, the primaries for several city elections took place. For readers unfamiliar with American politics, primaries are the elections that determine which politicians should be selected as the official candidates for the Republican and Democratic parties. In constituencies with dominant republican or democratic electorates, these polls are often more important than the actual election itself.

New York City politicians used a 'ranked-choice' voting system for this mayoral election. In this system, voters ranked candidates in order of preference, and the votes of candidates with the fewest votes were redistributed until one candidate received the most votes.

On primary election night, the electoral commission announced the results of the first preference votes for the Democratic candidate for NYC Mayor. As expected, no candidate achieved the majority of the vote. Unexpectedly, commentators were delighted with the unusually high turnout.

A few days later, the commission released the second-stage results, where the votes of the least popular candidates were given to the more popular ones based on the voters' second preferences. The count showed that the top three candidates were still very close in votes.

New York has some curious rules that mean not all votes must be received or finalized on election day. The first is that you can send your ballot by post. If it is postmarked by election day, the commission will allow the vote to be counted, provided it arrives within a week. The second is that voters can change their ballot if they think an error has been made. These two oddities are usually balanced between parties and do not make any material difference except in unusually tight elections.

A few hours after the second data release, the New York City Board of Elections announced that they had discovered an error with the new software. Unfortunately, it turned out that electoral officials had not deleted the 135,000 'test votes' they used during software testing to identify bugs. These test votes should not have been included with the actual votes, and their presence also explained the unusually high voter turnout.

As you can imagine, this revelation led to criticism from the candidates and the media, questioning the competence of the Board of Elections. Investigations revealed that many individuals appointed to oversee elections in New York City were chosen for their political affiliations rather than their qualifications. Newspaper reports even documented instances where these appointed employees would clock in for work and then promptly leave.

Despite the frequency of elections in the United States, this debacle highlights that the more elections you conduct, the greater the chances of encountering such errors.

****

On another day, when my children and their boyfriends were in town, we and some friends went to watch New York City's other baseball team, the Mets, play at their Queens' stadium.

Before the game, we ate in Jackson Heights, part of Alexandria Ocasio-Cortez's congressional district. This bustling enclave is believed to be the most culturally diverse neighborhood on the planet, with 100,000 residents speaking 167 different languages. Above us, the elevated 7 train line screeched every minute or so, briefly drowning out the sounds of the constant hustle and bustle below.

The boyfriends of Daughters #1 and #2 had barely visited a city before, so they were definitely out of their comfort zone in New York City. This feeling intensified when we chose a modest Kazak restaurant for our evening meal. The density of immigrants, the cacophony of indecipherable languages, and the foreignness of everything overwhelmed their senses. However, they quickly adapted.

We enjoyed the three-hour baseball game with our friends, mainly because we could watch Shohei Ohtani, the Japanese wonder player equally adept at hitting home runs and pitching a ball at 100 mph.

Although three hours to watch a sport may seem like a long time, baseball games can extend much longer. The longest baseball game on record was a Triple-A minor league game between the Rochester Redwings from New York State and Rhode Island's Pawtucket Red Sox. This historic game started on 18 April 1981 but got off to a poor start with a thirty-minute floodlight delay. The 1,740 spectators in Rhode Island were slightly disgruntled, anticipating that this game would take half an hour longer than usual.

Two and a half hours later, at the bottom of the ninth inning, the game was tied at one run each. Because Americans can't accept a sport without a clear winner and loser, the game continued into extra innings until one side emerged victorious.

Are We There Yet?

No further runs were scored until the twenty-first inning. Unfortunately for those eager to go home, both teams scored. Wade Boggs, a future Hall of Famer, scored the equalizing run for the Rhode Island team, although his teammates weren't pleased because they wanted to end the game. Despite their wishes, the game carried on.

Unfortunately, the umpire was working with an incomplete rulebook, missing the rule stating that the game should be suspended after 12:50 am. The early hours of that April morning in Rhode Island were bitterly cold, and the players had gathered broken bats and wooden benches from the stadium to build a bonfire and keep warm. A chilly, gusty wind blew back any ball hit into the air onto the field.

By 4 am, someone at the stadium managed to reach the league president by phone. He was astonished that the teams were still playing and promptly ordered them to end the game at the conclusion of the thirty-second inning. The umpires finally suspended the game at 4:07 am.

Only twenty spectators remained at the stadium, including one who was asleep. These fans received season passes for their devotion to their team though the sleeping man never went to another game in his life. When the married men returned home, their wives were deeply suspicious of their far-fetched story of watching baseball until 4 am.

Every baseball game must be completed. When these sides next played each other two months later, they resumed the game in the thirty-third innings. Red Sox won the game when they scored a run in front of six thousand people and one hundred and forty reporters.

This game broke nearly every record in baseball. It holds the record for the number of at-bats (219), strikeouts (60), and runners left on base (53). Most of the batters, in their fourteen or fifteen appearances at the plate, neither scored a hit nor a run during that time.

And that's what I love about baseball: they adhere to the rules, even when it's four in the morning and they're burning whatever wood they can find to keep warm. I wish I had been there.

****

We saved much of our exploration of Brooklyn for when we moved there from our previous Midtown base. An old friend generously let us use his townhouse.

Brooklyn is both the largest and most populous New York City borough. In fact, if each borough were a separate municipality, Brooklyn would be America's third-most-populated city after Los Angeles and Chicago. Similar to Queens, Brooklyn has a diverse ethnic makeup though each neighborhood tends to be dominated by a single ethnic group rather than mixed. For instance, approximately one-fifth of Brooklyn residents are Jewish, concentrated in five predominantly Jewish communities.

We were billeted in Brooklyn Heights just over the other side of the bridge. Along with DUMBO (Down Under The Manhattan Bridge Overpass), these two areas are amongst the most expensive and trendy neighborhoods in New York City today.

Some of the most breathtaking views in the city can be found at Brooklyn Bridge Park along the East River. The best experience can be obtained by securing one of the park's grilling areas, available for free on a first-come, first-served basis. It was common to see large gatherings, primarily comprised of Black and Dominican extended families. As with barbecue gatherings worldwide, the men typically took charge of the grilling. These pitmasters showcased their culinary prowess with an array of exotic offerings, from two-foot-long sausages to pork shoulder, and roasted goat. Meanwhile, the women enjoyed socializing, pleased that their men were finally contributing to the meal.

DUMBO also offers ferries to the now-hipster areas of Williamsburg and Greenpoint on the East River. These hipsters share these neighborhoods with the conservative Hasidic Jewish and Polish-American communities. I would strongly recommend taking a walking tour in Williamsburg that showcases this clash of cultures.

Two million Jewish people, primarily from Germany and Eastern Europe, immigrated to the US in the four decades spanning the late nineteenth century. Had they not done so, the number of holocaust victims would likely have been even higher. This Jewish exodus also explains why 42 percent of Jewish people worldwide reside in America.

Lorna and I explored Brighton Beach in South Brooklyn, a community often referred to as Russian but, in reality, home to immigrants from all the former Soviet Union nations. Its history began with Holocaust survivors and Jewish immigrants from Ukraine in the thirties and forties, saw increased arrivals during a temporary period of Soviet emigration in the seventies, and experienced its most substantial wave after the fall of the Wall in 1989 when ex-Soviets were freer to reunite with their compatriots.

Brighton Beach is a sensory shock. Every sign is in Cyrillic, and every voice you hear speaks Russian. This is for a good reason; 98 percent of its residents have Russian as their native language, and most are not proficient in English. It feels thousands of miles away from Manhattan, not just twenty.

We picked a restaurant randomly from the many under the elevated train tracks. Pre-Ukrainian invasion, I was planning a long self-guided trip to the former Soviet Union. However, on requesting a table, I realized I would be in trouble for this venture when I could not recall the Russian for 'two.' The Cyrillic script of the menu was similarly challenging.

Lorna ordered the special $10 menu of Russian salad, borscht, and minced chicken. I ordered some rye bread and the only vegetarian dish on the menu, *vareniki*. The bread was dry and unappetizing. A few minutes later, I was re-evaluating plans for our big Soviet trip when I tasted the cheese *vareniki*. These Ukrainian potato ravioli were sickly sweet, drowning in a vat of oil, and came with a *smetana* sauceboat of cold sour cream, so liquidy that it swayed from side to side when I passed it across the table. Lorna expressed interest in tasting these dumplings, and I was more than happy to move as many of these things off my plate to show the proud waiter that I had enjoyed his region's cuisine. After Lorna passed on a second *vareniki*, Mr. Bean-like, I looked for any opportunity to conceal these sweet heart-attack-inducing pockets of sweetened vomit. As Lorna said, who wants a plate load of these *vareniki*? Certainly not me, as I returned with much greater relish to the arid rye bread.

After the meal, I was famished. We stopped at *La Brioche*, a Russian bakery with hundreds of delectable pastries and cakes made from condensed milk. It was difficult not to over-buy at this store, especially when one has consumed only two *vareniki*. The street markets sold vegetables and fruits of every persuasion, and I noticed that the melons here were one-third of the price of those in Manhattan.

Brighton Beach is not your typical tourist destination; you won't find Kiss Me Quick hats or beach paraphernalia for sale here. It's more like a neighborhood transported from another continent into America. The people here looked like they belonged to the Soviet era, their faces weathered by decades of hard work and rugged living. In the park, older men played chess while women of the same age gathered to socialize and discuss the day's issues. I couldn't understand their conversations; it could have been about the district's plans to approve some new housing development or the shocking behavior of Mrs. Kruschev at number seventeen. Street musicians adorned the street corners, playing accordions and balalaikas instead of guitars as you'd find in the rest of NYC.

As we walked toward the beach, the apartments grew grander. You could see this town's origins as a getaway for New York's elite. Brighton Beach's name was given to it by its founder, William Engeman, who had modeled it on the English beach town of the same name.

On the beach, hirsute Russian men changed out of their tracksuits into tight-fitting speedos. We quickly averted our gaze and continued walking along the somewhat hazardous boardwalk from Manhattan Beach to Coney Island, once an actual island before the channel between it and the rest of Brooklyn was filled in. The heat had caused many of the boards and screws to become loose. We were wearing sturdy shoes, but I couldn't help but worry about those wearing flip-flops.

Lorna was feeling the effects of the scorching summer sun and complained of heat exhaustion. She wanted to find shade and rest in a lovely cafe on the seafront. Unfortunately, we had walked all the way to Coney Island by this point, with its many amusement parks. It was somewhat comparable to Blackpool but without the high culture.

Beaches were packed here, and people gorged on Nathan's hot dogs. It was only a few days until the 4 July hot dog eating competition at Coney Island. A couple of days previously, I had left the TV on after a successful England Euros match and found myself absorbed in a documentary about the sport of competitive eating. It concerned the rivalry between the two titans of the sport, Joey Chestnut and Takeru Kobayashi. Both competitors could eat over sixty hot dogs and buns in ten minutes. Yes, that's one hot dog, plus its bun, every ten seconds.

You might assume that the supreme athletes of this primarily American sport would be large folk; however, the leading proponents are relatively fit and trim. The governing body for this sport, the International Federation of Competitive Eating, organizes multiple competitive eating events in their Major League Eating Championship. In addition to hot dogs, they compete in consuming chicken wings, shrimp, pizzas, corn, sausages, pumpkin pie, tamales, strawberry shortcakes, baked beans, tacos, and spam. Curiously, all these competitions seem to be sponsored by purveyors of these fine foodstuffs.

In the documentary, the unctuous executive representing the sports body tried to explain why one of the sport's titans, the 2001 to 2006 winner of the Mustard Yellow Belt (presumably with some extra notches), was refusing to participate in any of the tournaments. Unfortunately, this left his American rival, Joey Chestnut, with little competition. Chestnut has since won fourteen of the following fifteen titles and increased his record to seventy-six hot dogs and buns.

It was a sweltering day with temperatures well into the mid-nineties. While at the restaurant, every cell phone had sirened in unison as we all simultaneously received an emergency notification that the New York electrical grid was under severe strain. The authorities urged us to stop using washers and dryers and turn off all microwaves and air conditioning units.

One wonders how much effect these warnings have. In the same way as panic buying, I wonder if people decide to make their homes a bit cooler just in case they lose power.

These emergency warnings and their startling sirens sounded every ten minutes for the rest of the day. A man on the train was warning anyone who would listen that he had been told that all subway trains would cease after 7 pm to preserve electricity.

****

It had been fifty-five years since the England soccer team had progressed to a major final. I knew England had an exciting young squad, but bitter experience had taught me not to be too optimistic about their prospects. I had selected a Brooklyn bar to watch the game with other fans, but I was disappointed to find their cable broken. Another frustrated New York soccer fan I met on the doorstep made several calls, and we found a nearby speakeasy showing the game.

Speakeasies were created as venues for the illegal distribution of alcohol during the Prohibition era. The term 'speakeasy' derives from the need for customers to 'speak easy' so as not to attract the attention of the authorities. Their entrances were often hidden behind secret doors and typically required a password or special knock for entry. The clandestine nature of the speakeasy offered a sense of excitement and glamor, with live music and dancing. Speakeasies attracted diverse people, including the wealthy, politicians, and celebrities. Their popularity demonstrated the limit on what a government can do to regulate morality.

Although prohibition banned the sale of alcohol, you could still get an alcohol prescription. When Churchill visited New York in 1932, his New York doctor prescribed a minimum of 250cc of alcoholic spirits at mealtimes for post-accident convalescence.

This 'member-only' speakeasy was located at the rear of a clothing store. The owner took pity on our predicament and let us in to watch the game. The bar was superb: compact but not tiny. Members joined as the game progressed until about fifteen people were watching it. I bought my new friend a drink and quickly made thirteen other new friends.

These new friends were educated professionals. During halftime and the numerous stops in play, they showed themselves as well-read people with curiosity and noteworthy experiences. One of the patrons observed something about British people and football. He said they watched the game dispassionately until their team scored and then went wild. He then gave his best impression of a celebrating Dick-Van-Dyke cockney.

Denmark tested my sang-froid when they took the lead with a free-kick. It was relatively early in the game, and I had mentally prepared myself for disappointment. I was calm. England then equalized, and I erupted with joy... but without any faux-cockney accent.

****

The borough of Staten Island has a poor reputation. For one thing, much of it—up until about a decade ago—was a colossal rubbish dump, appropriately perhaps called Fresh Kills landfill, but actually named after the Dutch name for a nearby estuary. When I say colossal, I do mean it. Many say this landfill is the largest manufactured structure by volume globally, although others claim that this accolade should be given to the Boeing Factory in Washington State. Either way, this landfill is immense. Its 2,200 acres of rubbish received all of New York City's trash for over fifty years, replacing the city's ten incinerators that previously had polluted its skyline. In 1948, the residents of Staten Island objected and won the right for this to be a temporary arrangement for only three years. In a warning to other 'it's-only-temporary' solutions, this stop-gap measure lasted for fifty-three years.

Almost immediately after the landfill was closed, it had to be reopened as a temporary examination site for 1.6 million tons of World Trade Center debris. Thousands of forensic detectives worked for a combined 1.7 million hours to recover the remains of the people killed in the Al Qaida attack. As a result, the workers recovered 4,257 human body parts, returning any unidentified remains to the National 9/11 Memorial in Manhattan.

Are We There Yet?

More serendipitously, this former landfill is being transformed into the second-largest park in New York City, behind Pelham Bay Park in the Bronx. Freshkills Park will not be open at the time of the publication of this book. Indeed, it is unlikely to be finished until around 2038. You can put the date in your diary fifteen years hence to enjoy the park's network of cycle paths, kayaking trails, and sports fields.

However, I managed to wangle a place on a guided tour of part of the unopened park. The guide showed how the trash was concealed in four large hills, with each layer of garbage covered by incinerator ash and then a layer of soil. This park will join 169 other Staten Island parks, occupying over a third of the island and sealing its status as the greenest borough.

When America was being colonized, there was a dispute over whether Staten Island should be incorporated into the New York or New Jersey colonies. According to legend, the Duke of York proposed that any small island be part of New York. He defined 'small' as an island a boat could circumvent in less than a day. As ships were powered by wind at that time, New Jersey was sure that Staten Island should belong to them. The duke, however, had different plans, hiring a British sailor who circumnavigated the island and completed the journey in just 23 hours.

A nice story. However, it is unlikely to be true. For one thing, there is no record of anyone telling this story until two hundred years after the alleged race. Even more compelling, however, is that New Jersey took the case to the Supreme Court in 1831, but New York refused to send lawyers to argue the countercase. The Chief Justice, fearing that the two powerful states would disregard any ruling, postponed the case until 1833. This delay provided future President Martin Van Buren, who was then vice president, with the time to orchestrate a compromise. New Jersey won the right to build docks on its shore, and a boundary line was drawn in the middle of the Hudson River. This line then diverted right so that New York could retain Staten Island.

People with a downer on Staten Island claim that New York lost both arguments. The city allowed ports to flourish in New Jersey and had to continue administering the lifeless Staten Island. Many New Yorkers seem to regard Staten Island in a negative light. I went there twice in a month, two times more than most New Yorkers in their lifetime, and thought it had some redeeming features.

On my first trip, I caught the subway to one of Brooklyn's extremities, a down-at-heel neighborhood without any sign of that traditional Big Apple excitement. Next, I took a bus over the two-level Verrazzano-

Narrows Bridge built in the sixties to connect Staten Island with the rest of New York.

I started at Fort Wadsworth, a strategically positioned defense fortification guarding Upper New York Bay. The British had initially constructed a fort here during their occupation in the Revolutionary War. After gaining independence, safeguarding the city became a top priority for the US government, determined to prevent any future incursions. Consequently, the US government constructed multiple forts along New York's waterways in the early nineteenth century.

In 1994, the US Navy left Fort Wadsworth, and the National Parks Service took over the running of the facility. The fort has terrific views of the Narrows, a body of water that links Upper New York Bay with Lower New York Bay, and the impressive bridge, still the longest suspension bridge in the Western Hemisphere.

I hopped on another bus to the start of the boardwalk along Staten Island's Atlantic Coast. Although the fourth-longest boardwalk in the world, this two-and-a-half-mile impressive wooden walkway is lightly used. I saw very few people that July day, and it didn't surprise me that Coney Island's boardwalk has nineteen times more pedestrians.

This is a pity because it is much more attractive than the kiss-me-quick one in Brooklyn. Walking along the boardwalk, I had excellent views over the beach and the Atlantic Ocean on my left and countless leisure activities on my right. I saw vacant basketball courts, roller hockey venues, shuffleboards, bocce courts, skateboard parks, and chess boards.

I could have availed myself of regular restrooms or purchased refreshments without waiting in line at the many food kiosks. If I had a car, I could have parked at one of the 6,950 open parking lot spaces. Instead, I exchanged greetings with the occasional dog-walker and nodded at the much faster-passing cyclist.

In the early sixties, before it was connected to the rest of the city by the Verrazano Bridge, Staten Island was a summer vacation spot for hard-working New York families. On this early July day, it was emptier than a vacuum in a black hole.

I came across several baseball diamonds. As in Manhattan's earlier games, the players had decided to take some exercise. This exercise was much needed on both sides, and there was a considerable age and girth range. The pitcher in the game I watched was having a nightmare. He had 'walked' six consecutive batters, with twenty-four erratic pitches and only one hitting its target. In response, the opposing batters had decided not to try to hit the ball, preferring the free walk to first base. This was sensible as many batters looked like the first base run would have been athletically challenging. Eventually, the pitcher's teammates took mercy on him and replaced him with another player, while the struggling pitcher retreated to the outfield, shaking his head in disbelief at the turn of events.

I eventually tired of walking (sic) and caught another bus to a more populated area of Staten Island. I must say, compared to the rest of New York City, public transport here was lacking. Buses were as rare as a mosquito at a citronella candle convention, and there was no connection to NYC's subway system whatsoever. This is one reason Staten Island is often called the Forgotten Borough. In fact, in 1993, Staten Island residents voted in a referendum to break away from New York City, but the incoming mayor, Rudy Giuliani, reversed their decision.

I alighted early from the bus to see the five-thousand-person Little Sri Lanka community. When President Johnson changed the immigration rules in the late sixties to favor non-European immigrants, a few Sri Lankan immigrants settled on Staten Island. This tiny group built a Buddhist temple, started a grocery store, and opened a Sri Lankan restaurant. Then, as their relatives and other Sri Lankans came to the US, they gravitated toward this small Sri Lankan community.

Incidentally, this change in immigration rules is one of the factors that has led to the browning of the US. Non-Hispanic Whites now account for only three out of five Americans, and more than half of those under sixteen identify as non-White. While the media often portrays the country as divided by race, there is ample evidence that America is becoming less racist. By way of examples: nineteen in twenty Americans approve of mixed-race marriage (compared to fewer than one in twenty in the 1960s); data from dating apps show that one in three couples are mixed-race; and more than one in ten babies is of mixed race.

Just beyond the Sri Lankan community, I stumbled across a bookshop and café where I bought a few books and had a very late cake-based lunch. With my feet throbbing from all the walking, I finally reached the Staten Island Ferry Terminal, the only place on the island that most New Yorkers have ever visited.

****

With the number of tourists to New York City still very low, Lorna and I took a ferry trip to Liberty and Ellis Islands in New York Harbor. Liberty

Island is home to the Statue of Liberty, while Ellis Island served as the primary entry point for immigrants until the mid twentieth century.

Under the 1832 agreement between New Jersey and New York, both islands fall within New Jersey waters but belong to New York. After this date, the Federal Government, which owns both islands, conducted extensive land reclamation on Ellis Island. New Jersey argued that these reclaimed lands should rightfully belong to them. In 1998, a more confident Supreme Court sided with New Jersey, confirming that the land reclaimed from New Jersey waters for the enlarged Ellis Island belonged to New Jersey. As a result, 83 percent of the sales tax income from the islands now goes to New Jersey rather than New York.

Ellis Island is home to a world-class museum. From its opening in 1892 to its closure in 1954, approximately fourteen million immigrants sailed past the welcoming Lady Liberty to enter Ellis Island's immigration portal. The majority of these immigrants came to America to reunite with existing family members who had prepaid their $30 tickets.

The museum's setup investigates each stage of the immigrant's experience. Each putative immigrant had to pass basic physical, mental, and honesty tests. The first Ellis Island immigrant was Annie Moore, a fifteen-year-old Irish girl traveling with her two younger brothers. Medical officials would have observed them briefly on entry into the Great Hall for any signs of poor health. Like most others, these siblings would pass this simple test, but a few unlucky ones would be marked with chalk and subjected to additional health screening.

At its busiest, Ellis Island processed about two thousand immigrants daily in roughly three hours—a processing time not too dissimilar to the speed at which tourists are processed today at Atlanta Hartsfield. Ellis Island handled passengers in steerage class, while those in first and second class were cleared on the ship.

Nearly everyone was admitted into the US to start their new life. About one-third would settle in New York, while the majority were directed to nearby train stations to begin their journey to various cities across the US. It's impossible not to marvel at the bravery and optimism of these immigrants, many of whom had no idea where they would ultimately settle.

A small number—fewer than one in fifty—were not immediately permitted entry. The unlucky 2 percent might be detained for weeks while officials reviewed their health or honesty credentials. If they didn't pass, these failed immigrants were returned to their country of origin. The largest immigrant group, the Italians, renamed Ellis Island *L'isola delle Lagrime*, the island of tears.

Incidentally, it is a myth that US immigration officials Americanized the names of the new immigrants. The information they used came directly from the ship's manifest, which the traveler had provided themselves. Many immigrants simply chose a new name for the new country.

Perhaps it was fortified by my recent conversion to a US citizen, but I found Ellis Island moving and informative. I would recommend it to anyone.

Famously, America is a nation of immigrants that continues to welcome new settlers. The fact that, at any one time, approximately one in six Americans is a first-generation immigrant has not only strengthened the nation's culture but also made diversity one of America's greatest assets. This diversity fosters a broader range of perspectives, which, in turn, fuels innovation and creativity. Each immigrant community both adapts to American culture and contributes its own traditions, resulting in a smorgasbord of cultural experiences for everyone.

In our era, many countries want to restrict (or eliminate) immigration, and electors vote for politicians who promote anti-immigration rhetoric. To some extent, public opposition to immigration is understandable: it can threaten cultural norms, and short-term inconveniences, such as strains on educational, medical, and welfare provisions, can quickly become urgent.

Perversely—rather than preventing hard-working, motivated immigrants from entering a country—those concerned about the future of their country might better focus on how to persuade those lazy, unskilled natives to emigrate.

Immigrants tend to be overwhelmingly good for a country. To avoid starving, immigrants are hungry. In the US, immigrants are much likelier to start businesses, and these enterprises create wealth and employ others. Despite representing only 16 percent of the population, one-third of engineers in America and more than one-quarter of other scientists were born outside the US. These first-generation scientists are responsible for three-quarters of patents issued at top universities and help develop new technologies that fuel new companies. Let me give you one specific example. Half of all American unicorns (start-ups worth more than $1 billion) were founded by first-generation immigrants.

Immigrants also bring intangible benefits. For instance, they encourage social structures to be more dynamic and fluid.

Contrary to fears, immigrants do not make native-born Americans less wealthy; they make them richer. There is a statistically significant positive correlation between immigration and both average earnings and GDP.

As natural birth rates continue to decline across the developed world, there will be intense competition for immigrants in the future. In this world, where countries will compete to attract immigrants, I expect America, which has welcomed immigrants since its formation, to perform rather well.

****

With both daughters and their boyfriends enthusiastic to see NYC's tourist attractions, it would have been churlish not to join them when they wanted us to pay. So, we wholeheartedly embraced some of the quintessential tourist experiences. We savored a vibrant meal in Chinatown, admired the architectural beauty of Grand Central Station, wandered through the picturesque streets of Greenwich Village, and immersed ourselves in the world-class art at MOMA, the Met, and the Guggenheim. These attractions are popular for a reason—they are nothing short of exceptional.

Are We There Yet?

Chapter 7 – Philadelphia and the First State

With a big enough bite taken from the Big Apple and another temporary home ahead of us, we drove straight outta Brooklyn to Staten Island over the Verrazzano-Narrows Bridge on the one-hundred-mile journey to Philadelphia.

I had been to Philadelphia once before on business. After those meetings, I managed a quick whistle-stop tour of the Old City area before catching my flight back to my then-home in the UK. Nevertheless, I had seen enough to realize I wanted to return for a more in-depth visit when time allowed. Fortunately, I now had that time.

Philadelphia is under two hours from New York City and Washington, DC. As a result, these three cities are among the most frequented cities by Americans. Surprisingly, Philly is much less frequented by foreigners, and I have encountered relatively few British travelers who have seen the city. In fact, Philly receives fewer than 10 percent of the international tourists that New York City attracts. This is unfortunate because Philadelphia has a great deal to offer; its history is rich, its streets are wide and inviting, and its prices are significantly lower.

Unlike many of America's great cities, Philadelphia is affordable. Therefore, if I were advising a young American professional on where to live, I would recommend they consider Philadelphia. It is a highly walkable city with numerous restaurants, a rich history, and, at least when we were there, precisely ninety-nine museums.

Similar to many other East Coast cities, Philadelphia has a long history. Its first inhabitants were the Lenape, also known as the Delaware Indians, who hunted and gathered here from about 8,000 BCE. The initial colonists were not the English but rather the Dutch, Germans, and Swedes. Peter Minuit, who had previously purchased Manhattan Island and was later dismissed from his role as Governor of New Netherlands by the Dutch

West India Company due to his upward management issues, first brought settlers to Philadelphia in 1638.

However, in 1664, the English crown claimed all Dutch lands in America when they sailed into New Amsterdam Harbor and politely requested the Dutch to surrender. Peter Stuyvesant, the Director-General of New Netherlands at that time, initially resisted but eventually negotiated a peaceful handover with minimal fighting. This marked the English takeover of the area.

William Penn, the eldest son of English Admiral William Penn, stood out from his privileged background. In Paris, he faced a duel challenge from a troublemaker for not showing enough respect during a first meeting. Penn won but chose an uncommon path by sparing his opponent's life.

Worse was to come from this peace-loving hippy. When in Ireland, supposedly quelling a rebellion, Penn met the founder of the Quakers, George Fox, and was immediately attracted to Fox's peaceful teachings. Penn's commitment to Quakerism led to his imprisonment in the Tower of London. During his time there, he wrote *No Cross, No Crown*, an influential book on Quaker beliefs.

King Charles II owed Penn's father £16,000, about $1.0 million in today's money. Upon the admiral's death in 1681, the King settled the debt by granting William Penn a vast tract of land in the New World, spanning 45,000 square miles, now encompassing Pennsylvania and Delaware. In a somewhat petty move, the King named the colony Pennsylvania (meaning 'Penn's Forest'), knowing it would irk the Quaker who preferred not to name places after individuals.

Penn founded Philadelphia on the Delaware River to exemplify his philosophy, naming it after the Greek for 'brotherly love.' His vision was a city plan resembling an expansive English shire town rather than a bustling metropolis, and his dream was to create a community where people of all religions could coexist harmoniously. To fulfill this visionary dream, he convinced skilled tradespeople, farmers, and merchants from Europe to join him in this grand endeavor.

Although he legally possessed the land based on the prevailing laws of the time, Penn made the conscious decision to compensate the native Lenape and established a treaty focused on peace and cooperation. In today's less forgiving world, Penn's reputation is marred by his ownership of enslaved individuals. Nevertheless, his Quaker principles led

Are We There Yet?

Philadelphia to become the first city in the New World to protest slavery in 1684 and, subsequently, the first to abolish it in 1780.

Despite constructing an impressive residence along the Delaware River and championing religious tolerance in the settlement, Penn ultimately found that life in the New World did not suit him. He returned to England and stayed away from America for more than two decades. Unpredictably, his absence played a pivotal role in the city's development. With no ruler to enforce strict rules or impose taxes, the colony thrived, and the town blossomed into a bustling cosmopolitan hub.

Penn led an affluent lifestyle and displayed excessive generosity toward others. He also borrowed beyond his means to fund the formation of Philadelphia. As a result of this profligacy, he was declared bankrupt and imprisoned in a debtor's gaol in 1707. During his time in prison, he experienced a series of incapacitating strokes, with the last one leaving him bedridden and unable to communicate for the remaining six years of his life. Penn died penniless at the age of seventy-three.

Just as we might inherit a chest of drawers from our parents, Thomas Penn, the younger son, inherited his father's colony. However, he had a different approach to fair dealings with Native Americans. He believed the colonists needed more land and convinced the Lenape to draw a new northern Philadelphia boundary eighteen hours' walk from Wrightstown. He chose Solomon Jennings, James Yeates, and Edward Marshall to represent the colonists for this walk, and several Lenape were selected to ensure fair play. However, the pace set by the three Englishmen was surprisingly fast. The Delaware Indians shouted at them, urging them to walk instead of run. They had assumed that the colonists would walk at a leisurely pace, taking breaks for a smoke or hunting, just as they did.

Jennings was the first to give up due to exhaustion, covering fewer than ten miles. Unfortunately, he never fully recovered from his efforts and died. A few hours later, Yeates collapsed on the trail, went as blind as a bat without its glasses, and died three days later.

Even though two Europeans and all but one Lenape had quit due to exhaustion, Marshall managed to walk a remarkable sixty-five miles during the Walking Purchase. While this might not sound like much today, the walkers had to traverse rivers and cut their way through dense undergrowth. Marshall was rewarded with five pounds and given five hundred acres of land, now known as Marshall's Creek. His journey had secured an extra 1,200 square miles of land for Penn Junior Junior.

The Delaware Indians resisted and declined to vacate their land. So, the colonists recruited the Lenape's enemies, the Iroquois, to forcibly remove them from their ancestral territories. The Lenape held a lasting grudge against Marshall for his role in this episode, leading to frequent attacks on Marshall's residence. These attacks resulted in the scalping of his wife and the death of one of his sons.

Despite the tarnishing of the Penn name among the Indians, Philadelphia was the world's second-largest English-speaking city and the most populous American city at the time of the US's initial census in 1790. It retained this distinction until 1800 when New York City surpassed it.

The city of brotherly love is primarily renowned for its pivotal role in revolutionary and constitutional history. It served as the planning ground for the American Revolution and the drafting of both the Declaration of Independence and the Constitution.

Philadelphia shared the role of America's capital with various other East Coast cities from the Declaration of Independence until 1790. Afterward, it briefly served as an interim capital before passing the torch to the newly constructed Washington, DC.

Philadelphia was the cradle of the American Dream. The first and second Continental Congresses were held in secret here, activities so treacherous that Benjamin Franklin was reputed to have said, "If we do not hang together, we shall surely hang separately." While the Founding Fathers famously declared independence on July 4, 1776, only John Hancock and Charles Thomson actually signed the document that day, with the former doing so both prominently and flamboyantly. This moment in history forever immortalized Hancock, as even today, people may ask for your 'John Hancock' on a document. Most of the remaining fifty-four signatures didn't appear until a month later, and one signature wasn't added until 1781.

The revolutionaries disseminated The Declaration of Independence across the colonies, igniting the War of Independence. In 1777, British troops swiftly recaptured Philadelphia. Nevertheless, less than a year later, as the French allied with the revolutionaries, the British abandoned Philadelphia and focused on defending New York City.

When independence was won, Philadelphia witnessed a significant influx of immigrants during the nineteenth century. The population, which stood at 40,000 in 1800, swelled to 1.3 million by the century's close. Immigration persisted into the early twentieth century, with African Americans also contributing to the city's growth during the Great

Are We There Yet?

Migration. By 1930, Philadelphia was home to nearly two million residents. This population boom necessitated the construction of new public buildings, with Philadelphia's architectural style favoring classical designs, in contrast to the skyscrapers of New York and Chicago.

Similar to many other Northern cities, Philly declined economically in the fifties, as poor-quality housing and gangland crime convinced around half a million mainly middle-class White residents to leave the city for nearby suburbs.

By the early nineties, Philadelphia faced significant financial challenges, holding the lowest debt bond rating in the US and running a substantial budget deficit. However, the city's fortunes began to change with the election of a reform-minded mayor in 1992, who initiated a positive transformation of the city's finances and began to attract private investment. The new millennium brought further investment and the gentrification of many of its city neighborhoods.

****

The Founding Fathers were the political leaders who played a vital role in the American Revolution and the establishment of the United States of America. They not only drafted and signed the Declaration of Independence but, more importantly, authored the Constitution, which still provides the foundation for how the US operates today.

During our time in Philadelphia, we couldn't help but notice that, at the time, the US President, the House Speaker, and the Senate Majority Leader were all in their eighties. In stark contrast, many of the Founding Fathers were in their twenties. This group of around fifty men from the eastern seaboard envisioned a new nation grounded in principles of democracy, liberty, and individual rights.

The Founding Fathers included four individuals who would later serve as president (Washington, Adams, Jefferson, and Madison), along with others who made significant contributions. Among them, Benjamin Franklin stands out as one of the most renowned. He was among the five authors of the Declaration of Independence and holds the distinction of being the sole Founding Father to have signed all four pivotal documents that laid the foundation for the United States.

Franklin, closely associated with Philadelphia, fled there at seventeen from his birthplace in Boston. He hailed from a large family, the youngest of fifteen children, and had only two years of formal education. A true

Renaissance man, Franklin excelled as an inventor, businessman, scientist, politician, and writer, achieving remarkable success in all these fields. His extraordinary longevity, living twice as long as most people of his time, allowed him to accumulate invaluable experience, which he later shared with the fledgling nation.

Taking each of these professions in order, Franklin was a prodigious inventor. He devised or introduced over a hundred inventions to the New World, including swim fins, the Franklin stove, lightning rods, the flexible catheter, the odometer, the glass armonica (a musical instrument), bifocals, library chairs, and an extension arm that allowed readers to reach books on high shelves. He also innovated public services, notably firefighting, street lighting, the 24-hour clock, and daylight savings time.

Franklin also proposed that Amerikan English eliminate the redundant letters 'C,' 'J,' 'Q,' 'X,' and 'Y'. I am sorri that has giust not kwite kort on.

Fortunately for the US, he was also an eighteenth-century open-source advocate who did not believe in patenting his inventions. In his autobiography, he wrote, "That as we enjoy great advantages from the inventions of others, we should be glad of an opportunity to serve others by any invention of ours; and this we should do freely and generously."

Despite not cashing in on his inventions, Franklin was a prosperous businessman who managed a range of public service enterprises. Among them, he operated a book publisher, a fire service, a print shop, a hospital, and a newspaper. Additionally, Franklin can be credited with inventing a standard business model widely used today—the franchise contract.

As a scientist, Franklin was a leading pioneer in electricity and weather. He discovered that electricity existed in storm clouds and revealed the existence of the Gulf Stream. He concluded that lead was poisonous to humans, that a concentration of electrical charges at the North Pole formed the aurora borealis, and that the common cold was spread aerobically to others.

Franklin was an early pioneer of vaccination, and a personal tragedy reinforced his interest in this field. During a smallpox epidemic in Boston in the 1720s, a man named Onesimus, who the rather uniquely named Cotton Mather enslaved, shared a method used in West Africa to immunize against smallpox. This method involved intentionally infecting communities with small amounts of this disease. As the smallpox epidemic in Boston continued to spread, Mather campaigned for a similar approach to inoculation.

Are We There Yet?

In those days, intentionally exposing oneself to a dreaded disease to gain immunity must have seemed counterintuitive. The Doctors at that time cautioned against the approach. However, as many of these were of the snake-oil-salesmen variety, people rightly had little trust in these 'experts.' Furthermore, church leaders raised religious objections, believing such practices went against God's will.

You may wonder how much has changed in the last three centuries. While today's vaccinations no longer require us to inject ourselves with the actual virus, a leap of faith is still needed to put a cocktail of secretive chemicals into our bodies. Most of us haven't earned degrees in biological science, and to be honest, many of us couldn't. But, realistically, what choice do we have? We could follow the advice of someone who has devoted their life to science or trust Billy who argues that such practices go against God's will.

Franklin's personal tragedy occurred a decade later as smallpox swept through Philadelphia. Franklin and his common-law wife, Deborah Read, had a four-year-old child who they unimaginatively called Franky. The couple decided to delay their son's inoculation, as he was suffering from a severe cold. Sadly, Franky contracted smallpox and died.

Perhaps given Franklin's firm conviction on inoculations, the fake news of the time spread that Franklin's son had died from the vaccination, not the disease. Franklin rebuffed this in the *Pennsylvania Gazette* and later became a leading advocate of inoculation, publishing many studies on the subject.

In other health areas, Franklin had unorthodox views. He refused to bathe with water, favoring the air bath, which involved walking around his house naked for the first hour of the morning.

Franklin was also a skilled statesman. He served as the US Ambassador to France for six years, during which time France was America's crucial ally and the primary supplier of its weapons. With the French seemingly ambivalent about Franklin's body odor, he successfully negotiated two significant treaties: the 1778 Treaty of Alliance with France and the 1783 Treaty of Paris, which formally acknowledged the United States as an independent nation.

Franklin founded what is now the University of Pennsylvania, Pennsylvania Hospital, and America's first insurance company. He also created the US's first lending library and the American Philosophical Society. On return to the US, Franklin engineered the US postal system and was its first Postmaster General.

Franklin was a prolific reader and writer. So he could save more money for books, he became a vegetarian at sixteen. In addition to writing for his own newspaper, *The Pennsylvania Gazette*, Franklin wrote hundreds of books. These included the famous *Poor Richard's Almanack*, his autobiography, and the specialist book *Fart Proudly*.

Franklin published his almanac for twenty-six years. It is highly influential in the American language today. You will perhaps have used some of his aphorisms:

"Early to bed and early to rise makes a man healthy, wealthy, and wise,"
"Don't throw stones at your neighbors if your own windows are glass,"
"No gains without pains," and
"There never was good war or a bad peace."

Franklin's autobiography was written in four separate periods. He began the initial part in 1771 during a week of leisure but didn't continue until 1784, when he had time on his hands as the Ambassador to France. The third part was penned in 1788-89 upon his return to the US, and the final section was completed in the last few months of his life in 1790.

Franklin died at eighty-four and was laid to rest in Christ Church, Philadelphia. You can tour his final resting place in the church's graveyard today. It's the one adorned with pennies tossed daily by admirers, a tradition inspired by one of his beloved almanac sayings, "A penny saved is a penny earned." In homage to his wisdom, I contributed one of my pennies to his collection, which adds about five thousand dollars to the church's funds yearly.

Franklin undoubtedly ranks among the greatest Americans and has been honored by being featured on the first US postage stamp and gracing the $100 bill.

****

A knowledgeable Philadelphian led us on a walking tour of historic Center City, taking us to the Constitution Center, which now houses the Liberty Bell. This massive one-ton bell was cast in 1751 to commemorate the fiftieth anniversary of William Penn's *Charter of Privileges*, an early version of Philadelphia's Constitution. Interestingly, it was produced at the same Whitechapel foundry that, a century later, would craft Big Ben, the renowned bell housed in the Elizabeth Tower of the British Houses of Parliament.

Are We There Yet?

This specific bell was one of twelve sent to the New World as part of a consignment. Unfortunately, unlike its counterparts, the Philadelphia bell had a flaw upon delivery, probably due to an excess of copper in the alloy, causing it to crack during initial testing. Some skilled American craftsmen later recast it, but the local community did not find its sound pleasing.

A new bell was ordered from Whitechapel in 1754, but this one—also in E-flat—sounded no better. The original Liberty Bell remained in the State House steeple to be rung for special events, while the new bell was housed in the State House cupola, striking on the hour to keep time for the industrious Philadelphians.

For nearly a century, the Liberty Bell rang out on significant occasions, such as the signing of the Constitution and the passing of Founding Fathers. Over time, it also evolved into a potent symbol for the emancipation movement, embodying freedom for the entire nation.

Regrettably, this iconic cymbal (sic) fell silent in 1846, when it was last rung to celebrate George Washington's 114th birthday. Tragically, an irreparable zig-zag fracture appeared on the bell, symbolizing a crack in the nation for many.

The Liberty Bell maintains its cherished position in Philadelphia. Though it no longer reverberates, it is still gently tapped on momentous occasions, such as when women gained the right to vote, on the 150th anniversary of independence, at the time of the Normandy beach invasions, and when the Berlin Wall was erected and later dismantled. Furthermore, every July 4, descendants of the signers of the Declaration of Independence symbolically tap the Liberty Bell thirteen times, once for each of the original thirteen US states.

During the Revolutionary War, in anticipation of the British invasion of Philadelphia, the rebels took the bell to Allentown, another Pennsylvanian city sixty miles away. The Revolutionaries feared the British would melt down their symbol of liberty for weaponry.

I had the opportunity to explore three museums in Philadelphia. One noteworthy museum was the Museum of the American Revolution, which provides a comprehensive look at the events leading to the Declaration of Independence and the subsequent war. The museum boasts a remarkable collection of artifacts, including General Washington's wartime 'tent,' which, in truth, would be more accurately described as an oval marquee. What's intriguing is the tent's subsequent history, which illustrates the interconnectedness of America's elite during that era. It eventually came into the possession of George Washington's step-great-granddaughter, who later married Robert E. Lee, the Confederate army's commander. During the Civil War, Lee's enslaved housekeeper, Selina Norris Gray, played a crucial role in safeguarding the tent and other Washington heirlooms when Union soldiers looted Lee's residence.

I also visited the much-renovated Independence Hall, the former capitol building where both the Declaration of Independence and the US Constitution were debated. Independence Hall was also the meeting location that eventually founded the League of Nations and the United Nations.

The final museum I saw was the Barnes Foundation, an art museum founded by Albert Barnes. Barnes sold his pharmaceutical company months before the 1929 stock market crash and plowed his cash into purchasing impressionist and post-impressionist works of art. As a result, the collection is vast and includes 181 paintings by Renoir and around fifty each by Cezanne, Matisse, and Picasso. If you appreciate Impressionism, you must seek out the Barnes Foundation.

I elected to watch England lose to Italy in the soccer final of the European Championships. Had I known the result beforehand, I would have instead spent my time in the Philadelphia Museum of Art with its exemplary Rocky steps.

We didn't spend all our time in museums. Instead, we enjoyed Philly's rooftop bars and outdoor restaurants, which were half the price of similar places in New York. There is a friendly competition between Philadelphia and New York about who lives in the better city. The walking guide, for example, was exemplary in every way other than his fixation on which city was better. The reality is that New Yorkers don't give a fig about Philadelphia. It's comparable to the soccer rivalry between Barcelona and Espanyol. That scarce person, an Espanyol supporter, hates Barcelona FC passionately. Unfortunately, that's not reciprocated by Barcelona fans, who reserve their rivalry primarily for Real Madrid.

We also enjoyed Philadelphia's calmer Chinatown and the uber-food court of Reading Terminal Market. Lorna has a rule that she must try the signature dish of each place we visit. In Ukraine, she asked for the local specialty and was given some bland breaded chicken, which we now know must be called Chicken Kyiv. In Philadelphia, the local dish is undeniably the Philly Cheesesteak, which they make from scratch at the Reading Terminal Market. The griller mixed the onions, minced beef, and cheese until it formed a sloppy mess. He then placed this unappetizing gruel into a demi-baguette. At that moment, I was delighted that I was a vegetarian.

Are We There Yet?

I consumed all my Chinese dumplings, while Lorna left almost all her Philly Cheesesteak untouched. She said it was inedible.

Despite this culinary misstep, we liked Philadelphia a lot. With ninety-six museums unvisited and the city specialty tasted and discarded, I am confident that we will return. First, however, we had a new state to call in on.

We had visited forty-five US states, with the remaining states being the two non-contiguous ones, Kansas, Delaware, and Nebraska. The latter often appears at the bottom of the list of states that tourists are interested in visiting, so much so that the Nebraska Tourism Commission once adopted the slogan, 'Nebraska: honestly, it's not for everyone.' In keeping with the humorous spirit of the people of Nebraska, we decided to save this state until last. Our journey to South Carolina allowed us to check off another state on the way, The First State.

What most know about Delaware is that it is small—ninety-six miles high by thirty-nine miles wide. Indeed, it is the second smallest state after Rhode Island. Its vehicle license plates sport the moniker First State, celebrating that it was the first state to ratify the Constitution. The state has only three counties, making it easy to compose the state anthem. The first three verses praise each county, while the last honors the state as a whole.

Delaware is renowned as an onshore corporate tax haven, with approximately two-thirds of Fortune 500 companies choosing to register their businesses in Delaware. This preference is due to the state's unique tax policies, where companies are exempt from income tax and pay a franchise tax instead. Delaware also offers a business-friendly legal environment, featuring an experienced and efficient court system and privacy protections. Accordingly, it is the only state with more companies than people.

There are also two hundred times more chickens than people, reflecting the importance of agriculture in the state. Bewitchingly, despite having a mere twenty-five thousand cows, Delaware's state beverage is milk, along with twenty-one other unoriginal states.

Delaware is President Joe Biden's home state. Like all states in the Union, Delaware sends two senators to represent its interests. However, Delaware and five other states with relatively low populations—Wyoming, Vermont, Alaska, North Dakota, and South Dakota—have fewer than one million residents. Consequently, these six states collectively have twelve senators, with each senator, on average, representing approximately four hundred thousand residents. In contrast, California, with its vastly larger population, has an average of twenty million residents per senator. It's worth noting that by 2040, it is projected that about half of the entire US population will reside in just nine states. This means that eighteen senators will represent half the nation, while the remaining eighty-two others will represent the other half.

All of this was a deliberate solution crafted by the Founding Fathers to ensure that smaller states would not be overshadowed or dominated by their more populous counterparts. The intention behind this system was to have senators who were seasoned, thoughtful leaders capable of adopting long-term perspectives in their decision-making.

On the other hand, house representation is based on population size, and the seven smallest states have only one representative each. They are elected every two years to respond to their electorate's mood. Unfortunately, this means they spend an average of twenty-five hours a week fundraising for the next election.

It is perhaps good fortune for Joe Biden that he was raised in Delaware—competition to be a senator is significantly less competitive in Delaware than in California. His presence in the state was, however, the result of bad luck. Biden's father had been born wealthy but experienced financial setbacks. As a result, Biden lived with his maternal grandparents in Pennsylvania for the first few years of his life. Then, Biden's father moved to Delaware to become a used-car dealer.

Uncle Joe was elected as one of the two Delaware senators when he was twenty-nine, just a few months before he was eligible to take his seat under the US Constitution. At that time, Republicans held a strong position in Delaware. Many Democrats in the state believed they couldn't defeat the well-liked Republican incumbent, so Biden was chosen as the Democratic candidate with little competition. Initially, Biden trailed his opponent by a significant 30 percentage points a few months before the election. However, his youthful vigor and dedicated campaigning began to narrow the gap. On election day, Biden secured victory by a slim margin of 3,162 votes.

A month later, tragedy struck when Biden's wife and their one-year-old daughter lost their lives in a car accident caused by a collision with a truck while she was driving. Biden has expressed that he felt as though God had played a cruel trick on him during that time. He even contemplated resigning from his newly elected position as senator to care for his two surviving sons, who had also been in the accident. However, the then-

Are We There Yet?

Senate Majority Leader convinced him not to take this step. In remembrance of his first wife and daughter, Biden never works on the anniversary of the accident.

Biden entered the Senate at a time when Japanese soldiers from World War II were still being discovered in remote jungles, as the Beatles made their final rooftop performance, and well before Dartmouth University admitted women. However, this long tenure in public service has provided Joe Biden with certain advantages—notably a deep understanding of history.

In 1975, Biden met his second wife, Jill. He credits her for renewing his interest in life. One snippet of oddness is that the happy couple spent their honeymoon at the admittedly lovely Lake Balaton, then behind the Iron Curtain in Hungary.

Joe Biden first stood as a presidential candidate in 1987. Had he been successful, he would have become the youngest president since JFK. Biden was well-positioned when a scandal hit his candidacy—he plagiarized a speech from Neil Kinnock, the famed windbag and unsuccessful former UK Labor Leader. Journalists then found previous addresses that bore remarkable similarities to those from RFK, JFK, and even Hubert Humphrey.

His initial setback in the quest for the Democratic presidential nomination proved to be a stroke of luck for his family. In February 1988, Biden experienced excruciating neck pain, later diagnosed as two brain aneurysms. His family believed that he would not have survived these conditions if he had still been campaigning.

Biden ran again as a presidential candidate in 2008 but was bested by a youthful and charismatic Barack Obama. Obama selected Biden as his running mate, and together, they led the executive branch of the government for eight years.

Toward the end of their second term, tragedy struck again. Biden's eldest son, Beau, died of brain cancer. This tragedy dissuaded Biden from standing as a presidential candidate in 2016. Most pundits believed that his long political career would end there. However, in 2021, at seventy-eight years old, Joe Biden became the oldest person to become president.

We decided to stay in President Joe Biden's Delaware vacation home of Rehoboth Beach and were eager to learn more about it. I love a museum, especially those in small towns. What's delightful is that most small American towns have a museum. Typically founded by local historians, they are often run on a shoestring by unpaid volunteers. While this lack of funding may limit the resources allocated to contextualizing what you see, there are advantages, too. They tend to have a more informal atmosphere, allowing visitors to interact with exhibits rather than merely viewing them through display cases. For example, schoolchildren can pass around an ancient Native American spearhead, marveling at its sharpness.

Small-town museums typically have an unwavering local focus. The assortment of artifacts is akin to a communal family album, meticulously assembling a shared history of the town. The curators understand that their museum serves as the primary custodian of their local heritage and dedicate themselves to vividly portraying their town's character.

While this might not have been the case in the past, nowadays, every local museum highlights the pre-colonial history of their region. In my experience, they confront the injustices of the past head-on. Many actively involve local tribes or marginalized communities in narrating their own stories. The abundance of these oral histories represents a valuable source of information and artifacts somewhat underutilized by academic historians.

Unlike some major museums, small-town ones are always thrilled to welcome visitors. They greet each new guest with genuine enthusiasm as if they didn't expect anyone to drop in that day. The museum staff is often knowledgeable and is as eager as a bird with a front-row seat at a worm parade to answer your questions about their passion. While the Vatican may be a magnificent museum, it's hard to imagine having a lengthy conversation with a staff member about the significance of what you see. Finally, as a passing tourist, connecting with locals is often challenging, but the museum is one place where this connection is encouraged.

Small-town museums are also manageable. In my twenties, I spent a year of Saturday mornings at the British Museum trying to work out the meaning of their jumble of artifacts. In a small-town museum, you can achieve this in ninety minutes or less.

Many American museums employ creative strategies to attract tourists, often featuring notable objects such as the world's largest pistachio, beagle, or hockey stick. In contrast, small-town museums have the liberty to delve into specific, often overlooked, subjects. For instance, in my last book, I discussed a Minnesota museum's collection of electric vibrators from the early twentieth century, which offered a blend of humor, intrigue, and social commentary. I'm sure the British Museum has an equally impressive collection of sex toys, but they are seldom displayed publicly alongside the Rosetta Stone.

Are We There Yet?

Some small-town museums choose not to chronicle their town's past but instead focus laser-like on a specific element of history. For example, in Missouri, you can explore the fascinating world of nuclear waste or visit the Hair Wreath Museum. If you have a penchant for toilets, Hawaii offers the chance to behold what is claimed to be the world's most scenic urinal, while Texas boasts the Toilet Seat Museum. Perhaps you're into sculpture? In that case, North Dakota's Enchanted Highway offers thirty-two miles of captivating scrap metal installations, or you can marvel at Carhenge in Nebraska or Foamhenge in Virginia. For agriculture enthusiasts, South Dakota's Corn Palace draws half a million visitors annually with its focus on Midwest farming. And if none of these pique your interest, there's always the Museum of Bad Art in Boston, Alabama's Unclaimed Baggage Center, Connecticut's Collection of Brains, the Salt and Pepper Shaker Museum in Gatlinburg, or Colorado's UFO Watchtower Museum.

So, what did I learn at the Rehoboth Museum? Thousands of years ago, Rehoboth Beach was located thirty miles inland from the Atlantic Coast when sea levels were much lower. However, by colonization, the ocean had risen to where it is today. Native American tribes, including the Lenape, inhabited and thrived in this area. In 1873, the town as we know it today was founded by Methodist churches as a camping area, with each house-sized plot priced at $50. The introduction of a new railroad made Rehoboth accessible to tourists from nearby cities, and in 1925, a highway further boosted tourism. Even long before Joe Biden's time, the town earned the nickname 'The Nation's Summer Capital' due to its popularity among DC visitors.

I had a lengthy conversation with the curator and told her I appreciated how the museum addressed some less attractive aspects of its history. Firstly, the museum's curation of its Native American history was commendable. Secondly, it didn't shy away from the fact that Delaware was a slave state despite its decision to remain in the Union. Thirdly, it highlighted Rehoboth's historical opposition to homosexuality, including campaigns such as 'Keep Rehoboth a family town' and attempts to regulate Poodle Beach, a clothing-optional beach popular among the gay community. It's heartening to see that things change over time, and today, the town has become one of the coast's most popular LGBTQ+-friendly tourist destinations. The curator seemed delighted someone had noticed her recent work in this area.

Rehoboth Beach is primarily a vacation town, with approximately fifteen hundred residents in the winter that swells to twenty-five thousand in the summer, thanks mainly to the influx of tourists known as 'Shoobies,' a somewhat derogatory term used by Delawareans. There are two schools of thought on the derivation of this word. The one with the better story is that day trippers would arrive by train with their lunch packed in a shoebox. Owners of restaurants would know that those with shoeboxes would not be spending a dime in their establishments. The other source for the name is that tourists would need to wear shoes on the scorching asphalt, while locals' feet were literally more hardened. Today's Shoobies may not carry shoeboxes, but you can identify them because they talk loudly and wear Hawaiian shirts, socks, and sandals.

The words may differ, but every tourist destination has a similar expression. For example, on the Jersey Shore, the non-native is called a Benny, the acronym for Bayonne, Elizabeth, Newark, and New York, the typical hometowns of these visitors. Some locals have 'Go Home Bennies' parties on their porches on Labor Day, the traditional last day of summer.

Some say these terms are racist. I'm not sure I agree, but they reflect mild annoyance at how these temporary visitors change their community. Perhaps the traffic is terrible, you can't get a table at your favorite restaurant, or they behave differently from the established norms of your community. Incidentally, I saw a bumper sticker in the Florida Keys earlier in our journey. It read, "If it's tourist season, why can't we shoot them?"

You're probably familiar with the concept of 'six degrees of separation,' which suggests that every person on Earth is connected to everyone else through a chain of no more than six mutual acquaintances. In other words, you could potentially meet anybody on the planet via a maximum of six handshakes… obviously pre-Covid. Surprisingly, Microsoft researchers analyzed thirty billion electronic messages and calculated that any two strangers are, on average, separated by precisely 6.6 degrees of separation.

In Southern Delaware, only two degrees of separation used to connect everyone. However, this is changing. Native Delawareans are disappearing from the beach towns. Out-of-Towners had bought all the beach property as second homes, and with tiny houses now selling at $2 million, it is unlikely the native Delawarean will return.

The pandemic appears to have accelerated this process. The locals told me their town had been full of outsiders 'working from home' that winter and complained that these AirBnBers had brought their Covid with them.

Are We There Yet?

Two Double Ds, a married couple who had both graduated from the University of Delaware, told me it was now impossible to find an affordable house in their hometown.

The people of Rehoboth were friendly to me. Maybe it was because I asked them questions, or perhaps it was my English accent. Either way, they were happy to talk and share their views. The one thing they seemed to disagree on was how to pronounce the name of their town. Some emphasized the first syllable, while others stressed the middle part of the word.

The locals told me that Delaware's local delicacy was 'scrapple,' a mush of minced pig's head, pig offal scraps, cornmeal flour, and spices—often referred to as 'everything but the oink.' This Amish-Mennonite delicacy is cooked in one-thousand-pound vats for two hours, and apparently, the aroma fills the neighborhoods where it's prepared. The mixture is then cooled overnight into semi-solid congealed loaves and distributed to restaurants and supermarkets. Finally, the product is sliced, fried, and served with eggs and condiments as a breakfast foodstuff.

This dish sounded perfect for Lorna. In keeping with her customs, Lorna was duty-bound to taste this specialty. From its description, I looked forward to comforting her as she vomited the meal into the toilet basin later in the day. I phoned several local restaurants before eventually finding one that had scrapple on its menu. They told me they only had Rapper Scrapple, which I thought sounded like a new R&B artist from South Central.

The restaurant was severely short-staffed, and the overworked waiter explained that locals were no longer interested in working in restaurants, and additionally, no J1 foreign visas were being processed. The menu clarified that this café offered Rapa Scrapple, the dominant Scrapple manufacturer in Delaware, made by a company formed by brothers Ralph and Paul Adams. Lorna disappointed me by eating all the scrapple and compounded this by complaining that it was somewhat bland and needed better seasoning.

Every shop and restaurant in Rehoboth had signs at their entrances indicating job openings, and many had to operate with reduced hours. This labor shortage was a widespread issue across all states. The primary cause was that many workers laid off in 2020 had found better-paid positions, while others had decided to retire, and a few were hesitant to return due to the risks of contracting Covid. Others who used to work multiple jobs found that the increased salaries offered by big-box companies allowed them to make a living with just one job.

With no restaurant tables available in town, Lorna and I ambled along the town's impressive mile-long boardwalk, ice cream in hand. The walkway dated back to the town's formation though it seemed from the many plaques that the wood had to be replaced regularly due to hurricanes.

The beach town had an old-fashioned fair and amusement arcade, a rarity here unlike in Britain. The Fasnacht family purchased the original 1930 arcade sixty years ago and renamed it Funland. It boasts offering today's rides at yesterday's prices. I would take issue with the modernity of the attractions because most people would describe the bumper-car-type activities as retro rather than modern. Nevertheless, the prices are still pretty good value. For twenty-five years, a ticket for a ride would cost only a dime. Unfortunately, inflation has ravaged Funland's cost base, and each never-expiring ticket now sets you back $0.60.

Still under the Fasnacht's ownership, we skipped the rides but enjoyed playing traditional arcade games. We tested our strength (not good), gambled unwisely on plastic derby horses, tossed the skeeball and goblet erratically, hooped the Coca-Cola bottle, and failed to grab the soft toy with that claw crane thing.

The most concise way to describe Rehoboth Beach is quaint, and Rehoboth was as quaint as a garden gnome's summer house. Its charming houses are New England style, with pristine wooden facias and white-painted balustrades. Its downtown offers wholesome food and noise-controlled entertainment, while its 1963 bandstand offers free music every Friday and Saturday evening.

****

As a long-time senator and Delaware resident, Joe Biden is not a Shoobie. But, in 2017, he bought a six-bedroom, five-and-a-half-bathroom house on the north shores of Rehoboth Beach for $2.7 million. You won't be surprised that this beach house is nicknamed 'the Summer White House.'

Biden seemed to be quite popular among the locals I spoke to. He had served as their senator for thirty-six years, their vice president for eight, and was now the first president from Delaware. The state park had even constructed a helipad to accommodate his weekend trips from the White

House. This new addition reduced the need to temporarily close roads to allow his motorcade to pass through unhindered.

One of the reasons for Biden's popularity is that, until relatively recently, he was not someone who used his position to amass immense wealth. For most of his career, Biden consistently ranked among the least wealthy senators. While some in Congress enter with pre-existing wealth, it's perplexing how many others accumulate tens or even hundreds of millions in assets while earning a comparatively modest salary of $174,000 per year. Certainly, the fact that they and their families can trade options based on privileged information may explain their financial success.

In his first year as vice president, at a time when the average senator had a net worth of $14 million, Joe Biden's net worth was less than $30,000. While this may raise questions about his financial management, it doesn't suggest corruption. Only in the years following his vice presidency did he capitalize on his position, earning $540,000 per year as a professor and commanding $100,000 per speech on the speaking circuit.

Some progressives believe that Biden's fifty years in politics disadvantage him because he is forced to defend his twentieth-century voting record to a new generation, some of whom see issues in black and white rather than gray. However, these former policy positions—on topics such as opposition to gay marriage and bussing children to better school districts—were mainstream for a Democrat then and are still somewhat palatable to undecided voters today. Most importantly, this longevity makes it difficult for his Republican opponents to portray him as a dangerous socialist.

****

We went wine tasting in Delaware's oldest winery. Similar to California, one has to pay for the wine-tasting experience; in this case, a token $10 per person. In exchange, we each received six small glasses of wine to sample from their selection of fifteen. Since I abstained from tasting, Lorna had the opportunity to sample nearly all the wines.

Lorna provided colorful descriptions of each wine. For instance, she characterized a 2019 Pinot Grigio as having pronounced overtones of urine… not undertones, but overtones. I didn't ask how she recognized it so readily, perhaps because I noticed that this description didn't deter her from finishing the entire glass.

The only other people there were a couple on a first date. The man sported a beard, was heavily tattooed, and appeared uncomfortable in his formal attire. His date was amply breasted, with a tight-fitting black dress that proudly showcased her prominent assets. The wine professional asked us about our music preferences, and the man chose country music, which was acceptable to us but not to his date's liking. In a pique of honest nervousness, the man admitted that he preferred beer and just didn't get wine. However, prompted by a stern glare from his date, he quickly added that he was very much open to learning new things. One felt their date was not going as well as he had hoped.

Fans of my previous book may expect descriptions of Lorna getting drunk at a new winery. Unfortunately, this did not happen. I asked her if the glasses were much smaller at this winery or whether she had become a more hardened alcoholic since the previous year. Perhaps in response, I noticed that Lorna did not drink the entire glass allocation as the tasting progressed. When I asked her what was wrong, she said she didn't want to be drunk in a second book.

****

We left Delaware and entered the bustling coastline of Maryland. Compared to the refined Rehoboth coast, the Maryland beaches were more packed, the accommodation was higher rise, and the mini-golf establishments were more frequent. The tourists here liked to ride roller coasters, devour ice creams and funnel cakes, and party into the early hours.

The drive over the Chesapeake Bay Bridge was spectacular. Mostly bridge but, in places, a tunnel; this eighteen-mile bridge-tunnel was built across the mouth of Chesapeake Bay in 1964. I was the passenger, so I could marvel at the view of the immense bay. As the driver, Lorna kept her eyes firmly on the road. This was a good thing because, of the fifteen vehicles blown off the bridge in its history, only two have survived.

We overnighted at our second Fayetteville in just over a month; this one was the North Carolina version. As with Rehoboth Beach, we stayed in a traditional motel rather than one of the more modern hotels next to the freeway.

The origin of the traditional motel is closely tied to the popularization of the motor car. The original concept was simple: you could park your car in front of the hotel room and walk no more than ten steps to reach the hotel door. The first was built in 1925 as soon as enough Americans owned their own vehicles. Before this, Americans had always desired to explore their beautiful country but were limited primarily to places connected by railroad. Suddenly, with tens of millions of Americans able to travel more freely by car, there was a massive demand for accommodation.

Over the following decades, the classic motel room perfected a standard layout. At one end of the rectangular footprint, you'll find a bathroom with an accompanying Norman Bates-style plastic shower curtain, a basin or two, and a toilet. In the main section, there will be a king-sized bed or possibly two queens if you're traveling as a family or group. Additionally, this section often includes amenities such as a microwave, fridge, and TV with access to several hundred channels.

The room is completed with four other artifacts. First, a folding luggage rack will raise your case off the carpet. Second, an ice bucket with an empty plastic sleeve will remind you to collect ice from the industrial ice machine in some shared central area. Third, there is an alarm clock, which the previous occupant had helpfully set at 5 am and neglected to turn off. Finally, an AC unit, as quiet as a mouse with a megaphone, blows ice-cold air onto the right-hand side of the bed, what I call Lorna's side.

Most of the motels were independently owned or at least only loosely franchised. Art Deco neon signs would lure you to their establishment rather than their rivals.

The traditional motel reached its zenith in the sixties, with around sixty thousand motels, coincidentally around the release of Hitchcock's Psycho. In reality, Eisenhower's expansion of the interstate system probably kicked in around this time, and the lodging industry had to invest in a slightly different design of hotels by these new roads.

I confess that I find the traditional motel comforting. As with many other things American, there is uniformity to the product. You know exactly—and I mean exactly—what you will get.

Tastes have evolved, and the dividing line between motels and highway hotels has blurred. It's no longer the case that you can park your car right in front of your hotel room. Instead, when you arrive at a franchised hotel, you must often park some distance from the central reception area. After checking in, you must navigate a circuitous route to your room while carrying your belongings that are too valuable to leave in your distant vehicle.

The hotels have added additional facilities that are must-haves for a new generation but, in reality, are seldom used. For example, all hotels now come with some tiny pool, have warmed cookies at 4 pm, and offer plastic-wrapped breakfasts of plastic food the following day.

Most of the old motels are long gone, but a few remain. Many of these holdouts have converted to weekly efficiencies for the almost homeless. However, a small number still cater to the weirdo motel lover like me.

Are We There Yet?

Chapter 8 – The Lowcountry of South Carolina

We arrived at our next month's home, an old—well, 1925—three-bedroom cottage set on three acres with its own extended dock by a river in South Carolina's Lowcountry. There were only a dozen other houses on this stretch of river. On the other riverbank was an island wilderness of bullrushes from which you expected Huckleberry Finn to emerge.

Like so many islands in the Lowcountry, it was mainly marshy, with some scattered oak trees standing on sturdy ground. Indeed, Beaufort is home to almost a quarter of the East Coast's marshlands. We had this magnificent waterway to ourselves most of the time and saw our neighbors only occasionally, usually when Dog #1 had jumped the high fence into their equally large yards to greet their dogs.

Our 250-foot dock was more like a pier than a standard boat dock and had many different parts. The dock had a couple of areas to lift boats out of the water; an outhouse; an expansive space for sunbathing and diving into the river; multiple sites to cast nets or dangle rods; and an outside kitchen for gutting all the fish... that Lorna never caught. The six-hundred-foot-wide river ebbed and flowed with the extreme tide. Three-quarters of this dock was fixed by piles to the land, and the remaining floating pontoon rose and fell with the tide. Its drawbridge was level at high tide as the floating dock rose up the wooden piles. However, the dogs used the steep slope at low tide as a playground slide.

In the last book, I wrote about the joys of an American lake vacation. A river vacation is similar, but swimming is more challenging. It was August, and the water was deliciously warm. However, you had to pay attention to the strong current, whether taking the elegant route into the water via a ladder or merely jumping in. If you didn't concentrate, you would soon find yourself at the neighbor's dock and face the walk of shame through their yard. So. we learned to have a buoy—which Americans inexplicably pronounce as boo-ey—ready to help the swimmer return to our dock.

When not working, Lorna spent most of her day fishing. The current was strong whether the tide was ebbing or flowing. The only constants were the velocity of Lorna's fishing bobby and the absence of any fish to consume. From time to time, Lorna would snare the odd errant stingray, but although they were perfectly edible, she found them unpleasant to prepare. Dolphins were frequent visitors and would regularly play under our dock. They would taunt Lorna with the bounty and diversity of their catch from this vast river.

The dock had other goodies. A crab contraption yielded almost no seafood, save for one grunt that inadvertently swam the wrong way one sunny afternoon. Dog #2 spent her time chasing tiny black crabs on the long dock, but these crustaceans generally successfully scurried away under the boards just before she reached them. Meanwhile, Dog #1 spent his time licking the semi-salty surface of the dock in the style of a gourmand at a Michelin-starred restaurant.

As the sun descended westward, the tranquil river mirrored the celestial scene above. Daughter #2 and Boyfriend #2, technically still teenagers, would spend their evenings on the dock eating junk food alongside the soft glow of the fireflies.

The dialog of the dolphins, the plop of nearby somersaulting fish, the divebomb of the pelican, and some classic seventies albums were the soundtracks to our days. The scent of salt, fused with the earthy freshness of the bullrushes, was the intoxicating perfume. As far as the sights, they were provided by the dock's weathered planks against the sunlight that shimmered reflections over the river's surface.

The daughters and their boyfriends were again with us for much of the month. In the evenings, we often played cards outside in the screened porch area, with the fan barely cooling the air around us. Boyfriend #1 was scandalized that our card games were so confrontational and unkind. Apparently, when he has his own children, he wouldn't be nearly so mean to them. Below-scratch golfer Boyfriend #1 played golf on the region's numerous golf courses while his girlfriend rode horses in the hundred-degree heat. One evening, we took everyone to the local indoor mini-golf and found that proper golf skills did not necessarily transfer to the shorter indoor game.

Are We There Yet?

I used my time reading and writing. I also found a nearby tennis club willing to tolerate my weak backhand slice and errant first serve. I had never played in this level of heat and humidity before.

Beads of perspiration formed on my forehead as I walked from the car to the court. As I warmed up, these beads trickled down my face, stinging my eyes and saturating my clothes. My sweat-soaked fingers struggled to maintain a firm grip on the racket, adding an element of uncertainty to every shot. As you see at Flushing Meadows, I dried my right hand with a large towel after each service point.

With each swing of the racket, the fully saturated air weighed down every stroke until I pushed through a dense wall of molasses. The sweltering heat and oppressive humidity extracted every ounce of energy from my body. The actual opponent was not the person on the other side of the net but nature itself. Each shot was an act of resilience. I just needed to get one more shot back. If I do, it will break my opponent's spirit.

At the end of each match, I was drained. No amount of water consumption could replace the sweat that had vacated my body. Whether I had won or lost the match, I felt I had overcome nature, at least until another day.

Summer was the season for thunderstorms. Most afternoons brought tremendous downpours and riotous rackets of thunder that made us retreat to the house and convinced diffident Dog #1 to flee even further for safety to the middle of the building.

The house's grounds had other wonders, too. It had a long driveway with rhododendrons and azaleas on both sides. The garden had a firepit, multiple swinging chairs, and tractor tire swings. This rural part of the world had plentiful wildlife. Our dogs, who unusually could roam free whenever they wanted, barked at foxes, deer, and coyotes.

Lorna invariably says whenever we travel somewhere new, "This place is nice. I could live here." She then promptly researches what we can afford in the new neighborhood. Sadly, I would have to sell a Bryson-load of books to afford one of these riverside homes.

There are two cities named Beaufort in the Carolinas. The one in North Carolina is pronounced as 'Bow-fort,' while the older one in the Southern state is pronounced 'Byoo-foot.' Both communities are named after the second Duke of Beaufort, who pronounced his name like the newer town.

Beaufort County, one of eight counties in the Lowcountry, holds the distinction of being one of the first parts of the United States to be settled by colonists. Situated on sixty-eight separate islands and boasting a naturally deep harbor, this county was discovered by the Spanish in around 1515, just a year after Ponce de Leon founded St Augustine. A decade later, the French dropped off thirty protestants on one of its islands, Port Royal. Unfortunately, these early colonizers were as argumentative as teenagers negotiating curfews; they quarreled amongst themselves, then clashed with the native Cherokee, and eventually built a boat with sails made from bedsheets to escape back to France. In 1566, the Spanish made a second attempt to colonize the area, leading to the construction of a fort on nearby Parris Island.

Sir Francis Drake, famous for repelling the Spanish Armada from English shores, torched St Augustine in 1586, forcing the Spanish to abandon their Port Royal settlement.

In the mid seventeenth century, the English established multiple settlements in South Carolina, including Charleston, Hilton Head, and Beaufort.

By the second half of the eighteenth century, Beaufort was specializing in shipbuilding, while Charleston had evolved into a significant trading center, rivaling the northern ports of Boston, New York, and Philadelphia in significance. Charleston's trade also included the trafficking of enslaved people, with White Lowcountry farmers responsible for 'purchasing' approximately half of the 0.4 million enslaved West Africans who were directly brought to the United States.

These Gullah Geechee people brought their language, culture, and food to the area. These immigrants—transported here against their will—retained their West African farming and cooking methods, which still influence much of the local cuisine today. This influence is evident in the prevalence of one-pot dishes such as gumbos, crab stews, squash casseroles, and shrimp and grits on Lowcountry menus. Another popular option here is the 'meat and three,' which includes dishes such as barbecued chicken or blackened fish served with three vegetable sides and cornbread or biscuits.

Gullah cuisine served as the inspiration for Southern cooking and later evolved into what we now know as Northern soul food when many formerly enslaved people migrated from the South in the early twentieth century.

Beaufort was the first Confederate city to be captured by Union troops in 1861. As Union soldiers invaded their islands, White residents abandoned both their properties and many of their workers. In 1862, Robert Smalls, an enslaved crew member of the Confederate Ship *The*

Are We There Yet?

Planter, led a mutiny with other Black crewmembers while their White co-workers were ashore. Smalls managed to rescue their families and sailed the ship into the hands of the US Navy. For his courageous actions, he was eventually put in charge of *The Planter* and, using the money he received as a reward for his exploits, purchased the mansion that had once belonged to his former 'owner.' Smalls later went into politics, serving as a Republican congressman for five consecutive terms.

Beaufort's capture marked an early trial for reconstruction in the United States, as the nation aimed to assimilate millions of newly liberated African Americans into society. This initial reconstruction effort, known as the Port Royal Experiment, included a school staffed by Northern educators to assist formerly enslaved individuals in adapting to their newfound freedom.

A little over ten years later, after the closely fought 1876 presidential election, federal armies left South Carolina, marking the end of the reconstruction era. By 1895, South Carolina voters approved a new constitution that excluded Black voters, and segregation laws known as 'Jim Crow' laws were reintroduced.

Beaufort's economy further declined after a series of misfortunes. First, in 1893, a hurricane hit the Lowcountry, killing two thousand residents and devastating the city. Then, a 1907 fire and a weevil infection of the cotton plant shattered an already declining economy and population.

The region's economy began to recover when the military established installations here. The two World Wars and the Cold War brought an influx of military personnel, leading to significant economic growth in the area.

Despite being many miles from Beaufort, we frequented it for food, entertainment, or sometimes just the drive. It is one of the most attractive places in America, and the enchanting landscape around it is a living canvas of marshlands and winding estuaries. I love the bridges that cross the vast expanses of water the most. If you stop at one of these bridges to look more carefully, you will see an intricate network of creeks and channels snaking through the reeds. It is where graceful herons wade, egrets take flight, and fiddler crabs scuttle across the mudflats. It is a place to rent a boat to explore the beckoning sun-kissed waters.

Although the antebellum plantations and the fields of tobacco, rice, indigo, and cotton are mostly long gone, the same house design is still widespread. The white, wooden houses are built upon pilings to protect them from the tidal environment, regular storms, and hurricanes. The large porches of these houses provide refuge from the heat and host multiple swinging chairs, where residents enjoy cakes and pitchers of sweet tea.

We became regulars at the farmer's market. These markets are abundant in America but seldom feature any farmers. They often have new-age-type individuals selling small pots of overpriced honey, exorbitant aromatic soaps, and pricey pastries. However, this Beaufort market consisted primarily of two groups of sellers: farmers who had harvested their products and chefs who had creatively concocted some charming chow. It was popular, too; cars were parked in every available spot, and crowds swarmed the various goods on offer.

There were long lines at the most popular vendors. I tended to buy non-standard mushrooms, such as maitake, enoki, and King Trumpet, which were not stocked in the supermarket. I would have purchased more fruits and vegetables, but the prices were extremely high compared to the supermarket. I understand that farmers have a tough time; they work all the hours, bear all the risks, and still usually come away with only a small net income. That being said, there is no way that I am willing to pay $10 for a simple loaf of bread, $12 for a few strawberries, or $30 for a loin of pork.

My hair had not been trimmed since Ohio. When I entered the Beaufort barbershop, my heart sank as I saw three men in the waiting area, all of whom I assumed were customers waiting for haircuts. To my surprise, one of the men inquired about what I wanted, and I suddenly realized all three were underemployed hairdressers.

I remarked that business appeared to be slow. However, this was precisely the wrong statement to make, and the barber lamented that he had hardly seen a customer all day. He had thought business was terrible when Covid first hit, and income had dropped by half. The business then returned to normal for the summer of 2020. However, with this new Delta strain, his clientele—mostly older men—were more frightened than ever, and his business was a quarter of what it used to be.

He blamed the Federal Government for scaring everyone, especially that Dr. Fauci. He spat out his name as if trying to evacuate feces from his mouth. Although the barber's clients had been vaccinated, they feared succumbing to this new strain. The hairdresser told me that he had been first in the line for the vaccination in February and didn't believe he was now at any significant risk. My stylist confessed that he doubted whether all pandemic casualties had truly died from Covid, sharing with me a story of one of his long-term customers and friends, Bob, whose passing had been recorded as a Covid death.

My barber said he used to attend Bob's house to cut his hair even before the pandemic, as Bob had been seriously ill. Bob had suffered multiple strokes and had so many leg infections that the doctors planned to amputate the limb. It was indeed a miracle that Bob was still alive before the pandemic started. I could have quoted the excess mortality rates showing that one million more Americans had died than expected, at a slightly higher rate than in Europe. However, I also understood that my barber was mainly expressing his frustration, and I was tired of discussing the pandemic.

****

The military is crucial to Beaufort's economy. Three military installations have their homes here: The Marine Corps Recruitment Depot, the Marine Corps Air Station, and the Naval Hospital.

I had heard about the public museum at the Recruitment Depot and was eager to visit, but the journey proved to be quite tricky. It was situated right in the middle of the vast Marine Corps training facility. The first challenge was clearing the armed guards who meticulously inspected every vehicle, verifying driver's licenses, vehicle registrations, and insurance against their headquarters' records. After a fifteen-minute inspection, I was given the green light. I then approached one of the guards for directions to the museum, but he explained that the route was too complicated to explain verbally and recommended using GPS navigation instead.

Following the advised route was indeed intricate, with few meaningful signposts. However, as is typical of landscapes in this part of the world, the views were stunning. Birds of prey supervised the river inlets and accompanying marshlands. On the more solid patches of ground, ancient trees, adorned with Spanish Moss, provided shade from the scorching one-hundred-degree heat for marine recruits and their instructors. The drill instructors wore wide-brimmed campaign hats that curved upwards, offering some protection from the sun. In contrast, their charges sported eight-point cover caps, which seemed to serve no purpose other than making them look somewhat comical.

I eventually reached the heart of the protected Marine town, which, like any other town, had shops, restaurants, a gas station, and a post office.

There were also recreational facilities, such as sports fields, a children's playground, a cinema, and a bowling alley complex. But there were also differences: the most enormous US flag I had ever seen flapped ferociously in the pre-storm wind, and a nearby bridge here sported the simple slogan, 'We Make Marines,' highlighting the primary focus of their work here. I also noticed some other Marines were parading in the morning's heat in a different type of comical hat. Since new Marine graduation was still a few weeks away, the only proud families at the base were those visiting their Drill Instructor children. The revelation that these tough sergeants had parents probably came as a surprise to the trainee Marines.

The museum had a bit of a slow start, featuring the typical exhibits you'd find in many museums, with ancient uniforms, hats, and armaments on display. What first caught my interest was an exhibition that focused on the significant battles the Marines have been involved in. The Marines take immense pride in being the first to arrive in conflict zones and being responsible for embassy security at all US embassies.

However, the best part of the museum showcased the training journey of a Marine. This training facility provides the boot camp for all enlisted recruits east of the Mississippi, while a second training facility in San Diego trains those from elsewhere. Each batch of recruits arrives by bus and assembles outside. They stand in the yellow footprints of the million Marines trained here since 1915 and are told they will soon be part of the world's finest fighting forces. They are advised that they will have to train as a team and should omit the word 'I' from their vocabulary.

Each recruit enters the main training doors of the Depot only once; the instructors have to go via another route. Upon entering the building, each budding Marine's first task is to call their family on a public phone. Each would-be Marine is handed a script to narrate, from which they must not deviate. This will be their last contact with their family until the end of training. This ten-second supervised script must be terrifying for the person on the other end.

"This is Recruit (Last Name). I have arrived safely at Parris Island. Please do not send any food or bulky items to me in the mail. I will contact you in seven to ten days by letter with my new address. Thank you for your support. Goodbye for now."

I projected that—had it been me delivering these words—I'm sure my dad would be replying, "Let me just get your mother."

The male recruit is then taken to the barber area to have his hair shorn. This haircut strips away his individuality. Women are not permitted to have their heads shaven; their regulations are much more complicated and differ depending on whether their hair is short, medium, or long, with those in the latter group having to pack it inconspicuously in a tight bun.

Probably influenced by the movies, I had the impression that military training deconstructs each recruit and then rebuilds their confidence after hitting rock bottom. According to this museum, this is not true at all. The main aims of the training are to build upon each recruit's previous confidence level and learn to trust their team.

The first week adapts the civilians to Marine life. The recruits spend their time on administration, medical evaluation, and simple fitness tests, whose aim is to build confidence. They also start martial arts training in *Jiu-Jitsu*, *Taekwondo*, and *Krav Maga*.

In the weeks following their arrival, the pressure steadily increases. The primary training objective is to cultivate resilience for the challenges they will likely face in the future. Recruits endure grueling conditions, including extreme heat, mud, and water, with minimal sleep and food. These conditions are designed to teach them how to make sound decisions despite sleep deprivation. They must also rappel walls, complete a three-mile run in under eighteen minutes, and perform thousands of push-ups. Furthermore, Marines must learn to be both supportive of and reliant on their team.

In the latter half of their training, recruits focus on acquiring military skills. Many readers may have seen movies where recruits must learn to disassemble and reassemble a rifle blindfolded in fewer than thirty seconds. After mastering this skill, they proceed to firearm training. Those with aptitude can achieve remarkable accuracy, hitting bullseye targets from distances of up to half a kilometer.

The greatest anxiety for the recruits is the Crucible, which occurs at the end of their training. This grueling fifty-four-hour field exercise tests all their skills. Many enlisted recruits fear they will fail their training at this final stage. However, the Drill Sergeant I spoke to told me that a mixture of their new skills and the team's solidity meant that almost everybody passed this final milestone test.

In the thirteenth week, the recruits graduate as Marines. Marines are encouraged to invite their families to visit them for their graduation ceremony. Having talked to a few Marine parents, I know this forty-eight-hour period is among the best days of the parent's life.

The training has not always lasted thirteen weeks. In times of war, preparation is abbreviated to deliver fresh Marines to the front. After Pearl

Harbor, for example, training was initially shortened to only four weeks to accelerate troops into the Pacific. However, the training period had returned to three months by the war's end.

I am not somebody easily swayed by the opinions of others. However, by the end of the museum tour, I was ready to volunteer for the US Marines. Therefore, unless you are of enlisting age, I heartily recommend this free museum to anyone.

The first graduating class in 1909 consisted entirely of white males. It wasn't until 1918 that women began serving as Marines, initially in US-based administrative roles. In 1948, women were granted admission to combat roles, and today, they comprise just under 10 percent of the 200,000 active Marines. During World War II, the Marine Corps began accepting individuals from diverse ethnic backgrounds, although initially, this was done on a segregated basis. Full integration, in alignment with broader American society, was not achieved until around 1960.

These basic-level Marines earn an annual salary of a shade over $20,000, and with some experience but no promotion, their pay can double. While this is still not great pay, having met a lot of former Marines in the US, you tend to find that, after their military career, they gravitate toward leadership positions.

Of course, these days, everyone in the military is a volunteer. However, this was not the case during the Vietnam conflict, as around one-third were conscripted through 'the draft,' which was notionally based on a mathematical lottery.

In the early stages of the conflict, young men were chosen for service by local draft boards. Unfortunately, these boards often succumbed to pressure from influential individuals, resulting in a situation where three-quarters of those drafted came from working-class backgrounds. Wealthier families found it much easier to secure college, medical, or other deferments for their sons.

This inequality prompted the federal government to reform the draft mechanism, making it genuinely random. On December 1, 1969, the Selective Service System held its first lottery to determine which young men would be called to serve in 1970.

The first lottery was amateurishly simple. Days of the year were printed on paper slips, put into opaque capsules, and placed in a shoebox. Another person then moved the capsules into a two-lidded glass jar, inverted this jar, and finally, the capsules were drawn.

Are We There Yet?

The first date selected was September 14. All men of draft age born on this date would be the first to have to report for a military medical. This drawing continued until the last capsule, June 8, was opened. In the 1970 draft, the first 195 birthdates were called to serve in the order they were drawn.

In a truly random drawing, one would expect a proportional distribution of birthdates across the months. However, in the 1970 draft, there was insufficient shuffling, resulting in a higher concentration of low draft numbers for birthdates in November and December.

This issue arose because the capsules were initially arranged in chronological order when placed in the shoebox, which meant that the later birthdates ended up at the bottom when they were later transferred to a glass jar. When the jar was inverted, most of the later dates moved back to the top.

By way of example, had my family been age- and gender-eligible for the 1970 draft, November-birthdayed Daughter # 1 and I, plus December-baby Lorna, would have all been selected for service. My father, mother, sister, and Daughter #2, all born in the first four months of the year, would not have been drafted.

Can you imagine today's uproar if people were selected for service in such a non-random way? It moved many families toward the Peace Movement.

The 1971 draft was a model of complexity but did correct the non-randomness. The National Bureau of Standards printed the first 365 positive integers 78 times. Twenty-five of these groups were selected randomly, converted into birthdates, and then placed in 25 separate envelopes. Meanwhile, a further set of 365 numbers were placed in another 25 envelopes. A Select Service Official then randomly chose two envelopes, one with all the birthdates and a second with the raw draft number.

These 365 birthdates and draft numbers were inserted into capsules and put into two separate drums. The lottery organizers then rotated the drums. They turned the birthdates' drum for sixty minutes. Unfortunately, the rotating mechanism on the second drum broke after only thirty minutes. The draft then took place, with September 16 being drawn first with draft number 139. That year, July 9 was paired with draft number 1. This meant all men born on July 9, 1951, were the first to report for their military medical in early January 1971.

Of the twenty-seven million men eligible for military service between 1964 and 1973, fifteen million were granted deferment for educational or medical reasons. Of the 2.2 million drafted, 0.2 million illegally resisted the draft, and 0.1 million deserted, with Canada as the favorite bolthole.

The US military transitioned to an all-volunteer force in 1973, but Congress retains the authority to reinstate the draft in a national emergency. The Selective Service System Agency still operates and requires all male US residents to register within a month of their eighteenth birthday. In a national emergency, any male between eighteen and twenty-five could be called to serve.

****

The shortage of workers and products throughout the United States was worsening by the month. American consumers were becoming accustomed to every call center, restaurant, hotel, and supermarket experiencing a staff shortage. Almost all supermarkets had taken the opportunity to transition to self-checkout, where you, the customer, take a very temporary, short-term job as a checkout worker. I thought it was only a matter of time before they extended this principle to the customer having to perform a stint in the unloading warehouse before being allowed to make a purchase.

These shortages became especially noticeable for us on water deliveries. Our rental home relied on well water rather than water pumped through pipes. It worked perfectly well for washing and cooking, but it wasn't the most appealing option for drinking. This was less of an issue for my wife and daughters—who enjoyed their alcoholic beverages—but it posed a challenge for me. The property owners had a water dispenser, similar to the ones you see in offices. Unfortunately, the water delivery company had neither the five-gallon water jugs nor staff available to pick up or deliver these large containers. This type of inconvenience was happening across the US for almost every product or service.

The media attributed the shortages of goods in every shop to a Japanese container ship, *The Ever Given*, getting stuck in the Suez Canal for six days in March. They argued that 12 percent of global trade flowed through this canal, with $10 billion worth of goods accumulating daily.

However, this sea delay was mostly a red herring. The principal causes of these supply chain issues were uneven American demand and the effect of the pandemic on container traffic.

Are We There Yet?

Covid lockdowns had cratered US consumer spending. When states later relaxed their Covid rules, Americans quickly started spending their stimulus checks and savings on manufactured goods, most of which came from Asia. These sudden shifts in spending patterns had disrupted the container industry. The world had enough containers, but unfortunately, they were in the wrong place.

Four hundred container ships, each carrying an average of 20,000 TEUs ('twenty-foot equivalent units'), were waiting for clearance in China due to their Covid rules. Meanwhile, Chinese exporters struggled to find containers to transport new goods because most empty ones were stranded in the US, delayed by labor shortages at Los Angeles ports.

The price of sending a container rocketed sevenfold, causing knock-on problems for the entire supply chain. Some Americans seemed to blame their president for these shortages, but, in truth, there was little he or anyone could do other than wait for the problem to unravel. In the meantime, this was one of many factors fueling inflation.

****

The place we were renting was a half-hour drive between two small cities. It was, however, much closer to a drive-in movie theatre. I love almost everything about a drive-in movie. To start with, I love being outside on a warm evening under the stars. Next, if it's an ancient drive-in facility, I love the low-tech audio from your car radio's speakers or the speaker stands. Finally, I love that people choose different ways of watching the movie. Some movie-goers watch from inside their car, others bring deck chairs, a dog, and a radio, while some couples watch the film from a mattress in the bed of their pickup truck.

It is a different experience from watching a film at the theatre, offering much more freedom. If the movie is as riveting as watching a snail marathon, the kids can meet with friends or stop by the concession stands. If you don't enjoy movie theatre food, bring your own foie gras, quinoa salad, or crunchy carrots. If you are the type of person who likes to text during movies, you can do that… provided others in the car agree.

The drive-in movie obviously couldn't be a thing until society had a lot of cars. So, unsurprisingly, the first drive-in movie was established in New Jersey in 1933. Only two decades later, there were four thousand of them. This was the golden era of drive-in movies. If George Lucas's *American*

Graffiti is to be believed, the yesteryear drive-ins were frequented by hot rods, heartthrobs, and roller-skating waitresses serving milkshakes.

The decline in the popularity of drive-in movies can be attributed to several factors. Initially, the rise of new technology played a significant role. The introduction of VHS allowed people to watch movies from the comfort of their homes, while digital projection made this home viewing experience more cinematic. With streaming services, audiences could watch anything they wanted at their convenience. However, a turning point for many drive-ins came when studios required digital projection and sound systems for their films. Unfortunately, the high cost of this technological upgrade led to the closure of many drive-in theaters.

In the subsequent years, the United States has witnessed a significant increase in the land value on which drive-in movie theaters are located. Faced with making a living from occasional patrons like me attending movies or selling their land to housing developers, most owners wisely chose the latter.

The place where you would have taken your date on a Friday or Saturday night in the fifties or sixties is now a rarity. Today, there are only 325 drive-ins remaining in the entire United States. Approximately 5 percent of them are available for sale if you want to purchase one from a retiring owner. The prices range from half a million to two million dollars, presumably reflecting mainly the intrinsic value of the land.

Catch a drive-in movie while you still can.

****

With our children happily occupied at their university and our dogs in the safe care of friends, we decided to spend the next few months of our nomadic travels in Europe. Fortunately, for this book at least, we chose countries with close associations with America.

Are We There Yet?

Chapter 9 – Taking French Leave

We should have opted for the €1.50 airport tram to reach our city apartment, but due to inadequate planning, we ended up squandering €48 on a taxi instead. Unlike most airports worldwide, Nice Côte d'Azur airport is situated by the beach close to the city. So—during one of France's many strikes—the Niçois would grudgingly trudge the four-kilometer seafront promenade to their Nice dwelling. You couldn't do this from Heathrow or Hartsfield, Atlanta.

We had booked our extended stay here at the last minute. The concern over Covid regulations meant that every Nice district had many bargain-priced choices. Lorna had discovered a *Les Baumettes* mansion block just off the beachfront road. This mansion had a fine courtyard and magnificent entrance halls, while our apartment had a chic living room, a spacious bedroom, and a full kitchen with every French accouterment. Best of all, it had two balconies from which you could eat dinner with a view of either the beach or the street below.

We traveled to France during the early weeks of it opening its borders to overseas travelers. All EU tourists possessed a *Passe Sanitaire*, which confirmed their vaccination status. Non-Europeans had the option to obtain this pass, but the process to do so was plagued by inefficiencies, resulting in a substantial backlog of applications. Fortunately, the pragmatic French authorities accepted our CDC vaccination cards, which was fortunate; otherwise, we wouldn't have been able to access museums, supermarkets, restaurants, or cinemas.

Lorna and I quickly fell into a routine. We swam in the Med on the public beach close to our apartment every afternoon. The pale turquoise azure of the Med is allegedly accentuated by the presence of giant pebbles, or *galets*, endemic to this part of the coast.

Regrettably, I had neglected to pack our water shoes. My feet were unaccustomed to walking on the rigid and sometimes sharp shingle. With each step, they sank to variable depths, making it surprisingly challenging to maintain one's balance. On the bright side, this encouraged us to venture into the water earlier rather than waiting until the last moment as one often does in cold seawater. So, Lorna and I swam unadventurously daily in the slightly cooler Mediterranean waters, all while admiring the view of Nice's grand architecture.

The free public beaches along the *Promenade des Anglais* were nestled among the more numerous private ones. Opting for the private option entailed a minimum €25 admission charge, which rewarded you with a beach chair, umbrella, and sometimes a bar or restaurant. However, since we frequented the beach daily, albeit briefly, during the off-season, and it was essentially the same stretch of beach, we were as frugal as coupon collectors at a discount store and chose to stick with the free public beaches.

France's fifteen hundred private beaches face a challenge, as the French Government has mandated unrestricted public access to the sea. Nevertheless, certain local authorities, including Nice, have devised a workaround by allowing 'temporary' beach installations. This restricts private beach operations to six months each year, requiring owners to dismantle the infrastructure at the end of each season.

France is not the only country where wealthy individuals want their own beaches. Fortunately, beach property law for most countries has evolved from Roman law, which regarded the air, running water, and the sea as things common to all humanity. The American civil law system is no exception, with most US states ruling that private ownership can only begin at the mean high tide line. This means if the tide wets the sand, it is probably public property.

The preferred swimwear for the French male is the Speedo, an Australian brand of racing brief that has made its way into the French language. In many anglosphere countries, these tight-fitting swim briefs are humorously referred to as 'budgie-smugglers.' Indeed, not even a Frenchman could believe he looks good in these banana hammocks. However, the main reason for the Speedo's popularity is that most French municipal pools prohibit all other forms of swimwear for men.

For centuries, the French have been crafting laws, and in 1903, with most other things already prohibited, the French parliament officially banned longer swimming shorts, citing hygienic and safety concerns. You might wonder what these hygienic and safety reasons are. According to the French, surf shorts or boardshorts are considered less hygienic than shorter trunks because the excess water they trap can lead to bacterial growth, potentially spreading infections. As for safety, apparently, French lifeguards find it more challenging to rescue the long-shorted swimmer.

Incidentally, it is also illegal in France to wear clothes on a nudist beach, which reminds me of a joke:
How do you spot a blind man at a nudist camp? It's not hard.

A more recent swimwear ban on burkinis was controversial. Many French municipalities adopted policies prohibiting wearing the all-encompassing swimsuit, favored by some Muslim women and an even more significant number of Muslim men. However, France's top court eventually overturned these bans because they violated the principle of government neutrality toward religion.

Of course, every country has its fair share of absurd laws, but France has a reputation for drafting some of the most ludicrous regulations in recent decades. For instance, President Charles de Gaulle passed a law in 1959 allowing the president to marry a couple even if one or both partners were dead.

Many of France's unusual laws relate to an attempt to preserve its culture. In attempting to protect their language, a 1994 law required radio stations to play French songs for at least 40 percent of their airtime, causing the unintended consequence of stifling innovation and creativity.

To combat obesity, the French government limited the amount of ketchup and dressing available at school meals. Another unusual French regulation is the lunch-break law, where workers are prohibited from eating lunch alone at their desks. Instead, they are encouraged to take a ninety-minute lunch break with colleagues, perhaps with a glass or two of wine.

While these laws may appear somewhat unconventional to those of us accustomed to unrestricted personal freedom, they are part of what makes the French… French.

****

Joyce, Nabokov, and Hemingway have all written extensively about the *Promenade des Anglais*, the four-mile palm-lined seafront that abuts Nice's elegant nineteenth-century mansions. I'm sure you're all eager to hear my thoughts.

It is said that *Promenade des Anglais* acquired its name from the *Niçois,* who were perplexed by the wealthy nineteenth-century English tourists' habit of promenading with parasols in hand. Notable figures, such as Queen Victoria and Winston Churchill, enjoyed their view of the *Baie des Anges* during their seaside walks here. Less fortunately, Isadora Duncan, the denaturalized American-born dancer, met a tragic end on the bustling four-lane road opposite the promenade. Throughout her life, Duncan had a troubled relationship with automobiles. In 1913, her infant children drowned, alongside their governess, when their vehicle plunged into the Seine. Duncan herself survived two severe car accidents in 1913 and 1924. Tragically, just outside the Hotel Negresco, Duncan met her demise when her own silk scarf became entangled in the wheels of an open-top Bugatti. The dashing driver had been demonstrating the sports car's impressive acceleration when a gust of wind caused her scarf to be sucked into the rear left wheel. This propelled Duncan out of the vehicle into the space between the mudguard and the wheel, severing her spinal column.

I relished my daily morning run along the promenade with other exercise fiends, most of whom were younger and speedier than me. These fitness freaks pounded the pavement, determined to shave off another percentage point of body fat. Cyclists were even more abundant, speeding from one end of the promenade to another, overtaken only by electric scooters racing along the cycle lane. Some agile young skaters glided effortlessly, not with the clunky two-column wheels of our childhood, but with inline wheels that mimicked the grace of ice skates. Some busy mothers often joined in, gracefully skating with their little ones comfortably ensconced in those fashionable three-wheel prams. Life on the promenade unfolded at a brisk pace for these young passengers. Some multi-tasking female hipsters pushed their foot scooters while simultaneously taking care of their overnight emails and early-morning WhatsApp calls. On the other hand, dog owners strolled alongside their canine companions, and a few even carried their furry friends in pouches within their backpacks, heading for the same destination—the pebbly dog beach.

Some Niçois were exercising on the beach itself. Some swam open-water style, a few snorkeled, but most just trod water aimlessly in the tranquil sea. Those who had finished their natation enjoyed the sturdy showers while they watched the occasional hardy woman performing her yoga in isolation on the beach's unyielding pebbles.

Are We There Yet?

Men of Chinese origin were fishing for their lunch with rods and nets in the *Baie des Anges*. It is said that one such angel was the patron saint of Nice, Saint Réparate. This fifteen-year-old Caesarea girl is said to have been beheaded by third-century Palestinians and placed on a raft to be devoured by birds. According to legend, her body arrived untouched in Nice, blown by angels from the Holy Land.

While busy during the day, the promenade came alive at night. Along with the nocturnal exercisers, a broader population was on show. Sure enough, the most significant clusters were couples swaying slowly along the promenade, walking off a few of their evening meal carbs. The promenade is also an outdoor pick-up joint for would-be couples, with small groups of fashionable men seeking a mate from covens of similarly well-attired young women. Youngsters who didn't yet want to pair up congregated in communal circles on the stony beach below, with the more disaffected of them blasting their music to their friends and the rest of the promenaders.

The more reflective promenaders had stopped walking and sat upright on one of the hundreds of blue chairs or benches that overlooked the water. They could hear the lapping of the waves on the shore but could no longer determine the color of the Med, which earlier in the day had been a crystalline turquoise. There were always a few vagrants sprawled on benches; a few seemed full-time, but most looked more likely to be hotelless travelers, judging from their pristine Manchester City tops.

It is apt that this modern-day homeless population used the benches as their beds for the night, as an earlier generation of vagrant people constructed the Promenade des Anglais. The British began coming to Nice around the 1760s, and at that time, the only places for a post-prandial walk were the narrow streets of Vieux Nice.

The Reverend Lewis Way raised money to fund a promenade next to the sea. This money also employed the local vagrant population, whose poverty the English found upsetting. This *Camin dei Anglès* was later widened and extended in the nineteenth and twentieth centuries. Soon, foreigners constructed mansions and hotels along the city's new attraction, and the entire Nice community enjoyed the amenities. When wealthy American tourists arrived in the late nineteenth century, the architectural styles of the buildings broadened, and lifestyle opportunities expanded even further.

Our main pastime in Nice was food shopping. After two years of overprocessed American food, it was a joy to shop in a French supermarket. You have probably seen older women wheel their groceries back from the stores in a fabric food trolley—our apartment had the deluxe model, the Range Rover of its class. While the basic model had only two wheels, our advanced model featured both insulation to keep the food fresh and six wheels, making it easy to lift onto the curb or navigate the rough terrain of Nice's *trottoirs*.

While we enjoyed the supermarket, exploring food products from specialist shops and the local market was far more enjoyable. Our primary shopping destination was the *Marché de la Buffa*, France's oldest covered market, which had seen better days. Built in 1925, it once boasted 125 pitches and stores, making it the largest covered market in Nice. Unfortunately, it was now only about one-eighth occupied. When I inquired about the fate of the hundred or so other businesses that once thrived in the market, our trusted grocer explained that these market traders had retired. This was true but only partially so.

A little research through back editions of *Nice Matin* revealed that the building the market occupied had been purchased from the city in 2008 by a company that wished to convert it into a residential block. This developer had then bought out all but twenty-five businesses. The holdouts demanded higher payments to move, but the acquirer refused. The last decade had seen a stalemate between the owner of the building and the remaining merchants. The owners refused to repair the ground floor infrastructure, and the market traders declined to cooperate with the building owners. Our favored *poissonier* was the leader of the holdouts. From time to time, the Nice government attempted to broker an agreement between the two sides, who were no longer talking to each other.

France's specialist stores elsewhere in Nice also seemed to be in mild decline. You could still find them easily but perhaps not on every street as used to be the case. Nevertheless, independent shops continue to do well in France, unlike the United States, where chain stores dominate the retail landscape.

There are several factors contributing to this phenomenon. To start with, the consumer culture in each country is fundamentally different. American consumers prioritize convenience and lower prices, while French consumers value higher-quality products and personalized service. Next, the business culture in the two countries also varies significantly. The US has a capitalist growth perspective, where successful small businesses often aim to expand and increase profitability through franchising or acquiring new outlets. These American companies focus on improving processes, supply chains, and marketing, leading to the proliferation of large chain stores and making it challenging for smaller independent shops to compete.

In contrast, while French supermarkets follow this US model, many small independent shops are family businesses passed down through generations. Finally, French regulations are designed to support small companies, with stricter zoning, planning, and business licensing requirements that limit the growth of big-box stores. In the US, regulations are typically more laissez-faire.

Like many men, I do not particularly enjoy shopping. I find greater happiness in experiences rather than accumulating more possessions. One shopping experience I have always enjoyed is grocery shopping, where I take pleasure in discovering high-quality products at reasonable prices.

In Nice, I was in my element, scouring various specialist shops and market stalls to find the ingredients for that day's meals. My daily shopping excursion would include visits to the *boulangerie, patisserie, fruteria, poissonerie, and boucherie or charcuterie*. Within just a few days, I began establishing connections with the individuals who regularly served me. Lorna would buy fish from the ringleader, a different type of seafood each day, while I frequented the vegetable and fruit stall run by our partially truthful greengrocer. We gradually gained the trust of this band of renegades. I imagine it would take many years to build a similar rapport with the Aldi checkout person, who skillfully speeds through scanning my purchases.

The local gelateria owner was a master of customer engagement. He was not only an artisan in crafting delicious ice creams but also an expert in charming every customer, regardless of age or gender. In the United States, ice creams are often served quickly, and spending too much time with one customer might mean missing out on potential sales. However, here in France, the role of the server was to cultivate a lasting relationship with each customer, ensuring their return.

His ice creams were not standard fare. The Italian couple ahead of us had already sampled half his extensive selection of hand-crafted creations. He was flirting with them obscenely but without quite ever being obscene. When it was my turn, I expressed interest in trying the pear ice cream, a flavor I had rarely encountered. He described it as *magnifique*, a fusion of pear, ginger, and pepper. While I found the ginger too pronounced, I appreciated the kick from the crushed peppercorns. My wife, who always favors pistachio, found her choice overwhelming—its nuttiness was too intense for her delicate palate. After declining the pear sample, I selected his hazelnut delight; I felt the glacier had sacrificed a thousand hazelnuts for one boule of icy perfection.

The French—outside of Paris, at least—are known for their friendly disposition. While they can be passionate and animated, I generally find them more relaxed compared to Americans. This cultural difference might help explain why American (and British) doctors often prescribe twice as many antidepressants as their French counterparts.

Famously, George W. Bush was once said to have proclaimed that the problem with the French is that they didn't have a word for 'entrepreneur.' This amusing line feeds into our prejudices about both the intellectual rigor of the forty-third president and France's sometimes ambivalent attitude toward capitalism. Regrettably, the British politician Shirley Williams fabricated the entire quote.

However, it does underscore that France operates a different model of capitalism to America. The United States adheres to a purer form of free-market capitalism, resulting in more efficient labor markets where the connection between workers and employers is relatively unimpeded by unions and regulations. One outcome is that hiring and firing American employees is much easier than in most European countries. While this means that there is relatively little genuine job security for most in America, it also fosters an environment where companies can innovate, startup businesses can thrive, and job seekers have a good chance of finding employment.

Most European governments have robust employment regulations that protect those already in work, and, in some cases, these are so stringent that laying off employees becomes nearly impossible. Unfortunately, these same regulations encourage companies to be extremely cautious about hiring. On a macro level, European unemployment rates tend to be about twice that of those in the United States, resulting in a quarter to one-third of Southern European youth being without jobs.

Many Europeans have confidently told me that the US government does not offer welfare. This simply isn't true—in fact, at any one time, one in five Americans receives welfare aid from a federal program. While some welfare elements vary somewhat by state, in most states, someone who has lost their job receives up to six months of unemployment benefits. However, these welfare programs come with time limits, and Americans are expected to seek new employment actively. Except during the most severe recessions, finding a new job tends to be relatively straightforward, which may explain why Americans often appear more nonchalant about being laid off compared to their European counterparts.

Academics have observed a correlation between parents and their children's welfare use, which social scientists label as 'intergenerational welfare dependency.' Despite numerous studies, it is challenging to establish definitively that a parent's welfare status directly causes their children to have a higher likelihood of relying on benefits. External factors are more likely to influence both the parent and child. These factors may include adverse living environments, inherited health issues, diabolical schooling, substance addiction, and involvement in criminal activities.

Many British people believe some families have been unemployed and on benefits for multiple generations. They think this because politicians from different parties have told us so. For example, Prime Minister Tony Blair in 1997 and Work and Pensions Minister Iain Duncan Smith in 2009, among others, told us there were countless families where three or four generations had never worked.

The Joseph Rowntree Foundation attempted to prove these statements. They sought to interview some of these three or four generations of families who had never worked. Of course, proving that something does not exist isn't easy; just because nobody reliable has ever seen an Abominable Snowman doesn't mean that a Yeti doesn't exist. The Labour Force Survey showed that 15,000 British families had experienced long-term unemployment (0.3 percent). This means that three and four generations of idlers must be even rarer. Despite years of research in some of the most impoverished communities in Britain, the Rowntree researchers could not find a single family where nobody had worked for three or four generations. You might question where these politicians get their data from. One wonders if other commonly held views on welfare are also incorrect.

OK, if there aren't three generations of layabouts, surely many benefits are claimed fraudulently? A poll found that the British public believed over a quarter of benefits were fraudulent. According to the Department for Work and Pensions, the number is likely around £2 billion, less than 3 percent of welfare spending.

If generations of malingerers don't exist, and there is little fraud, some say that migrants come to the UK because we are a soft touch and pay far more in benefits than elsewhere in Europe. This is also untrue. In reality, the UK's spending on benefits is approximately in line with the EU average. In fact, it is about 12 percent lower than France's, the country from which most migrants cross into the UK.

If there aren't three generations of deadbeats as idle as sloths on a Sunday afternoon, no widespread fraud, and UK benefits aren't stupidly generous, there must be loads of mums on benefits with dozens of children, all of whom have different fathers. In 2011, there were only 130 families claiming benefits with more than ten children. Indeed, only 8 percent had three or more kids.

OK, no multiple generations of ne'er-do-wells, relatively low levels of fraud, EU average benefit payments, very few mums popping out sprogs every five minutes, there must be people with large families claiming over £100,000 housing benefits per year. Finally, we have found something that is true. There are five such families in the UK.

The concern in all countries is that welfare payments may weaken work incentives and create an underclass. While this is potentially true in some cases, many other analyses also suggest that when families receive predictable support for more extended periods, it can lead to better outcomes for their children and increase the likelihood of breaking the cycle of poverty.

So, how does the United States compare in terms of intergenerational welfare dependency? It's approximately twice as high as the European average, with discrimination and lack of access to quality education as the main challenges for poor Americans.

Turning to regulation, one historical economic advantage American companies have held over their European counterparts is lower levels of regulation. While American regulations are not flawless, they tend to place fewer burdens on businesses than those within the European Union. In the US, most states tend to adopt business-friendly regulatory approaches, while Europe typically places a stronger emphasis on consumer and societal protection.

Obviously, some regulation is necessary. It defends public health, provides a structure that encourages competition, and protects the environment. However, over-regulation also dampens economic growth. For instance, it is believed that part of Europe's relative economic decline is caused by overregulation by the European Union, implemented by politicians who often lack a business background. The US may now be heading in the same direction, albeit from a much lower starting point. The number of federal regulations has doubled in the last fifty years, and in

Are We There Yet?

2021, American federal, state, and city governments introduced a staggering twelve thousand new business regulations.

Another dampener on economic growth is taxation. Although on an upward trend in the US, Government expenditure in America is much smaller than in any other industrial country. The US spends 37 percent of its GDP on federal, state, and local government, a figure that has increased steadily since the end of World War II. However, the comparative figure in France is 57 percent, the highest in Europe.

This higher level of government spending in France implies a reduction in work incentives. So, maybe one of the reasons US productivity is more elevated than France's is because Americans have extra incentives to work harder.

One area of the economy seldom associated with productivity is the public sector. In his inaugural address, US President Ronald Reagan struck a chord with Americans when he declared, "Government is not the solution to our problem; government is the problem." In a later news conference, he elaborated on this by stating, "The nine most terrifying words in the English language are: 'I'm from the Government, and I'm here to help.'"

These quotes may come across as provocative to some Europeans, many of whom have a touching attachment to the role and competence of government, often leaning towards the idea that government should assume greater control as the default response to any problem.

However, you don't have to be Ayn Rand to question whether the government has the skills to manage multiple complicated projects in a complex world. In most of the free world, the press bombards us with data about the government's lack of competence. Scarcely a day passes without reports of bureaucratic incompetence, overspending, missed targets, and political dithering that permits the continuation of programs that self-evidently offer poor value for money. Indeed, we are surprised when something goes well, such as a Covid vaccination program.

Obviously, the people who work in government are not inherently incompetent. Having spent many years in the public sector, I can attest that I encountered mostly intelligent and dedicated professionals. However, we should acknowledge the substantial influences that can constrain the capabilities of government entities.

First and foremost, these government enterprises typically enjoy a monopoly in what they do, which can lead to complacency and a lack of innovation. Without the threat of competition, there is often a low incentive to provide better services and improve efficiency.

Secondly, government entities are subject to the shifting priorities of politicians, irrespective of their political affiliations. This can result in a consistent emphasis on short-term political objectives over long-term economic goals. Furthermore, government agencies tend to develop highly bureaucratic structures to navigate the complexities of these political whims. While bureaucracy can provide stability, it often hinders agility, resulting in slow decision-making processes and operational inefficiencies.

Lastly, government workers do not usually have the same incentives to achieve their goals as their private-sector counterparts. As a result, poor performers are often tolerated, and strong performers are not adequately motivated.

France has more fully- or partly-owned state enterprises than any other Western country. The French government essentially controls a wide range of sectors, including energy production, railways, transportation infrastructure, major airlines such as Air France and KLM, healthcare, automobile manufacturing, telecommunications, postal services, universities, public broadcasting, as well as the defense and aerospace industries.

This ownership model is closer to China than the USA, where very few large business entities are permanently owned or controlled by the US Government. The two American enterprises best known for being federally run are the Post Office and Veteran Affairs, neither of which enjoys a good reputation. I wrote about the Post Office in my previous book. Unfortunately, even though I still appreciate its convenient service and my daily interaction with the mail carrier, its financial performance remains as lucrative as a squirrel's retirement plan.

The Department of Veterans Affairs (VA) provides health care, loans, and education to eligible military veterans and their families. Non-Americans—and many Americans, as well—often lament that the US lacks a centralized, integrated healthcare system like every other developed country. However, this isn't entirely accurate, as the VA offers healthcare services to approximately twenty million veterans via a nationwide system of hospitals, medical centers, and clinics. Additionally, there is a second centralized healthcare system, the Indian Health Service, which covers around 2.6 million Native Americans.

Are We There Yet?

Unfortunately, the government-run VA has a historically poor reputation. Despite being free for many and significantly cheaper for all, two out of every three eligible veterans choose not to use the service. Instead, they prefer to pay more for their own private insurance. This choice is often driven by excessive red tape, inconvenient locations, and long wait times.

The VA's competence is held in such low regard that it often becomes a topic of discussion during presidential elections. Regular reports highlight issues such as excessive spending, inadequate healthcare, and a revolving door of leadership, with ten heads in the last thirty years.

There have been efforts to enhance the performance and efficiency of the VA in the last decade, including a recent doubling in annual funding to $325 billion. To provide some context for this funding, it's worth noting that the VA's healthcare budget is only 40 percent less than the total healthcare budget for the UK, despite serving fewer than one-seventh of the UK's population. However, with VA hospitals facing a shortage of forty thousand doctors and nurses, work is still needed to ensure veterans receive the timely and high-quality care they deserve. With the United States engaged in endless conflicts, the demand for VA services is on the rise, not declining.

In any case, comparing VA outcomes with those of privately insured individuals may be unwise. This is because the VA serves a challenging customer base, many of whom face complex mental and physical health issues resulting from their military service. For instance, an alarming statistic reveals that twenty US veterans commit suicide daily—that's seventy-nine thousand over the past twelve years. Interestingly, the vast majority of sixty-nine separate studies that have attempted to adjust for similar patient bases have shown that the VA performs as well as or better than the American private sector in terms of safety, effectiveness, and efficiency. These studies challenge the view held by many Americans that government healthcare does not work.

****

Nice is a blend of older Italian architecture and newer Parisian-style buildings, reflecting its history as a predominantly Italian city until 1860. The Greeks were the first to establish a settlement here; they called it Nikaia, after the goddess Nike, the deity of plimsolls. During the Middle Ages, Nizza was part of the Germanic Lombard Kingdom of Northern

Italy, but, by the fourteenth century, it had become part of the Kingdom of Sardinia under the rule of the House of Savoy. Then, in 1860, France annexed Nice under the Treaty of Turin after a referendum as dodgy a vegetarian's review of a steakhouse. This annexation was the price Italy paid to France for protection against the Austrians. Despite some irredentism from Garibaldi and others, the Niçois were compelled to adopt the French language, and their Ligurian dialect, Nissa, became a relic of history.

Nice has since remained French, except for a brief period of occupation by the Italians and, subsequently, the Germans during World War II. American paratroopers and local resistance fighters finally liberated Nice in August 1944, and, as a tribute, a portion of the *Promenade des Anglais* was renamed *Le Quai des Etats-Unis*.

To bring us up to date, Nice has experienced decades of economic growth since the war, primarily under the corrupt mayoralties of father and son Jean and Jacques Médecin. As a result, Nice is now France's fifth-largest city and second-most visited by tourists.

I had curated a list of museums and sites on the *Côte d'Azur* for us to visit, with roughly one activity planned daily. Our initial area of focus was Nice's charming old town, *Vieux Nice*. Reflecting its rich Italian and French histories, Nice offers a remarkable mélange of architecture, food, and culture from these two countries. Within the medieval walls, you'll find two distinct areas: the first retains its Greek and medieval character, while the second consists of sixteenth-century terracotta buildings that dominate narrow, winding alleyways. As with many old towns, *Vieux Nice* is a joyful place to wander. While the daily market street of *Cours Saleya* is now geared mainly toward tourists, you can still purchase vegetables and flowers here if you don't mind the slightly elevated prices. The nineteenth-century neoclassical *Opéra de Nice*, inspired by Milan's *La Scala*, offers a more authentic glimpse into the city's cultural heritage.

The old town also houses the sixteenth-century Jewish ghetto, one of the oldest in Europe. We joined a walking tour of the synagogue and surrounding area and learned about the historical confinement of Jewish people within this walled area by the Duke of Savoy. Interestingly, this was often against the wishes of the local Niçois, who clandestinely dug passageways under buildings, enabling the internees to bypass the guarded gates and move freely throughout the city. Several centuries later, however, many *Niçois* collaborated with Nazis to deport some four thousand Jewish people to concentration camps. Very few of those deported survived the war.

Any penitent collaborators could have sought subsequent absolution from priests in Nice's seventeenth-century, pink Baroque cathedral dedicated to Saint Réparate. Had they done so, they would have marveled at the church's marbled sculptures and intricate stained-glass windows and departed from the church—suitably absolved of all sin—to enjoy the vibrant cafés of *Place Rossetti*.

In *Vieux Nice*, the open spaces feature several unique structures. Above the checkered pavement of *Place Masséna*, seven ten-foot Buddhas, each representing one of the seven continents and symbolizing peace and harmony, gracefully tower over the square on lotus-flowered plinths. These plazas also feature abundant water features, designed on the dried-up and covered-over riverbed, making them perfect for toddlers to enjoy on a summer day. Notably, *Place Masséna* hosts the Sun Fountain, adorned with impressive nude Greek statues with equally impressive manhoods that once sparked protests among the conservative women of Nice. Their objections prompted the city government to make adjustments, leading the disgruntled sculptor to delicately reduce the statues' offending members' size.

At precisely midday, a cannon shot booms over *Vieux Nice*. The story behind this tradition is both a curious anecdote and illustrative of British influence in Nice at that time. Sir Thomas Coventry, inappropriately from Scotland, had become frustrated by his wife's lack of punctuality for lunch. So he asked the Nice mayor for a cannon to be fired at noon to remind his wife that she should join him for lunch as was the custom in his home Scottish village. When Sir Thomas returned to Scotland many years later, he took the cannon with him. By then, the Niçois were so used to the midday alarm that they asked the city to continue the tradition. One midday, when we were in *Vieux Nice*, the cannon resounded in its customary fashion, and a young blonde tourist next to me leaped like a startled butterfly, shredding her mortal shroud in an instant.

A street musician was playing the theme from *The Third Man* on a Zimmer outside the Société Générale Bank in Avenue Jean Médecin, the site of a famed heist in the seventies. Former special services officer turned portrait photographer Albert Spaggiari tunneled into the bank vault from the sewers below with twenty Marseille associates. The robbery was meticulously planned. For instance, Spaggiari had planted an alarm clock inside his safety deposit box to test if there were any seismic detection alarms inside the vault.

The burrowing was arduous; the men spent two months waist-deep in human excrement, with the proceeds from the digging in their pockets, *Great Escape* style. The men scrubbed themselves clean with massive quantities of bubble bath every evening.

After two months of excavating twenty-six-foot upward, the men finally broke into the vault during the three-day Bastille Day weekend in 1976. They had welded the vault door shut from the inside, and in true French fashion, they celebrated with a picnic featuring pâté, baguettes, and red wine. Over the weekend, the gang emptied 371 safety deposit boxes before making their getaway early Monday morning, carrying an estimated €29 million in cash and valuables. When the police eventually opened the vault, they found the words, "*Sans armes, ni haine, ni violence*" painted on the wall.

Unfortunately, one of Spaggiari's accomplices foolishly abandoned his wife soon after the heist. In revenge, she ratted the gang out to the police.

Spaggiari's trial was held in a stiflingly hot second-floor courtroom. Spaggiari asked the judge to open the window for some air. While the judge was distracted by a fictitious, coded document, Spaggiare hurled himself out of the window, breaking his leg on the car roof below. He hobbled onto a waiting motorcycle while waving at the gaping judge and attorneys. Spaggiari escaped to Argentina, and the heist proceeds were never recovered.

We visited everything on the list in Nice. We sounded out hundreds of musical instruments at the Baroque Palais Lascaris, clambered up the walls of the ruined *Colline du Château* for the best panoramic view of the city, marveled at the botanical gardens, birds, and insects of Parc Phoenix, and wondered at the region's flora and fauna in the Museum of Natural History.

In the late nineteenth and early twentieth centuries, Nice was a magnet for art and literature. Nietzche wrote *Thus Spoke Zarathustra* here, and Chekhov completed *Three Sisters*. Meanwhile, Chagall, Dufy, Matisse, Picasso, and countless other painters enjoyed Nice's soft light.

We devoured much of this art at eight separate museums. These galleries ignited our imaginations, stirred our souls, and softened our default detached cynicism. Each stroke of the brush, every sculpted form, and carefully constructed installation seemed to breathe with life, evoking feelings that simple words struggled to capture. The walls became our teachers, educating us on historical events and the culture of our ancestors.

After all that introspection and contemplation, we often found ourselves as hungry as wolves at a sheep convention. Fortunately, Nice is renowned for its fresh cuisine. One of Lorna's favorite dishes is *Salade Niçoise*. In Nissarde cuisine, this dish typically includes tomatoes, olives, tuna, anchovies, and hard-boiled eggs, all generously dressed with an olive oil-based vinaigrette. You can enjoy this specialty on a plate or tucked inside a round, crusty bap as a *Pan Bagnat* sandwich. However, Lorna still preferred the Anglicized version of this dish, which included added potatoes and green beans. Nice also offers culinary delights such as *Pissaladière*, a flavorful pesto soup, and Ratatouille—a delightful medley of tomatoes, eggplant, zucchini, peppers, and onions—all of which originate from this vibrant city.

However, as with many other great cuisines, Nice has borrowed popular dishes from elsewhere and claimed them as its own. *Moules marinières*, probably Belgian and ideally served with French fries, is another of Lorna's favorites. *Socca*, a beloved street food in Nice with roots in Genoa, is a humongous charcoal-grilled pancake made from ground chickpea flour and olive oil. Its crispy outside contrasts with its creamy interior. As Stoppard might say, "We ate well in Nice, though not necessarily skillfully."

****

With the notable exception of Marseille, the South leans to the right in French politics. This inclination can be traced back to the end of the Algerian War in 1962 when 700,000 French-settling *Pieds-Noirs* returned from Algeria, deeply disillusioned with the French Government for capitulating. Many of these settlers chose to establish new roots in the South of France. Similar to Florida in the United States, this tendency toward right-wing thinking is further accentuated by a climate that attracts senior citizens, who are likelier to hold conservative views.

Although the French have numerous political parties, the Presidency was traditionally held by one of the two main blocs: Socialists or Republicans. However, with both main groups as popular as a clown at a funeral, centrist Emmanuel Macron disrupted this two-party system in 2017 with his hastily improvised '*En Marche!*' political party. This significant shift has given the radical right hope that they can gain national power.

Le Front National, a nationalist party focused on promoting traditional French values and opposing immigration, was founded by Jean-Marie Le Pen in the seventies. It has since been rebranded as *Rassemblement National* to appeal to a broader electorate beyond the working class, and it is now led by his estranged daughter, Marine Le Pen. With both traditional political blocs still unpopular, she has been the main opposition to Macron in the two most recent presidential elections. She was trounced in the 2017 election (66-34 percent) and experienced another convincing loss in the final-round 2022 election (59-41 percent).

Le Front National built its support base in the right-leaning South of France, winning power first in mostly rural Southern towns and then the Provence-Alpes-Cote d'Azur region. Other right-of-center parties have also performed well in the area.

Extremism is rising, and France has been significantly affected by major terrorist incidents in recent years. In January 2015, the Charlie Hebdo attack occurred, where Islamist gunmen murdered twelve office workers at a satirical magazine. In November later that year, a series of coordinated terrorist attacks took place in Paris, resulting in the loss of 130 lives.

On Bastille Day in 2016, a Tunisian truck driver drove into crowds on Nice's *Promenade des Anglais*, resulting in the tragic deaths of eighty-four people. His truck traveled for a mile, mowing down revelers until police apprehended and killed him. Since then, numerous terrorist attacks and beheadings committed on French soil have made terrorism and immigration key election issues.

In pursuit of a colorblind republic, it is illegal for the French to gather information about a person's ethnicity, race, or religion. France enshrined this principle in their constitution after Vichy France had used government data to identify and deport Jewish people to concentration and extermination camps. As a result, we do not have precise data on the number of Muslims living in France. Estimates vary between four and six million.

While it is a noble and sometimes liberating concept to declare that every citizen is simply French, the lack of data also conceals the likely extent of discrimination against Muslims in employment, housing, and welfare provision. In practice, it is straightforward, if inadvisable, to visit a Parisian suburban group of tower blocks. Here, most residents have

North African origins, unemployment is prevalent, and economic hardship is pervasive.

Unsurprisingly, this situation creates a fertile recruiting ground for radical Islamists. Like some other European countries, France has a problem with radicalization. For instance, two thousand French citizens chose to join jihadists in Syria, which is twice the number from the UK.

While many Americans believe the United States is disintegrating, the French have a more profound sense of pessimism about their country. Opinion polls indicate that three-quarters of them believe France is falling apart, and nearly half believe it is on the verge of civil war. There is an undeniable sense of unease among the citizens of France.

Some of this is partially self-inflicted. In my lifetime, the French have been known for belligerent resistance to any changes in their rights. In a typical year, French farmers block roads or set fire to British agricultural trucks, French air traffic controllers ground all aircraft, and the railways cease operation. The French strike as much as a clock with a grudge against time, more than seven times as often as other Europeans.

While in Nice, we witnessed protests against mask-wearing, the Algerian war (which ended over sixty years ago), and the proposed raising of the pension age. This latter topic has been a matter of conflict in France for over four decades.

France allocates nearly a third of its GDP to welfare, with almost half of that expenditure dedicated to pensions. President Emmanuel Macron has proposed raising the retirement age from 62 to 64, a move met with resistance and ongoing national strikes, as over two-thirds of the French population oppose this change. Nevertheless, French demographics make this change a manifest necessity, as France is aging rapidly. A healthy worker-to-pensioner ratio is typically between 3 and 4. Currently, in France, it stands at 1.7, and if no action is taken, it is projected to decline further to 1.3 by mid-century.

Oddly, the retirement age used to be 65 in the early eighties until President François Mitterand lowered it to 60. His successor, Jacques Chirac, failed to raise the pension age against the backdrop of paralyzing strikes in 1995, but in 2010, President Nicolas Sarkozy resisted renewed protests and increased the retirement age to 62.

Britain thinks of itself as having a 'Special Relationship' with the US. However, the original American special relationship was with France.

Early French settlers integrated quickly into American society, bringing their farming methods, cuisine, and etiquette into the emerging American culture. In 1778, Benjamin Franklin met Voltaire, resulting in crucial treaties that established France as America's first ally. This pivotal alliance led to France providing essential funding to the newly independent USA during the War of Independence, with many of its military leaders actively supporting the United States in battle.

After the war, the two countries remained close, and France continued to help the new country. For instance, French-born artist Pierre L'Enfant was the architect of the new nation's capital, Washington, DC.

French influence has endured in various ways. For instance, Thomas Jefferson deeply appreciated the French dish mac' n' cheese, even serving it at a state dinner in 1802. Today, this culinary delight is immensely popular in the United States, with a staggering two million boxes—yes, they are indeed sold in boxes—being purchased daily.

Amity between the two countries deteriorated after the French Revolution when France's primary interests were focused on the European continent. When Founding Father John Jay negotiated a trade agreement with Britain in 1794, it upset the French. Their navy began attacking American merchant vessels, leading to a *de facto* state of war between the two nations. France's euro-focus deepened when France sold off most of its American territory in 1803 with the Louisiana Purchase, further distancing the special relationship between the two countries.

Nevertheless, French people continued to immigrate to the US. Approximately half a million came directly from France, and an additional one million arrived from French Canada during the second half of the nineteenth and early twentieth centuries. Due to the high birth rate of those amorous French Canadians, more than ten million American citizens today claim French ancestry, primarily in Louisiana and New England. Surprisingly, 1.3 million Americans still speak French at home, with an additional three-quarters of a million speaking Creole, a language derived from French.

The French 'special relationship' has, undeniably, experienced many rocky patches over the years. Although the Americans liberated France in World War II, President De Gaulle opposed much subsequent anglosphere policy, including France's withdrawal from NATO in 1966.

Are We There Yet?

Moreover, the French have shown admirable resistance to 'coca-colonization,' not just in terms of Coca-Cola but also regarding many aspects of American culture. As a result, American cultural influence has spread more slowly in France than in other Western European countries.

****

In the last book, I pointed out that the combined market capitalization of the largest one hundred publicly listed companies on the UK stock exchange was less than the largest US company, Apple. However, despite a significant decline in the value of all tech companies, I have to report that another giant, Microsoft, is set to surpass the total worth of the UK's top 100 companies. This issue isn't limited to the UK alone; Apple also exceeds the combined market capitalization of the top 100 companies in France and Germany.

This did not happen suddenly. In 1984, a young Californian executive told a French TV interviewer that governments made poor investors and entrepreneurs need to be given a second chance if they failed. The interviewer, skeptical of this view, scoffed and listed several highly successful French companies. Unfortunately, since this time, European companies have generally faltered. Ironically, the company founded by that young executive, Steve Jobs, has thrived.

In the eighties, Europe accounted for 30 percent of global GDP. Today, that figure has dwindled to less than 17 percent, with Asia and the US claiming larger shares. This decline has, if anything, accelerated since the turn of the century when Western Europe boasted forty-one of the world's hundred most valuable companies. Two decades later, that number has shrunk to just fifteen. While Chinese companies have gained ground, the USA has seen the most significant growth, now boasting sixty-one of the top hundred.

Europe has struggled to establish globally competitive technology companies. Not too long ago, the continent boasted several technology giants. Consumers might have owned Finnish Nokia phones, Dutch Philips TVs, or German Siemens dishwashers. However, European consumer electronics hardware companies are nearly non-existent in today's landscape. No notable European companies manufacture PCs, gaming consoles, smartphones, TVs, cameras, drones, or hardware for mass-market Virtual or Augmented Reality.

European companies have also struggled in the services and software sectors. The global infrastructure for cloud computing and content distribution is dominated by American companies, except for China, where Chinese companies lead. Similarly, the platform layer that enables software, such as operating systems, search engines, app stores, web browsers, and social media platforms, is predominantly American or Chinese.

European success stories are mostly limited to the application level, where a deep understanding of cultural behavior often plays a significant role. However, apart from the notable exception of Sweden's Spotify, most European companies offer single-product, often single-country solutions. For many European tech startups, the realistic ambition is to be acquired by one of the large American tech giants.

What about technology companies of the future? If we look at the number of unicorns—private startups valued at more than $1 billion—the US has 704, China 243, and India 85 unicorns. The first-placed European country is the no-longer EU member, the UK, with 56 unicorns. France and Germany have twenty-something, while the other European countries have fewer than ten each.

The obvious question is, why is this so?

First, despite Europe having roughly twice the population of the US, it remains a highly fragmented market, with each country having its own languages, rules, and customs. Achieving critical mass can be faster in the homogenized markets of the US or China.

Second, European governments impose more stringent regulations, including higher taxes, fewer incentives, stricter labor laws, tighter privacy rules, and more bureaucratic red tape.

Third, European startups often face challenges in raising capital for growth. In Silicon Valley, a robust ecosystem of support services helps propel companies to their next growth stage.

Fourth, American culture fosters greater support for technological innovation. American tech companies are generally more willing to take significant risks, understanding that failure can be a prelude to eventual success. Conversely, Europe sometimes exhibits a cultural aversion to risk-taking and entrepreneurship, with a tendency to focus on the potential negative aspects of new technology.

Finally, and likely linked to the previous four challenges, Europe experiences a significant brain drain of engineers and technology entrepreneurs to the United States. As an example, at a recent US Artificial

Intelligence conference, two-thirds of the speakers were first-generation US immigrants.

If there's a silver lining to Europe not having technology giants, it's that it is politically easier to introduce stringent regulations, since they don't significantly impact home-grown companies. Therefore, regulation is the one area where Europe leads the world in technology.

In contrast, America's more laissez-faire approach to regulation empowers US technology companies to disrupt existing processes and business models. Take the taxi business, for instance, where innovations in mapping and other technologies enabled Uber and Lyft to introduce a popular new service that disrupted the traditional industry. The absence of new regulations and the selective enforcement of existing rules in the US allowed these companies to grow quickly. As a result, some European countries and cities have protected their local taxi industries, leaving only the low-revenue micromobility industry as one of the few opportunities for European startups.

Many of Europe's largest companies are entrenched in traditional industries. I occasionally hear European politicians express the belief that Europe can maintain dominance in sectors such as banking, car manufacturing, energy, utilities, and consumer goods. I fear this is myopically incorrect. It's widely acknowledged that technology is the primary driver of economic growth, and as new technology infiltrates every industry, the old sectors are bound to undergo substantial disruption, leading to a probable decline in European companies' prominence. In fact, we are already witnessing this trend, with numerous European companies experiencing significantly slower revenue growth compared to their American counterparts.

At the time of writing, the US had well over a hundred companies with a market capitalization of over $100 billion. France has only six such mega-companies, the largest four of which are fashion houses.

This European underperformance is a tragedy with far-reaching implications. It's terrible news for consumers who need more alternatives to the mega American technology companies. It's a calamity for Europe, which will likely secure an even smaller share of the world's GDP. But perhaps most significantly, it could be a catastrophe for young Europeans.

In many parts of Europe, many young people will likely face challenges in finding well-paying jobs that enable them to afford homes and start families. The underlying problem lies in Europe's tendency to prioritize preserving social benefits for its aging population over fostering innovation and economic growth. Consequently, Europe risks becoming primarily an open-air museum for Americans and Asians, where European youth serve as tour guides, hoteliers, and servers.

In the meantime, the real battle for commercial and technological dominance will be between America and China, with no other country or blocs of nations even in the picture.

A decade ago, the prevailing belief was that China's success primarily came from copying technologies from other sources and creating low-value technological solutions. It was widely believed that the Chinese had limited commercial innovation capabilities, relied heavily on foreign technology, and would face high license fees and a talent exodus.

I must confess that I believed in this idea for a while, perhaps because I wanted it to be true. Before living in Hong Kong, it aligned with my experience of Chinese products and people. However, the Chinese themselves were more self-aware, acknowledging the limitations of their education system and recognizing the need for a different set of behaviors to achieve long-term economic success.

I remember when Daughter #1 and I teamed up with three Chinese college students to take on a Shanghai escape-room challenge. It was an interesting experience, and it would have made for fascinating psychological observation, not just because of my daughter's then-unconventional teamwork skills.

First, there was a language barrier. I spoke very little Chinese, so communication between my daughter, the Chinese students, and me was a mix of basic Mandarin and English. Second, it became evident that the Chinese students had never played an escape-room game before, and their education didn't seem to emphasize lateral thinking. For those unfamiliar with escape rooms, the goal is to work as a team to solve cryptic puzzles, often involving opening combination locks, to escape from a room.

When we proposed a solution, one of the Chinese students would invariably respond by saying they would never attempt such a thing in China. Yet, when we went ahead and tried our solution anyway, it often worked, leaving our Chinese teammates utterly bewildered. I'm confident that if we had relied solely on their approach, we would probably still be stuck in that room.

However, the more I learned about China, the more I revised my view. During a tour of Peking University in Beijing in 2010, I was amazed to discover that China graduated nearly five million students annually with degrees in Science, Technology, Engineering, or Math (STEM). This number was five times higher than that of the US and a staggering forty times more than France or the UK.

What was inescapable (apart from rooms with combination locks) was that ethnic Chinese communities in all of Asia displayed remarkable entrepreneurial spirit and achieved impressive success. Additionally, Chinese-made technology products were gaining recognition on a global scale, earning accolades for their innovation. What struck me most was that the Chinese individuals I collaborated with possessed the same level of creativity as anyone else; they simply hadn't been encouraged to innovate until then.

So what had changed?

In the last decade, China has transitioned from imitator to innovator, taking the lead in the most advanced technologies. According to the Australian Strategic Policy Institute, China and the US rank first or second in all 44 'new technologies,' with China leading in 37 of them. Notably, there was a substantial gap between these two countries and the rest of the list in each new technology category.

In 2010, the Information Technology and Innovation Foundation (ITIF) estimated that China's technology capabilities were 58 percent of those of the US. In ten years, this gap has closed to 75 percent. Perhaps these capabilities will be almost equal by 2030. One metric that might suggest this has already happened is the number of new patent applications, where China has 40 percent of the global total, twice that of the US.

So, what has propelled China's remarkable momentum? How has this nation, which in the eighties had over 95 percent of its population living in abject poverty on less than $2 per day, become a commercial superpower so swiftly? The answer is multifaceted.

First, the Chinese government has the authority to shape industrial policy through its five-year plan mechanism in a much more coordinated manner than any Western country. They have invested billions of dollars in research and development and subsidized their technology industry. This system has some advantages over those driven solely by short-term opinion polls. While some strategic mistakes have been made, they have gotten more right than wrong.

Secondly, as of the end of 2022, China has the world's largest population. Its burgeoning middle-class demographic is a massive domestic market for technology companies to tap into. Once these successful companies have established success in their home market, they can expand their reach to customers in other countries.

Thirdly, as already noted, China has a large pool of STEM workers and a culture of entrepreneurship and hard work. This combination of expertise and work ethic is ideal for fast-growing startups and companies.

Fourthly, Chinese technology companies have excelled in establishing strategic partnerships or buying foreign companies or skillsets to acquire capabilities they don't possess.

So, China now boasts technology mega-companies that can rival American giants. Tencent, a social network and provider of almost any app, boasts over a billion users and a market capitalization greater than Facebook. Alibaba, often described as a combination of Amazon, PayPal, Twitter, and YouTube, operates in 200 countries. Huawei dominates the telecom market, selling more phones than any other company and providing telecom infrastructure in 170 countries. Baidu serves as China's default search and mapping engine, and Xiaomi is a prominent consumer electronics manufacturer.

These Chinese companies and many others are going global and competing successfully. The West may ban them from operating in their markets as some have with Huawei and as they look likely to do with TikTok. However, these companies will likely be the giants where they are allowed to compete.

The fourth industrial revolution is upon us, marked by a convergence of technologies such as Artificial Intelligence, Big Data, 5G telecommunications, nano- and biotechnologies, robotics, blockchain, the Internet of Things, and possibly even quantum computing. This revolution is poised to reshape the world, just as the first industrial revolution propelled Britain to global dominance and dramatically increased productivity. Artificial Intelligence is likely the primary battleground, with companies that master it gaining a competitive edge, much like their predecessors did in the first industrial revolution. There will be an almighty battle for pre-eminence between Chinese and American companies, with other nations likely needing to align with one of these giants.

****

We caught the bus to the Cimiez area of Nice, situated high in the hills above the city. This community was once a favored winter destination for

Are We There Yet?

the British upper class and continues to be an affluent neighborhood. Modern apartment blocks now stand in the former gardens of the once-grand Belle Époque palaces. Despite the transformations, remnants of the nineteenth-century British influence remain visible, including grassy fields that were used for croquet and tennis.

Our initial destination was the Franciscan monastery. Before visiting this museum, I was confused about the various Catholic religious orders. While I knew they all embraced vows of chastity, poverty, and obedience, I hadn't delved into the specifics of their histories. This museum provided a comprehensive explanation, albeit primarily in French.

Son of a wealthy merchant, St. Francis of Assisi founded the Franciscan order in 1209 with the approval of Pope Innocent III. Today, they are the largest religious order and perhaps the most evangelical. These friars and sisters take a vow of poverty and work primarily with the poor. If you see a friar or nun in a leper colony, it will likely be a Franciscan. They wear a uniform of a brown, coarse woolen tunic, a white corded rope around the waist, and open-toed sandals. However, in Britain, their tunic was gray, which is why they were called Grey Friars. There are cloistered sisters in this order, too, known sometimes as 'Poor Clares.'

The museum explained the other major Christian orders. The *Dominicans*, sometimes called the Franciscan Irish Twins, were formed a decade later. Their purpose is to preach in parishes and schools. The Society of Jesus—or *Jesuits* as they are better known—was founded to bring educational rigor to the church. Finally, the *Benedictines* are a monastic community. Their goal is to ascend to heaven through hard work and prayer. If you have heard singing at a monastery, Benedictines probably provide this communal liturgy.

While the Franciscans may maintain tidy minds, their gardens were surprisingly unkempt. Nevertheless, these gardens provide breathtaking views over the city. True to her nature, Lorna was as eager as a squirrel at an acorn convention to visit the labyrinthian Cimiez cemetery adjacent to the monastery. At first, it appeared small, with sepulchers, crypts, tombs, and graves crammed next to and on top of each other. However, around every corner, we discovered another array of monuments for the deceased, including the tombs of Nice artists Raoul Dufy and Henri Matisse.

Invigorated by our tour of Matisse's final resting place, we ventured to the former law clerk's museum, accompanied by a group of enthusiastic French schoolchildren. At the tender age of twenty, Matisse's mother gifted him a set of art supplies to aid his recovery from appendicitis, and thus began his lifelong passion for painting. The museum is situated in one of the many seventeenth-century villas adopted by British winterers on the prime real estate of the city hills. This museum, plus the nearby *Chapelle du Rosaire de Vence*, are the world's only places dedicated to the work of modern-art influencer Henri Matisse.

While we enjoyed the Matisse collection, we preferred an exhibition of the work of his youngest son, Pierre. Peculiarly, this did not feature any of Pierre Matisse's own art. Although Pierre Matisse founded one of the lesser-known '–isms,' emotionalism, he was better known for his work as an art dealer acting as a go-between for European artists and American buyers. Therefore, this exhibition focused on his collections for those he represented, including Picasso, Miró, Chagall, Giacometti, Derain, Le Corbusier, and his father.

The final destination of that day was the second-century Roman amphitheater in the *Jardins de Cimiez*, which once held gladiatorial contests in front of five thousand spectators. Its weathered stones stood as silent witnesses to the whispered secrets of gladiators and the thunderous applause of a long-vanished crowd.

Elsewhere in the park, beneath the azure sky, weathered Niçois gentlemen had discovered their ideal haven for a spirited game of boules. With the lush gardens, ancient Roman remnants, the charming cityscape of Nice, and the sparkling Mediterranean as their backdrop, it was a scene straight from a postcard.

****

On another day, it was early, and the view over neighboring Villefranche from the bus as we crossed the hill was exceptional. The sunshine shimmered off the Med and glistened like stars in the sky. It was the type of view that made you realize that those impressionists and post-impressionists were spot-on in how they saw the world. This small town was idyllic without its regular thousands of cruise ship day-trippers, and the mid-September temperature was already touching 80°F as we breakfasted at a port cafe.

There was a hive of quotidian activity in the port. Tethered fishing boats and leisure speedboats bobbled up and down and swayed starboard and port on the lapping waves. A sun-kissed beach bum-ette paddle-boarded her way out to an anchored craft while a bronzed, ponytailed god of a man prepared rental boats for eager adventurers.

Are We There Yet?

A tiny three-wheeled van delivered crates of Orangina while a larger vehicle transported cases of beer. An overweight, perspiring man arrived in a substantial truck, unloading stacks of Coca-Cola bottles. Amidst the commotion, a tiny Pomeranian wandered off its leash, scavenging for any crumbs carelessly dropped by diners. Fortunately, Lorna had ordered a baguette and jam, and the dog spent some quality time beneath our table, eagerly cleaning up after her.

Some early-rising sun-seekers, skin still shriveled from the previous week's scorching sun, made their way toward the beach. It wouldn't be long before the small sandy cove was crowded with fellow sun worshippers. On one of the docks, a young woman, dressed in black shorts, black sunglasses, and a black t-shirt, her sunburned skin only slightly lighter, engaged in her morning exercises. She lifted weights, lunged, and stretched, capturing my furtive interest. On the other hand, my wife probably longed for a bare-chested Tony Curtis lookalike tending to his nets on the rocky shore.

High above the town, a train approached Italy over monumental viaducts. I selected a chocolate milkshake from the menu while Lorna drank her second cappuccino. Finally, I settled down with my daily *Nice Matin* while Lorna responded to emails. This was the South of France at its best. We liked our apartment in Nice, but, in these no-cruise-boat times, Villefranche had suddenly become irresistible.

On another day, we traveled by tram and train to the nearby beach community of Antibes. Lorna had her wallet stolen, so we spent much time there attempting to contact numerous banks. The reality is that the thieves would have taken the cash from her purse and then thrown the wallet into a nearby garbage can. It took an eternity to contact each bank and cancel each card. It's as if they had never had such a call before.

We visited Antibes's Picasso Museum, one of eight devoted to his work in Europe. Picasso once said, "Give me a museum, and I'll fill it up." He seemed to live up to it, and it is estimated that Picasso produced almost one-hundred-and-fifty-thousand pieces of art in his ninety-one years.

Upon his death, Picasso left behind an astonishing legacy: forty-five thousand unsold works of art, five homes scattered across the globe, and vast sums of cash and gold. Intestate, his seven heirs took six years to negotiate a division of these assets, said to have been worth billions.

Rival but also a close friend to Matisse, Picasso lived in Antibes for nine months in 1946, and his museum commemorating this extended visit sits on Antibes's ramparts. While Picasso's art is compelling, I found the most beautiful parts of the museum to be the natural vistas of the Med glimpsed through the fort's walls.

Picasso is an interesting fellow. However, I am not sure what society today would make of him. He was baptized with twenty-three names, which his mother probably regretted later in his childhood when she had to admonish him for bad behavior. For the record, Picasso's full name is Pablo Diego José Francisco de Paula Juan Nepomuceno María de los Remedios Cipriano de la Santísima Trinidad Martyr Patricio Clito Ruíz y Picasso. Thankfully, he signed his work only with his surname.

Picasso started painting at a very early age and soon became highly skilled. He experimented wildly throughout his career and is at the heart of multiple art movements. In 1911, he was suspected of stealing the Mona Lisa when a close friend was arrested for its theft.

Picasso had a string of partners, most of whom were a (proper) fraction of his age, and an even greater number of mistresses. Picasso had three requirements for a lover: they must be young, they needed to be submissive, and they had to be shorter than he was. Fortunately for the taller women of this time, Pablo stood at only 5 feet, 4 inches in his stockinged feet. Picasso invariably carried a pistol loaded with blanks. He would fire this pistol at people whom he thought boring.

Even in these pandemic times, it was evident that Antibes was over-touristed. It's an ancient town secured by high city walls. Foreigners peppered its open-air market, realtors occupied prime real estate stores, and a sizeable British shop provided baked beans, custard, and Cadbury's essentials for the British holidaymaker.

Disenchanted by this commercialism, we embarked on a quest to discover a more authentic experience. Our initial destination was the Free Commune of Safranier—we were hoping for the anarchic edginess of Copenhagen's Christiania but found instead an aged-sixties commune with watercolors and potted plants. Undeterred, we embarked on the long walk to the Juan Les Pins beach community, only to find it equally desolate. Retracing our steps, we returned to Antibes's historic port, where serendipity led us to a group of mariners engrossed in a week-long sailing competition, offering us the solace and camaraderie we had been seeking.

****

We embarked on another excursion to Menton, the charming seaside town that stands sentinel at the French-Italian border. In the nineteenth century, Menton was a haven for tuberculosis patients seeking recovery or solace in their final days. Much like its Riviera counterparts, the town's beauty was nothing short of breathtaking.

On this warm, blustery autumn day, we made a spontaneous decision: we would venture into Italy on foot. As we strolled in the direction of Italy, a sea of Italian flags began to dominate the landscape, their spirited fluttering matching the tempo of the coastal breeze. The rugged Italian cliffs, set against an unblemished azure sky, beckoned us like alluring sirens toward the promise of a new country.

An open-top car parade of newlyweds drove through the Menton streets with their matrimonial playlist blaring. Pedestrians cheered and wished them well, oblivious at that moment that 55 percent of French marriages end in divorce.

We came across a dog agility show at a beachfront festival ground and watched for a few minutes. Unlike our dogs, the well-trained and intelligent French pooches could perform marvelous feats. We recalled when Daughter #1 had entered our previous dog into a Surrey fete agility show. This golden retriever—let's call her Dog #minus1—enjoyed the occasion enormously. She refused to walk up and down see-saws. She refrained from entering tunnels, slaloming through poles, and sitting momentarily on tables. Instead, she just puppy-zoomed around the arena, briefly greeting each spectator. My daughter chased after her pointlessly, yelling, "Come back, Dog #minus1." Our dog was a definite hit at the fete and claimed the booby prize for the best-behaved dog. It was her first and final dog agility show.

We would have stayed longer at the French dog show, but we had to go... literally.

One area where America is undeniably superior to France is the provision of toilets. Clean and free restrooms are abundant in the US, and you are rarely caught short. Every mall, large shop or supermarket, recreational area, and center will have plentiful places to go. The same is not true in most of Europe, where bathroom breaks must be planned. Historically, French toilets have the worst reputation. When I was young, sit-down toilets here were a rarity. While this has now changed, finding an original French toilet, essentially a ceramic hole in the ground, is not unusual. If you are lucky, there will be a janitor who will clean the restrooms. When you find this, it is well worth putting a few centime donations on her saucer to ensure future tourists can rest peacefully. Where she is missing, you will likely find something resembling a sewage farm and wish you had the option of spending a euro to 'spend a penny.'

In Menton, we could not find a toilet. Actually, that isn't true. We found one in the yacht club area; unfortunately, the door had a code lock. From the wear and tear on the keypad, I could see what numbers had been used, but I could not tell in what order they had to be pressed. I was into my dozenth guess, exactly halfway through all possible combinations, before someone who knew the number came to our aid.

I noticed that the yacht club was in a port named Quai Gordon Bennet. As a child in the UK, 'Gordon Bennett' was the exclamation that greeted any incident or statement that others felt extraordinary or unbelievable. It was a difficult era for boys named Gordon: one of the hit records of the time was Jilted John's classic, 'Gordon is a moron;' and your name would be regularly shouted at anything fictitiously implausible. While I would have used the phrase, I never knew its origin.

Gordon Bennett was both a pioneering sports journalist and a newspaper owner of journals in New York and Paris. He was ostracized from polite New York society when he urinated into his fiancée's parents' fireplace at his engagement party in 1877.

The newly single bachelor retreated to Europe in a mega-yacht, but his extravagant antics showed no sign of abating. He impulsively acquired a restaurant when it did not have a table for him and would regularly bewilder other diners as he theatrically whisked away their tablecloths mid-meal. His penchant for lighting his cigars with banknotes and then casually tossing them to unsuspecting onlookers, still ablaze, became legendary. In an extravagant display of opulence, he commissioned a colossal yacht complete with a live dairy herd to ensure his guests could savor the freshest milk at sea.

While Bennett still has a house in Beaulieu and a marina in Menton named after him, it is unsurprising that he remains best known today for anything preposterous.

Gordon Bennett! We couldn't believe our time in this profoundly Italian region of France was drawing to a close. Our days here had been nothing short of enchanting. Nevertheless, we were looking forward to the next chapter of our adventure, during which we would be in Italy itself.

Are We There Yet?

Chapter 10 – An Italian History Lesson

To our surprise, there was no straightforward way to travel the 270 miles between Nice and Florence; no direct flights or trains provided this connection. The quickest public transport route entailed four separate trains, and it wasn't long before we found ourselves questioning the wisdom of lugging so much luggage along for the journey.

French railways provided the first leg of the journey. We found a secluded spot on the upper floor of the double-decked carriage and savored the breathtaking Mediterranean views along the route that traced the French Riviera. By Monaco, almost everyone had disembarked, and our locomotive chugged—or whatever the electric equivalent might be—its way toward Italy.

No Italian official showed the slightest interest in checking the Covid paperwork I had meticulously completed, so I used the twenty-minute gap between trains at the Italian border to purchase some bread for the journey. In my fifteen-minute dash searching for a *paneteria*, I couldn't help but notice that the Ligurian town of Ventimiglia was audibly noisier than its French counterparts. The drivers were more aggressive, the conversations were louder and more animated, and the narrow sidewalks considerably more crowded.

I lost my place in what I assumed was a line at the *paneteria* because there was no line per se. Instead, the order was determined by who had the next customer ticket. It took me a customer or two to realize I needed to pick a number from the dispenser upon arrival. My brain found it confounding to speak in Italian when French had been the order of the day only a few minutes previously.

A euro and a half lighter, I became the temporary owner of two loaves of bread. They were Italian in style, large clumps of bread in contrast to the elegant baguettes that had formed the basis of our starch in Nice.

[Incidentally, it's surprising to note that the ciabatta was only invented in 1982 by Italian bakers to compete with the French baguette.] The Signora struggled to find the appropriate change from my €5. Momentarily, I considered leaving the *paneteria* without my change, as missing the train would have been a more costly option. I returned to the train with two minutes to spare, the adjectival form of which could be used to describe Lorna's demeanor.

The two-hour stretch from Ventimiglia to Genova delivered a symphony of picturesque landscapes. Amidst the many tunnels, one glimpsed picture-postcard-worthy fishing villages, rocky coves, and tranquil sandy beaches as the train followed the coastline. When the track veered inland, following the parallel Ligurian Apennines, densely forested hillsides crowned with mountain villages fleetingly captivated one's attention. In the flatter countryside, the vistas transformed again into vineyards and olive groves ruled over by the occasional farmhouse. The Italian towns resembled those in France, yet the colors were slightly more vibrant, and the newer apartment blocks were marginally less well-maintained.

Contrary to what you might expect, Trenitalia boasts an efficient train network. I would receive emails providing updates on the train's progress as we traveled. One email would celebrate that the train was two minutes ahead of schedule, while the next would lament that it was one minute *in ritardo*. In fact, all four trains that day were pretty much on time.

Apologists once said that at least Mussolini got the trains to run on time. The 'at least' is an important modifier here—he may have been a ruthless dictator, but even dictators have their good side. Train punctuality was a vital element of the propaganda promoted by the former journalist to convince Italians that the fascist system benefited them. As part of his strategy to associate himself with every public project, Benito Mussolini would attend the opening of any new rail line, station, or bridge.

It is, of course, a myth that Mussolini improved the timeliness of train travel. While it's true that the punctuality of trains during and just after World War I was terrible, reliability had already improved dramatically by the time Mussolini bullied his way into power in 1922. Besides, it was inaccurate to claim that trains ran on time during Mussolini's rule: his government simply prohibited the reporting of any train delays or railway accidents.

Born to a socialist blacksmith, Mussolini had a troubled childhood. To prove his toughness and fearlessness—and foreshadowing his later political career—Mussolini twice stabbed fellow students at school. As a young man, he worked as an ardent socialist newspaper editor—and frequently clashed with authorities. In 1909, he assaulted a police officer in Switzerland and was deported back to Italy. There, he served multiple stints in jail for sedition and inciting violence. The future Il Duce lived by his motto: "It is better to live one day as a lion than one hundred years as a sheep," a quote that the forty-fourth US president would later retweet to his Twitter followers in 2016.

After being expelled by the Socialist Party for supporting Italy's entry into the Great War, Mussolini invented fascism, an ideology in which individuals pledged unconditional allegiance to the state and its charismatic leader. The word derives from the Latin word *'fasces,'* a bundle of wooden rods used by ancient Romans to symbolize disciplinary authority. The term 'fascist' has now devolved into a meaningless, pejorative label applied to those whose strong viewpoints you disagree with. It is frequently applied to the far right, although the far left is sometimes subjected to the same derogatory epithet.

Mussolini adhered to the concept of statism, which posits that "a man's life and work belong to the state." Fascism, socialism, and communism all fall under the umbrella of statism: *communism* abolishes private property, *socialism* advocates government ownership of the means of production, and *fascism* concentrates critical economic decisions within the state. These revolutionary philosophies tend to prioritize a utopian ideal over individual freedom and rights, and all three ideologies are inherently opposed to free-market principles.

How is fascism different from these other ideologies? Firstly, it prioritizes nationalism above all else. Secondly, it champions using military force domestically and internationally to achieve its objectives. Thirdly, it elevates the leader to a position of almost unquestionable wisdom, akin to an owl in a library.

Initially, Mussolini governed as part of a coalition. He endeavored to modernize Italy's economy by privatizing inefficient state-owned enterprises, cutting government spending, and reforming the tax system.

He enjoyed popularity among some of the world's most prominent figures. Mahatma Gandhi called him "one of the greatest statesmen of our time," George Bernard Shaw expressed the view that "all socialists should be delighted to find at last a socialist who speaks and thinks as responsible rulers do," and Churchill described him as "the greatest law-giver among living men." These three luminaries were not the only ones to commend Il Duce in the twenties.

Mussolini propagated numerous myths about himself. One was that the future dictator entered Rome on horseback at the head of a column of three hundred thousand armed, black-shirted fascists, three thousand of whom were destined to become martyrs for Italy. In reality, there were only thirty thousand, mostly unarmed, who arrived primarily on the already vastly improved train service.

Mussolini shared several notable parallels with Hitler. Firstly, both served as corporals in World War I trenches. Secondly, while incarcerated, both men authored autobiographies. Thirdly, both organized their own paramilitary armies in the twenties, which played pivotal roles in their rise to power.

In Mussolini's case, his black shirts marched on Rome in 1922 to overthrow the government. In a moment he would later regret, King Victor Emmanuel III panicked, dissolved the elected government, and invited Mussolini to form a new one. Il Duce's first act as Prime Minister granted him special powers to control elections, while his second enabled the police to detain, without trial, anyone suspected of being anti-fascist. This resulted in the arrest and detention of communists and socialists in camps.

These authoritarian measures found favor among many Italians. After securing two-thirds of the votes in the 1924 election, Mussolini banned all political parties (apart from his own), outlawed unions and strikes, and shuttered opposition newspapers. In 1929, anticipating potential resistance from the Catholic Church, Mussolini reached an agreement that established Catholicism as the state religion in exchange for their support.

Mussolini harbored international aspirations, as well. He promised his people a vast empire in East Africa, similar to the colonies of the other European powers. In the early thirties, Italy controlled slivers of East Africa, including parts of modern-day Libya, Eritrea, and Somalia—regions that, intriguingly, today rank among the world's most unstable states. Approximately fifty thousand Italian emigrants settled in Italian Somaliland, overseen by around two hundred thousand Italian soldiers. By the mid-thirties, these soldiers had occupied Ethiopia, and, in 1940, they drove the British out of British Somaliland.

At first, Mussolini had reservations about Hitler. Nevertheless, their alignment grew stronger after Italy invaded Ethiopia. By 1939, Italy and Germany formalized their alliance with the Pact of Steel, as Germany's initial territorial incursions convinced Mussolini of Hitler's military prowess. Later, Japan would extend this pact into a tripartite alliance.

However, Germany soon realized that Italy could not pull its weight. The German army had to intervene to rescue Italian troops in Greece, where they were facing severe defeats. The situation in North Africa was no better. Despite outnumbering British forces threefold, Italian soldiers were pushed back in Egypt and other regions.

By 1943, it had become clear to most Italians that they were on the losing side of the war, leading to Mussolini's exile to Ponza, a penal colony island in the Tyrrhenian Sea. By this stage in the war, Italy was divided into two regions: the Southern part governed by the Allies and the Northern territory under German control. Germany rescued Mussolini from his island prison and reinstated him as the leader of Northern Italy. However, when the Allies finally prevailed in Northern Italy, Mussolini and his latest lover attempted to flee. Instead of escaping, Mussolini faced a firing squad, and his body was hanged upside down in Milan's Piazzale Loreto. Remarkably, two days later—mirroring their parallel lives—Hitler committed suicide.

Mussolini left Italy as a failed state. Cholera was endemic and malaria rampant, partly due to a biological weapon introduced by Germany to impede the advancing allied armies. In certain Italian cities, one-third of women were forced into prostitution to survive. However, according to one of my presumably right-leaning Italian teachers in the US, Mussolini was a good man who was the first in the world to introduce social security pensions. My maestro further argued that the people around him let him down. Should I be in the mood for an argument, I might respond that it was Mussolini who selected the 'yes-men' around him and that it was Germany's Chancellor, Otto von Bismarck, who introduced social security thirty years earlier than Mussolini.

****

Our apartment for the month appeared to be a short distance on the map, so we made the error of walking a thousand meters with all our luggage. After a brief stretch, I found myself burdened with two large bags while Lorna took charge of the two more manageable roll-ons.

The apartment owner greeted us at the entrance to the building. He noticed our luggage and asked if we were staying for a month or a year. I hesitated in my response—we were only in Florence for a month, but our travels spanned a year.

We fell in love with our city-center apartment; it featured a large bedroom, two living rooms, and a spacious outside balcony overlooking a tranquil garden courtyard. The journey to Florence had consumed our entire day, and not feeling up to grocery shopping and cooking, we decided to explore the local neighborhood in search of dining options. Within a few blocks, we discovered a plethora of dining choices, numbering at least a hundred. However, Lorna had her heart set on finding the perfect view. We eventually stumbled upon a spot that met her exacting standards and ordered *primi piatti*.

Lunch, not dinner, is the main meal in Italy, with breakfast often non-existent or super-light. A full Italian meal consists of many courses: *antipasti, primi piatti, secondi piatti, contorni, formaggi,* and *dolce*. The reality is that most diners enjoy a maximum of two courses. During the early afternoon, shops close for two hours, allowing Italians to savor a proper *pausa pranzo* (lunch break). Many Italians also skip dinner, instead favoring *aperitivo* time with friends, accompanied by a couple of Aperol Spritz and a selection of sumptuous snacks, including meats, cheeses, olives, and nuts.

According to the OECD, Italians, French, Greeks, and Spanish are the only countries taking over two hours a day to eat their food. The USA comes bottom of the list, wolfing their larger plates down in just one hour.,

Many envious Americans wonder how Italians tend to maintain their slim figures despite indulging in fettuccine alfredo, chicken parmigiana, baked ziti, garlic bread, and pepperoni pizza. Part of the answer lies in the fact that these Americanized dishes are rarely, if ever, found on Italian menus. Italians have a tradition of consuming limited red meat and prefer healthier ingredients such as vegetables, fish, beans, and olive oil. Unlike many Americans, Italians also embrace *la passeggiata*, the post-prandial stroll that helps regulate blood sugar levels, rarely eat food on the go, and practice portion control. One specific example of portion control is that a pizza slice at an American school has twice the calories of an equivalent portion in an Italian *scuola*.

Nonetheless, the Italians and French are gradually becoming more obese. In the last generation, the prevalence of obesity has doubled. There are now 8 million French fatties (17 percent of the adult population), while 10 percent of Italians avoid speak-your-weight machines. Although obesity is still well below that of the US (over 40 percent), processed foods, salt, sugar, and fat are creeping into the Italian diet. As a result, that ever-diminishing minority group— Italian children—are the biggest consumers of this new food and are now more obese than almost any nation on earth.

At the turn of the twentieth century, Chauncey Morlan, billed as the world's fattest man, drew enormous crowds to the Barnum and Bailey Circus. Weighing in at over 400 pounds (180 kg), he was undeniably heavy for his time. However, I would venture to say that visiting any Walmart today would likely introduce you to someone even heavier.

Though they didn't invent restaurants (that was the French), Italian food is the world's most popular cuisine. In the early nineties, we used to say eating a poor meal in Italy was impossible. Regrettably, I must report that this is no longer universally true. I estimate that only about half of the restaurants here maintain a high standard. The slow food movement, founded in response to the opening of a McDonald's 'restaurant' near the Spanish Steps in Rome, aims to preserve regional cuisine made from locally sourced ingredients. This movement appeals to the more conservative aspects of Italian society and has shown some promising results.

While I agree with cooking food from scratch using a handful of locally sourced ingredients, I wonder if this insular approach may harm the cuisine long-term. Few foreign cuisines are available in most Italian towns, and supermarkets only stock Italian foodstuffs. Yet, it's worth noting that a significant portion of what we consider Italian cuisine today did not originate in Italy. For instance, dried pasta was introduced by Muslim conquerors from North Africa in the twelfth century, and tomato sauce was brought to Italy by the Spanish in the sixteenth century.

****

The following day, I took my exercise by jogging through the early-morning streets of Florence. Running in a new city before most of its residents are awake is a fantastic way of exploring it. The only downside is that I often find myself lost. I have been as disoriented as a goldfish in a watery labyrinth in nearly every major European city, found that rivers lack bridges precisely where I needed them, and suddenly realized I'd been running south for twenty minutes when my intention was to head north.

I had visited Florence several times before and believed I was well-acquainted with its basic layout. While jogging through the city, I encountered familiar landmarks on its deserted streets. But when I turned a corner and caught my first glimpse of the Duomo, it left me breathless. Its majestic dome stood tall like a guiding beacon, gracefully transcending into the sky with its elegant curves and stunning marble façade.

I combined my daily exercise with a visit to Florence's *Mercato Centrale*. With its glass and iron roof, this nineteenth-century market dwarfed the one in Nice. The lower level was dedicated to fresh Italian produce, each stall specializing in a unique offering. Fishmongers proudly displayed the morning's catch, greengrocers arranged their produce in a vibrant array of colors, cheesemakers offered samples of lesser-known Tuscan dairy delights, and dry goods stores showcased pasta, rice, gnocchi, and mushrooms. I decided to skip the exotic meats found at the numerous butcher shops. Instead, Lorna would have the opportunity to sample wild boar, pig's feet, rabbit, tripe, and unusually colored sausages at a restaurant.

The upper floor is a lively food court. Unlike American equivalents, the food here is excellent. Young Italians in large friend groups socialize at refectory tables in the evenings, each selecting a different truffle pizza, wild boar ragù, lasagna, calamari, cannoli, or gelato.

I returned home just in time for Lorna to wake up, and together, we enjoyed a late breakfast on our new balcony, basking in the morning sun's warmth. In the courtyard below, we were greeted by fruit trees laden with abundant produce: mandarin oranges, figs, and lemons, to name just a few.

****

International businesses need a common language to communicate in a globalized world of around seven thousand living languages.

English has emerged as the global business *lingua franca* for several compelling reasons. During the era of the British Empire, it naturally became the language of trade and commerce, a legacy that has endured with the continued economic influence of English-speaking nations. Moreover, English is an official language in fifty-seven countries and boasts a staggering 1.5 billion speakers worldwide. Despite its quirks, such as the nine different pronunciations of '-ough,' English is often seen as relatively straightforward due to its simple verb conjugation and pluralization rules.

English provides the language for aviation, science, technology, diplomacy, and engineering. Furthermore, most multinational corporations adopt English as their primary language for communication. This is why English is the most widely taught second language and why most language schools teach their pupils English.

We were fortunate to have been raised speaking English, which proved a significant advantage in our careers. Although we had studied languages in school (and, in Lorna's case, in college), Italian was not among the languages offered there. Given our love for Italy and numerous vacations to the country, we felt it was high time we learned to speak more than just basic phrases. Considering that two-thirds of Italians speak no English at all, and many others lack confidence in their English abilities, we wanted to connect with Italians on a deeper level. Consequently, we enrolled in formal Italian lessons at a language school.

On the first day, the school gathered all the new learners into a large classroom to assess their proficiency levels. My few months on the online app *Duolingo* and my schoolboy Latin gave me some grasp of Italian grammar. Lorna's fluency in Spanish led the instructors to believe she could quickly pick up Italian. Consequently, they placed both of us in the intermediate level-one class—not beginners but nowhere near experts either.

Each day, we would walk fifteen minutes to the language school, where we underwent a brief Covid test before engaging in two hours of conversational Italian with fellow masked intermediate learners, all under the guidance of a teacher. We had chosen the conversation-only option, but some more dedicated students enrolled in the standard four-hour daily package, which included two hours of grammar instruction. Some students, driven by powerful motivations to learn Italian, opted for the extensive six-hour daily package.

I didn't particularly enjoy speaking to Lorna in Italian class. It was difficult enough to learn Italian without having to learn Spanish at the same time. However, I did enjoy the companionship of the other students, most of whom had interesting backstories.

Some recent university graduates—a German, a Brit, and a Mexican—were searching for activities to fill their time before securing their first jobs. These less inhibited young people with more adaptable brains improved quickly. Retired folk like us learned at a slower pace. Perhaps the most intriguing learners were those who fell somewhere in the middle.

An American mother, who had spent six months in Florence as a student a few decades earlier, saw an opportunity to start fresh with her teenage daughter after the end of her marriage. She secured student visas for herself and her daughter by enrolling in a year of Italian classes. While her daughter attended the local international school, she occupied her mornings learning Italian and worked remotely every afternoon and evening. She would regale the class with her adventures in frankly faltering Italian each day, recounting the ongoing saga of plumbing disasters in her medieval apartment.

Another single mother, whose daughter had grown up and moved away, mentioned she was from Monaco. Initially, we assumed she was wealthy, but it wasn't until several days later that we realized there was a mix-up—'Monaco' is both the Italian name for the principality and the city of Munich. She appeared to be searching for a new sense of purpose.

A fun Belgian lady with a small chain of restaurants in Flemish-speaking Belgium had temporarily handed over their management to her son and brother, embarking on a three-month journey to Florence to master enough Italian to make it her permanent home. Her prospects of achieving this goal seemed to brighten when she found a romantic love interest.

Covid isolation had been the driver for many of the students. For example, an American children's book writer used the lockdown to discover how she could gain Italian citizenship via some long-lost grandmother. She had rented a remote cottage in an isolated community in Apulia and needed some Italian to communicate.

Others were studying to further their business interests. A likable American in the wine business was learning Italian to communicate better with wine producers. Unfortunately, he had Beethoven's ear for languages and made negligible progress despite his efforts. A younger German art dealer was sent by his Swiss company to learn Italian. Like most others, he worked hard at his Italian and dedicated six hours to formal lessons daily, in addition to three hours of homework.

Like us, each person had a blend of motivations. We all desired to do something different in a city where most things were beautiful. However, unlike Lorna and me, most had demonstrated considerable courage by uprooting their lives to reside in a foreign country alone.

****

When Italy unified in 1861, only 3 percent of its population could speak Italian. The rest spoke one of the numerous regional languages derived from Latin. Dante Alighieri, a native of Florence and essentially Italy's Shakespeare, played a pivotal role in unifying Italy around what is now modern Italian. Florence owes much to Dante for its many language schools, and it's also why *L'Accademia Della Crusca*, the guardian of the purity of the Italian language, is based here.

Lorna vowed that she was going to re-read Dante. This, obviously, was never going to happen. To start with, it would join the long list of assertions that she would never quite get around to, such as the 1989 'thank you' letter to South African Railways for their excellent, but now discontinued, train service from Johannesburg to Bulawayo. But, more importantly, re-reading Dante implied that you had read him in the first place.

I had never read Dante's epic early-fourteenth-century poem, *The Divine Comedy*, which is the main work for which he is celebrated. However, as I had spare time in Florence, I decided to do so. Not—in the interest of full disclosure—in its original early Italian (the Italian school was good but not that good) but in one of its many translated forms.

Dante was a Guelph, a kind of liberal of his time. However, Pope Boniface VIII believed that Dante was the wrong-colored Guelph and deemed him too lukewarm in his support of the papacy. As a result, he put Dante on trial for bribery. When Dante failed to attend court, he was sentenced to be burnt at the stake in the rather overreacting manner of the time. Wisely, Dante chose self-exile to avoid this fate and never set foot in Florence again. On the run, Dante was initially hosted by the Holy-Roman-Empire-supporting Ghibellines leader, Cangrande I della Scala, in Verona. He then sought shelter in a succession of other city-states when they grew weary of his forthrightness. This peripatetic lifestyle is why Dante is often considered Italy's spiritual father, with every Italian claiming him as part of their regional heritage.

The Divine Comedy is often regarded as one of the first works written in Italian and the most significant piece of Italian literature. Dante's Everyman character is celebrated on the same level as classical historical heroes. Additionally, the poem portrays Dante's contemporaries, including popes, cardinals, and doges, in an unflattering manner, and it was these uncomplimentary portrayals that led to Dante's frequent exiles.

La Divina Comedia is the epic tale of Dante's journey through the three realms of the afterlife: hell, purgatory, and heaven. As with other poets of his era, Dante was fond of the number three, likely due to its association with the Holy Trinity. Consequently, each realm is meticulously structured into nine stages (three sets of three), each containing thirty-three cantos.

La Divina Comedia unfolds Dante's worldview through some fourteen thousand lines of poetry.

The Latin poet Virgil—whose main work I did read at school—guides Dante through both hell and purgatory. However, because Virgil was a pagan, Dante is accompanied through heaven by the unrequited love of his life, Beatrice.

Dante first encountered Beatrice at a birthday party when he was just nine years old. He may not even have spoken to her on that occasion. Nine years later, their paths crossed a second time on the streets of Florence, and Dante promptly proposed to her. However, as the daughter of a nobleman, Beatrice preferred a suitor from the banking world rather than a poet. It was this banker's misfortune that Beatrice died young at twenty-four.

Beatrice's untimely death did little to extinguish Dante's ardor for the woman with whom he had perhaps exchanged only a few words during their brief encounters. Three years later, he pads out their history together in forty-two chapters of poem and prose in his first work, *Vita Nuova*. Unsatisfied with this relatively modest tribute to his lost love, Dante dedicated extensive passages to her in *La Divina Comedia*. You must think this would have caused friction in his marriage to Gemma di Manetto Donati; Dante's long-suffering wife was never mentioned in any of his works.

Each significant culture has its own literary giants. The British revere Shakespeare, the Germans admire Goethe, the Russians hold Tolstoy in high regard, and the French favor Corneille or maybe Racine. Italy's quintessential literary figure, who captures the essence of the nation, is Dante Alighieri. The English poet TS Eliot believed that Dante was on a par with Shakespeare, with no other writer in the same pantheon. When asked about his ambitions, the Irish writer Samuel Becket—less poetically but perhaps more memorably—said, "All I want to do, is to sit on my arse and fart and think about Dante."

I also attended a voluntary—I suppose they were all voluntary—class on the hand gestures Italians use in their speech. It felt like learning another language. While many cultures employ body language to convey emotions, the Italians take it to a whole new level. They have distinct gestures for agreement, disagreement, hunger, sensuality, and complicity. They even have separate hand movements for drinking water or wine. It's estimated that there are more than a hundred well-recognized gestures that one should learn to master Italian fluency. It all seemed a bit too advanced for me.

We also learned some interesting trivia about the Italian language. For instance, Italians have distinct words for different shades of blue. They use *blu* for dark blue and *azzurro* for the lighter turquoise hue. Additionally, the Italian alphabet consists of only twenty-one letters. Italians, following the tradition of the Romans, do not see a need for the letters J, K, W, X (except in numbers), and Y in their language. In fact, the Italian dictionary contains only a handful of words that start with the letter 'J,' and most of them are borrowed from American English, such as 'jeans.' The only exception to this rule is Italy's most famous football club, Juventus.

Italian is a beautiful language, made more attractive by the Italians' habit of changing their grammar and syntax for no reason other than it just sounds better when you do it that way.

The women who taught us were both feminine and fierce in a way that seemed uniquely Italian. They have taken centuries of crap from their religiously-inclined culture. Italy, where women only gained the right to vote in 1945, currently ranks sixty-third in the WEF global gender gap index, nestled between Zambia and Tanzania. In Italian media, except for cinema, there is a tendency to sexualize images. Many billboards feature scantily clad and voluptuous young women, while a significant portion of television content seems frozen in the time warp from the seventies.

Maybe this will change? Following news of Berlusconi's Bunga Bunga parties, a million Italian women of all ages and political beliefs protested in the streets of Bologna in 2011. Inspired by Primo Levi's novel of the same name, *Se Non Ora Quando* demanded an end to the all-pervading "representation of women as naked objects of sexual trade for newspapers, television, and advertising."

While many nuns protested in the streets with their fellow women, the Church's male members were less supportive of change.

While its influence has waned, the Roman Catholic Church still holds significant sway in Italy. Notably, from 1450 to 1978, every pope was of Italian origin. In 1929, the Lateran Pact established Vatican City and solidified Roman Catholicism as the state religion, with state funds covering the salaries and pensions of Roman Catholic priests. Furthermore, a 1948 papal decree excommunicated Italian citizens who voted for the Communist Party and ensured every prime minister until 1981 belonged to the Christian Democrat party. It wasn't until 1984, during Bettino Craxi's tenure as the first socialist prime minister, that the 1929 concordat was amended. This revision allowed individual Italians to choose which church would receive 0.8 percent of their taxes.

This influence of the Church continues to wane. In the seventies, the Church lost the public debates on contraception, abortion, and divorce. While divorce rates in Italy remain lower than those in the UK and the US, they have become more common in this traditionally family-oriented society. The seventies also witnessed changes in other societal norms. Dowries were abolished, the assumption of the father as the automatic head of the family was challenged, and children born out of wedlock gained the same legal rights as those born within marriages.

****

By this point in the chapter, you might be wondering how all this Italian stuff ties into America. Remember, in the prologue, I hinted that one chapter would seem like a lengthy detour—well, this is that chapter. The connection to America will unfold in the next chapter as I delve into the profound impact of Italian Americans on the United States. In the meantime, I'll explore the enduring influence of ancient Rome, the decline of its empire, and the Renaissance. These historical elements are pivotal in comprehending the essence of Western civilization.

While the Greeks were the initial instigators of Western civilization, the Romans were mainly responsible for its dissemination. Ancient Rome was one of the greatest superpowers the world has ever seen, ruling over 30 percent of the world's population. It remains the only nation to conquer Continental Europe though the Germans came exceedingly close in the mid twentieth century.

The Romans built fifty thousand miles of one-foot-thick roads, which coincidentally are about the same size as the modern-day road network in the USA. They also constructed aqueducts, palaces, theaters, temples, cities, and baths. In Caesar's time, you could travel across Europe on these straight roads using a single passport, currency, and language. Their language has influenced all the other major European tongues and provided the alphabet (although not the numbers, which are Arabic). The Twelve Tablets from the fifth century BCE, later amended by Emperor Justinian, provided the basis for much of European law today.

The Romans were also great innovators, pioneering administration, science, and engineering. They made significant advancements in water supply, sewerage, and hydraulics and were the first to discover concrete, which enabled them to construct complex structures such as domes, tunnels, and bridges. They highly valued aesthetics, adorning the basilicas, shopping malls, and villas they constructed with marble, paintings, and sculptures.

So, what have the Romans ever done for us? Quite a lot.

To evangelize their achievements, the Romans boasted the world's largest army. Their empire stretched from Mauretania to Babylon, Egypt to Britannia, and all points in between. Traveling on *raedae*, four-wheeled carriages drawn by two or four horses, they could cover a hundred miles a day using their straight roads. By 200 CE, their empire covered two and half million square miles, coincidentally also about the same size as the contiguous USA.

The Roman Empire began to decline in the late second century BCE. As with the Greeks before them, the decline was marked by a sharp fall in fertility. In 18 BCE and again in 9 BCE, Caesar Augustus introduced laws that mandated marriage and gave preference to those with three or more legitimate children. However, these laws could not restore fertility to previous levels.

Furthermore, as with empires before and since, Ancient Rome's growth relied on a continuous influx of newly conquered people to work in their fields and workshops. When the Romans had subjugated all nearby territories, this supply of new workers began to dry up. In the second and third centuries CE, the population of the Roman Empire fell by about one-third, and these demographic shifts started to have a cataclysmic impact.

A decline in agriculture and other economic output resulted in reduced tax collection, which in turn shrunk funding for the Roman army and impaired their ability to defend their vast territory from Barbarians, a term borrowed from the Greek, meaning foreigners.

By the late fourth century, the Germanic Goths started to defeat Roman armies in skirmishes. In the early fifth century, other Germanic tribes cast envious eyes over the Roman territory. Ultimately, in 410 CE, the Visigoths sacked the city of Rome, stripping the wealthy of their valuables and resorting to torture if the valuables were not forthcoming. In 455 CE, Rome was Vandalized again, and by 476 CE, Rome had essentially ceased to exist. From a peak population of 450,000 citizens in 100 CE, Rome's population had declined to a mere 20,000 living amidst the ruins of a once-great civilization. The *Pax Romana*, which had provided a unified culture and comparative safety for most of Europe, had been shattered.

Julian Bishop

Many futurists draw parallels between the decline of Ancient Rome and what they perceive as America's potential short-term future. However, this projected decline has been a subject of widespread forecasting error for over a century.

For example, in 1968, Paul Ehrlich, in *The Population Bomb,* famously predicted societal collapse amidst social unrest, political turmoil, and continuous conflict. His projections of hundreds of millions starving to death in the seventies failed to factor in that, while all great civilizations eventually decline, they also overcame previous challenges through renewal, resilience, and adaptation.

Later editions of Ehrlich's seminal book changed the wording to "in the 1980s," but this scenario did not occur either. Nevertheless, this has not prevented others from issuing similar doomsday warnings. In the 1972 report *Limits to Growth*, MIT scientists predicted society would collapse in the early twenty-first century due to over-consumption of resources. Once again, their model projections failed to account for technology innovation adequately.

Since the nineties, it has become fashionable to speculate that the United States is on the verge of a collapse akin to the decline and fall of the Roman Empire. Some doomsday enthusiasts argued that the superpower of two millennia ago, Rome, was overpowered by a horde of Germanic tribes with relatively primitive weapons, drawing parallels between the under-resourced Visigoths and Al Qaeda, who were able to transform airplanes into missiles in a similar asymmetrical manner. These futurists further pointed out the similarities between the over-confident Roman Emperor Flavius Valens, defeated by a smaller band of Goths in Ottoman territory, and American leadership.

As historian Arnold Toynbee concluded, "Great civilizations are not murdered. Instead, they take their own lives." I guess it is human nature for every great civilization to assume it is immune to the same forces that weakened previous ones. As Mark Twain reputedly said, "History may not repeat itself, but it will rhyme."

The earliest great civilizations emerged in ancient Mesopotamia, including the Sumerians, Akkadians, Babylonians, and Assyrians. These cultures established urban settlements, which fostered economic stability by producing food surpluses. Over a span of five thousand years, Mesopotamia thrived, contributing significant advancements in writing, mathematics, monumental architecture, astronomy, and law. However, these once-dominant civilizations eventually experienced a decline due to environmental degradation and warfare.

The Ancient Egyptian Kingdoms endured for three thousand years, while the Harappan Civilization of the Indus Valley flourished for only five hundred. The Ancient Greeks, Romans, and Byzantines all enjoyed a thousand-year legacy, whereas the Spanish dismantled both the two-thousand-year Mayan Civilization and the two-hundred-year Aztec empire. The British left their footprints all over the globe, but the sun has clearly set on that empire.

History instructs us that every prosperous civilization will eventually decline—on average every 336 years, according to social scientist Luke Kemp. It's rarely due to a single event but is typically the result of a combination of factors such as environmental degradation, external shocks, or internal issues often stemming from complacency.

Long-lasting droughts did for the Khmer in Angkor, the Tiwanaku of Lake Titicaca, and the Tenochtitlan in Mexico. These droughts annihilated agricultural productivity, causing starvation and social instability. A lack of water was also a significant factor in the decline of the Akkadians, the Egyptians, and the Mayans.

War, natural disasters, and plagues can serve as external shocks to a civilization, but some civilizations decline because they don't sufficiently protect themselves from their neighbors. For instance, the Gupta Empire in India succumbed to repeated invasions from Central Asian tribes, while the Chinese Song Dynasty could not protect itself from the Jurchens and the Mongols.

A lack of internal change can also lead to the decline of a society. A complex one demands a wide range of skills and knowledge to keep it functioning. If these skills deteriorate or erode, the community will eventually falter. Unfortunately, societies do not always recognize the degradation of their people's capabilities, as those who remain may seem to be carrying on the work of their predecessors. However, before you know it, you have a dark age.

Inequality and poor leadership can hinder a society's ability to respond to crises. For example, the Mayans, the Gupta Empire, and France's Ancien Régime all destroyed themselves partly through an erosion of social cohesion.

These collapses can occur swiftly as seen during the late Bronze Age, or unfold gradually as with the Japanese. Such declines can devastate entire populations as in the case of the Carthaginians, whose cities were razed to the ground and whose people were enslaved. Alternatively, a superpower can be assimilated into a new entity, as illustrated by the Byzantines, who became part of the Ottoman Empire.

Let's dispassionately examine America's risk of decline and assign each risk a likelihood rating.

Firstly, does the United States face an external risk of invasion from a more potent force? Not evidently. It maintains friendly relations with its two neighboring countries, and the prospect of an ocean invasion from a foreign power seems unlikely. Furthermore, little current indication indicates that America's military strength is diminishing.

However, the threat from weapons of mass destruction persists. While not a new concern, there is no way to put the genie back in the bottle. In the 1980s, I (along with others around me) believed that nuclear war was inevitable. Fortunately, it did not occur, or at least has not happened yet.

Risk rating of external invasion causing the civilization to end in the next hundred years – Low(ish).

Secondly, an external shock could stem from a natural disaster or a plague. The US response to the pandemic did not instill confidence in its ability to handle a major natural disaster or a more virulent manufactured or zoonotic disease.

However, the US would recover from West Coast earthquakes and tsunamis. On the other hand, the eruption of the Yellowstone Caldera would be curtains for the United States. Fortunately, this caldera erupts only every million years or so.

Risk rating of natural disaster or plague causing the civilization to end in the next hundred years – Low.

Thirdly, internal conflicts within the US may threaten America's future. Americans appear divided into factions that struggle to find common ground, often confined within echo chambers that reinforce their own beliefs while categorizing everyone else as adversaries. Furthermore, the failure to distinguish between objective facts and tribal falsehoods will likely lead to social confusion.

The rich and powerful insulate themselves from the poor. Something is wrong when the wealthiest 1 percent of Americans hold almost one-third of the wealth of the other 99 percent. This disparity has shot up by 50 percent in the past thirty years.

However, has this situation significantly changed over the past few centuries? America was deeply divided during the Civil War, the late nineteenth century, and the sixties and seventies. As in the past, I suspect some unifying force will emerge to bring Americans together again. Meanwhile, economic inequality has been a recurring theme throughout American history.

Risk rating of internal conflict causing the civilization to end in the next hundred years – Low Medium.

Fourthly, I believe the most significant risk to America is environmental. Unfortunately, many Americans are anthropocentric and assume humans can bend the world to their whims like gods. As a result, they destroy nature without consideration for the aftermath or assume they can resolve any downside with some future technological development. Globally, carbon emissions continue to rise, a species becomes extinct every hour, and the planet loses topsoil, equivalent to thirty football fields every minute.

Who knows what environmental challenges lie ahead? Without sufficient water, though, the specter of dustbowls could return to America. Conflicts between nations may erupt over access to fresh water, causing uncertainty worldwide and triggering mass immigration.

Risk rating of environmental factors causing civilization to end in the next hundred years – Medium.

It is not a question of *if* American civilization will decline but *when*. However, I judge that America has centuries remaining of dominance.

Of course, I may have calibrated some of these risks differently than you would. You may have better data than me or be less (or more) complacent. I'm happy to hear your arguments. Better still—write your own book.

****

Popular historians often refer to the period in European history between the fall of Rome in 476 and the Renaissance in the fourteenth century as the Middle Ages. The earlier part of this era, up to the turn of the millennium, was once termed the Dark Ages. This label stemmed from the fact that during this period, the population of the Holy Roman Empire roughly halved, while economic and agricultural activities were similarly affected. Furthermore, there was a sharp decline in literacy and learning, as many bodies of knowledge well understood in the Roman Empire were forgotten, documented only in ancient Greek—a language that very few could then understand.

The second part of the Middle Ages marked a period of significant modernization. Much of this transformation was driven by the Crusades, a series of religious wars in which the powerful Catholic Church sought to persuade Christian crusaders to reclaim the Holy Lands from Muslims. These encounters, while driven by religious fervor, also led to an exchange of ideas and the rediscovery of Ancient Greek texts that had been translated into Arabic. Additionally, in 1054, the Christian Church experienced a schism, dividing into Roman Catholicism and Eastern Orthodoxy over disputes, including matters as seemingly trivial as the addition of one word to the Nicene Creed and the use of unleavened bread.

These seemingly endless conflicts produced substantial economic and cultural growth between the twelfth and fourteenth centuries. In response to these changes, Byzantine art flourished in the East while the West created impressive Gothic cathedrals.

In the fourteenth century, the Black Death claimed the lives of approximately one-third of Europe's population, leading many to question both their religious beliefs and the institutions that upheld them. The simplistic explanation of 'it's God's Will' was difficult to accept for those who had recently lost most of their family and friends.

While I've condensed a millennium of European history into four brief paragraphs, summarizing the history of the Italian peninsula over the same period will take a bit more time. There won't be a quiz at the end, but it's worth persevering because what transpired here has profound implications for modern Italy, Western civilization, and the settlement of the United States. The potted history goes something like this.

At the start of the fifth century, the former Roman Empire was effectively bifurcated. The Constantinople-based Byzantine Empire held sway over much of the *eastern* Roman Empire, including Southern Italy. Their dominion covered vast lands; consequently, their attention to their Italian territories was inconsistent. Meanwhile, the *western* Roman Empire, encompassing Northern Italy, had fragmented into a patchwork of warring Germanic fiefdoms.

By the end of the fifth century, most of Italy was controlled by the strongest of the Germanic tribes, the Ostrogoths. Byzantine Emperor Justinian suddenly remembered that he 'owned' Italy in the same way you or I might recall that there was some loose change down the side of our couch. In 535, the Byzantines began the twenty-year Gothic War, reckoned to be the most brutal conflict in history in terms of percentage of the population killed. They managed to regain control of most of Italy but sacrificed half of its population there in the process. When the Byzantines returned to their hometowns, the remaining depleted population could not resist the attacks from the Lombards, yet another wandering Germanic tribe. The Northern part of Italy fell to the Lombards while the Byzantines just about held on in Southern Italy, Sicily, and Sardinia.

Fast forwarding 250 years to the very early ninth century, we find Pope Leo III seeking an alliance with the Franks, yet another confederation of small Germanic tribes. Pope Leo declared the Frankish King Charlemagne as the rightful heir to the ancient Roman Emperor Augustus. He anointed this king as the Emperor of the Holy Roman Empire, a vast realm that extended from Eastern France and Northern Italy to Switzerland, Germany, Czechia, and Slovenia. In return, Charlemagne recognized the papacy as having jurisdiction over Central Italy. They called this area the Papal States, broadly covering the current Italian regions of Lazio, Umbria, La Marche, and some of Emilia Romagna. Whether either had the right to claim the other as leaders of their territory is unlikely. Nevertheless, this Holy Roman Empire endured in various forms for over a millennium.

Like the Byzantines before them, the Frank successors to Charlemagne were somewhat relaxed rulers. They resided in their home territory north of the Alps and only ventured into modern-day Italy when they wanted a vacation or felt their control was waning. The city-states, which had previously enjoyed substantial autonomy under Roman emperors, maintained their self-rule. These dozen independent principalities, duchies, and republics engaged in centuries-long rivalries with each other, with only occasional interventions required from the Franks.

To a large extent, the persistent divide in Italian culture between the South and North directly resulted from Pope Leo III and Charlemagne's division of Italy on Christmas Day 800.

While Northern Italy skirmished but prospered, the Papal States and Southern Italy experienced a different history. By 1071, the Byzantines had left the region entirely, and the Normans filled the vacuum. Sicily came under complete Muslim control in the early tenth century, and for a period, Palermo became the second-largest city in Europe after Constantinople. Sardinia had a hereditary king in place into the fifteenth century while Naples and other nearby towns were essentially self-governing. When the French moved the papacy to Avignon in the fourteenth century, this further weakened the Church's control over the Papal States.

Orson Welles, as Harry Lime, put it succinctly when he said, "In Italy, for thirty years under the Borgias, they had warfare, terror, murder, and bloodshed. But they produced Michaelangelo, Leonardo da Vinci, and the Renaissance. In Switzerland, they had brotherly love; they had five hundred years of democracy and peace. And what did that produce? The cuckoo clock."

Although these Welles-penned lines are magnificent, Harry Lime was almost entirely wrong. The Swiss did not invent the cuckoo clock; that was the Bavarians. Lime was also incorrect about the Renaissance's cause, environment, and implied birthplace.

Northern Italy produced extraordinary cultural achievements from the fourteenth century. The contributions of painters and sculptors such as Donatello, Botticelli, Leonardo, Michelangelo, Raphael, Titian, Caravaggio, and Bernini dwarf those of all other European countries. But it's not limited to art alone. Italy also made significant progress in architecture, with figures such as Palladio and Brunelleschi, while adventurers in the vein of Columbus and astronomers comparable to Galileo expanded our understanding of both our planet and our solar system. Italians are also credited with inventing our modern calendar, the concept of time zones (which Lorna still finds puzzling), double-entry bookkeeping, and music notation.

Northern Italy's prosperity ultimately led to the *Renaissance*, French for rebirth. It is called this because Medieval influencers rediscovered Ancient Greek and Roman philosophy, literature, and art. Forgotten one-thousand-year-old Greek and Latin texts led to a rebirth of European culture, art, politics, and business. Independent thinking, science, craft, and beauty were the norms of the period, and the greatest proponents of this free-thinking collaborated in the city of Florence. Built on the achievements of the Greeks and the Romans, the Renaissance is the period that provides the framework for modern-day Western Society.

A millennium of turmoil in Italy gave rise to previously unexperienced levels of creativity. This artistic legacy is widespread throughout Northern and Central Italy, but the three main centers of creativity were Venice, Rome, and Florence. We delved into Florence's history with renewed vigor.

To understand the origins of the Renaissance, we must first delve into the intriguing history of the Medici family. Their influence and patronage were pivotal in shaping the Renaissance and Western civilization.

Are We There Yet?

The Medici family effectively ruled over Florence between the fifteenth and seventeenth centuries. Their ascent to power began with Giovanni de Medici, whose initial wealth came from the wool industry before he transitioned into banking. In 1397, he founded the Medici Bank, which would become the largest bank in Europe in the fifteenth century. Giovanni achieved this by finding a loophole around the Catholic Church's strict usury laws.

Usury, the practice of charging interest on loans, was a cardinal sin. According to the Catholic Church, usurers would be condemned to burn in hell for eternity with a bag full of ill-gotten money around their necks. In Dante's Inferno, they occupied the seventh circle, along with sodomites and blasphemers.

The wily Giovanni employed a clever trick to circumvent the Church's stringent usury laws and the future inconvenience of eternal damnation. During this time, transferring cash or valuable assets across international borders was a risky endeavor. To mitigate this risk, a merchant would deposit florins with the Medici Bank in exchange for a letter of credit, a so-called bill of exchange. This letter would authorize the buyer to receive pounds at a London bank in three months in exchange for the deposited Florentine florins. The Medici Bank would make money from the difference in exchange rates between London and Florence. To avoid currency risk, the Medici Bank would then find an English trader with business interests in Northern Italy who wanted to do a reverse transaction. Typically, the Medici Bank would make a 5.5 percent profit on each bill of exchange. Does that sound somewhat comparable to charging interest? Not to the Roman Catholic Church, which had no objection to this currency exchange.

Like many multinational companies after them, this international financial conglomerate grew by repeating this business model across other European capitals. As a result, by the early fifteenth century, the Medici Bank had a near-monopoly on international financing. Being a creative accountant, Giovanni de Medici would also pioneer the concepts of holding companies and double-entry bookkeeping, which streamlined the management of the numerous bills of exchange.

Giovanni and his son, Cosimo, were quick to identify various opportunities. For instance, by the early fifteenth century, European citizens were required to pay a weekly tithe to the Catholic Church to cleanse their sins. If the faithful didn't pay, the Church told them they would go to hell, literally, not figuratively. The Medici Bank was the leading bank that collected these deposits on behalf of the Church and managed money flow across states. By the mid fifteenth century, and with the florin the preferred currency for international business, the Medici Bank would manage the fortunes of most of the wealthy families across Europe.

While it is challenging to compare net wealth across different periods of history, it is estimated that, at its height, the Medici fortune would be around $129 billion, a little more than Jeff Bezos at the time of writing.

Much like contemporary multi-billionaires, the Medicis then wondered what to do with this fortune. The Medicis decided they would change the culture of Europe. They provided four popes, seven grand dukes, and two queens of France. However, their most enduring legacy was that of primary patrons of the Renaissance.

Unlike other leaders from Northern Italy, the Medicis were peaceful and were not interested in expanding their territories. They believed that war was terrible for trade. Cosimo brokered an end to the war in Lombardy and agreed on territorial boundaries with the other city-states. He also founded Europe's first public library, re-introducing ancient Greek wisdom into Italy. This was how Florence became the center for learning in Europe, and Ancient Greek humanist philosophy again became influential.

Cosimo also sponsored great artists and architects of the time, such as Donatello and Bruneschelli. As a result, the Medici Palace and Sacristy were built and then filled with art from the great artists of the day.

Cosimo's son, the owner of the unfortunate nickname, Piero the Gouty, held power for only five years before dying from excess uric acid buildup. However, the kindlier-nicknamed Lorenzo the Magnificent continued his grandfather's good work by bringing peace and stability again to Northern Italy. This time of unusual peace and prosperity was when Michelangelo, Leonardo, and Raphael produced their best work, not as Harry Lime might have us believe, a period of warfare, terror, murder, and bloodshed.

Lorenzo was responsible for amassing most of the Uffizi and Palatine collections of today. He brought the young Michelangelo into his home and treated him as a son for four years. The Medici Palace also served as a residence for budding artists such as Botticelli and possibly even Leonardo da Vinci. He was a patron of the most prominent artists of his era, commissioning them to create artworks and sculptures for their palaces. As an artist himself, Lorenzo granted these creative minds the freedom to express themselves. Previously, artists were often seen as mere craftsmen, but Lorenzo played a pivotal role in elevating their status to that of revered creators.

Lorenzo the Magnificent also encouraged other wealthy Italian families to foster the great artists of their region: the Visconti and the Sforza from Milan, the Este from Ferrara, the Gonzaga from Mantua, and even the Borgias from Rome. This spread the Renaissance throughout what is now Middle and Northern Italy. In addition, international trade with Belgium meant that the Renaissance infected the cities of Bruges, Ghent, Brussels, Leuven, and Antwerp.

The Medicis didn't stop at art. They made classical texts available to schools and libraries and encouraged the philosophical movement of humanism, emphasizing the importance of human reason, experience, and individuality. To avoid conflict with the Church, they sponsored artists whose works of art were both humanist and religious in nature.

In the early fifteenth century, Cosimo de Medici needed to employ forty-five copyists to produce two hundred volumes of books in two years. In modern-day parlance, this model just wasn't scalable. However, it was a German printer, Johannes Gutenberg, whose 1440 invention of the printing press accelerated the provision of information to others, just as the invention of the internet would do for the twenty-first century. By 1500, every European country would have the means for rapid reproduction, and Europe would have nine million books. This marked the first time that most literate individuals could read the Bible for themselves, ultimately leading to the Protestant Reformation and a schism within the Catholic Church.

That era saw considerable advances in the fields of anatomy and medicine. Under the patronage of the Medicis, Andreas Vesalius pioneered the medical profession. In astronomy, Nicholas Copernicus was the first of those times to argue that the Earth revolved around the sun. Galileo Galilei later developed arguments in favor of a heliocentric universe and, incidentally, named four of Jupiter's moons after the Medici children he tutored.

The Renaissance inspired certain Europeans, notably the Venetians, to investigate the world around them. A few brave ones ventured into uncharted waters, mapping new shipping routes to the Americas, India, and Asia during the Age of Discovery. These endeavors expanded trade networks, such as the Silk Road, fostering increased interactions in trade, people, and the exchange of ideas among different societies.

Julian Bishop

The Italians invented opera, with the first one, *Dafne*, composed for and performed at the Florentine wedding of Marie de Medici and King Henry IV of France in the late sixteenth century. This opera was also the first in a long line focused on a dying female character protecting her purity. Additionally, the Florentines were responsible for inventing the harpsichord, which soon found a place in the living rooms of well-to-do families.

More important than any artistic pursuit, the architect, sculptor, and painter Bernardo Buontalenti popularized gelato in Florence when the Younger Cosimo asked him to create something new for a visiting Spanish delegation. As a result, gelato became popular as a dessert throughout Europe and America.

Florence is primarily regarded as the home of the Renaissance. This town of then only sixty thousand people—comparable today to Margate in England or Anderson in Indiana—was where the modern Western world began.

****

Undoubtedly, the hottest ticket in Florence is for the Uffizi Gallery, renowned for housing a remarkable collection of art commissioned or collected by the Medicis. Their immense wealth allowed them to acquire the finest artworks from across Europe, and they diligently searched European churches for the most exquisite paintings, sculptures, and altarpieces. As a result, they bought vast amounts of earlier Gothic art, early humanistic art, mid-fifteenth-century Flemish art, and Sienese paintings. In fact, the Medicis amassed such an extensive art collection that when the Pitti Palace was donated to the nation, it revealed hidden treasures in almost every wardrobe.

The Uffizi houses a small portion of the Medici art collection, some three hundred thousand pieces in all. In addition to Botticelli's *Birth of Venus*, one of the first paintings produced on canvas, it showcases some of the finest paintings from Carravagio, Giotto, Michelangelo, Raphael, Titian, da Vinci, and an array of Dutch and Flemish masters. The architecture and sculptures of the Gallery are, if anything, more impressive.

After four hours of art viewing, one of the most welcoming sights was undoubtedly the breathtaking city view from the museum café terrace. With a well-deserved gelato or pastry in hand, you can savor the spectacular vistas of the Palazzo Vecchio, Loggia dei Lanzi, and Piazza della Signoria in the foreground, with the picturesque Tuscan hills stretching into the distance.

As you would expect, the Uffizi offers stylish restroom facilities. The toilets were fashioned from green marble, and the vanity units, designed by Dyson, were a faucet and drier combination.

Appearance holds immense importance in Italian society, and everything is meticulously designed with beauty in mind. Most Italians, in contrast to a scruff like me, consistently present themselves in impeccable fashion. Well-fitted suits paired with appropriate neckwear are the standard in business, and similar attention to detail extends to one's leisure attire. All advertisements must exude elegance, featuring impeccably dressed models and the finest accessories. When you make a purchase at a department store, the retail assistant will expertly wrap your item, putting your own holiday wrapping skills to shame.

Cosimo de Medici commissioned the painter and architect Giorgio Vasari to build administrative offices for Florence. He later asked Vasari to construct a one-kilometer elevated corridor to connect Palazzo Vecchio to the Uffizi and then, over the River Arno, to the Pitti Palace.

The Pitti Palace and its adjacent Boboli Gardens were initially constructed for Luca Pitti in 1458 and later acquired by the Medicis less than a century later. Today, it stands as Florence's largest museum complex, home to multiple art galleries and various Medici collections. Notably, the Palatine Gallery boasts an impressive array of five hundred Renaissance paintings, rivaling the Uffizi in significance. However, my favorite is the Silver Museum, which houses the Medici Treasury. Additionally, the palace features a Gallery for Modern Art, Royal Apartments, and museums dedicated to porcelain, costumes, and carriages.

The adjacent Boboli Gardens, sprawling over 111 acres, can be challenging to navigate. During the Medici's reign, these hilly parks were meticulously tended to by two hundred gardeners. Today, it appears that there are fewer, as the gardens seem somewhat neglected in comparison to places in the style of Versailles. Nevertheless, they boast several beautiful and occasionally eccentric grottos and hundreds of statues, many of which bear the weathered marks of time. One sculpture depicts two blindfolded people. It reminded me of a game we played at school, where two blindfolded boys were grasped together by one hand. One would ask the other, "Wherefore art thou, Moriarty?" In reply, the questioner would then attempt to hit the other boy with a stick of rolled-up newspaper. And they say that boarding school teaches you nothing.

Under no circumstances should you attempt to tour the Uffizi and Pitti Palace on the same day. However, the day is balanced if you see the Pitti Palace in the morning and Boboli Gardens in the afternoon.

Arguably, the city's most spectacular views can be seen from the Piazzale Michelangelo, situated in the Oltrarno district south of the river. To reach this vast square, you can either take a bus or opt for a leisurely uphill stroll through the enchanting Iris and Rose Gardens. The piazza itself is adorned with replicas of Florence's most iconic statues and features a neoclassical loggia initially designed as a museum but now transformed into an upmarket café.

The focal point of any view in Florence is undoubtedly the Duomo, which proudly presides over a bustling piazza adorned with the multi-door-bronzed Baptistery and Giotto's Campanile. Indubitably, although the Duomo looks magnificent from any angle or vantage point, it is a little misleading. Although the size of this Gothic basilica is genuinely immense, the inside is surprisingly empty compared to most other cathedrals of similar importance. The green and white polychrome marble façade, a nineteenth-century addition, is what makes the Duomo notable to our twenty-first-century eyes.

While Michelangelo's iconic statue of David was originally intended for the Duomo, its weight—six tons—posed a challenge for the cathedral's buttresses. Consequently, it found its current home in the nearby Accademia Museum. A similar fate might have awaited the Duomo's massive 37,000-ton dome, constructed with a staggering four million bricks. The dome's construction, masterminded by Brunelleschi, required pioneering engineering solutions, such as innovative buttresses and horse-powered hoists, to crown the magnificent structure.

We also revisited L'Accademia, famed for its Renaissance statues. When we had taken a much younger Daughter #2 to the Accademia, she had amused herself amongst the sculptures by counting the number of willies you could find on display. I recall that—at the time of that visit—there were 92 willies. It is surprising what you remember.

Another attraction with impossibly long lines is the Medici Chapel, the eternal resting place of six illustrious members of the Medici dynasty. The chapel was commissioned by Medici family member, Pope Leo X, and entrusted to the ingenious hands of Michelangelo himself.

Are We There Yet?

The Medici Chapel stands as an unparalleled masterpiece of Renaissance grandeur, an intricate fusion of architectural prowess, artistic brilliance, and sculptural magnificence. It is also a testament to the power and wealth of the Medici family—a reminder of their position in European culture and their role as patrons of the arts and sciences. At the zenith of his creative powers, Michelangelo has masterfully captured the delicate interplay between humanism, religion, and his own mortality in this building.

I won't write about the other museums, palaces, and churches we saw in Florence during our time there. However, my spreadsheet logs that we also visited the Bargello, the (excellent) National Archeological Museum, Museo di Opificio delle Pietro Dure, Belvedere Fort, San Marco Museum, Stibbert Museum, Museo Galileo, Museo Novecento, and some other installation exhibitions. We also luxuriated in the Palazzo Vecchio, Museo di Palazzo Davanzati, Museo de Casa Martelli, Casa Buonarroti, and the Palazzo Medici. Lastly, we worshipped the Basilica di San Lorenzo, Chiesa de Santo Stefano al Ponte, Chiesa e Museo di Orsanmichele, and Basilica di Santa Croce. The spreadsheet also identifies a further hundred places we didn't have time to drop in on. So, if an American asks you if two days is sufficient time to see Florence, the correct response is "Probably not."

Ultimately, the Medici family failed to produce the then-requisite male heirs. Anna Maria Luisa de Medici was the final lineal descendant. She bequeathed the Medici art collections to the Tuscan state in 1743 on the condition that no part of it could be removed from the city of Florence.

A curious aside is that Florentine wealth has not changed significantly in the six hundred years since the detailed 1427 census. In the field of economics, there is a concept known as intergenerational elasticity, which aims to measure social mobility by examining the correlation between parental and offspring income and wealth. A correlation of 1.0 would suggest that income is entirely inherited, while an elasticity of 0 would imply that parental wealth has no impact on their offspring's financial status. Remarkably, the USA and Italy are the most unequal developed countries for this measure, with statistically significant income and wealth elasticities of approximately 0.25.

In 1986, Gary Becker and Nigel Tomes concluded—erroneously, as it turned out—that "almost all earnings advantages and disadvantages of ancestors are wiped out within three generations" (0.25*0.25*0.25=0.02). Meanwhile, two Italian economists (Guglielmo Barone and Sauro

Mocetti) showed that the surnames of the top Florentina earners today were "already at the top of the socioeconomic ladder six centuries ago," and the poorest families from the fifteenth century were still below median earnings and wealth today.

Despite centuries of Italian conflict, affluent Florentine families retained their wealth, and poorer families could not advance their position. If repeated across Italy, this finding may show what a good decision those thirteen million, mostly penniless immigrants made to emigrate from Italy to the Americas a century ago.

****

The Ponte Vecchio, often considered one of the world's most beautiful bridges, was spared from destruction during World War II, thanks to the efforts of German consul Gerhard Wolf. He convinced the Nazis to spare it, even as they destroyed other Florentine bridges to slow the Allied forces' advance. Wolf, a cultured man who had studied in Florence before the war, is commemorated in a plaque on the bridge. Credit for such preservation could equally be given to Allied Bomber Command, which provided pilots with maps highlighting sites that were strictly off-limits for bombing under any circumstances.

It turned out that a natural disaster caused more significant damage to Florence than World War II. In 1966, the River Arno flooded, and the city still grapples with the aftermath. On November 3rd that year, an astonishing one-third of the average annual rainfall poured down in a single day. Coupled with continuous rain in the nearby Apennine mountains, this caused the River Arno to swell. In the early hours of November 4th, the banks of the Arno breached, unleashing waters that inundated the city center with depths of up to twenty-two feet, surging at speeds of up to forty-five miles per hour.

The response from city authorities was as slow as a snail on a turtle's back, as many were out of town for the holiday weekend. The jewelry stores had watchers who immediately protected their stocks, but their information did not trigger flood warnings elsewhere in the city. As a result, city residents were compelled to climb onto their roofs as their houses filled with water.

The flood claimed the lives of dozens of people and left tens of thousands homeless. However, the most significant loss in Florence was to art and culture as approximately 600,000 tons of mud, sewage, and oil were mixed with the water, causing damage to four million rare books and fourteen thousand works of art. In the aftermath, art and book restorers, as well as amateur volunteers worldwide, rallied to Florence's aid. Within a fortnight, two thousand overseas *angeli del fango* (mud angels) salvaged works of art from submerged rooms and commenced the painstaking process of cleaning the mud and sewage from each precious artifact. It was challenging work; these primarily young volunteers had to wear gas masks to shield themselves from the overpowering stench of decaying leather bindings and sewage.

The Franciscan Basilica of Santa Croce—a marvelous place to visit, by the way—was among the most severely flooded buildings, with water levels rising to twenty feet. Consequently, two significant works suffered extensive damage. Giovanni Cimabue's wooden crucifix was submerged to Christ's halo, and Giorgio Vasari's Last Supper was wholly immersed in sewage for twelve hours. The wooden crucifix had absorbed so much water that it had doubled in weight, and two-thirds of its original paint had been lost. The poplar wood was repopulated in a ten-year restoration, and the color was meticulously reapplied. The restoration of the Last Supper proved to be an even longer and more complex endeavor. The five waterlogged wooden panels had to await the development of new technology before restoration could be completed. However, it was recently unveiled again on the fiftieth anniversary of the devastating floods.

Water can cause severe damage to paintings as it loosens the priming layer, leading to the dissolution of colors. Blisters bubble up, and flecks of paint fall off the panel or canvas painting. To mitigate this, movable works of art were promptly transferred to huge low-humidity treatment facilities, where they were carefully wrapped in rice paper. Frescoes were trickier because they couldn't be moved quickly. Consequently, restorers drilled holes in the wall from the back, bottom, and top of the fresco, and heaters gradually reduced the moisture content within the artwork. Only when completely dry could the fresco be detached from the wall, marking the commencement of the more detailed stage of the restoration.

The most significant damage occurred to historical manuscripts and books in Florence, particularly at the *Biblioteca Nazionale Centrale*, equivalent to the UK's British Library or the US Library of Congress. This esteemed institution houses every book ever published in Italy, and it bore the weight of over a million damaged books in the aftermath of the flood. To salvage these valuable works, bindings had to be carefully cut, and each page underwent a meticulous cleansing process to remove sewage and mud. Subsequently, the pages were dried using various methods, including kilns, tobacco barns, washing lines, sawdust, or blotting paper (you might want to look that one up, kids). A team of dedicated book restorers implemented a comprehensive nine-step process to manage this complex operation, which included carefully separating each page before sending it to the improvised 'laundry' facility at Santa Maria Novella Railway Station.

If you recall Boris Johnson losing his place in the infamous Peppa Pig speech when the pages of his speech were not page-numbered, think of the challenges with this exercise. This process enabled the restorers to repair a hundred books daily. I'm sure some of you are beginning to do the calculations in your head. If 4,000,000 books are restored at a maximum rate of 100 per day, how long does it take Giuseppe to fix all the old books and manuscripts? The answer is 110 years. There are warehouses still full of books and manuscripts waiting to be processed.

Different restoration processes had to be employed for sculptures, wooden furniture, firearms, swords, bronzes, and precious metal *objets*. On a positive note, this tragic event transformed Florence into a global hub for art restoration, with the *Opificio delle Pietre Dure* serving as a great visit to understand the restorer's work.

While the flood was a human and artistic calamity for Florence, it was also a coming-together of a global community, including hundreds of Americans. There was a shared feeling from the international art community that the home of the Renaissance had to be saved. It should also act as a cautionary tale of professional hubris. Why, for example, did the *Biblioteca Nazionale Centrale* keep most of their books in the basement in a city renowned for flooding regularly?

The River Arno, which Dante charmingly dubbed "that cursed and unlucky ditch" 650 years ago, has undergone significant alterations. Italian engineers have constructed dams upstream and raised the riverbanks within the city with the intention of preventing such a catastrophe from recurring. When you visit Florence next, watch for plaques commemorating the historic flooding. However, they're not at eye level; you may need to crane your neck to look fifteen feet above your natural gaze.

Are We There Yet?

The Renaissance movement faltered in 1494 when the unaffable King Charles VIII of France invaded Florence, leading to the exile of the Medicis and the occupation of their palaces. Regrettably, this event also marked the end of relative peace among the city-states in Northern Italy. The Italian Wars erupted in the late fifteenth century as the French, Spanish, Swiss, and Germans launched frequent incursions into the Papal States and Southern Italy. Germanic tribes again sacked Rome in 1527, raping nuns, murdering priests, and executing wealthy people. Shockingly, it is believed that they murdered a quarter of Rome's population. Eventually, the Spanish emerged victorious from these conflicts, and their enduring cultural influence continues to shape Southern Italy to this day.

A resurgent Catholic Church viewed humanism as a challenge to its authority, leading to the reintroduction of censorship and the persecution of those who propagated humanist ideas. Over the following five decades, numerous texts that nourished the Renaissance and their inspired artworks were banned. In 1545, the Council of Trent formally endorsed the Inquisition and declared any viewpoints that questioned the Church as acts of heresy, punishable by death.

While the Spanish retained control of the South and Sicily, there were significant changes in the governance of Northern Italy's city-states. Notably, the Kingdom of Savoy expanded its borders in the first half of the seventeenth century by capturing Sardinia and other parts of Northern Italy. Meanwhile, the Austrians were granted control over Venice and Milan, ending their thousand-year history of independence.

In 1796, Napoleon emerged on the scene when the French once again invaded the Italian peninsula, resulting in the establishment of several new republics. Three years later, the Austrians retook control of these newly-formed republics with some assistance from the Russians, only for Napoleon to re-conquer them in the early nineteenth century. Following Napoleon's downfall (and more on him later), the Congress of Vienna essentially restored the former Italian Kingdoms under the rule of conservative leaders.

With their feudalist way of thinking, these conservative leaders were as popular as a math test on a Friday afternoon. Guiseppe Mazzini, a nineteenth-century social influencer primarily based in London, formed one of many secret societies aiming to create a unified Italian state. The first uprisings were repelled by the conservative leaders and their Austrian enforcers. However, after the French defeated the Austrians in 1859,

Italian unifiers made a resurgence. The charismatic and courageous military leader Giuseppe Garibaldi played a pivotal role in the Risorgimento, the movement for a united Italy. He assembled a force of one thousand men to overthrow the Bourbon monarchy ruling in the Southern part of Italy. Despite being vastly outnumbered, they achieved an unlikely victory, and the remaining Papal States quickly joined the new Italy.

After nearly two millennia, Italy was finally united once again.

Are We There Yet?

Chapter 11 – A Reunited Italy

Not all historians believe Italian reunification was a good thing. Some from the *Mezzogiorno* (Italian for midday and nickname for the South) believed that the North's occupation of the South led to economic decline and mass emigration, while some Northern-based ones wondered if a united Northern Italy might be more prosperous and mafia-free.

You might also wonder how this Italian history is linked to America. While it's true that many of the founding fathers of the 'New Italy' (including Garibaldi) received their education in the US, the most significant connection lies in the fact that, after reunification, approximately one-quarter of Italy's population emigrated from the newly-formed Italy for economic reasons.

Although Italy industrialized quickly, this modernization was concentrated in wealthier North Italy. The South remained chiefly agricultural, with farmers scraping by on peasant incomes on farms with low-quality land owned primarily by Northerners. In addition, Italy's modernization brought higher tax rates, disproportionately affecting the poorest. Southern Italians, therefore, felt little allegiance to the Italian government, which was mainly run by Northerners, and retreated to a *la-famiglia* loyalty.

This period was marked by numerous natural disasters in Southern Italy. Cholera and malaria epidemics were frequent, and the volcanoes of Etna and Vesuvius erupted. In 1908, a devastating earthquake and tsunami struck Sicily and Puglia, resulting in the loss of 75,000 lives in Messina alone. Another factor that drove migration was the compulsory seven-year military conscription of the era.

During that post-Risorgimento period, nearly half of Italy's population chose to emigrate, and most of these eleven million migrants were men from the South. According to the Italian Ministry of Foreign Affairs, two-thirds of this number went to the US and Canada.

At the turn of the century, the illiteracy rate in Southern Italy stood at a staggering 70 percent, nearly ten times higher than in any other European country of the time. Consequently, many Italian immigrants in the US obtained low-wage jobs in the construction industry.

Many 'birds of passage' took advantage of the *padrone* system, in which Italian middlemen (*padroni*) facilitated transportation, lodging, and employment for a fee. An American teacher who had previously studied in Italy was deeply troubled by Italian immigrants' working and living conditions, so she formed the Society for the Protection of Italian Immigrants.

Many Italians initially came to the US intending to return to Italy. As the time for a three-thousand-mile ship journey accelerated, some would even commute to the US for the summer, returning to Southern Italy for the winter. Although statistics from the period are notoriously unreliable, around two-thirds stayed in the US, forming mini-Italian communities in their new homeland. Ultimately, these new Little Italies would become permanent homes for their wives, children, and extended families.

Early Italian immigrants brought a strong sense of respect for family and elders but also harbored a deep suspicion of organized authority and other communities. Unlike the Irish Americans, Italian Americans were slow to organize into larger organizations and voting blocs. Their identity was attached to their village of origin rather than Italy as a whole.

This slow integration coincided with a deep prejudice against Italians. Newspapers often propagated pseudo-scientific theories that depicted Italians as congenitally inferior to their Northern European counterparts. Italians were blamed for crime, the Mafia, and socialism. Anti-immigrant groups, such as the Ku Klux Klan, gained support, leading to frequent attacks on Italian buildings and people.

For instance, in New Orleans in 1891, the mayor wrongly accused Sicilian gangsters of assassinating the chief of police. He rounded up a hundred Sicilian Americans, and nineteen were eventually put on trial. When they were found not guilty, a mob of ten thousand people broke into the jail, forcibly removed eleven Sicilians from their holding cells, and publicly lynched them.

The 1920s marked a significant decline in Italian immigration. The 1921 Emergency Quota Act and the 1924 Immigration Act both imposed discriminatory restrictions on Italians. These laws favored Northern

Are We There Yet?

Europeans, with Germans receiving a thirteen times larger quota than that of Italians. Despite these stringent limitations, Italian migrants still constituted one out of every sixteen new immigrants.

Italian Americans often harbored a distrust toward formal education, which influenced the trajectory of upward mobility for future generations, leading many into small businesses rather than professional occupations. There were, unquestionably, exceptions. For instance, Italians with banking experience founded the Bank of Italy, which later evolved into the Bank of America, now one of the largest banks in the world.

By 1920, as Italians became more integrated into American society, they began to secure higher-skilled positions as police officers, firefighters, and skilled tradespeople. With these better-paying jobs, many moved away from the Italian districts, while the large number of Little Italies became more prosperous.

In the twenties and thirties, Italian Americans started making significant contributions to broader American culture through classical and popular music, movies, sports, the wine industry, and the labor movement. These early pioneers paved the way for more celebrated figures in the forties and fifties to thrive. It is difficult to imagine music without the contribution of Bennett, Como, Darin, Martin, and Sinatra. In cinema, Capra, Kazan, Makiewicz, Minnelli, Sturges, and Wise have directed many of America's favorite movies, while Brando, Dean, Lewis, Lollobridgida, Loren, Newman, and Sinatra (again) have acted in them. A world without Tom & Jerry and Woody Woodpecker would be poorer, not least because they inspired dozens of other Italian cartoonists and animators.

Italian Americans played pivotal roles in a wide range of fields, including academics, architecture, design, diplomacy, fashion, journalism, law enforcement, literature, the military, politics, and science. These innovators in every area of human endeavor were typically second-generation immigrants who descended from the mainly illiterate Italians who came to the US around the turn of the century.

So, when you hear someone talking about admitting only highly skilled immigrants to your country, remember that almost no Italians from this period would have been admitted under these criteria, and America would be much poorer for it. These vast numbers of destitute immigrants from Southern Italy were proof points that anyone could achieve upward mobility through hard work.

When America finally joined World War II, FDR's Executive Order 9066 classified some 0.6 million unnaturalized Italians as enemy aliens and restricted their movement. The Federal Government interned one thousand unnaturalized Italian Americans in military camps, and ten thousand others were forced to move inland from their West Coast homes.

A lingering sense of wariness toward other communities often led Italians to naturalize slower than other immigrant groups. This delay affected their integration into American society. However, during World War II, many Italian Americans chose to expedite their naturalization rather than risk being labeled as enemies of the state. Consequently, more than a million Italian Americans—about 10 percent of the total armed forces—would serve to fight for America.

While Italian immigrants had a low arrest rate similar to other immigrant groups, a small minority introduced a different subculture. Initially, the Mafia preyed on their own community, extorting protection money from Little Italy businesses.

However, when the Fascists came to power in Italy in the early 1920s, Mussolini prioritized dismantling the Mafia. Consequently, hundreds of mafia henchmen fled to America to avoid prosecution. Coincidentally, their arrival corresponded with the era of Prohibition, which presented economic opportunities for gangsters willing to engage in illegal activities—albeit those enjoyed by a significant portion of Americans.

The most infamous mafia gangster was Al Capone, whose parents emigrated from Naples in 1893. Capone was born in Brooklyn and became involved in crime early, having dropped out of school in the sixth grade after assaulting a teacher.

Capone relocated to Chicago at the age of 20. Within six years, he had become the most influential mafia boss there, taking control of alcohol production and distribution and amassing an annual income of approximately $100 million (equivalent to around $1.5 billion in today's money). Capone saw it differently, describing himself as a simple businessman who gave people what they wanted.

Capone had utterly compromised the Chicago law enforcement community. Consequently, President Hoover directed Federal Agencies to restore law and order. Eliot Ness and his team of 'Untouchables' designated Capone as Public Enemy Number One and focused their efforts on dismantling his criminal enterprises.

Famously, Capone was not convicted for traditional mafia activity but rather for tax fraud, as he had neglected to pay any income tax between

1925 and 1929. Capone eventually pleaded guilty to tax evasion and was sentenced to eleven years.

Capone was incarcerated in Alcatraz. He suffered from syphilis of the brain and, on early release from prison in 1939, endured ill health until he passed away in Florida seven years later.

In the fifties, Congress passed legislation granting new powers for witness protection and modern surveillance techniques against the Mafia. Two young Italian-American prosecutors—Louis Freeh and Rudy Giuliani—harnessed these newfound powers to pursue mafia bosses. Louis Freeh successfully prosecuted the Gambini crime family before serving as a Federal Judge, eventually rising to the position of FBI Director. Rudy Giuliani established an organized crime unit focused on dismantling the Mafia in New York City. He would later be elected its mayor before, much later, thoroughly discrediting himself by becoming Donald Trump's personal lawyer.

You may be wrong if you think prejudice against Italian Americans has disappeared. The TV and movie industry has regularly depicted the Italian community overwhelmingly negatively. *The Godfather*, *Goodfellas*, *The Sopranos*, *The Jersey Shore*, and even *Shark Tale* portray an Italian-American community full of violent criminals and sociopaths. According to the Italic Institute of America, two-thirds of movies about Italian Americans present them negatively, and an average of nine new mafia movies are produced annually. These one-sided portrayals would not be tolerated for other ethnic groups.

The truth is, of course, quite different. According to FBI estimates, there are approximately 3,000 Italian-American mafia members and associates in the US today, roughly one in every 6,000 individuals who identify as Italian Americans.

However, the Mafia is still highly prominent in Italy, and any discussion of the country would be incomplete without an overview of its four main mafia groups.

The *Cosa Nostra* from Sicily is the most well-known, primarily due to its frequent portrayal in movies. Its main operation involves offering protection to roughly three-quarters of shop owners in Sicily in exchange for a small payment, known as *'pizzo.'*

The *Ndrangheta* is the largest crime syndicate globally, comprising around 160 family clans and engaging a further estimated 60,000 global associates. Clan leaders, known as the *Madrine*, are expected to maximize their offspring, with sons joining the family business and daughters marrying into other *Ndrangheta* clans.

Until the mid-seventies, the *Ndrangheta* restricted itself to extortion and blackmail primarily in the toe of the boot of Italy. Then, it successfully diversified into kidnapping, capturing around two hundred people, including the soon-to-be-one-ear-less John Paul Getty III. Since that time, it has continued to diversify and expand internationally. Today, it is considered the fifth-largest enterprise in Italy, generating annual revenues of up to $80 billion, approximately 3.5 percent of Italy's GDP.

Over half of *Ndragnheta's* money comes from dominating Europe's cocaine industry. They are the preferred business partners of the Columbian cartels. So, if you have sniffed some blow, you will likely have the *Ndrangheta* and their sophisticated blend of violence, financial controls, and supply chain management to thank. Their other significant business is illegal garbage disposal, which generates around $20 billion. Its previous core businesses of extortion, embezzlement, gambling, public work contracts, arms trading, prostitution, and counterfeiting are now legacy businesses.

Given that the *Ndrangheta* is essentially a family business, Italian authorities have found it challenging to infiltrate this mafia group. This dynamic began to shift with the appointment of Nicola Gratteri, a fellow native of Calabria, as an Anti-Mafia prosecutor three decades ago. In 2019, a massive operation involving three thousand police officers led to the arrest of three hundred and fifty *Ndrangheta* associates from the Mancuso clan after four years of collecting evidence.

In 2021, the largest mafia trial in three decades commenced, with politicians, businesspeople, and lawyers on trial in a specially constructed courtroom. The world's most extensive courtroom—converted from a former call center and guarded by the Italian Army—accommodates the defendants, their lawyers, the prosecutors, and about a thousand witnesses. Remarkably, this maxi trial focuses solely on one clan from two small communes in Calabria. However, it is anticipated that further trials involving other families will follow.

The first defendants opted for 'speedy' trials, resulting in the conviction of seventy individuals. The fate of the remaining alleged mafia members will be determined in the coming years.

The preceding maxi trial in 1992 resulted in the assassination of its two lead prosecutors. In the first attack, the *Cosa Nostra* targeted Giovanni

Falcone, blowing up the motorway he was traveling on. In the second incident, Paolo Borsellino's car was bombed.

The current prosecutor has lived under police protection for thirty years. Fifty-eight state witnesses from this trial have recently joined him, including Nicola Bonaventura, son of one of the bosses. A recent alumnus of one of Italy's prisons after being convicted of multiple murders, his wife persuaded him to testify against the *Ndrangheta*. I certainly would not be selling either of them life assurance.

Eager to maintain a lower profile, there are two additional sizeable mafia communities. In the Naples area, a hundred or so *Camorra* gangs involve themselves in various criminal activities. In Apulia, the *Sacra Corona Unita* is the fourth largest and most recently formed. Founded only in 1981 by former *Camorra* members, its principal business is smuggling drugs, cigarettes, weapons, and people from Albania across the Adriatic.

How important are all these mafia families to the Italian economy? On a net basis, they likely have an overall negative impact on economic output. However, they still account for approximately 5 percent of Italy's GDP.

****

We shopped at the market daily for ingredients. Our kitchen was well-equipped but had one drawback. Although our induction stove top had four separate hobs, we soon learned there was a limitation to the total power that could be applied. While each hob could theoretically heat from 0 to 10, the sum of all hobs could total no more than 12. This meant that if one hob needed more power, another had to be adjusted lower. Managing power consumption became even more challenging when using other electrical appliances simultaneously.

With cooking finally accomplished, we decided to catch a movie. There's a joy in experiencing everyday activities in different countries. While some things are the same, I enjoy spotting the differences, as they often reveal a defining feature of a culture. Italian showings often have a break in the middle—with films now so long, this is literally a much-needed relief. However, Italians use this pause to refill their glasses.

After the movies, we enjoyed late-night walks in the city. The young would congregate on their Vespas in piazzas on Friday and Saturday nights, entertained by classical buskers demonstrating their violin or ballet skills.

Julian Bishop

I began to play tennis illegally at a local Italian club. Illegally, I hear you ask. Do you mean you made some questionable line calls? No doubt. However, my 'crime' was that I failed to provide a *certificato medico* with ECG (both at rest and during exercise) from a specialist sports doctor before participating in any exercise or sporting program, as required by Italian law. It's just one of the many regulations that specialists have advocated for, all in the name of their profession's benefit.

Few members of this club spoke much English besides the many English terms used in Italian for the tennis game. The exception was Valentino, the president of the club. He was a generous man whose first girlfriend was English. They had met on vacation in Greece and continued the relationship for a year, visiting each other's country every month. Ultimately, she wanted to remain in the UK and he in Italy. I wondered if—somewhere in England—a late-middle-aged woman was also lamenting what could have been.

It seemed important for Valentino to shower together after each match; for him, it was part of the ritual. Consequently, I started bringing my clean clothes to the club instead of walking the thirty minutes home in my sweaty tennis attire. He was proud of his club and the changing rooms that he had provided for it.

As I strolled to and from the club in the late evening, I couldn't help but notice the constant shortage of parking spaces. Italians have a unique approach to parking; they expertly maneuver into impossibly tight spots, and it's not unusual to see cars double (or even triple) parked on sharp bends, all done with the precision of ensuring every vehicle can theoretically escape its position. Bus drivers demonstrate immense skill in navigating through the narrow openings left by these parking acrobatics. Meanwhile, mopeds seem to form a never-ending line, almost like they're waiting for a James Bond car chase to sweep through and scatter them like pins in a bowling alley.

People who are lightly traveled often believe that routine things are done the same way the world over. In reality, they can vary significantly. Take something simple, such as the collection of trash from your home. This is quite different in Florence from other places where we have lived. In the cities, huge receptacles are buried in the ground of each street: one for general waste, another for paper, and a third for plastics. Each householder simply takes their garbage and deposits it into the appropriate slot. Then, the sanitation workers simply and efficiently empty each central receptacle daily.

Are We There Yet?

This differs from the UK, where every householder has many separate bins for each type of waste they have to put outside on different days for the dustman to collect. In the US, we have learned that refuse collection varies widely by city. In our previous residence in Georgia, a free-market approach allowed multiple waste management services to compete for customers. This was good because the service was cheap, a third of that of the nearest city with a monopoly provider. However, it would have been good to have one day of the week when the trucks did not wake you as they collected your neighborhood's garbage.

My former business school professor received a hard lesson in culture in his first week in Switzerland. Although he had received written instructions not to put out his garbage until 6:00 pm, he decided to be proactive and did so at 5:40 pm. To his surprise, a policeman knocked on his door at 5:50 pm, informing him that a neighbor had complained that he had taken his garbage out before the appointed time. The police asked my friend to bring his garbage container back into the confines of his house, by which time it was 6:00 pm, and he could legally take it outside again. It was an unconventional introduction to his new neighbors.

While Switzerland, Austria, and Germany are renowned for their strict adherence to the rules, Italy is equally famous for both breaking rules and being the home of an intractable bureaucracy.

Part of the reason for this bureaucracy is that Italy is one of the most demographically decentralized countries in the world. Even the largest metro area, Milan, only has 7 percent of the total population, and over half of Italians reside in towns with fewer than twenty thousand inhabitants.

Italy has four layers of government: national, regional, provincial, and municipal. While the US has similar layers, it's usually clear what level of government is responsible for which activity. In Italy, on the other hand, there are times when all four levels appear to have jurisdiction over the same matters.

Using policing as an example, Italy's law enforcement system consists of five national police forces, a hundred provincial police services, and approximately eight thousand municipal police departments. These police authorities are funded and overseen by different bodies, operate independently of each other, and maintain their own rules of engagement.

Although Italy has this unwanted reputation for bureaucracy, this isn't necessarily across all layers of the government. Several municipal, provincial, and regional governments have efficiency levels comparable to other European countries.

Robert Putnam, a Harvard political scientist, correlated a range of regional Italian data with measures of good government. He found that those provinces and municipalities with more extended periods of self-rule in the Middle Ages tended to have higher social capital—what the Italians call *civismo*—which generally led to better local government performance.

While there are a few bright spots in some former city-states, Italy performs poorly on most government efficiency measures. Its famed bureaucracy makes it a nightmare for *businesses*. In the most recent World Bank's *Ease of Doing Business* rankings, Italy ranks 98th in the world for starting a business, 128th for paying taxes, and 122nd for enforcing contracts. On this latter measure, resolving a commercial dispute takes an average of just over three years: that's 10 days to submit paperwork, 840 days for the trial, and 270 days for the judgment and enforcement. Predictably, Italian companies often avoid making significant changes due to the lengthy and costly contractual uncertainties involved.

Dealing with the government is bewildering for the *individual*, as well. Although he wouldn't have known it then, Dante's words, "Abandon hope all ye who enter here," perfectly describe the experience of visiting Italian government offices, post offices, and police headquarters. Simply finding the appropriate office and its often-limited opening hours can be difficult, and when you have, you'd better strap yourself in for a long ride whether you have to declare your presence in a municipality, renew your driving license, file your taxes, or register a new car. According to Facebook expat pages, spending hours waiting in line is common, only to discover that they have run out of that application form.

This day-to-day bureaucracy—much worse in the South than the North—affords many opportunities for government officials at all levels to supplement their meager income during their (brief) careers. How many of us would spend days in government offices when an official could expedite the process for a minor consideration?

Some may call this behavior corruption. However, many Italians might describe it slightly differently.

Verità is the Italian word for truth. As with many other words, it has its roots in Latin. Enigmatically, *verità* is also the Italian word for version, a more than slightly different concept.

This linguistic ambiguity may reflect the Italians' renowned adaptability. For example, in most Western democracies, it's relatively uncommon for politicians to switch political parties. While we can all think of a case where someone has moved from Republican to Democrat or vice versa, or a similar shift from the Conservative to the Labour Party in the UK, such instances are infrequent. However, in Italy, party-switching is almost customary. For example, during the 2008-2012 legislature, 100 out of 650 deputies changed parties.

In World War I, the Italians changed sides from the Triple Alliance to the Allies in 1915. They repeated the trick in World War II when they again sided with the Allies in 1943 despite having been a founder member of the Axis for the first four years of the conflict.

Why commit to a point of view on any issue when you can be confident of being on the right side by waiting a bit to see which option will prevail? Italian leaders have honed the skill of delivering news while keeping their options open. They refer to this behavior as '*garbo*,' behaving elegantly.

Visitors to Italy are initially perplexed about how they should line up for a service, for example, to use public transport. After a while, the visitors figure out how things are done and adapt accordingly. "When in Rome...," or should I say, especially in Rome.

Italians are famed for skipping the line. In Italian, it is called *fare il furbo*. '*Furbo*' is a flexible word. As with many other Italian words, it has multiple meanings: cunning, sly, or crafty. These aren't positive words, but they are not entirely negative either. Indeed, many Italians see you as a *fesso* (idiot) if you pay full price for a ticket or tell the tax man your actual income. It seems that many Italians divide others into the *furbi* and the *fessi*.

Many moons ago, I was the HR Director for a business unit of a large multinational company. Our company had a global policy of force-ranking employee performance by giving better performers higher bonuses. However, only one in five employees could receive the highest compensation, with a further one in ten condemned to receive a small bonus (which the company hoped would nudge them to look elsewhere for work). As you can imagine, it was quite a stressful experience for everyone concerned. Nearly every manager wanted their team to receive high bonuses, leaving no one in the lowest bonus category. To make the process manageable, I tasked each country with force-ranking their employees and facilitated these difficult discussions. Every country eventually provided a ranking of employees by performance—except for Italy.

The Italian managers moaned that this wasn't how you did things in Italy. I would retort by saying it was how our company did things worldwide. Very slowly, I managed to facilitate them in making the required distributions. It was hard work, and I had to drag them every inch of the way.

This company had a computer database where you recorded the performance level of each employee. For some reason, this system had a cut-off time, after which these ratings were locked forever. In the first year of forced-ranking performance, the Italian HR person reluctantly went into the system and entered the bonus levels of the Italian consultants. I recall checking the system to ensure they met the required distributions at 10 pm and sent an email congratulating the Italian managers for their hard work. However, sometime before midnight, someone revisited the system and altered all the rankings to their preferred arrangement, where most people received the top bonus award. I only discovered this the next day. At that point, there was nothing I could do. There was a collective shrug of shoulders, and Global HR performance experts informed me that this was how the Italians did things. Nobody wanted a big argument.

The following year, the situation was very similar. Once again, the Italian managers dragged their feet about making the required compromises. Eventually, they complied. The Italian HR manager entered the appropriate bonus levels into the HR system, which I approved. I sent a congratulatory email. Someone in Italy then went back into the system to change the bonus levels back to their preferred non-distribution at 11 pm. However, on this occasion, I revisited the system at 11:30 pm to restore the bonuses to the agreed-upon compliant levels. The next day, I anticipated the mother of all arguments. However, it was the opposite. I had out-*furboed* them and could sense a higher level of respect for doing so. This is one of the many reasons I love Italy.

There is a similar gray area in telling the truth. Being creative with *la verità* is endemic and sometimes admired.

One widely venerated example occurred during the Cold War when the Italians were apprehensive about the presence of Soviet bloc troops amassed in their former Istrian territories. The Italians created an almost entirely fictional 300,000-person brigade, the *Terzo Corpo Designato d'Armata*, that was supposed to patrol the Northeast of Italy. The idea was that the mere presence of this pretend army—and its equally fictional tanks, artillery, and weapons—would deter the Soviets from invading. The army wasn't entirely imaginary; it had a general and small staff whose job was to leak false information about the brigade to the Soviets. These staff worked tirelessly to generate copious amounts of paperwork for these 300,000 fictional soldiers. Remarkably, this ruse hoodwinked Soviet intelligence, who believed the unit was real and thought it a genuine threat to their troops.

You might expect me to unearth some data about sexual cheating. Unfortunately, no comparable data on infidelity exists, so I cannot determine whether Italians are more faithful to their partners than other nationalities… or otherwise. However, Vodafone, the cellular phone carrier, used to have a product called *Alter Ego*, where the subscriber had two phone numbers on one SIM card, effectively enabling the user to keep their spouse's communications entirely separate from their lover's. This service was only available in Italy and was described as "a local market initiative with only significant demand in one country."

Cheating at school is commonplace. In one survey, three-quarters of all pre-teens reported that they had cheated at school. Predictably, the first business enterprise that Silvio Berlusconi established was an essay-writing service that allowed students to submit essays written by others.

To aid scholastic cheating, Italian fashion houses have designed a specialist form of clothing, *la cartucciera*, a cotton belt that sits under your shirt and enables the wearer to conceal multiple *bigliettini* (crib sheets). The digital era has widened the opportunity to be *furbo*; many students have watches and pens capable of concealing electronic *bigliettini*.

Cheating is wrong, but you would be a *fesso* if you didn't participate when all others do so.

Cheating on the *maturita*, which is similar to the SAT/ACT and determines university admissions for eighteen-year-olds, is so widespread that education authorities have been forced to take extreme measures to combat it. In the past, one could purchase these tests illegally on the dark web weeks before the examination day. Today, the examination board sends access codes to schools only thirty minutes before the start of the exam.

Another place where cheating is rife is in the criminal justice system. For just €100, you can buy the services of a witness who will swear on oath that you were driving within the speed limit or on the right side of the road. The more serious the offense, the higher the cost. Given that testimony is often as reliable as a screen door on a submarine, Italian authorities must resort to alternative methods to secure convictions. One such method is the extensive use of wiretaps—Italy authorizes one hundred times more per capita yearly than the US.

Unlike most European countries, the Italian legal system is not based on the Napoleonic code and does not employ juries. Instead, it prefers a small panel of professional judges. However, this system does not result in a more efficient court process. On average, it takes 3.4 years for criminal cases and 5.5 years for civil cases to move from indictment to conviction. Compared to the United States, Italian penalties are notably lenient; the average murderer serves just twelve years, while an embezzler spends only sixteen months behind bars. Moreover, the likelihood of going to jail is low if you are over seventy years old.

This is assuming you are even convicted in the first place. Italian law guarantees two appeals, which can take about eight years to process. Except in cases of murder and mafia collaboration, most convicted individuals are not incarcerated until the second appeal is finalized. Often, by this time, the statute of limitations has been reached.

These lenient penalties not only embolden individuals and companies to take action first and seek permission later but also foster corruption. It's often more convenient to offer a *bustarella* (a wad of notes) to achieve immediate results, knowing that future consequences will likely be minimal or nonexistent, rather than navigating the correct but endlessly protracted bureaucratic processes.

Data analysis shows that first- and second-generation Italian Americans commit crimes in the US at the same rate as British, Scandinavian, and German immigrants. This is because the same strict deterrents are in place for each group, and statutes of limitations are lengthy.

Another common form of corruption is nepotism. This comes from the Italian word *nipote*, which means both grandchild and nephew. According to the OECD, more than twice as many Italians than other OECD countries obtain their jobs through who they know rather than via formal recruitment processes.

In 2015, Italy sat at the bottom among European countries in Transparency International's *Corruption Perception Index*. It also ranked 102nd out of 144 countries in the World Economic Forum's indicator on ethics and corruption and 95th in control of corruption. This corruption was estimated to have cost about 4 percent of GDP.

Even more challenging was the detrimental effect this corruption has on economic growth. Corruption tends to deter domestic and international investment, stifles competition, hampers entrepreneurship, and results in inefficient government spending. All of these affect economic growth.

Are We There Yet?

There is a light on the horizon for Italy. Recent data indicates a slight decrease in corruption in Italy, resulting in its ranking rising above that of some Eastern European countries.

****

At the end of World War II—with Italy firmly on the winning side—King Victor Emmanuel III attempted to save the Italian monarchy by abdicating in favor of his son, Umberto II. However, Victor Emmanuel's earlier support for the fascists was still profoundly unpopular, and after the people voted to abolish the monarchy in a 1946 nationwide referendum, the House of Savoy was compelled to go into exile in Egypt and Portugal.

Like most other countries in Europe, Italy has multiple political parties. This pluralism stands in contrast to the UK and the US, where the two-party system is now the norm. It's worth noting that the two-party system was not the intended system in America. Founding Father John Adams once wrote, "There is nothing I dread so much as a division of the republic into two parties, each arranged under its leader and concerting measures in opposition to each other."

However, with so many parties in Italy, no party ever attains a majority, so coalitions of semi-liked-minded individuals are forged to rule the country.

The 1946 election was pivotal. At the time, Italy had the largest Communist Party membership in Western Europe, and there was intense international pressure on them to avoid a leftist coalition that might align them with the Soviet Union.

US President Harry Truman pressured Italy to exclude the Communist and Socialist Parties from government. The CIA funded center-right political parties and fabricated letters that 'proved' the Soviets financed the Italian Communist Party (it did, but not to the extent claimed). US federal agencies also funded propaganda radio broadcasts, books, and articles warning of the dangers of communism. Furthermore, Italian voters received ten million letters from Italian Americans urging them not to vote for communist candidates. But, perhaps most persuasively at the time, the Vatican told its congregations that voting for the Communist Party would be a mortal sin punishable by excommunication.

The Christian Democrats (DC) alliance resoundingly won the 1946 election, with both the Communist Party (PCI) and the more moderate Socialist Party (PSI) receiving 20 percent of the vote.

For most of the rest of the century, the Christian Democrats governed Italy. For almost all of this period, the opposition was consistently led by the strongly supported Communist Party,

Italy was active in international politics, serving as a founding member of NATO, the United Nations, and the organizations that would later evolve into the European Union. It was also a strong ally of the United States. The funding Italy received from the Marshall Plan propelled Italy into unprecedented economic growth.

In the early fifties, one-quarter of Italian families were reckoned to be destitute, with only half the houses in the South having access to running water. However, over the next two decades, Italy experienced a *miracolo economico*. During this period, its economy grew strongly while those of Britain and France languished. By 1970, per capita income in Italy had nearly caught up with that of the UK.

By the seventies, however, the Christian Democrats looked out of touch, as their traditional Christian values jarred with a modernizing Italy and were forced to rule with increasingly broader coalitions with other minority parties.

The prime minister for much of the seventies was Giulio Andreotti. He failed to resolve Italy's main challenges of the time: an unrestrained Mafia, inefficient social services, and massive inequality between the North and South.

Italy introduced laws that increased spending in the South and improved social services. They imposed restrictions on businesses that refused to guarantee jobs, increased fringe benefits to unprecedented levels, and aligned pay with inflation. As a result, real wages rose by three-quarters in the seventies without the requisite increase in productivity. By the mid-seventies, Italian workers were the best-paid, most protected, and had the most generous welfare provisions. Perhaps the worst political decision was made by two-time prime minister Mariano Rumor. To woo public sector workers, he allowed state employees to retire after nineteen-and-a-half years of service, with women who had children being able to retire five years earlier.

As in many other European countries, the student movement in the seventies protested against Italy's system of government and occupied large businesses. These led to extremist riots from both left and right. This turbulent period, gli *anni di piombo* (years of lead), was characterized by bombings, assassinations, and other acts of terrorism. The most infamous incident was the kidnapping of former Prime Minister Aldo Moro by the

Are We There Yet?

Brigate Rosse (Red Brigade). Resolutely, Prime Minister Andreotti refused to negotiate with terrorists for his release, and tragically, Moro was found guilty in a 'people's court.' Due to the absence of any protracted appeal process, the brigadistas stuffed his lifeless body into the cramped trunk of a Renault 4.

The PCI was the best-performing communist party in a Western European democracy. It consistently outperformed the more moderate PSI due to its better organization and grassroots support. Over time, it gradually grew in popularity but only once attracted more than a third of the votes. When the PCI eventually surpassed the Christian Democrats in 1984, it was the more moderate Socialist Bettino Craxi who became the first prime minister not to come from the Christian Democrat Party. His Socialists preferred an alliance with the Christian Democrats over being a supporting partner in a Communist-led government. In just four years, this centrist Government presided over a massive increase in Italian debt.

Italian for Bribeville, *tangentopoli* was a series of investigations that exposed rampant corruption in every political party (except for the Communist Party). Companies seeking government-sponsored contracts were forced to pay kickbacks to politicians in exchange for winning those contracts. These illicit funds not only financed political parties but also found their way into politicians' personal bank accounts. Understandably, these revelations sent shockwaves through the political and business establishments, ultimately marking the end of the First Republic. This scandal shocked even Italians and resulted in the disbandment of most existing political parties and a referendum that changed the voting system. The next set of elections led to a 70 percent turnover in deputies and senators.

The New Republic sought to hold former politicians accountable through Milanese judges known as the *Mani pulite* (clean hands). Andreotti—or Uncle Giulio as the *Cosa Nostra* knew him—was tried for having close mafia connections and being involved in several assassinations. He was acquitted in his first two trials, primarily because much of the evidence fell outside the legal statute of limitations. However, Andreotti was eventually convicted of consorting with the Mafia to kill a troublesome journalist, Mino Pecorelli. The lower court sentenced Andreotti to twenty-four years in jail, a penalty upheld by the first appeal court. However, in 2003, the Italian Supreme Court overturned the judgment, and Andreotti died a free man a decade later.

The main casualty of *Mani pulite* was Bettino Craxi, who was pelted with coins by angry Romans as he left the Piazza Navona hotel where he lived. Rather than declaring his innocence, Craxi contended that everyone else was equally guilty. To evade nine years in prison, Craxi fled to Tunisia, a nation to which he had illicitly funneled *tangentopoli* funds in 1987.

In practice, it was unlikely that he would have ever gone to jail. Although approximately half of the five thousand people investigated by the *Mani pulite* were indicted, only four ever served time in prison. The low conviction rate can be attributed to a combination of factors, including the slow court process, law changes, frequent amnesties, and statutes of limitations.

Another incidental victim of *Mani pulite* was Silvio Berlusconi. Installation artist Gianni Motti created a bar of soap allegedly from the waste fat from one of Silvio Berlusconi's many liposuction operations. Wittily, he named the soap *Mani pulite*—clean hands.

In the Second Republic, entirely new political parties were established. Silvio Berlusconi started his Forza Italia party less than a year before he came to power, some say as a mechanism to protect his businesses from scrutiny. Berlusconi was a protégé of Craxi—indeed, Craxi was godfather to one of Berlusconi's children and best man at his second wedding. More sinisterly, Berlusconi also paid 23 billion lire (about $34 million in today's money) into Craxi's offshore bank account for approval of his media empire.

Initially positioned on the center-left of the political spectrum and attracting former-socialist voters, the seemingly candid Berlusconi elevated political imagery to new levels. Relentlessly optimistic about Italy, the fashionably attired Berlusconi ruled as prime minister for over a decade.

Berlusconi organized other parties, too, particularly those involving hundreds of very young, professional women. In 2010, Berlusconi's then-wife issued a statement saying that her husband was a sick man who consorted with minors. Subsequently, video and audio recordings emerged of him engaging in pillow talk with underage girls at these infamous Bunga Bunga parties. A year later, Berlusconi resigned as prime minister but continued to exert significant influence on Italian politics.

Like his recent predecessors, Berlusconi avoided jail time for many offenses. He didn't join the ten Italian ex-presidents and prime ministers imprisoned since 1900, a world record incidentally, easily surpassing

Are We There Yet?

Pakistan's meager eight. However, he faced investigations and trials for a wide range of charges, including money laundering, false accounting, forming a cartel and violation of anti-trust laws, embezzlement, mafia association, complicity in murder, paying underage girls for sex, and bribing judges, lawyers, politicians, and the police. Quite some rap sheet, making America's forty-fifth president look like a model citizen. Most of these charges were timed out, with Berlusconi and his companies benefitting greatly from many laws he changed as prime minister.

The mafia associations date back to the late seventies and early eighties when the former cruise ship singer Berlusconi allegedly received 99 billion lire (about $116 million) to build his media empire. Berlusconi exercised his right to silence. On gaining power—partly by winning all sixty-one Sicilian seats in parliament—Forza Italia softened jail conditions for mafia members and reduced the confiscation of their property. How extensively did Italian news report this? Not much. Berlusconi owned or influenced 90 percent of free-to-air TV news and numerous newspapers during his time in power.

Like that other mafia associate, Al Capone, Berlusconi was eventually convicted of some €7 million in tax fraud, with a further €55 million having fallen foul of the statute of limitations. He was ultimately sentenced to four years in jail. However, as Berlusconi was over seventy years old, three years were automatically wiped off his sentence. The remaining year could be served as community service, and he chose to volunteer four hours a week at a care home. If someone tells you that crime never pays, they obviously haven't thoroughly studied Italy.

At times of greatest crisis, Italy adopts technocratic governments formed chiefly of ministers with some competence. It is an interesting idea, but these Italian governments rarely last long.

The Italians are often derided around the world for their chaotic national governments. In the 78 years since WWII, Italy has had 67 governments, with an average duration of 1.16 years for those who prefer not to do the math.

While true, this is a little misleading. In Italy, each coalition government comprises politicians from multiple parties. The prime minister wields executive power through a Council of Ministers representing all coalition parties. According to Italian law, a change of government is mandated every time there is a reshuffle of this Council. Often, a new government does not necessarily imply a new prime minister but rather a change in the composition of this cabinet. Thus, a new government must be formed if one of the smaller political parties exits or enters the coalition. This regular turnover keeps the Head of State, the President, as busy as a bee in a beehive with a packed schedule. So, while there have indeed been 67 separate governments, there have only been 31 prime ministers, roughly one every two and half years.

Since the establishment of the Second Republic, several anti-establishment right-of-center parties—such as the Five-Star movement, the Northern League, and the National Alliance—have been formed. Some of these parties garner enough votes to join a coalition and exert an influence on policymaking.

At the time of writing, the latest prime minister is Georgia Meloni, who secured a quarter of the vote in the 2022 elections. Her recent success continues the shift of European politics toward the right. A mere decade after the SNOQ movement was formed, this professional politician became Italy's first female prime minister. As with several prime ministers before her, she swiftly ascended from relative obscurity to lead the *Fratelli d'Italia* party (Brothers of Italy).

Raised by her romance-writing mother, Meloni is an unmarried mother herself. Unlike most other Italian politicians, Meloni does not aspire to gain universal approval. She asserts that, from a young age, she recognized the importance of having enemies as this quote might illustrate:

"In a political world where everyone's saying one thing and doing another, our system of values is pretty clear. You may like it or not, but we aren't misleading."

Statements of this nature create a perception of honesty and a commitment to explicit action in the eyes of right-of-center voters. Meloni promotes Christian values and gender norms while also opposing 'woke orthodoxy' and the globalist left. Unlike most other coalition partners in her government, she supports international organizations such as NATO and the EU. This pragmatic stance could be correlated with the desire to receive $200 billion in post-Covid EU recovery funds.

Time will tell how long Meloni will be Italian prime minister, one of the most challenging jobs in the world. According to The Economist Intelligence Unit, Italy is classified as a flawed democracy marked by high degrees of fragmentation, instability, and short-lived coalitions. Over the past two decades, the country's economy has stagnated, with its GDP, once on par with Britain's, now nearly 50 percent smaller. Italy faces an exceptionally high level of debt, coupled with structural, cultural, and demographic issues, suggesting that its economic outlook will remain grim.

****

Italy is a wonderful destination for numerous reasons, but one aspect that often goes unnoticed is that its people actively welcome children. Whenever we visited Italy with our young kids, we noticed Italians always doted over them. It was also apparent that there were usually not many Italian children for them to play with.

Italy has a severe demographic problem; its birth rate is around half its death rate. In fact, the average fertility rate for Italian women has remained at approximately 1.2 children for decades, just slightly above half of the natural replacement rate.

You might wonder how these good Catholics adhere to the Church's teaching on contraception—the answer is that they don't. Italy's birth rate fell below the natural replacement rate soon after birth control was legalized in 1971. Despite their admirable reputation in the love-making arena, young Italians face challenges in hooking up, as three-quarters of those in their twenties continue to live at home with their parents.

This puts constraints on romantic opportunities. Many years ago, I vividly recall walking past a long line of cars parked on a Sunday afternoon in Napoli. Each vehicle had its windows covered from the inside with newspaper, and each bounced up and down, with the occupants enthusiastically testing its suspension.

In 2012, Italy recorded the lowest level of births since it became a state in 1861. And ever since then, a new record low has been hit yearly.

For a few decades, net immigration into Italy balanced the deficit in net births. However, although immigration from Africa and elsewhere persists, seven times as many young professional Italians now opt to live abroad compared to thirty years ago. In both 2020 and 2021, Italy's population declined by over one-third of a million people, roughly equivalent to the city of Florence each year.

Italian schools have lower rolls than they used to. It is not difficult to find schools that incorporate a wider range of ages in a class or have uncommonly small class sizes.

The Italian workforce is also shrinking, and this trend is expected to accelerate in the coming years as fewer adolescents enter the workforce compared to retiring adults and emigrants who are leaving it.

This decline in the working population will decrease tax revenues just at a time when a previous baby boom retires. With higher borrowing levels unaffordable, social programs will have to be cut. Meanwhile, companies will likely face increased labor costs and further economic stagnation.

Italians have other fears about their future. A decline in the number of young people in the workforce could hinder innovation, ultimately diminishing the country's competitiveness. A smaller next generation might also eventually lead to a loss of cultural identity, and the effectiveness of the Italian army might decrease further.

There are multiple reasons for Italy's low birth rate. The primary factor is economic. Italy's declining birth rate is considered both a symptom and a cause of its persistently stagnant economy. Numerous surveys indicate that the average Italian woman still desires to have at least two children but cannot envisage ever being able to afford them. Unemployment remains high, and the available jobs are primarily on poorly paid short-term contracts. With both housing and childcare prohibitively expensive, half of Italians in their twenties say they can't imagine ever owning their own home or starting families. It is difficult to fault their analysis.

Italian President Sergio Mattarella has described Italy's demographics as "a problem that threatens the existence of our country." Previous Prime Minister Mario Draghi echoed these sentiments, "Without children, Italy's fate is to age and then disappear."

Most of Italy's social security is directed toward pensions and health for the elderly rather than the young. In 2021, the government finally passed a $25 billion Family Act aimed at encouraging childbirth. This legislation now provides a monthly $300 allowance for each child, offers financial support for young people to buy a home, extends family time off, and doubles the number of nurseries. It's not enough, but Italy hopes to enhance these incentives further when it receives $200 billion from the EU Pandemic Recovery Plan.

Unless some of these programs start to work, Italy's population will likely almost halve by the end of this century. Net migration could help, but Italy is not renowned for welcoming immigrants.

Openness toward immigration is difficult for most countries. The fear that some alien culture will limit natives' opportunities and diminish their quality of life is common. Throughout most of its history, the United States has embraced immigration. However, this hasn't always been the case.

In the 1850s, the US had a third major political party, known as the 'Know-Nothings.' With vehemently anti-immigration policies, mainly targeting Catholics, this political party managed to secure over 20 percent of congressional seats and controlled several cities and municipalities. Its manifesto was part-progressive, advocating for issues such as anti-slavery, the expansion of women's rights, and improved labor laws. However, it also supported immigration restrictions and a requirement of twenty-one years of residency before granting citizenship.

The party's original name was the Native American Party, which was curious because its membership consisted entirely of colonists. The 'Know-Nothings' was a semi-secret society. When asked whether they were a member, they invariably replied, "I know nothing."

Anti-immigration rhetoric experienced a resurgence in the 1920s, leading to the enactment of a series of restrictive immigration laws. This rhetoric has re-emerged more recently, notably from figures such as Donald Trump, who opposed immigration from Central and South America and often conflated illegal immigrants with criminals such as rapists and drug runners. Trump later expanded his opposition to legal immigrants, arguing that an "influx of foreign workers depresses wages, increases unemployment, and poses challenges for low-income and working-class Americans."

****

The reality is that, in almost all areas of Italian life, it seems to be very difficult for Italy to make the radical changes it probably needs. The double whammy of a culture that rejects rules and a system with an aversion to change means that Italy will likely be slow in adopting change.

However, perhaps they are only recent exceptions, but Italy is making some progress in introducing and enforcing new rules. Who would have thought the Italians would be as effective at reducing smoking as their Teutonic neighbors? While an Italian car may still be just inches away from your bumper, it seems to drive slower these days. Obviously, Italians don't strictly adhere to the speed limits, but they do speed less quickly.

I had anticipated mask mandates to be lightly policed in Italy. Instead, all indoor activities required *il green pass* for admission. Almost all Italians seemed to adhere to mask-wearing with good humor. If the Italians aren't careful, they will lose their well-deserved reputation for anarchy and disorder. As in Key West, you would see someone riding their moped with *mascherina*. You might think this excessively cautious, except that many were riding their bike the wrong way along a busy one-way street. It seemed acceptable to all, including the local *carabinieri*.

Furthermore, Italy is surprisingly unified for a country that is only one hundred and fifty years old, and thanks to television and military service, almost all Italians now speak the same language. Moreover, unlike many other European countries, support for separation from the mother nation appears to be diminishing. Cultural experiences such as soccer and the Catholic Church provide Italy with a shared set of values.

Incidentally, it's soccer—and not Catholicism—that is the primary religion of Italians. Despite not reaching the finals in the past two World Cups, Italy has won the World Cup four times. *Gli Azzurri,* who adopted their blue colors from the House of Savoy, are beloved by all. As that quote-machine, Churchill, famously said, "Italians lose their wars as if they were football matches, and football matches as if they were wars." Three daily newspapers are entirely devoted to *il calcio, La Gazzetta Dello Sport, Corriere Dello Sport, and Tutttosport*. Between the three titles, these account for one-quarter of all newspapers sold.

****

While the United States did not invent democracy—that credit goes to the Greeks supported much later by the Magna Carta—it was an early adopter of democracy, albeit limited to white males for almost the first hundred years.

For over one hundred and fifty years, autocratic governments remained the norm, and the United States stood as a relative outlier. By World War II, the USA was still one of only seventeen democracies. However, thanks to America's influence in rebuilding post-war Europe and Japan, democracies began to flourish.

Europe was rebuilt with the American-funded Marshall Plan, while Japan received aid through GARIOA and the Dodge Line. However, one of the most significant contributions to the rest of the world was what some call *Pax Americana*. America protected Western Europe from the Soviet Union and, using Japan as a strategic base, countered expansionary ideologies in much of Asia. Without these efforts, there would likely be far fewer democracies worldwide.

Today, America appears to be returning to its pre-World War II policy of isolationism. If so, this shift could have significant implications for those who seek global peace. Russia, China, and many others appear resolute in pursuing their regional interests without American intervention. If I were a betting person, I would wager that they will eventually succeed in their quest.

I remember a conversation I had almost two decades ago who had been involved in efforts to rebuild Afghanistan. He emphasized that Afghanistan's biggest challenge was the lack of trust its people had in their institutions. According to him, Afghanistan faced a bleak future without this crucial trust.

The Edelman Trust Barometer surveys 36,000 citizens in 28 countries every year. They report that institutional trust has declined in almost every country but is particularly pronounced in Western democracies. In its most recent 2022 survey, two-thirds of respondents believed they were being lied to by journalists, heads of government, and business leaders.

The belief in the trustworthiness of public officials and professionals is fundamental to the strength of a country's institutions. When the public suspects politicians of abusing their powers, journalists of failing to report the truth, and professionals of exploiting their positions, the very foundation of representative democracies begins to erode.

Those politicians as slippery as eels in a bucket of oil don't inspire trust. While celebrated for their communication skills, figures of the caliber of Tony Blair and Bill Clinton are often viewed as adept at concealing the truth. The British people did not believe the famous Iraq case for war, and the Americans did not trust that Clinton did 'not have sexual relations with that woman.' While both individuals may have escaped the immediate consequences of their untruths, the long-term cost is an erosion of trust in future leaders—either that or the election of non-slick politicians.

We have witnessed a decade marked by significant electronic data leaks, revealing widespread corruption at the highest levels. The 2013 Snowden unauthorized disclosure of NSA files, the 2014 and 2015 Luxembourg and HSBC Switzerland tax breaches, the 2016 exposure from a Panamanian law firm, and the leaks in 2017 and 2021 of Paradise and Pandora Papers give the impression that every wealthy or influential person is corrupt.

The divide between the American elite who run the country's institutions and the average American citizen is widening. The general population increasingly views the elite as corrupt and self-serving, while the elite often perceives the electorate as being influenced by shadowy forces. Obviously, this isn't just an American problem—Britain, France, and Italy, to name just three, have the same issue.

Julian Bishop

Our language classes' day-to-day routine had left us weary, so we escaped for a long weekend to Elba, Italy's third-largest island. Despite its modest dimensions—less than twenty miles in width and just over ten miles in height—it boasts a rugged coastline stretching for ninety miles and features sizable hills in its interior.

Elba was the source of iron for the weapons of Roman centurions and the origin of the granite for Rome's magnificent Pantheon. This mineral wealth has made Elba a coveted prize for numerous neighboring nation-states throughout history, and its ownership has changed with the regularity of one of the stations in Monopoly.

Despite the absence of visible remnants from its industrial history, Elba still bears two distinct reminders. Firstly, its capital bears the name Portoferraio, meaning 'port of iron.' Secondly, the island's hills are so rich in iron deposits that compasses of passing ships often go haywire.

Although one can reach the island by a small plane or private boat, the most common means of arrival is by ferry. When the two ferry companies to the island merged, the locals formed a new company in competition. So, in solidarity with these anti-monopolists, we caught the local boat. Conveniently, it was twenty euros cheaper.

Since World War II, Elba has transformed remarkably from an industrial heartland into a tourist island. It's great for hiking, biking, and beaches. You can walk the ninety-mile *La Via dell'Essenza* that circumnavigates the island or take off-road trails on your mountain bike if you are a daredevil. For most visitors, though, the island's numerous picturesque bays and curvaceous coves are the attraction. While some beaches can be reached by hiking trails, others are only accessible by sea.

Elba is a summer destination, bustling with Italian beachgoers in July and August. While on one of the beaches, we watched a sizeable Italian friend group smoking weed in a beachside café. These friends watched an older couple from their group alternating between skipping stones into a flat sea and snogging on the beach. They jeered good-naturedly at their two middle-aged friends who were undoubtedly reveling in the first throes of a new relationship.

It reminded me of something a French person had recently told me, "The Italians are like the French, only happy."

It was the end of the season for the café owners—their very last work afternoon of the year. The staff were eating leftovers from lunch and invited us to join them. They hugged each other passionately, celebrating a successful summer of business after the previous year's Covid washout.

Are We There Yet?

We braved the hotel's large pool that overlooked the port. I dove into the cool waters while Lorna put herself through the agony of inching into the pool's salted water. A lone dive master and pupil, suitably wet-suited, were surprised to see anyone else in the pool. "It's 18 degrees," they shouted in Italian, with a mixture of disbelief and admiration.

Our hotel hosted a giant bike-fest. Hundreds of motocross aficionadi had pushed their motorcycles to the limits and conquered Elba's inland dirt paths. As the sun descended and a warm glow set across the horizon, these bikers enjoyed the hotel hospitality as the air filled with laughter, camaraderie, and exhilaration. Plates of Italian cuisine and cheap wine rejuvenated their tired bodies.

The next day, we were determined to learn more about Napoleon's time on the island, so we visited a couple of his houses.

After the defeat in the Napoleonic Wars, France's allies exiled Napoleon to Elba under the 1814 Treaty of Fontainebleau. It was a messy compromise, the type of agreement where no party is happy with the outcome. The treaty established Elba as an independent principality he could rule over until his death. Napoleon was allowed to retain his title as emperor but had no powers in France or any of its territories—indeed, he was never permitted to leave the island. Napoleon took with him almost a thousand of his elite military, along with a navy ship, to defend himself from attack and assassination. France also agreed to pay Napoleon a salary of two million francs annually (about $25 million in today's money).

Napoleon once said, "History is a set of lies that have been agreed upon. Even after I am gone, I shall remain in people's minds… My name will be the war cry of their efforts, the motto of their hopes." However, he was desolate at his humiliation at this point in his life. He attempted suicide with an overdose of opium but vomited the contents of his stomach. By morning, he had changed his mind about his future.

The islanders welcomed Napoleon. However, unsurprisingly, he despised his fate and, consequently, loathed the island. He had been accustomed to commanding an army of half a million men, and the small brigade, along with an assortment of mules and horses, was a significant demotion. Nevertheless, in his short time on the island, Napoleon initiated the construction of new roads and bridges, modernized agriculture, and enhanced water and waste infrastructure.

When King Louis XVIII reneged on the annual stipend and with other elements of the Treaty of Fontainebleau not adhered to, Napoleon felt no compunction to comply with the restrictions placed on him.

Julian Bishop

On 27 February 1815, in the absence of the British commissioner, Napoleon's navy slipped out of Portoferraio. The British and German navies had been taking turns guarding Napoleon by patrolling the island with gunboats. However, on the day of Napoleon's escape, it was France's responsibility.

Neither of the French frigates patrolling Elba and guarding against Napoleon's escape spotted his flotilla. Two days later, Napoleon landed in France near Antibes. Just eighteen days after his landing, Napoleon reached Paris and embarked on his second term as the ruler of France. Surprisingly, not a single shot had been fired on his return.

After a mere ten months of captivity on Elba, Napoleon had managed to escape and regain power in France. Fewer than three months later, he would lose the Battle of Waterloo despite a significant military advantage. This forced him to abdicate once more, leading to his exile on St Helena, a remote island in the middle of the South Atlantic. He remained there until his death six years later.

We visited Napoleon's primary residence, a relatively modest palazzina situated at the hill's summit in the island's capital town. The architect, Paolo Bargigli, redesigned the upper floor of this house into an apartment for Napoleon's wife, Maria. However, she never joined him; this apartment was occupied by Napoleon's favorite sister and bonne viveuse, Pauline.

It is worth spending a couple of paragraphs on Pauline Bonaparte. Her story could easily be the plot of one of those captivating BBC Sunday evening serials. Pauline was renowned as a beauty in her time and remained highly flirtatious and promiscuous throughout her life. She is often delicately described as having absolutely no intellectual leanings, code for dumb as a bag of hammers. From thirteen years old, she engaged in a series of affairs with military leaders, most of whom soon found their careers foundering when her big brother learned of their liaisons. Then, in 1803, she married Prince Camillo Borghese, the renowned Roman nobleman. The couple had a son, but tragically, while the child was under Borghese's care during her absence at a spa, the six-year-old succumbed to a fever. Astonishingly, Borghese attempted to conceal their son's death from her. It's unclear how long he expected to get away with this deception, but Pauline thereafter bitterly referred to him as 'the butcher of her son.'

Borghese commissioned Antonio Canova to sculpt Pauline posing as Venus to woo her back. Pauline insisted that the sculpture portray her in the nude. Borghese was appalled by the finished statue and consigned it, no doubt, to one of his many attics. When asked whether she was uncomfortable posing nude before Canova, Pauline replied, "No, there was a fire in the room." Understandably, Canova took his time with the sculpture, completing the statue after three years of grueling modeling. Today, *Venus Victrix* is regarded as his masterpiece, and you can admire it at the Galleria Borghese in Rome.

Unfortunately, her husband's attempt to win her back proved futile. Pauline embarked on two decades of affairs with both men and women before finally reconciling a few months before she died in 1825. During Napoleon's first exile, Pauline sold the Hotel de Charost to the British Government. In a twist of irony, The Duke of Wellington used it as his residence in Paris, a tradition continued by all subsequent British ambassadors to France.

****

We chanced upon a chestnut festival high in the hills of western Elba. Parking in this hilltop town was problematic, and a policeman, whose organizational skills rivaled those of Daughter #2, was deputized to coordinate it. We were then shuttled back into town on the school bus, each seat bearing the current student's name.

Without a clear idea of what awaited us at the end of the line, we patiently queued for our green passes to be inspected. Whether young or old, Italians have an undeniable proclivity for festivals, and it seems every municipality, regardless of size, hosts several each year. All we guessed was that the food would be chestnut-based.

We had participated in Italian festivals before in our travels. One especially memorable experience was when we spent a week's vacation on Monte Isola, located in the middle of Lake Iseo, during carnival week. Every evening, all the islanders gathered in the main town for a communal meal and raucous entertainment. During that particular event, we were the only non-Italians on the island.

This festival bore many similarities to the one on Monte Isola, as it appeared that the entire island had gathered to celebrate. Beneath the scorching autumn sun, I savored my mushroom and chestnut tagliatelle while Lorna devoured her *castagna* with polenta. Unlike our experience on Monte Isola, the Italian rock band's repertoire mainly consisted of English songs.

Julian Bishop

As our time in Italy drew to a close, a familiar bittersweet feeling enveloped us, a sensation we experience year after year. The sun-kissed days and enchanting nights in this land of art, history, and pasta were about to become cherished memories. But we took solace in knowing we would return the following year to explore a different corner of this diverse country, accompanied by our children and their ever-expanding entourage. Despite its challenges, Italy is so perfectly imperfect.

Chapter 12 – Bouncing Around Florida

We returned to the UK to spend a further week with our relatives, and as expected, the dreary British weather had settled in for the long haul until spring. The British climate is seldom extreme; it's neither too hot nor too cold. No hurricanes or F-3 tornadoes will ever wreak havoc here, and Britain isn't exactly renowned as a winter sun vacation destination… or a summer one, for that matter.

A typical British day will deliver plenty of cloud cover and regular light rain. The British become animated when the sun momentarily emerges from behind the cloud: "Do you remember last Tuesday's weather? It was glorious." However, when you research the weather conditions on the day in question, you will likely find just ninety minutes of relatively clear skies.

With so many other conversation topics off limits, the British talk incessantly about the weather. "Turned out nice again," one might say to another during the briefest interlude between showers. More often than not, though, they'll simply remark, "It's raining again." This serves as a safe opening line for the socially reserved Brit, as the response can provide valuable clues about the other person's mood. If both parties find common ground, perhaps the pair can indulge in Britain's national pastime of grumbling.

Here's a tip for foreigners: always agree with the British person's perspective on the weather. For one thing, because they talk about it so much, many consider themselves experts, even though most couldn't differentiate between an isobar and an isotherm. More importantly, it's a matter of etiquette to agree with an opening statement aimed at establishing common ground.

The British find immense satisfaction in simple pleasures. My parents, for example, are never happier than when someone pours them a mug of hot weak tea. They practically reach the zenith of delight if a humble cookie joins this modest feast. It's not typically an exciting biscuit, mind you, but one that can be comfortably dunked in their milky tea. Perhaps it will be a Rich Tea, a Nice Biscuit, or a Digestive— you couldn't invent more unassuming names for these unambitious cookies if you tried.

Now, I'm not saying that simple pleasures lack merit. Quite the contrary, the ability to find contentment in the uncomplicated is indeed a gift. Nevertheless, it wouldn't hurt to embrace a touch of pastry ambition— perhaps a biscuit with some chocolate covering or something with flavored cream inside? It perplexes me how Britain once ruled over most of the planet for so long, although perhaps this colonization was carried out by people who tired quickly of insubstantial hot beverages, malted milk biscuits, and incessant conversation about the weather.

Rural England felt like an anticlimax after Florence, though to be fair, most places would pale in comparison. We cherished time with each of our relatives, visiting traditional British pubs and eating underwhelming food. After Italy's outstanding cuisine, it was a challenge to muster enthusiasm for processed pub fare that had been overcooked in the microwave and served with chips and gravy.

With travel still subdued, London Heathrow was as empty as a Prince Andrew book signing. The few people still traveling had grown unused to air travel. The security lines were slow, with four out of every five travelers leaving something in their luggage that required security inspection.

We ventured into the airport lounge, where, in an unusual departure from this airline's usual demeanor, they greeted us with the warmth reserved for long-lost relatives. I won't mention the airline by name, but if you'd like a hint, it brands itself as the world's 'least favorite airline' or something along those lines.

As non-US residents were still not permitted to enter the United States due to Covid regulations at that time, the plane was only one-tenth full. However, the airlines had to keep flying despite this low demand to preserve their landing slots. Lorna and I chose seats in different rows of the plane because we could.

I often found entering the US as a visitor to be an unfriendly experience. The immigration and customs officials are as suspicious as cats near a bathtub—I guess that's how they get the job. However, this was our first time entering America on our new US passports, so it was no longer "Welcome to the USA," but rather, "Welcome back, Sir." It felt good to be back.

On arrival at Miami Airport, I immediately noticed a significant shift in the proportion of people wearing baseball caps. It's fewer than 1 percent in Europe, but here, it seems fifty times greater. For some, these caps are fashion accessories, albeit ones rarely seen on Milan's catwalks. For others, they are a concealment. Many women I know wear one when they haven't washed their hair that day, while men I have known for months often surprise me with their male-pattern baldness when I finally see them capless. For many, the logo on the hat communicates their identity; you may be proud that you hail from New York, belong to a yacht club, or align yourself with the forty-fifth US President.

In the early days of baseball, players wore whatever hats they could find. Early sports stars donned hats of various brims: boaters, pillboxes, fedoras, or deerstalkers. Then, around the turn of the century, the baseball cap emerged as the standard. In 1901, the Detroit Tigers were the first to promote their logo. The twenties saw longer visors, and by the forties, the cap looked pretty much as it does today.

****

The pre-industrial Florida coastline was surrounded by islands, almost all of which have now been incorporated into mainland Florida via road bridges. As a result, most coastal Florida destinations offer both oceanside and bayside views, giving visitors the choice of preferred water outlook. This topography has also created an Intracoastal Waterway that encircles most of Florida. In fact, you can take your boat on the Great Loop, an almost six-thousand-mile circumnavigation of the Eastern USA, which includes the Canadian and New York State Canals, Atlantic Intracoastal Waterways, the Gulf Intracoastal, the Mississippi, and the Great Lakes. Traveling at an average speed of ten miles per hour, most adventurers take six months to complete this continuous waterway loop.

Most Floridians have a clear preference for either the East or West Coast. The East Coast group prefers a faster pace and is likelier to hail from New York and surrounding areas, whereas the West Coasters have a higher proportion of Midwesterners and, as a result, tend to be a little more laid-back. Additionally, the bodies of water on the two coasts differ; the mighty Atlantic Ocean crashes onto the East Coast, whereas the calmer Gulf of Mexico mostly laps onto the West Coast.

The great city of Miami, with its ethnically diverse and younger population, dominates the East Coast. A succession of retirement and vacation cities then stretches northward four hundred miles to the state's top.

This coast is home to Cape Canaveral and the Kennedy Space Center. The choice of this East Coast location in 1950 was strategic: rockets receive a 914-mph boost from the Earth's west-to-east rotation, a crucial advantage when you need to achieve a speed of 17,000 mph to enter the Earth's atmosphere. In contrast, a West Coast site would pose greater challenges for launching missiles over populated areas.

The Elon-Musk-owned SpaceX and other companies launch their rockets from Cape Canaveral. You see them frequently in the sky, even from the West Coast of Florida.

Thanks to SpaceX, the United States still leads the space race. In 2022, the US launched seven times as many objects into space as all other countries combined. The US dominates the low Earth orbit, with SpaceX accounting for three-quarters of all satellites in this region. However, increasing space debris has necessitated the regular replacement of Starlink satellites.

NASA's primary focus is the Space Launch System, which aims to ferry astronauts to the Moon. Additionally, NASA has successfully sent five robotic vehicles to Mars in journeys that take seven months. These vehicles utilize radioactive plutonium decay to power their batteries, enabling the rovers to maneuver around the planet, search for signs of past microbial life, and transmit images and data back to Earth for analysis. Thanks to these missions, we now have concrete evidence that Mars once boasted abundant water in its lakes and rivers.

In keeping with the new world order, China is just behind America in the number of launched rockets. In 2021, it successfully sent its first robot to Mars and seems to share similar ambitions for human colonization on Mars as the Americans.

Obviously, space is unfathomably infinite. For perspective, there are more stars in the universe than there have been heartbeats from all the humans who have ever lived on Earth. If that's still hard to grasp, consider this: there are also more suns in the universe than grains of sand on all the beaches on our planet. Therefore, establishing dominance in space will be a formidable challenge. Nevertheless, the tiny sliver of space near Earth is likely to be pioneered first by the United States. The US government and

Are We There Yet?

private American companies invest approximately three times more in space activities than China, India, or Europe combined.

****

We've been visiting Florida for thirty years, and while we've occasionally flirted with the East Coast, we are decidedly West Coasters. We've stayed in almost every town south of Tampa and thought we knew the Gulf Coast well. How wrong we were. For the next two months, we rented a house on Longboat Key, a narrow barrier island now connected by bridge to other islands on Florida's Gulf Coast. The neighborhood was as quiet as a library during nap time, and our rental house had a dock almost on Sarasota Bay.

In 1877, at the end of Reconstruction, Florida was home to only a quarter of a million people. Today, it boasts a population a hundred times larger, making it the third-largest state in the US—and it's still growing. According to the 2020 census, Florida's population increased by 2.7 million over the previous decade. More recent data from the first eighteen months of the 2020s, gathered by Florida's Division of Motorist Services and Daughter #2's occasional employer, U-Haul, suggested that an additional net 0.6 million people have chosen Florida as their new home during this period. Surprisingly, of the 840 daily new migrants, two-thirds were Millennials, rather than the retiree profile you might have expected.

Four factors appear to be drawing people to Florida. Firstly, as one of America's warmest states, it is appealing to residents from snow-bound regions. Similarly, other Sunbelt states—from Arizona to North Carolina—have also seen significant population increases.

Secondly, Florida's favorable tax environment is a significant draw. It is one of only nine states with no state income tax, a sharp contrast to states like California, where the wealthiest residents pay 13.3 percent in state taxes in addition to the top rate of federal income tax of 37 percent. Additionally, other taxes in Florida, such as property tax, are notably lower than elsewhere. For instance, Florida's property tax rate, which is less than 1 percent of property values, is considerably lower than the 2.5 percent rate in New Jersey. Therefore, moving from your million-dollar home and professional job in New Jersey to a similar property and employment in Florida could save you approximately $20,000 annually in total taxes.

Thirdly, Florida's cost of living is roughly at the national average for US states. In contrast, New York State boasts a cost of living that is 20 percent greater, and in California, it's a staggering 40 percent higher.

The fourth factor is state governance. Florida's (non-Disney) business-friendly policies seem to be attractive to migrants. A recent example of this can be seen in its approach to Covid regulations. While Florida initially imposed restrictions at the start of the pandemic, it had largely reopened by the summer of 2020 and even prohibited its cities from implementing mask mandates. This approach sharply contrasted with the policies of more liberal states, which implemented various lockdowns, restrictions, and mask mandates.

Some economists take a negative view of individual states having their own laws and regulations consistent with the US Constitution; they argue that too many different rules will eventually undermine America's single market. However, I can see many advantages. A highly centralized government often produces unpopular policies because decision-makers located far from their constituents may not anticipate their unpopularity until after imposing the policy. Another potential benefit is that one state can serve as a testing ground for new policy ideas, allowing other states to learn from these experiments. However, what I appreciate most is that the US can offer a variety of experiences to cater to different preferences—similar to Europe. In theory, one can live in a region that aligns with one's values.

After World War II, the primary rivalry emerged between California and New York, the two then-most-populous states. This rivalry sparked a miniature clash of values between the East and West Coasts.

By the nineties, Texas had overtaken New York as the second-largest state. As California shifted more liberal, Texas emerged as a counterpoint with its prevailing conservative politics and values. This rivalry endures today, as Texas continues to draw more businesses and people away from California.

In 2014, Florida surpassed New York to become the state with the third-largest population. While Florida shares some similarities with Texas, it also has notable differences. It tends to be less socially conservative, less religious, and more ethnically diverse than Texas. The primary reason for this is that only one-third of Florida residents are native to the state, with the remaining two-thirds being first-generation immigrants or migrants from Northeastern or Midwestern states. This pattern of migration also contributes to a less homogenized population.

Are We There Yet?

The primary state rivalry has recently shifted to California and Florida, perhaps because the two states have many similarities geographically. One area to receive scrutiny is their relative pandemic performance.

As of the time of writing, the performances of these states have been somewhat similar despite pursuing vastly different policies. California chose lockdown and school closing, while Florida opened everything up. Ultimately, California has a marginally lower death rate per 100,000 people than Florida, but this could be more than explained by the 7-percentage point lower vaccine take-up, a significantly higher percentage of seniors, and warmer weather in Florida.

Several academics calculated an age-adjusted Covid death rate that showed both states had nearly identical death rates. Meanwhile, one Los Angeles newspaper modeled that Florida could have had three thousand fewer deaths if only they had adopted California's policies.

Another point of comparison is net migration, where, in 2022, California lost more than Florida gained, causing conservative radio host Rush Limbaugh to comment, "Californians are voting with their moving vans."

This mostly friendly rivalry does have an impact on democracy. The 1929 Permanent Apportionment Act restricted the number of voting House Representatives to 435. As the American population has grown, the average constituency size has expanded to three-quarters of a million people, the largest in the world. After each census, House seats are redistributed from slower-growing states to faster-growing ones. In the past few decades, the sunbelt states, which trend red, the color of the Republican party, have gained more representatives, while rustbelt states have fewer. The 2020 census will further apportion, with Texas receiving two extra House seats and Florida, North Carolina, Colorado, Montana, and Oregon each gaining one seat. Conversely, California, Michigan, Ohio, Pennsylvania, New York, Illinois, and West Virginia will each lose one seat.

Some mean-spirited individuals view California's current challenges through gleeful eyes, hoping that this majority-liberal state will falter. However, reports of its demise are exaggerated. Since the Gold Rush, California has attracted people worldwide to its shores. Starting in the 1910s, the motion picture industry attracted those passionate about performing, and after World War II, Americans flocked to Southern California during a spectacular post-war boom period. For the past fifty years, Silicon Valley has enticed anyone with a passion for technology.

Although the population has leveled off over the past decade, California remains one of the most dynamic places on Earth. In fact, if California were its own country (which some advocate for), it would boast the world's fifth-largest economy.

California is fighting back. Unexpectedly, the state appears to be doubling down on its social positioning. Instead of trying to entice back some of the recent exiles by, for example, replicating Texan policies, it is promoting its state as having 'social policies you can believe in.'

Ultimately, I suspect California's campaign is misguided. Except for Texas, the states most Californians are choosing to move to also have liberal state governments with similar social policies. In reality, the decline in California's population share can be attributed to the high cost of living and taxes, both of which remain unaddressed by Californian politicians.

To position its Governor as a viable presidential candidate, Florida has introduced legislation that restricts teachers from discussing sexual orientation and gender identification with children under the age of nine, commonly known as the 'Don't Say Gay' bill. Meanwhile, California is introducing different legislation that guarantees women from any state the right to obtain an abortion in California. The state is reportedly offering to cover the woman's expenses, including airfare, lodging, childcare, and the abortion procedure.

While people will fight these social issues on both sides and forlornly try to convert the other side to their opinion, I find it quite attractive that choices are available. Americans can choose to live in slightly more regulated communities or ones that lean more libertarian. Unless your main aim is to control others' lives, why would you object to these elements of choice?

In any case, this decentralized political system is by deliberate design. The Founding Fathers believed competition between states would foster innovation, entrepreneurship, and good governance. They thought states would be better governed when residents and businesses could relocate to another state.

This practice is still evident today, as Chambers of Commerce actively vie for businesses and residents by promoting their state's or city's tax regimes, tax incentives, legal regulations, and amenities. Many business-friendly states have no or low state income taxes and labor laws that limit unionization, while a handful of states provide high-quality universities with affordable in-state tuition.

Are We There Yet?

We noticed one thing that was once rare in Florida: Californians. Hitherto, there had been little incentive for them to drop in on Florida. California offered its own beaches, amusement parks, and palm trees, making a two-thousand-mile journey to Florida unnecessary.

Based on conversations with numerous Californians, it became evident that they saw Florida as a haven of freedom. Californian after Oregonian complained it was impossible to relax in their own states. They told me that brigades of self-appointed enforcers seemed to relish dictating the behavior of those around them, and the pandemic had provided them with a new stick with which to beat them.

****

The bulk of Americans—and that is, indeed, the collective noun for Americans—regards three fundamental American values to be sacrosanct. While most people share each of these values, what receives less attention is the cost associated with upholding these values.

Individual freedom was the cornerstone of the Founding Fathers' thinking and is ingrained within the Constitution that forms the foundation of America's political, legal, and cultural framework. However, the price Americans pay for individual freedom is *self-reliance*. It also explains why Americans can be so forthright and why the most extensive section in any US bookstore is the self-help section.

The second fundamental value is *equality of opportunity*. Some members of today's younger generation may question the authenticity of this value, asserting that it's self-evident that individuals from disadvantaged backgrounds and those with certain skin tones do not enjoy the same opportunities as their more privileged peers.

However, it's possible to hold firm beliefs while simultaneously failing to uphold them consistently. Thomas Jefferson is a classic example of this. Although he opposed slavery, believing it to be a "hideous blot on the American character," he still owned slaves himself. When Thomas Jefferson, influenced by the European Enlightenment movement, penned the phrase, 'All men are created equal,' he likely intended to convey that 'all of humankind is created equally.' He might have used this wording if he had access to a more extensive thesaurus and hadn't been constrained by the presence of the other slave-owning Founding Fathers reviewing his work.

In any case, while Americans don't believe in equality of outcome, I would posit that they do believe in equality of opportunity, or meritocracy, as it's often called here. Naturally, the price of meritocracy is *competition*, a fundamental element woven into every aspect of American culture. Competition inherently fuels the cultural components of free enterprise, innovation, technology, and the distinction between winners and losers.

The third fundamental American value is the *American Dream*. The price of the American Dream is *hard work*, and this drives the American cultural behaviors of individualism, mobility, productivity, and a belief that humans can and should control their environment, irrespective of others within their ecosystem.

Twice as many Americans as Europeans disagree with the statement that forces beyond our control largely determine success in life. Nearly every American I speak to believes in the American Dream. It is an integral part of the United States' identity and has inspired millions of immigrants to come to America, giving them a sense of purpose during times of significant challenges.

The term 'American Dream' was first used in 1918 to describe the immigrant aspiration. However, the historian James Truslow Adams popularized it in his 1931 book *Epic of America*. Adams believed that everyone should have an opportunity to succeed, regardless of their background. At a time when despotism was on the rise in Europe, Adams thought that the USA had lost its way in prizing money above all other values. Therefore, his definition of the American dream was not principally about money but about the notion that every citizen could achieve their fullest potential through hard work.

Martin Luther King developed his famous speech from Adams's work when he wrote:

"I still have a dream. It is a dream deeply rooted in the American dream. I have a dream that one day this nation will rise up and live out the true meaning of its creed: 'We hold these truths to be self-evident, that all men are created equal…'

I have a dream that my four little children will one day live in a nation where they will not be judged by the color of their skin but by the content of their character."

These days, many commentators incorrectly define the outcome of the American Dream as becoming a multimillionaire. But, of course, without massive inflation, not everyone can succeed in this quest. Moreover, hard work does not necessarily guarantee success. This is particularly true for first-generation immigrants who often pour everything into their children so that their children may achieve the American Dream.

While the concept may be American—as I pointed out in *High, Wide, and Handsome*—the USA has roughly similar levels of occupational upward mobility to other OECD countries. The Hamilton Project, which also seemed to take a narrower view of the definition of the American Dream, found that a child born into the bottom 20 percent of the income distribution had only a one in twenty-five chance of rising to the top 20 percent.

The main thing I abhor in the UK is the class system—it is so inefficient and wastes so much talent. Many Americans believe that they don't have a class system. However, profound economic inequalities exist between the affluent and disadvantaged in America. Children born into poverty in the United States are just as unlikely to rise to the top as their British counterparts when they become adults. In both countries, a 'glass floor' also prevents the less-talented offspring of the wealthy from experiencing downward mobility.

Pew Research regularly measures public belief in the American Dream. According to their surveys, the majority of Americans report that they have either achieved the American Dream or are well on their way to achieving it, with only 17 percent stating that it is beyond their grasp. Incidentally, Adams would be pleased to learn that respondents self-define the American Dream in line with his preferred definition, with freedom of choice in living, having a good family life, and retiring comfortably being deemed most important. Encouragingly, becoming a multimillionaire is deemed the least significant definition.

*****

Reunited with our excited dogs, we quickly readjusted to American life.

On our first day back in the US, my baseball team, the Atlanta Braves, won the World Series, so-called because one Canadian team gets to participate. In 2021, the winning teams from the six divisions joined the next-best six sides in a playoff series of knockout matches. The Atlanta Braves, who had dominated baseball in the nineties but had only won one World Series, emerged as the unexpected winners. They had the fewest wins of any playoff team and, early in the seven-game World Series, were reduced to only two starting pitchers, the most crucial position in baseball.

Like other American sports, baseball prioritizes the owners' commercial interests. In an antithesis of meritocracy and likely breach of anti-trust principles, no team can be either relegated or promoted. In every American sport, the owners have increasingly pushed for more teams to qualify for the postseason opportunity to win the ultimate prize. As a result, the regular-season games have become less critical, and the owners of all sports teams have become multi-billionaires... which, I am sure we will all agree, should be the primary goal of sports. Basketball is the most extreme example, where two-thirds of NBA teams now take some part in postseason play. This gives the regular-season game the air of a pre-season friendly, as the result of each individual game is close to meaningless.

Nevertheless, despite my structural misgivings, I was delighted for the Braves.

We also enjoyed other sports in Florida. Our favorite US sport is high school football. Even though we no longer have children in the school system, we spent Friday fall evenings enjoying the outside warmth of a game. Because we had watched them the previous year when we took a month's vacation in that town, we decided that our Florida team would be Venice High School, located an hour or so from where we were staying.

The world has thirteen towns or cities called Venice. One, the oldest, is apparently in Italy. Additionally, eleven US states boast a city called Venice, and Canada has a twenty-two-person hamlet of the same name.

Only two of these Venices have high school football teams. If you have seen the 1978 movie *Grease*, you might recognize the stadium for Venice High School in Los Angeles, where the Gondoliers play their home games. Considering the elevated land costs in LA, it is a relatively modest stadium that can accommodate just over three thousand spectators.

In the very first play of our opening match, the receiver for Venice High School in Florida caught the ball from the opposing team's kickoff and sprinted the length of the field untouched. I turned to Lorna and predicted it would be 0-50 by halftime. I was mistaken; the score was 0-49, still a shellacking in football terms. In such situations, it's a tradition for the dominant team to give their backup players a chance to play in the second half of the game.

It was an excellent year for playtime for Venice's second-stringers. In the last seven games of the season, Venice scored 47 points per game, almost all of them in the first half, and allowed only one score from their opponents.

Are We There Yet?

Americans love a winning team, and American English even has the somewhat inelegant adjective 'winningest' to describe the best team. I promise not to use it. As each week passed, we needed to arrive progressively earlier to secure parking and seats in the five-thousand-seater stadium. By halftime, many spectators decided they had seen enough and left. This latter feature seemed to be Lorna's favorite part of the game.

Belonging to the winningest team was an unusual experience for me. I support Torquay United, a hapless team in the fifth tier of English soccer, and my cricket county is Somerset, renowned for being one of the only three counties that have never won the County Championship.

What do I appreciate about high school football? Firstly, it's a fast-paced game, unlike the college and professional versions, which are heavily influenced by advertisers. Where the game has sold its soul to advertisers, ads often dictate its pace, leading to frequent delays. In the high school version, the game flows smoothly, and you typically reach halftime well before the end of the first hour.

That's not to say there are no advertisements. The massive video scoreboard will play ads whenever there's an opportunity. For instance, if an injured player is lying on the ground waiting for treatment, the local hospital screens an advert promoting its rehabilitation services. Other natural breaks in the game will see ads for local restaurants, building services, and the Structural Engineers Association. I'm not entirely sure why the latter organization advertises, but if I ever need the assistance of a structural engineering association, I'll undoubtedly consider giving them my business.

Secondly, the game is easy to understand. There aren't frequent technical rulings on the field that necessitate video referrals by officials. The offensive team throws, runs, or occasionally kicks the ball while the defensive team tries to stop them. The simplicity allows even casual fans to appreciate the exceptional moments of skill displayed by players who make a difference.

Thirdly, I cherish the family-oriented nature of the game. Around two thousand children from the high school attend, many of them spending the entire game socializing on the sidelines. However, I enjoy sitting next to the players' parents. The father wants his son to have the football career he did not have, while the mother cringes at the sight of her son lying prostrate on the ground at the end of a play as an insensitive ad selectively targets only her about the local hospital's rehabilitation services. I especially enjoy sitting just above the Huber extended family because the game really matters to them. They cheer with all their might when their courageous but somewhat pedestrian son thwarts an opposition play.

One of the early games we attended was the senior grade appreciation event when the school honors those young adults who would be graduating that year. The stadium displayed full-sized posters of every final-year student around the ground, and during halftime, each senior who wasn't involved in the game, along with their parent(s), was introduced to the crowd. The announcer would share a few words about what each person planned for the future while the spectators expressed their appreciation by jangling cowbells.

Fourthly, I value the technology. Football is fast-paced, and critical plays are reshown on the video screen for those who blinked momentarily. The quality of the footage is excellent, thanks to multiple cranes positioned around the stadium to capture footage for local TV.

Fifthly, the game is affordable. College football—at least that played at my daughters' university—can be outrageously expensive, costing several times more than Premier League soccer. The professional game is a little cheaper, but a single ticket will still set you back well over a hundred dollars a game. High school football, on the other hand, costs less than ten bucks.

Finally, I enjoy the high school band. These large bands encourage their respective teams and supporters with well-timed tunes just before crucial plays. However, after the first few Venice scores, I noticed the opposing team's band was largely silent or perhaps giving their rendition of John Cage's best-known work.

As the season progressed, Venice inched closer to the Championship. In the 2021 State Championship, Florida's two best high school football teams battled to determine the victor. The Venice Indians prevailed over the Apopka Blue Darters 35-7, finishing the season with a flawless 15-0 record.

For many of these young men, football is of paramount importance. College recruitment professionals meticulously record and scrutinize every move they make in a game. Most starters on a successful team like Venice will receive full university scholarships, and the top players become starters on their college teams, achieving remarkable fame at just twenty years old. If they can avoid injuries, the very best may make it to the professional level, earning enough to retire by their mid-twenties.

Are We There Yet?

Football wasn't the only sport we watched. In fact, for a city with no major professional sports teams, Sarasota offers a surprisingly wide range of sporting options. We began attending the regular Sunday polo matches with our horse-loving Daughter #1's interests in mind. Florida's dominant lawn is the practical yet somewhat spikey St Augustine grass, designed to withstand torrential rain, hurricanes, scorching heat, 100 percent humidity, and salt water. However, it was a pleasure to stroll on the Sarasota polo fields covered with Bermuda grass turf, similar to a cricket pitch.

Polo is undeniably a sport associated with great wealth. Throughout its history, it has been a pastime of kings and nobility. While marginally less expensive than Formula 1, it remains a niche sport in the West primarily enjoyed by the affluent. I am sure that some in polo want to introduce the sport to the masses, but your average guy from the ghetto will never be able to afford the eight polo ponies required for the sport. Its main contribution to general society is the all-pervasive polo shirt, worn initially by Indian players in the mid nineteenth century but popularized by polo-ace Lewis Lacey in the 1920s.

The most substantial expenses in polo are the horses. A basic horse will cost around $100,000, while a high-class one will cost much more. Typically, an individual player will probably bring at least six horses to each match. Consequently, a normal match will require around sixty horses, each demanding training, feeding, health care, and proper shelter.

The economics of the sport are somewhat elusive to me. The $15 admission and no television coverage mean ultra-wealthy patrons must subsidize the sport. In return, they often promote their companies by catering to the fabulously wealthy, of whom there are plenty on this coast.

Polo is one of the world's oldest sports, with the first documented game played between the Persians and Turkomans dating back to 600 BCE. Undoubtedly, the game is even older than this, as ancient art from centuries earlier portrays groups on horseback wielding mallets to strike decapitated heads.

The sport eventually traveled with the Byzantine Empire from Central Asia to India in the thirteenth century. Here, the British quickly adopted the game and made it their own. They named the sport 'polo,' drawing inspiration from the Tibetan word for a ball, 'pulu.' Like many other sports, the British formalized the rules of the game through the Hurlingham Club, which also played a role in establishing the rules for croquet, another mallet-bearing sport.

In the West, the game is played now wherever there are rich people who like horses. The most thriving countries for the game are the UK, the US, and Argentina, which is known for producing many of the best players. These Argentinians are sponsored by wealthy amateurs with names such as Josh, James, Margo, and Hannah.

The sport features many traditions. For example, one local rule at Sarasota Polo Club requires that if you fall off your horse, you have to buy the other players a beer. More sinisterly, a more modern tradition is its discrimination against one specific minority group: the 10 percent of the population who are left-handed. Since 1974, all players must play right-handed.

A chukker, spelled the American way, I'm afraid, lasts for seven and a half minutes. This duration is the maximum time a horse can run, covering roughly four miles in one stretch. Riders are required to switch horses at the end of each chukker, while the more skilled players change horses mid-chukker without dismounting.

The ideal polo pony stands at 15.1 hands (that's 61 inches or 155cm in height). While any horse breed can be used, Clydesdales are rarely seen on the polo field. Polo ponies must possess a combination of speed, stamina, agility, and temperament. In particular, they must be comfortable with the idea of a ball being hit near them and riding alongside a player wielding a large mallet.

The ponies begin training at around three years old, and many continue to play until their late teens. They gallop at speeds of about 35mph for most of the chukker, after which they will have completed their work for the day.

From what I could tell, it appeared that the horses genuinely enjoyed the sport. As in horseracing, they seem to relish competing in groups, striving to outpace their peers.

From the get-go, it was evident that some players were more adept than others. Apparently, about two-thirds of this is due to the quality of the horses. To avoid one-sided games, most polo matches employ a handicap system. The governing body assesses each player's horses, skills, and sportsmanship and assigns them a handicap rating on a scale from minus 2 to plus 10. It's quite a skewed sport, with two-thirds of all players rated at 2 or lower and only a handful, currently nine players (of which eight are from Argentina), boasting a 10 handicap.

For many games, the handicapping is calculated by subtracting one team's total handicap from the other. If a team has a combined handicap two points lower than their opponents, they will begin the game with a two-goal lead.

To be candid, polo is not the greatest spectator sport due to the challenge of tracking the ball. The polo field is the largest in all sports, measuring three hundred yards in length and one hundred and sixty yards in width, equivalent to the size of nine football fields. Furthermore, the organizers must add extra space for horses to run over the boards and off the field. As a result, most of the action unfolds at a considerable distance from the spectators, making it difficult to follow the ball or even discern the colors of the team jerseys.

After each goal, the teams change ends. If you're not paying close attention, this can be confusing, and it's easy to find yourself inadvertently cheering for the wrong side. Watching a game is somewhat akin to watching seven-year-olds playing soccer, with the ponies clustered together around the ball, moving up and down the immense field in unison. Allegedly, players have positions. There is a forward and another offensive player who score most of the goals... and probably go home with most of the girls. There is also a defensive player whose job it is to stop them and a playmaker in the middle of the field.

In any case, most of the crowd is too sloshed to notice or care. Indeed, in this regard, I should commend Lorna and Daughter #1 for doing such an admirable job of blending in. It appears that the primary purpose of this sport is to provide a venue for tailgating for the wealthy, with the main distinction between polo and American football enthusiasts being their preferred choice of beverage.

****

In contemporary times, the two-month holiday season kicks off with Halloween and includes celebrations such as Diwali, Thanksgiving, Hanukkah, Christmas, and Kwanzaa before culminating in New Year's Eve. Unless you are a schoolchild or work in a progressive office, you won't celebrate all of them, of course, just those that are culturally relevant to you.

The one holiday that everyone celebrates is Thanksgiving. Families will adorn their front doors with wreaths, doorsteps with lanterns, and window sills with candles. Inside the house, fall-themed throw pillows and blankets are draped over sofas, seasonal books are placed on coffee tables, and the fire is lit... even in Florida. Fall fruits such as persimmons, apples, and pomegranates are given pride of place in the fruit bowl alongside a few pinecones. Chrysanthemums, Peruvian lilies, and sunflowers fill out amber vases. Finally, the guest rooms are spruced up with plaid pillows, holiday bedding, and fancy soaps to celebrate one of the few times they will be occupied in the year.

With Daughter #1 holidaying with her in-laws, we stayed with the family of Daughter #2's best friend. Our hosts had set Thanksgiving-themed tableware: pumpkin-shaped napkin rings, autumnal base plates, and orange/brown-colored condiment holders, all arranged against the crisp white tablecloth. They also extended an invitation to friends without families to join us for the day and had prepared a large meal centered around a gigantic turkey. Similar to us, our hosts weren't big on watching TV, so we spent most of the day playing parlor games.

You've probably heard the origin story of Thanksgiving. It's the tale of Pilgrims from my birth town of Plymouth, England, thanking God at Plymouth Rock after their first year in the New World. These God-fearing early colonists invited a few Native Americans who had helped them survive their initial year in a hostile environment. It's a nice story, but unfortunately, most of it is untrue. More importantly, it is not the true origin story of Thanksgiving.

Thanksgiving traditions were part of many early Christian churches, with numerous historical Thanksgiving records existing in Europe before 1621. For the Pilgrims, Thanksgiving would have been wholly devoted to fasting and prayer. This kind of deprivation is decidedly not what modern-day Thanksgiving is about. The 1621 event that gave birth to the contemporary holiday was likely a rejoicing ceremony involving eating, drinking, and shooting. Additionally, the Wampanoag tribe was not initially invited to the party; around ninety of them came to the rescue of the Pilgrims when they heard the repeated sound of guns firing. They assumed an unknown enemy was attacking the Pilgrims and gathered around to help their allies.

Contemplative thanksgiving ceremonies, rejoicing parties, and harvest festivals continued for the next two hundred years. However, it wasn't until 1841 that Reverend Alexander Young linked all three together to form the concept of modern-day Thanksgiving. Two decades later, Sarah Josepha Hale, the author of the poem 'Mary Had a Little Lamb,' proposed a day of American unity based upon Thanksgiving. She was raised in New Hampshire, which celebrated an annual harvest festival holiday, and she used her position as editor of the highly influential *Godey's Lady's Book* to persuade about half of the US states and territories to observe a Thanksgiving-type holiday. Confederate President Jefferson Davis declared two Thanksgiving Days in 1861 and 1862 when the Civil War was going well for the South. In 1863, when the tide had turned in favor of the Union side, Abraham Lincoln announced Spring and Summer Thanksgivings.

Many Americans associate Thanksgiving with American football, and this tradition has been a part of the holiday for almost as long as Thanksgiving itself. While you may think that NFL football, the professional format of the game, is as American as apple pie (parenthetically, neither American nor part of a traditional Thanksgiving dinner), college football first established the association with Thanksgiving.

The first college football games were played on Thanksgiving less than a decade after it became a national holiday. This timing made sense because Thanksgiving provided everyone with time off work. As Abraham Lincoln introduced Thanksgiving during the Civil War, many Southerners ignored the holiday for decades. However, the popularity of college football is credited with helping popularize the holiday of Thanksgiving in the South.

Why anyone would enjoy football at the time is unknown. In the 1880s, the patience of Yale and Princeton fans must have been sorely tested when three consecutive Thanksgiving games ended scoreless.

A few high schools also play matches on Thanksgiving Day, particularly those in the Northeast. The oldest high school in America, Boston Latin, founded in 1635, has played its rivals, Boston English, every Thanksgiving since 1887. In 2021, Boston English won a rare victory, reducing their deficit to only 38-83, with 13 ties.

You have probably seen the *Friends* episode where the six main characters play tag football on the street. This amateur football is not at all an uncommon tradition. Many extended families, college fraternities, or local churches have their own Turkey Bowl traditions.

However, for most people, the NFL's version of the game best represents Thanksgiving. In an attempt to attract new fans after their team moved from Ohio in 1934, the Detroit Lions started playing on Thanksgiving. The Lions always host the midday game, and fans who want to attend the game in person will either have their Thanksgiving meal as part of tailgating in a freezing parking lot at 9 am or at the stadium itself.

The Dallas Cowboys joined Detroit in this tradition in the sixties when they saw an opportunity to gain more national prominence by appearing in fans' living rooms. The Cowboys have a long-standing association with the Salvation Army, for whom they have raised $3 billion. Its players drop in on Salvation Army homeless shelters on Thanksgiving morning to serve meals. More recently, a random third NFL game is also played on Thanksgiving, giving dedicated football fans around twelve hours of TV viewing.

Other Thanksgiving traditions have come and gone. For example, at the end of the nineteenth century, it was a tradition to wear masks on Thanksgiving. The wealthy would host masked balls, while those less fortunate in society would don masks and go door-to-door to ask for food. A little later, some boys would dress in girls' clothing, and children of all genders would wear rags. This tradition of dressing up was so popular at one point that Thanksgiving earned the nickname 'Ragamuffin Day.'

At the end of the Great Depression, Democrat President Franklin D Roosevelt moved Thanksgiving a week earlier to stimulate economic activity. In November 1939, there were five Thursdays, and he wanted Thanksgiving to be on the fourth Thursday that year rather than the final Thursday. This change disrupted football schedules, causing a great deal of consternation. That year, along partisan lines, twenty-two predominantly Democratic states celebrated Thanksgiving on November 23rd, while twenty-three Republican states celebrated it a week later. You might wonder what happened in the other five states. Party-loving Texas, Colorado, and Mississippi celebrated it on both dates, while Alaska and Hawaii were not yet states at that point. The confusion over which day to celebrate continued for a few years. Congress failed to legislate in 1941, with the House proposing the final Thursday in November and the Senate countering with the fourth Thursday. It wasn't until 1956 that all states aligned on the fourth Thursday in November.

A few politically motivated Americans refuse to celebrate Thanksgiving, arguing that it marks the genocide of Native peoples. This perspective is understandable, as Thanksgiving offers a platform for discussing their political cause in various media outlets throughout November. However, as the origin story is inaccurate and Thanksgiving is not about the early colonists and their relationships with the First People, it is a bit misguided. Personally, I relish this family holiday, where we give thanks for all the good things in life.

Are We There Yet?

Regarding the meal itself, Thanksgiving is somewhat reminiscent of a traditional British Christmas meal, but there are some notable differences. Americans will enjoy mashed potatoes, green bean casserole, mac and cheese, sweet potato casserole, creamed corn, and pumpkin pie. In contrast, a typical British Christmas meal features roast potatoes, roast parsnips, and pigs in blankets. The only shared traditions between the two are turkey, Brussels sprouts, cranberry sauce, and stuffing.

****

One of the challenges of being a nomad is the limited opportunity to be surrounded by good friends. I am fortunate to travel with my best friend, my wife. However, sometimes, you long for a broader circle of close friends.

Robert Dunbar, an anthropologist at the University of Oxford, is a pioneer in the academic field of friendship. His early research revealed a positive correlation between the dimensions of a primate's brain and the size of its social group. Building on this work, he predicted that a human can maintain a maximum of five intimate friends and no more than one hundred and fifty 'stable relationships,' a concept known as the Dunbar constant.

He corroborated this prediction when his team studied six billion reciprocated phone calls from 35 million Europeans in 2007. This data analysis showed an average person had 4.1 intimate friends, 11 close friends, 29.8 casual friends, and 129 acquaintances. I'll give you a moment to calculate whether you are averagely gregarious.

Using a slightly different definition of friendship, the International Social Survey Programme examined friendship habits globally. Their findings showed that Americans scored third highest, with only Australians having more mates and Norwegians having more drinking buddies. British people fell within the global average of friends, while those more inclined toward solitude were from Hungary and Spain.

However, it appears that the number of friends is beginning to decline slightly in the US. Currently, half of Americans have three or fewer close friends, compared to only one-quarter with such close-knit groups thirty years ago. This decline can be attributed to Americans now spending twice as much time with their children as they did in the past.

Finally, a longitudinal study of young Americans wins the 'No-Shit-Sherlock award' for the blindingly obvious. It found that the personality traits of openness and extraversion are positively correlated with increased friendship.

Fortunately, I find it easy to make acquaintances. For example, I will rock up at a tennis or bridge club and ask to play a game. In a way that jeopardizes my long-term membership of being English, I am happy to strike up a conversation with strangers at a dog park, supermarket, or (gasp) even on public transport.

The internet has made it easier for extroverts to make friends. Personally, I've found *Meetup*, a social media platform that connects you with groups of people of similar interests, to be particularly useful, and I joined a couple of groups that offered regular meetups for cyclists, kayakers, and hikers. These groups attract people like me who are new to the area and seeking companionship.

As with every other temporary location, I played tennis three times a week and gradually got to know the other men at the club. From my unscientific research, I'm not convinced that groups of male tennis players differ significantly worldwide. They playfully tease each other over every missed volley and offer only mild admiration for an exceptional shot from an adjacent court.

On the other hand, Lorna preferred more solitary activities, such as fishing. She found joy in catching catfish from our sunny dock. Additionally, we both loved kayaking and boating from our rental house, which was only a quarter of a canal away from Sarasota Bay—a fifty-six-square-mile estuary fed by three inlets from the Gulf of Mexico. We would venture into the bay, navigating the mangroves, fishing in the seagrass, and observing marine life. Then, at low tide, the sandbars would transform into temporary beaches, where we enjoyed some beach time in the heart of this vast bay.

Pods of dolphins would frequently swim by our boat to say hello, or perhaps to inform Lorna that they had already eaten all the fish. Alternatively, we might (figuratively) run into giant manatees wallowing in deeper waters. Unfortunately, human activity makes these manatees' lives challenging, as nearly all of them bear the propeller-blade scars from speeding motorboats.

However, our favorite activity was watching the seabirds dive-bomb into the water from the deep blue sky. A recent bird count in Sarasota Sound tallied 153 separate species and concluded there were more American Wigeons, ospreys, and egrets but fewer eagles and vultures than before. Lorna and I almost agree on our favorite bird. Mine is the pelican,

Are We There Yet?

which I can watch for hours. Lorna prefers the American White Pelican, essentially the same bird, just one that dresses for dinner.

Back in our temporary two-month home, we noticed water marks halfway up the kitchen cabinets above the newly tiled flooring. It dawned on us that these marks were probably caused by flooding from perigee tides, which occur when the Moon is closest to Earth. During one such evening, I found myself knee-deep in saltwater when taking out the trash. This was why three houses on our street, early victims of rising sea levels, were being rebuilt on top of ten feet of topsoil.

Sarasota was designed in 1885 by Scottish architects in Edinburgh, and its early settlers were Scottish immigrants who were taken aback by the dramatic weather change. If you look hard enough, you will find vestiges of Scottish heritage, including the impressive Riverview High School Kiltie Band and a shop selling British produce, including kilts.

Sarasota is undeniably an attractive city. The modern downtown condo blocks that rise above the bay, basking in its two-hundred-and-fifty-one days of sunshine, are a magnet for young professionals. In addition, the city sees an influx of four million tourists, drawn in by the allure of America's number one beach, Siesta Key, known for its 99 percent quartz-crystal sand. But, for the record, I personally believe that the beaches of nearby Anna Maria are superior.

Sarasota has many art facilities: an opera house, several theaters, a ballet, an art film theatre, the *Ca' d'Zan*, and several art museums, including the surprising Ringling. It is not New York, but it's not Newton Abbot, either.

In this part of the world, many people socialize with others on their respective boats, perhaps on an inland beach or sandbar. If you enjoy the sun, (country) music, sandbar volleyball, and beer, you might find it quite enjoyable, too. However, this vibrant boating culture has raised concerns for Longboat Key. Water is an efficient reflector and refractor of sound waves, allowing sound to travel greater distances. As a result, the town commissioners recently voted unanimously to impose stricter rules. In residential areas, boats are now restricted to 60 decibels from 7 am to 10 pm and 55 decibels from 10 pm to 7 am. For context, a whisper measures at 30 dB, while a normal conversation is 60 dB.

As you know, we love a parade. On the West Coast of Florida, there's a specific variant that we enjoy: the night boat parade. Several times a year, communities along the Intracoastal organize these boat parades, attracting dozens of boat owners. These boats, playing music at nearly 125 dB, are adorned with lights resembling firework displays, turkeys, or Christmas trees, depending on the holiday the parade celebrates. The boaters enthusiastically wave at the landlubbers who line the banks three or four deep while, in return, the spectators cheer on the parading mariners as they enjoy copious amounts of beer.

With so much drinking on the water, the US has a specific crime that is not common in the UK. Boating under the Influence—or BUI—carries similar penalties for drunk driving in the UK. This, and the occasional hurricane, means that there are plenty of wrecks in Florida's bay areas. These wrecks form havens for fish, where even Lorna can catch something.

****

I scoured the three Longboat Key complimentary weekly newspapers, but, in truth, there was little newsworthy content. My favorite part was the burgeoning letters section, where, in the first week, thirty-two residents had taken the time to write to the Editor of *Longboat Key News*. Sixty percent had written to protest against various proposed housing developments (often in forensic detail), 25 percent related to complaints about the horrendous traffic, 13 percent asked when the holiday lights would be turned on (an absurdly early November 1st), and 6 percent were about bees. Unfortunately, the two apian-related letters were as opaque as a foggy mirror after a hot shower.

Most local newspapers carry a police log of all crimes committed in the local police district. Crime in most parts of the US is minimal, certainly much lower than in Europe. Nevertheless, one notable exception to this trend is murder rates, which are significantly higher in the USA, primarily due to the widespread availability of firearms. From 1991 to 2014, however, America witnessed a halving of its homicide rate, partly attributed to more diligent policing and increased incarceration rates.

Unfortunately, since 2020, violent crime in the US has increased by about a third, primarily in big cities. This surge can be attributed to three main factors. Firstly, the aftermath of the 2020/21 'Black Lives Matters' protests has resulted in both reduced confidence in the police and less assertive policing. Secondly, gun sales spiked once again in 2020, with seven million Americans buying guns for the first time—half were women, and two-fifths were Black or Hispanic. A firearm makes everyone equal, so they say. Thirdly, the pandemic may have played a role. Schools shifted to virtual learning, teenagers had fewer distractions, and social services became scarcer. Some also argue that the chaos surrounding the pandemic created a 'moral holiday,' with many disregarding societal norms and laws.

However, judging from the police reports in Longboat Key, crime remained exceptionally low, and the good people of Longboat Key seemed to be, well, good.

In our first week, Longboat Key Police responded to nine incidents. The most serious was a custody dispute between a former couple concerning their child and a cellular phone. The other issues included a complaint about broken crosswalk lights, a report of a strange noise coming from a garage, an unusually parked vehicle, and a suspicious person with a bucket. Incidentally, this latter bucket-wielding maniac turned out to be pest control. Meanwhile, a concerned citizen had pursued another car he thought was driving recklessly with his hazard warning lights on. The responding officer arrived promptly but found no evidence of reckless driving. Another report concerned an injured raccoon on the road, but regrettably, the responding officer in this case was as slow as a snail on a coffee break and had to relocate the by-then deceased raccoon to the roadside. Finally, one householder had reported to the police that his water was not working, while a second had balanced this by registering a broken sprinkler head that was spurting water.

In the subsequent weeks, the frequency and severity of crimes appeared to decrease. Much of the 'crime' was animal-related. One officer had to "escort a very large, dead dolphin to a work truck," while another was dispatched to help a pelican with one leg. When this second officer located this one-legged seabird, he approached it, and the pelican flew away. Elsewhere, a negligent person had left their garage door open while a young female was warned for taking her dog onto the beach. Meanwhile, there was a traffic offense. An Uber passenger had fallen asleep, and the driver could not wake her. Finally, a man had fallen into the canal while fishing. His panicked wife called the police, fearing he might drown. However, when the police arrived, they found the husband in an outdoor shower, tending to his barnacle scrapes.

I wondered how many police officers this eight-thousand-person town of Longboat Key might need. It turned out that is twenty-one officer per four hundred people or one officer per 0.45 weekly incidents.

Elsewhere in the newspaper, I chose not to join the dinner meeting for the Republican Club of Longboat Key, where the key speaker was its

Chief of Police. It beats me how he found time away from the crime-infested town to attend. I was heartened, however, to learn that the Democrats and Republicans of Longboat Key met for lunch to promote dialogue and reduce conflict.

****

We enjoyed breakfast on several occasions in a nearby Amish community in Sarasota. While Amish communities are common in about half of the US states, this Florida community is where the Amish go on vacation.

In late-seventeenth-century Switzerland, a small group of Anabaptists led by Jakob Ammann split from their church in Switzerland. Interestingly, the Anabaptists initially intended the name 'Amish' as an insult to this bunch of renegades. About five hundred Amish came to America at the beginning of the eighteenth century, and an additional fifteen hundred joined them just over a century later.

Almost every one of the approximately 360,000 Amish and Mennonite people in the US today can trace their background to these two thousand immigrants. As the Amish are not evangelical, they have achieved this entirely through procreation. Indeed, only seventy-five people not born into an Amish family have ever joined the church.

The Amish community is one of the fastest-growing on the planet. With each couple having an average of seven children, the Amish population roughly doubles every eighteen years. If this high birth rate continues, its numbers will reach 0.7 million by 2040 and 1.4 million by 2060. The Amish don't tend to use birth control, not because it is forbidden, but rather because they view large families as part of God's purpose.

Amish communities are typically small and located in rural areas, with each church consisting of two or three dozen families. This rapid population growth leads to the establishment of around twenty new Amish communities each year, often in previously uncharted regions. Currently, thirty-one states have sizeable Amish communities, with the largest in the mid-west states of Pennsylvania, Ohio, Indiana, Iowa, Kansas, and Illinois.

As with many other things, it is difficult to generalize about the Amish. The primary reason for this is that each community develops its own rules, known as 'Ordnung' (the German word for order). Every church member participates in discussions and agrees on these rules every six months.

Since the *Ordnung* is developed independently, albeit with the guidance of the same Biblical reference book, the specific rules may diverge by community. These variations in interpretation can encompass crucial matters, such as deciding which new technologies to adopt, as well as seemingly less significant issues, such as determining the maximum permissible width of the brim of a hat.

The second reason generalizing about the Amish is challenging is because there have been numerous schisms driven by differing interpretations of the Bible. In the mid nineteenth century, *Amish Mennonites*, who, in simple terms, favored some adaptation to technological changes, separated from *Old Order Amish*. However, in the early twentieth century, *Swartzentruber Amish* broke away from the Old Order, believing this latter group was becoming too attached to new technologies, such as indoor plumbing and milking machines.

Two further less-conservative breakaway groups also disconnected from the Old Order in the twentieth century. The *Beachy Amish* preferred speaking English, worshiping in churches rather than at home, and using electricity. A fourth group, *New Order Amish*, also sought greater use of technology in farming and their homes, were more relaxed about dress codes and beard grooming, but abstained from alcohol and tobacco.

These Amish/Mennonite churches exist in a continuum, ranging from the most conservative Swartzentruber to the most liberal Mennonites. As outsiders, we can observe that they share many things in common, but insiders tend to focus on their substantial differences.

The most noticeable distinction between the Amish and the broader population is their appearance. Amish communities are readily identifiable due to their plain and uniform clothing. Amish men typically don dark suits, hats, simple shirts with suspenders, and black brogues. Married Amish men sport beards but not mustaches, as they associate the latter with the military, which conflicts with their strict pacifist beliefs.

Amish women wear bonnets and homemade dresses in uniform colors. They abstain from wearing jewelry, believing that the focus should be on God rather than material possessions. Additionally, women are not allowed to cut their hair. So, that business idea you had for a hairdressing salon in Amish communities may not be lucrative.

The Old Order prohibits what they consider the most dangerous new technological elements: buttons and zippers, both of which are seen as too flashy. Instead, all clothing should be fastened with pins. In contrast, the

New Order Amish flaunts its progressive side by allowing its members to wear buttons.

A second noticeable difference is their language. Although the Amish can speak English, they will typically talk to each other in 'Pennsylvania Dutch,' not actually Dutch but rather an old form of High German (*Hoch Deutsch*).

A third defining feature of the Amish is their resistance to new types of technology. In truth, this is an area where there can be a high degree of divergence. The Amish do not necessarily see new technology as inherently evil, but they tend to be wary of it due to its potential impact on their community and relationship with God. Hard work is highly valued because it is seen as a way to maintain a close connection with God, whereas labor-saving devices are generally discouraged, following the same principle. As a result, many Amish communities shun electricity, tractors, and motor cars. However, there is a line between hard work and unnecessary suffering. In most Amish communities, electricity may be used to keep farm-produced milk cool or to accommodate individuals with disabilities who require electric wheelchairs.

Anabaptist literally means 'later-baptism.' In keeping with other Anabaptists, church membership begins when someone is christened as an adult. Children can be raised as Amish, but they must make the deliberate choice to embrace the Amish way of life as adults.

Amish children attend Amish schools where instruction is typically delivered in English and takes place in traditional one- or two-roomed schoolhouses. Following a 1972 Supreme Court ruling, almost all Amish children finish school around the age of fourteen. Of course, informal education continues beyond eighth grade, primarily through on-the-job learning.

After formal schooling, many Amish have a period of *Rumspringa*, Swabian German for 'jumping around.' This rite of passage is when Amish adolescents decide whether to continue living in the Amish world. In many cases, these teenagers are encouraged to experience the non-Amish world. By the way, the Amish call this outside world 'the English world' and refer to all non-Amish people as 'English.' This is quaint and has the additional benefit of annoying Scottish people.

This period of *Rumspringa* may last only a couple of weeks or several years. However, in the end, approximately nine out of ten teenagers opt to become Amish. Some Amish teenagers join less strict sects, which the Amish refer to as 'getting their hair cut.' Ultimately, most Amish are baptized and formally join their church between seventeen and twenty-one.

The extent to which there is genuinely free choice is a contentious issue. Some argue that free will may be illusory in all societies and that sociological influences often constrain our choices. While our brains may create the perception of conscious choice, the reality is that decisions are frequently made within a limited range of options or are determined retrospectively.

The most contentious issue in Amish communities—and the cause of many schisms—is the practice of shunning. For British readers, this is akin to 'sending someone to Coventry' or punishing them by refusing to talk to them. For American readers, Coventry is somewhere you don't want to go. It rarely appears on tourist itineraries because the German Luftwaffe bombed it repeatedly during World War II.

Most Amish communities employ shunning as a means to uphold Ordnung, whereby disobedient church members face social isolation until they amend their behavior. In some Amish groups, teenagers who decide to leave the Amish community may face permanent shunning. It requires a strong-willed teenager to sever ties with their heritage and family.

A second thing that happens when you are an Amish teenager is dating. This starts with *Singings*, where adolescents sing fast-paced hymns in mixed-gender groups.

Amish communities have no arranged marriages, as the Amish believe in most tenets of free choice. Instead, many communities practice a tradition called *bundling*. This practice involves teenagers who are interested in each other lying side by side in separate blankets within the same bed and engaging in conversation throughout the night. Sexual contact is not permitted.

Amish couples typically announce their upcoming marriage a few weeks before the wedding day. It's common for their parents to purchase a bedroom suite as a wedding gift, and their communities become actively involved in preparing for the impending celebration. In certain communities, it is customary to construct a house for the newlyweds shortly after the wedding.

The Amish excel in various professions. While traditionally known for their farming, with approximately one-third of US dairies being Amish-owned, most now prefer to work in construction and furniture building. Their reputation for honesty and strong work ethic has made their services highly sought after. Additionally, the Amish operate a diverse range of commercial businesses. For instance, my preferred local supermarket, Detwiler's, is Mennonite-owned and still refuses to open on Sundays.

As you may recall from the film *Witness,* the Amish do not appreciate having their photo taken. This preference stems from their interpretation of the second commandment, which, as you may recall, prohibits the creation of graven images. It also aligns with their principle of *Hochmut,* which emphasizes the rejection of practices promoting vanity and individualism. Contrary to some misconceptions, however, the Amish do use mirrors for practical purposes, such as shaving or ensuring their hair is neatly arranged.

Most Amish communities do not permit insurance because it does not show sufficient *Gelassenheit,* the practice of submitting oneself to the will of God. This embraces health insurance, including government-run programs for Medicaid (poor people) or Medicare (old people).

Within each Amish community, every member contributes approximately $100 per month to a communal fund. When individuals require medical attention, they receive a diagnosis and a treatment plan from their healthcare provider. Subsequently, they consult their community to determine if the communal fund can cover the cost. Conglomerates of Amish communities often negotiate lower rates with local hospitals. These hospitals are willing to do so because they have confidence that, unlike insurance companies, Amish patients will promptly settle their medical bills in full, often within days of receiving the invoice.

The Amish are nevertheless suspicious of health authorities. The God complex of many doctors often clashes with the God's Will of the Amish. My Ohio judge friend told me that he regularly had to rule on disputes between health authorities and the Amish.

One consequence of the limited Amish gene pool is the increased prevalence of genetic health issues within their communities. While it's true that many Amish marriages now occur across distant communities to mitigate these concerns, serious genetic conditions can still occur. Most Amish individuals accept these conditions as part of *Gottes Wille*, and any child born with a disorder is embraced by the community and provided with tasks that align with their abilities. It's worth noting that other symptoms of *Gottes Wille* include a reluctance to install smoke alarms and a low rate of Covid vaccination.

Contrary to common misconceptions, the Amish do pay taxes but are exempt from social security, since they do not utilize its benefits.

Are We There Yet?

Additionally, they choose not to claim unemployment and welfare benefits. Addressing another misconception, some people believe that the Amish don't vote. However, my friend, the Judge, informs me this is inaccurate, particularly on local matters.

Historically, the Amish have refrained from using courts to settle disputes among themselves, aligning with their interpretation of God's Will. However, the significant increase in accidents involving speeding vehicles crashing into their slow-moving buggies has prompted a shift in their approach on disputes with 'the English.' Many Amish individuals now choose to pursue legal action against the speeder, using any financial compensation to support the establishment of new communities.

Amish cuisine is known for its wholesomeness though it can be quite calorific. Dining at an Amish restaurant offers excellent value and is undoubtedly a worthwhile experience if you happen upon one. In Amish communities, it's not uncommon to spot a horse-drawn buggy at a McDonald's drive-thru. However, you will never see them at a Taco Bell—not for religious reasons but because the Amish have standards.

In the 1920s, a few Amish and Mennonite families moved to Sarasota to grow celery, a crop they use instead of wedding flowers. Regrettably, this agricultural endeavor proved unsuccessful, and an Amish vacation town was created instead.

Around ten thousand Amish people visit Sarasota every year for vacations, resulting in Pinecraft becoming a melting pot of different Amish groups who intermingle in a relaxed manner. Some have dubbed it the 'Amish Las Vegas,' and, to that analogy, what happens in Pinecraft stays in Pinecraft.

It's not uncommon for some Amish elders to spend their winters here, effectively becoming Amish 'snowbirds.' At the other end of the age spectrum, many youngsters enjoy *Rumspringa* in a controlled manner. In this vibrant seasonal community, everyone will enjoy playing shuffleboard, listening to bluegrass music, and consuming ice cream from the excellent Big Olaf's Creamery.

After breakfast, we strolled through the local community. Each mailbox sported German surnames such as Yoder, Hochstetler, and Stoltzfus. Everyone we came across would exchange friendly greetings with us. Depending on their age, many would be on rented bikes, electric bikes, or tricycles. Others would be sitting on their front porch, cleaning something, finishing some needlework, or just talking.

You could see that this was a mélange of different communities. While they may have appeared similar at first glance, closer observation revealed subtle distinctions. Women wore bonnets and pinafores of varying colors, while men sported shirts of different hues and exhibited varying degrees of beard grooming.

I talked to a few Amish people as I had done elsewhere. Their American accents seemed incongruous with their dress. They seemed content to indulge this 'English,' but, when I left, they returned to their conversations in Pennsylvanian Dutch.

The businesses here were either Amish-owned or Amish-friendly. The local laundromat was bustling, like a bee on caffeine, and its distinguishing feature was the availability of outdoor drying lines. Meanwhile, we patronized Big Olaf's Creamery, which was celebrating its twentieth anniversary and offering its ice creams at 2001 prices.

On another of our visits, we had the good fortune to witness the arrival of six buses packed with Amish vacationers hailing from Illinois, Ohio, and Pennsylvania, judging from the vehicle tags. These newcomers, wearied by a grueling twenty-hour bus ride, were warmly welcomed by the entire community. Among them, I spied three teenage Amish boys, set apart from the others, diligently examining each bus for potential future spouses. Much like teenagers at a disco, they would giggle and share their preferences with their Amish friends when they saw someone they liked.

****

Daughters #1 and #2 visited us with their respective boyfriends during their extended semester break. Together, we enjoyed boating, kayaking, fishing, and relaxing on the beach, blending in with the other tourists at the beginning of Florida's high season.

On Christmas Day itself, we opted for a traditional American Jewish Christmas by dining out at a Chinese restaurant, followed by a movie. With both venues packed and the food and film disappointing, this was a one-time experiment we won't be repeating.

Christmas in the US just isn't the extended holiday that it is in Europe, with even Christian Americans only celebrating Christmas Day itself. I was curious about the reasons behind this and decided to do some research.

American Puritans banned Christmas Day between 1659 and 1681. More than a hundred years later, Christmas Day 1789 was notable only as the first time Congress sat in session. Christmas Day itself didn't become an official US public holiday until 1870.

As a relatively recent holiday, the US has adopted most Christmas traditions from the UK and Germany. As a result, Christmas in the US feels quite familiar. The Christmas traditions of the tree, meal, markets, music, cards, wreaths, stockings, and Santa's Grotto are more or less the same experience.

Some things are different, though, and some of these features have been exported to Europe. For instance, Santa Claus originally donned green and white attire until the forties when Coca-Cola altered his outfit to the now-iconic red, reflecting the company's colors. The power of American communication channels meant Father Christmas ultimately had to change his outfit in Europe.

Another influence is Christmas lights. For decades, American neighborhoods have competed against each other for the most over-the-top lighting displays. Other notable exports include poinsettias and being allowed to open one gift on Christmas Eve before bedtime.

Perhaps surprisingly, the traditional entertainment at Christmas is more high-brow in America than in the UK. American children will have to sit through a performance of the Nutcracker ballet, while British children will be scarred for life by being forced to watch a dreadful pantomime performed by actors last seen in Eastenders.

It's not surprising that the religious component of Christmas is more pronounced in America than in Europe. While Christmas Day is by far the busiest day for church attendance in an increasingly secular Britain, most Americans do attend church services to celebrate Christ's birthday. In contrast, one British tradition notably absent in America is the school nativity play, which is not permitted here because American public schools are prohibited from offering any specific religious education.

****

In early New Year, we relocated a few miles north to the neighboring barrier island for the next month. This new home was situated on the seven-mile-long Anna Maria Island. Although slightly smaller than Longboat Key, it is partitioned into three separate city jurisdictions. The southernmost is the 1.1-square-mile Bradenton Beach; the central municipality, Holmes Beach, covers 1.9 square miles and has the most people and amenities; and the most exclusive community is the 0.9-square-mile, two-piered, and one-theatred Anna Maria.

Despite their tiny populations, modest surface areas, and obvious similarities from sharing the same small island, each city has its own mayor and commissioners. These officials are responsible for managing separate police departments, waste management services, building regulations, amenities, and other aspects of local administration.

Unfortunately, the three municipalities have recently been involved in significant disputes with county and state authorities. These conflicts have arisen due to differing interests between residents, who wish to preserve their idyllic way of life, and the broader county population, which seeks to make the exceptional beaches accessible to others.

Residents of the city of Anna Maria voted to ban all short-term vacation rentals, which they saw as destroying their community. Anna Maria elected officials backed down from their plans when county officials threatened them with jail. When we first visited in the nineties, we vowed to retire to this paradise. However, we changed our minds when nearly every house had been purchased by investors and converted into weekly vacation rentals.

Holmes Beach residents are angry about traffic. In season, twenty-five thousand cars come to their beaches daily, and the single entrance and exit road is often gridlocked. After the briefest period of Covid lockdown, Holmes Beach unilaterally closed most of its public parking and restricted street parking before 5 pm to residents only. The County Commissioners demanded that Holmes Beach City reopen its parking, at least to other Manatee County residents. They argued that the County funds the beach replenishment and, therefore, all County residents should have access to the beach amenities.

This dispute escalated when Holmes Beach was slow to address the parking restrictions. Republican State Representative Will Robinson introduced a bill to override Holmes Beach and construct a 500-car parking garage on the island. He has further hinted at the possibility of consolidating all three city-governments and placing the entire island under the jurisdiction of Manatee County Commissioners.

Finally, Bradenton Beach recently resolved its dispute with the County when the current City Commissioners and the former Mayor won a court case against six former Commissioners from the now-defunct Concerned Residents of Bradenton Beach movement. These former commissioners incurred significant fines and legal costs because they violated the Florida

Are We There Yet?

Sunshine Law, a state statute mandating that all government meetings in Florida must be open to the public.

It generally makes sense for most local decisions to be made at the local level. The federal government would never cede its jurisdiction to the United Nations; individual states will fiercely protect their Constitutional powers; and counties and municipalities want to determine the most appropriate solution for their localities. Likewise, most individuals desire maximum personal freedom. However, a highly decentralized system of government can pose challenges when considering the broader picture or during times of crisis. It can also result in some peculiar decisions. For instance, Longboat Key's opposition to new cellphone towers can make finding a robust cellular connection nearly impossible. As a consequence, some traffic heading to the neighboring island consists of individuals seeking a better cell phone signal.

We enjoyed some of the facilities provided for the dwindling band of full-time Anna Maria residents. For example, the dog park provided a space for us to connect with fellow dog owners, the library an opportunity to meet like-minded knitting, origami, Mahjong, and ukulele enthusiasts, and the various sports facilities a chance to enjoy tennis, pickleball, or competitive angling.

With so many weekly vacationers, Anna Maria has transformed into a land of golf carts. A vacation isn't considered complete without being able to swap your regular car for a smaller, doorless one. It's of no consequence that the roads are congested for both types of vehicles, and parking options for any kind of automobile are scarce.

I conducted a forensic analysis of the three separate police reports found in Anna Maria Island's two weekly newspapers and concluded that Anna Maria Island is slightly more lawless than its neighbor. While the overall number of crimes was still absurdly low, unlike Longboat Key, they at least resembled actual crimes. In January, Anna Maria had one example of both vagrancy and Driving Under the Influence (DUI).

Meanwhile, one man was apprehended by a member of the public for an offense that wasn't clear, and a second individual was arrested for marijuana possession and driving on an invalid license. Additionally, there were some incidents related to mental health. One car had struck a building at low speed. Although the DUI test returned negative, it later came to light that the driver had recently stopped taking anxiety medication. Elsewhere on Anna Maria Island, a former employee had locked himself in the bathroom. When the police spoke to him through the toilet walls, the man said the bathroom had the wrong type of toilet tissue.

Of course, Anna Maria is fortunate to have two local newspapers. According to Pew Research, the US has 6,700 local newspapers, down about one-quarter since its peak in 2004. Unfortunately, each week, a further two newspapers fold. This situation is similar in relative size to the UK, which now has fewer than 1,000 local newspapers, also down just over one-quarter in the same period.

Newspaper revenue has more than halved in the last decade, primarily due to the migration of advertising revenue to digital media. Classified ads were first to shift to Craigslist and then Facebook Marketplace. This decline in revenue has also resulted in a halving of newspaper journalists. Although newspapers moved to digital to reduce production and delivery costs, most have struggled to maintain readership.

While some blame Google and Facebook for the decline in local journalism, it's difficult to overlook that the most significant cause of their decline is the reader, whose number has halved in the past two decades. Indeed, only 14 percent of Americans have paid for a local newspaper in the previous year. According to Pew Research, just 27 percent of Americans born after 1976 ever read a newspaper, compared to 55 percent of those born before 1947.

This decline in readership has unfortunate side effects. One of these is that the media's mission is to serve as a check on government, which is why the freedom of the press is integral to the First Amendment. The Founding Fathers recognized that a robust media was critical in educating the population and holding those in power accountable. Since most American government is deliberately local, a thriving local press is vital to democracy and good governance. When local news dwindles, accountability declines and civic corruption increases. Britain faces a similar issue, with two-thirds of all local authorities now lacking a local daily newspaper.

Regrettably, the unintended side effects of dwindling local newspapers get worse. The decrease in its readership is associated with declining engagement with local democratic life. Over the same period, America has witnessed a significant reduction in the number of political candidates running for local elections, resulting in two-thirds of more than half a million elected offices in the US going uncontested.

And worse again. Local communities rely on newspapers as trusted sources of information. Unlike the national media, the local press tends to be politically neutral. Therefore, a further reduction in local news is likely to increase political polarization further.

So, what can be done? Some have proposed public funding for journalism or subsidies from billionaires. It's challenging to see how either of these solutions could be implemented without bias. Australia attempted to ban social media companies from publishing local news content without compensating the news' source but capitulated when Facebook threatened to ban all news content.

****

We spent a significant part of November, December, and January on the beach. When New Year's resolutions were made, Lorna had two goals: figure out what she would do with the rest of her life and to go swimming in the ocean at least twice a week. I also embraced the goal of ocean swimming to support her in achieving this more specific objective.

It took Lorna precisely five days to game her second objective. She wanted to know if she could bank one of her swims if she swam three times in the first week. Fortunately, as it was also part of my objectives, we had agreed on the detailed rules. Firstly, evidently, you couldn't bank swims for the coming weeks—otherwise, the goal would have been 'swimming one hundred and four times in the ocean in 2022.' Secondly, what exactly was a swim? A mere toe-dip in the water wouldn't suffice. After some discussion, we eventually compromised on supporting ourselves in the water with at least twenty consecutive swimming strokes. Granted, in January, Florida's sea could be a little chilly. However, when I examined the record highs and lows, I discovered that Southwest Florida's lowest Gulf temperatures were consistently warmer than our native South Devon's summer highs.

Thirdly, when did the week begin and end? My view was that Sunday was the first day of the week, while Lorna was firm in her stance that the week did not start until Monday. She had some logic on her side. For example, in many languages, Saturday and Sunday are collectively referred to as the weekend. More persuasively, at least for European engineers, according to ISO 8601, the European-dominated international standard on the representation of dates and times, Monday is unequivocally established as the first day of the week.

However, Americans uniformly regard Sunday to be the beginning of the week. Consequently, they configure paper and online calendars, so

Sunday is in the first column. The origins of Sunday as the week's first day are undoubtedly religious. This goes back to ancient Egypt, where Sunday, the week's most important day, was firmly at the start of the week. Ra—the Sun God—had it set aside in his honor. Sun-day.

Later, in Jewish and early Christian traditions, it was believed that God created the Earth on a Sunday, which, by definition, was considered the first day. As you might recall from Sunday School, God rested on the seventh day, making Saturday holy. Post-Constantine Christians followed this tradition but preferred to have Sunday set aside for worship and rest.

In the end, I prevailed. This is partly because we both lived in and were citizens of the USA but mainly because Lorna is more conciliatory.

Are We There Yet?

Chapter 13 – Venice, The Florida One

My wife possesses numerous strengths, including an impulsive tendency when it comes to house hunting. In the morning, we would prioritize various criteria for an ideal property, finding that we shared similar preferences for a detached house within walking or cycling distance of a beach town. By the afternoon, she would have set her heart on some remote condo, which I know she would have impulsively purchased had I not intervened.

With this chapter only one paragraph old, you are probably already accusing me of hyperbole. "Nobody has ever bought a house as an impulse purchase," I hear you shouting. Well, it's not true. I have a British friend who has only ever bought homes on a whim, often in countries he was accidentally visiting or indeed had never visited.

Just last weekend, while we were viewing an open house outside our budget, a passing driver stopped to take a look. This bored, wealthy passer-by liked what he saw and made a binding contractual offer. By the next day, buyer's remorse had kicked in, and he was fortunate that the seller did not enforce the contract.

Of course, we Americans vary greatly by personality, behavior, and decision-making processes. However, the American Psychological Association found that Americans are likelier to make quick decisions without thinking than any other nation. Their findings also concluded that Americans were more inclined to engage in risky behaviors, such as driving recklessly, starting fights, or shoplifting.

Other studies have shown that the majority of purchases made were not envisaged when customers entered the store. This is why shop assistants are trained to upsell and cross-sell and why stores often offer promotions, such as Buy-One-Get-One-Free or Buy-Now-Pay-Later options. Certainly, online stores attempt to recreate environments that encourage impulse purchases, such as grouping related products together. However, only 6 percent of Americans report making an impulse purchase online compared to 79 percent in a physical store.

While two-thirds of Americans claim they lack the savings to cover an unexpected $500 car repair, the average American spends over $3,000 annually on 156 separate impulse purchases. Moreover, most Americans have indulged in impulse buys exceeding $1,000 at some point in their lives. As the saying goes, 'Moderation is for monks.' Yet, which demographic of Americans tends to be the most impulsive? Unfortunately, it's the younger and less affluent among us.

A $5,000 watch tells the same time as a $50 one; a Toyota will drive you just as far as a Mercedes; and a crocodile wallet will hold the same amount of money as a cheap plastic one. These examples underscore the adage that the holes dug for us in the cemetery are all the same size—except for those in America, where they may need to be a bit larger.

Why do people buy impulsively? The allure of immediate, pure pleasure can be compelling. That unexpected treat serves as a pick-me-up on a bad day or a zing for a boring one. After all, who among us hasn't enjoyed picking up an unplanned pizza on our way home from work?

Excessive shopping isn't the sole consequence of spontaneous behavior. Impulsive individuals may also partake in various activities, including binge eating, excessive drinking, gambling, shoplifting, arson, self-harm, and emotional outbursts. The most severe cases of impulsivity are often linked to mental health conditions such as bipolar disorder, ADHD, or other impulse control disorders. A National Institute of Mental Health study found that Americans exhibit these impulsive personality traits more frequently than people from other nations.

So, why are Americans so impulsive?

Firstly, with a disregard for future consequences, the consumerist culture inundates Americans with ads promoting immediate purchases. Secondly, easy access to credit encourages impulsive buying. Finally, the individualistic ethos fosters excessive self-assuredness and risk-taking. This is evident, for instance, in polls that show almost half of all Americans, including my wife, believe in their ability to land a jetplane safely during an emergency.

A comparative survey of Britons' and Americans' attitudes toward potential hand-to-hand fights with animals revealed greater American confidence across the board. Glossing over the finding that one-third of weedy Brits did not believe they could defeat a rat or cat, this perhaps explains why, when faced with hypothetical scenarios, a notable 8 percent of Americans think they would triumph over a lion—an outlook that might gain a sobering dose of reality within the confines of an actual lion's den.

****

Inflation reached its highest levels since the early 1980s. Americans were frustrated at the devaluation of their savings and how expensive everything was in Publix. A shortfall in the production of new cars meant many used cars appreciated. Meanwhile, gas prices soared, and many Americans descended on Aldi for the first time.

Central banks believed that inflation was transitory, attributed to supply shocks caused by the pandemic and the Russian invasion of Ukraine. To some extent, this assessment was accurate. Pandemic restrictions had led consumers to redirect their spending from services to physical goods. Unfortunately, the global supply chain couldn't adapt swiftly enough to meet the heightened demand, resulting in price increases for these material goods.

Meanwhile, the (transitory?) war between Russia and Ukraine increased the price of oil, grain, and fertilizer. Consequently, most central banks judged that inflation would unwind quickly. However, other economists correctly surmised that inflation resulted from a combination of supply shocks and excessive aggregate demand growth, such as the multi-trillion-dollar stimulus packages provided by many governments.

Other economists claimed that companies were price gouging. A New York Times analysis showed that profit margins were well above pre-pandemic levels as company profits boomed. However, as Jason Furman from the University of Michigan retorted, "Blaming inflation on corporate greed is similar to blaming a plane crash on gravity… technically correct, but it entirely misses the point."

Companies naturally aim to charge the highest prices possible, but competition typically acts as a check on these prices. In the absence of a government-controlled economy where prices are set by the state, higher demand for a diminishing supply will almost invariably lead to price increases.

In a matter of months, you would have to shell out over five bucks for a dozen eggs rather than the customary $1.50. The egg industry attributed this price increase to Avian Flu, which affected fifty-eight million American hens, and analysts confirmed that the total number of layers was down 13 percent from the previous year. Scrambled in their thinking, the same economists as in the last paragraph cried fowl play, and the New Yolk Times declared this another example of big business making eggregious 40 percent margins.

Some questioned why the price of eggs had more than tripled when supply had only fallen by 13 percent. Unfortunately, markets are rarely perfectly elastic. Specifically, there isn't a one-to-one relationship between the number of live layers and egg prices (it's the intersection between two curves, not a 45° line). Unfortunately, demand for eggs had risen at precisely the same time as supply had fallen. If a supermarket's egg supplier suffered an avian incident and had to remain closed for six months, the supermarket would then need to negotiate a new contract with a new supplier at the new market price.

In any case, consumers were eating more eggs because other protein sources were even more expensive. In the fifties, the advertising industry urged British people to "go to work on an egg," a phrase coined by British author Fay Weldon. It turns out it was also true that you should "work at home on an egg," perhaps because it is such an easy meal to cook.

American offices still had sparse attendance. Some locations were empty, including Apple's spacious Californian headquarters, which cost $5 billion to build (about twice as much as the UK's national health service spends on medical supplies each year). Some workers chose not to return to the office, having relocated to idyllic places.

One of these destinations was Florida, where the housing market was on fire. Or, as realtors would describe it, there were a lot of buyers in the market for precious little inventory. This shortage was particularly true for the places where we were searching.

With almost no houses for sale, those few that did appear on the market sold within hours to cash buyers, often for prices well above what mortgage companies would lend. Furthermore, given the scarcity of available properties, homeowners were understandably hesitant to sell and move.

I wanted to continue nomading around and had a preference for spending the winter in Mexico and California. However, Lorna was tired of moving around continuously. Therefore, I reluctantly agreed to revert to our earlier plan of wintering in Florida and spending the summers in Europe.

We leased an unfurnished property in Venice Island for two years. Its location was perfect for us, situated in the 'historic district,' just two blocks from town and three from the beach. We retrieved our remaining worldly possessions and efficiently furnished the two-thousand-square-foot home. Our dogs were content; they had half an acre of fenced yard to roam in.

****

Although Calusa and Seminole Indians had inhabited the region for twelve thousand years, Venice's modern history began in the early twentieth century when Bertha Honore Palmer, a wealthy Chicago widow, acquired 140,000 acres of Florida wilderness, roughly equivalent in size to Merseyside in the UK. In 1925, Dr Fred Albee bought a small portion of this land and hired John Nolen, a Harvard-educated landscape architect, to design a city with wide boulevards, abundant parks, and communal pedestrian areas. Nine weeks later, Albee quintupled his investment by selling the city of Venice to the Brotherhood of Engineers, who intended it to serve as a retirement community for its members.

The initial work on the city started in the 1920s, but the Great Depression curtailed much of the new town's development. In the thirties, the Kentucky Military Institute made Venice its home, and then, during World War II, the Air Force built a training base at Venice. It wasn't until the fifties that the town began its construction in earnest, following the original Nolen plan.

In the early sixties, Ringling Brothers and Barnum & Bailey circuses made Venice their permanent winter home. The town's museums feature magnificent photos of elephants walking across its bridges, and there's even a picture of a waterskiing elephant. Sadly, the circus left town for good in the early nineties, leaving behind only a circus training facility and a home for retired clowns.

As befits a city named Venice, most streets are named after places in Italy. We have streets called Milan, Turin, and Firenze, to name just three. However, when the planners ran out of Italian city names they were familiar with, they turned to Iberian place names instead. The influx of first- and second-generation Italian immigrants to Venice began in the mid twentieth century, creating a thriving Italian community. In fact, Venice now boasts over twenty authentic Italian restaurants, with ten conveniently located within easy walking distance of our house.

We began attending weekly Italian classes at Venice's Italian American Association. In our classes, most other learners were Italian by birth, upbringing, or marriage, and some could speak their dialect fluently but wished to learn formal Italian. With their Latin background, Italians love grammar, and these enjoyable and well-structured lessons filled in the gaps from our conversation-heavy classes in Florence.

The Italian American Club hosted *bocce*, a boules game similar to British bowls or French pétanque. Every morning, dozens of Italian men gathered to test their tactical wits against their friends. The women took center stage on Friday nights, serving New York Italian food rather than the authentic Italian cuisine we preferred. These gatherings would draw in hundreds of Italian Americans.

****

Tennis is widely popular throughout Florida, and it's estimated that the state has around ten thousand tennis courts. Although every Florida town and each sub-division has multiple floodlit courts, I opted to join a tennis club where finding a game and meeting people is made easy.

For most of the year, the weather is warm; it is common to play tennis in 85°F heat (30°C), and it's a blessed relief when it falls to the 70s. While the temperatures don't increase significantly in the summer, the humidity rises to 100 percent quickly, causing your tennis attire to be soaked with perspiration within seconds of your first forehand drive. Consequently, almost everyone opts for doubles rather than singles, and most choose to play early in the morning.

While the cost of a used racket and some balls is not high, tennis in Britain is primarily considered a sport for the middle or upper classes, possibly due to the unpredictable English weather and the high cost of indoor courts. Despite this, there has been a post-Covid resurgence in British tennis participation, with numbers increasing by almost half. However, the UK still has a long way to go to match US participation rates. Over one-quarter of the world's 87 million tennis players reside in the US, and thirty-five times as many Americans play regular tennis than Britons.

The two hundred members of my club were all friendly implants from the Northeast or the Midwest. I quickly received multiple daily offers to play, but I restricted my playing schedule to four times a week to safeguard my body from premature wear and tear. Despite being one of the younger club members, many of the older players were highly skilled at placing the ball exactly where they wanted. The only way to beat them was to make

Are We There Yet?

them run. I joined a tennis league and enjoyed playing competitively again.

In search of an intellectual challenge, I decided to join the town's duplicate bridge club. Although I had not played for a decade, I was allocated a partner, a snowbird from Massachusetts. I enjoyed his company and tried my best to grasp his intricate bidding system.

Unfortunately, the pandemic had devastated in-person bridge clubs worldwide. Having so many older people sitting inside opposite each other was just what the doctor had not ordered. The nearby Sarasota Bridge Club once boasted a massive facility with over 300 tables, reportedly one of the largest in the USA. However, when Covid struck, the club's income vanished overnight, leading to its inability to cover the rent for such a vast facility.

Venice's club was desperately hanging on. As with its neighbor, it also had spacious premises, but only about one in ten tables were in use. Pre-pandemic, one needed to book a seat online to guarantee a game. Now, the club was desperately beseeching people to come back. However, many were still Covid cautious, and virus-proofing in-person duplicate bridge is probably impossible. If one person carries the virus, there's a significant risk of transmission to everyone else in the club.

The owner had raised the table stakes to a hefty $10 per person to cover his rent, but this high cost deterred some from playing. A more significant issue was that the club owner was not naturally welcoming. As low participation continued, his gloom deepened as the lack of players threatened his livelihood. While I liked some individual members, his nature created an unfriendly atmosphere, and I felt no compunction to attend once my partner had returned northward at the end of the season.

While there are roughly the same number of bridge and tennis players globally, I believe that bridge will likely dwindle in popularity in my children's lifetime. Today's generation of children is not exposed to card games as we were in our youth. My sister and I would spend hours playing cards, partly because fewer alternative activities were available. Modern children have a multitude of more enticing distractions, such as interactive video games. When this generation retires, they may not have the same passion for card playing to fall back on, and the game will probably become a niche activity.

Card games are ephemeral. In the eighteenth and nineteenth centuries, whist was the most popular card game. Bridge, a more sophisticated whist variant, gained popularity in the early twentieth century. The Golden Age for bridge in the US was in the thirties and forties when almost half of US households played the game and when duplicate bridge—a variation that reduces the role of luck of the deal—was invented. However, by the mid-century, canasta briefly eclipsed it in popularity. In recent decades, the cool kids have taken to playing poker, and, indeed, twenty times as many Americans play it rather than bridge.

Americans love a holiday, and they celebrate a much more comprehensive array of them than the UK. Take, for example, St Patrick's Day. Understandably, this is a big thing in Ireland, but it is huge here, too, due to the presence of so many who identify as Irish Americans. In the US, Chicago dyes its river green, and many cities hold a parade. Everywhere, it is a commercial opportunity for businesses: shops promote their Irish products, restaurants take reservations for St Patrick's Day, and my Amish supermarket gives away a free cabbage to every customer. At the bridge club, my opponents wished me Happy St Patrick's Day and commended me for wearing green, just as they had done. I didn't like to tell them that I was wholly unaware that it was St Patrick's Day and also oblivious to the fact that I was wearing green.

Venice Beach offers free beach yoga three times every day. It is a popular activity in season, with several hundred bendy people attending each session. Lorna developed a ritual where she cycled the short five-minute ride to the designated part of the beach with a yoga mat securely strapped to her bike. It mystified me how yoginis are so trim, as the exercises appear deceptively simple and light. Upon her return, Lorna would enthusiastically demonstrate the latest moves, such as standing on one leg. I thought Lorna might be over-egging this 'exercise' when she bought a sports bra specifically for these yoga classes.

Gradually, I found myself attending these sessions, first as a warm-up for tennis and later as an early-morning exercise in its own right. Lying horizontally on the soft sand, gazing up at the deep blue sky, and listening to the soothing waves was a magnificent way to start the day. As the crowds grew, latecomers would extend half a football field from the center, unable to hear or even see the instructor. Instead, they would mimic the movements of those ahead of them.

The beach offers the usual array of activities, including beach volleyball, beach tennis, and watersports of every kind of propulsion. However, a more unusual American activity is the drum circle. Supposedly rooted in African and Native American cultures, drumming has been used for storytelling in communities for millennia. It was the

Are We There Yet?

sixties hippie movement that revitalized it in America. During that time, musicians would gather in public spaces to engage in improvised jam sessions. Today, every beach community seems to have its own drum circle, where drummers express themselves through rhythm, and non-drummers lose themselves in dance to these mesmerizing beats.

Angling is often thought to have the highest participation rate of any British sport. But, of course, this is a misconception; only two million Britons have the patience to sit by the side of a murky canal in the rain. In fact, three times as many Britons go running regularly than fish. Fishing is far more popular in the US. Although the US population has just under five times that of the UK, twenty-six times as many Americans enjoy the sport in its seas, lakes, and rivers.

Lorna often took herself fishing on the pier or jetty, both ideal vantage points for boat watching and popular spots at sunset. She would wheel her trolley filled with rods, bait, a chair, and a flask (of wine). Optimistically, she also carried an ice bucket to deposit her catch for later consumption. There is a fine line between fishing and standing on the shore like an idiot, one which Lorna frequently crosses. Nevertheless, she appeared to relish the sun and the camaraderie of fellow anglers.

Fishermen were also a common sight on the beach, with their rods securely placed in holders and their lines cast far out to sea. From time to time, we would see someone catch a shark. These were extended struggles, perilous catches, and poor meals. When the jubilant angler removed the hook from the shark's mouth and attempted to return it to the ocean, the shark's teeth often left a lasting reminder of their encounter.

The latest craze involves collecting seashells. In the past, women would take their early morning walks at high tide, strolling along the beach in search of natural treasures. However, a simple yet innovative gadget—akin to the metal detector of our era—has now enticed men to join in on this pastime. This device consists of a prismatic, meshed attachment affixed to a broom handle. The user thrusts the implement into the sandy shore at the water's edge to gather the ocean's bounty, lifting it out to let the water and sand drain through the meshed metal. What remains is then sifted, with shark's teeth and intact marine mollusks saved, their purpose often a mystery.

Our New Year's resolution to swim in the sea twice weekly was quite a challenge in January. However, one day in mid-February, it suddenly became delightful as temperatures soared into the eighties and beyond. A gentle sea breeze caressed my skin, and the rhythmic ebb and flow of the warm waves washed away the world's worries. Against the backdrop of the vast cerulean sky, I marveled as small planes gracefully soared from the former military airfield over the pier. The hum of their rudimentary engines, blending with the soothing sounds of waves lapping onto the beach, created a melody that resonated deep within me. I remained in the water for hours.

As the waters warmed, our beach grew more crowded with sunseekers lugging all sorts of paraphernalia: umbrellas, windbreaks, tents, picnics to feed an army, and music to annoy their temporary neighbors. In stark contrast, our kit is relatively minimal, consisting of one beach chair and book each, along with a shared towel and soda.

We relished gazing out into the Gulf, spying on a sea kayak gracefully gliding through the waves, a recreational fishing boat returning from its day's work, and an occasional jetski polluting the tranquility. On windy days, parasailers demonstrated their skills with daring jumps and impossible turns while sailing boats, tilted at 45-degree angles, raced each other for supremacy.

Dolphins were frequent visitors, and their presence suggested a potential prize for the shore anglers. They came by so regularly that I'd almost grown accustomed to their company. Almost, but not quite.

Squadrons of pelicans flew in formation, skimming about fifteen feet above the sea. They plunged deep into the water and invariably emerged with a fish in their gullet. The fishermen couldn't help but lament the loss of yet another potential catch.

As the weeks passed, we graduated to the dog beach for all our shoreline needs. It allowed us to bask in the sunshine and simultaneously give our dogs the exercise they needed.

The dog beach provided endless entertainment. On good-weather days (which is pretty much all of them), it hosted dozens of dogs engaged in various activities, from sniffing each other's butts to pursuing balls and playing chase. Just occasionally, conflicts arose. One dog would feel that another had encroached on its territory and started a barking dispute, sometimes even resorting to nipping the perceived intruder.

The owners of the dogs involved in these altercations demonstrated their parenting skills by promptly intervening. Both dogs were placed on a temporary 'naughty leash,' where they remained for ten minutes to reflect on their behavior.

Both our dogs enjoy the beach differently. Dog #2 is genetically programmed to corral other dogs. When the owner of another canine guest throws a ball, frisbee, or stick, Dog #2 will give chase to the dog in pursuit. However, she shows absolutely no interest in the object being thrown. Similar to an American cornerback, her sole focus is to prevent the other dog from reaching its goal. In football terms, she is playing interference.

Dog #1 adores the smell of newborn puppies—they are like catnip to him. He will investigate every small dog to see if they have that brand-new dog smell. When he finds one with this odor, he will play with the newborn pup, taking in their aroma until satiated (which he never is). In a human world, he would definitely be on a list.

Let's finish this section with a dog joke.
How can you tell a dog a knock-knock joke?
You can't. It will just start barking.

****

During one of Daughter #1's many visits, we spent time at Venice's showjumping facility, which is part of the professional Florida circuit. Showjumping possesses all the hallmarks of a fantastic spectator sport: the fundamental rules are easy to understand; the rider must not fall off; the horse must not refuse or hit a fence; and the victors are the duo that completes the course in the quickest time.

Moreover, it is compelling for other reasons. The sport has a low-cost entry fee for spectators, guaranteeing you a seat near the action under the still-warm evening skies. The resonating sound of hooves galloping vigorously on the dirt serves as a reminder of the inherent dangers of this sport.

I know these riders are typically the offspring of the extravagantly wealthy, some of them the daughters of American tech billionaires. These professionals exhibit the same level of skill and dedication as athletes in other sports. I can observe the paroxysms of joy on the rider's face after a clear round, but conversely, I am just as likely to witness the extreme dejectedness of someone who has clattered into numerous fences. In either case, I know I do not possess the bravery or the skill required for this sport.

Not all horse sports are exclusive to the upper echelons of society; we also ventured to the state's rural heartland to watch professional rodeo events. Since we had parked some distance from the stadium, a golf cart ferried us to the arena. The driver inquired whether we had previously attended a rodeo, and Daughter #1 had the rare opportunity to reply truthfully that this wasn't her first rodeo.

Julian Bishop

I enjoy the unapologetic Americanness of a rodeo. At the event's outset, the compère proudly declares that America is the greatest nation the world has ever known. He then asks those responsible for safeguarding our freedoms—veterans and active-duty military—to rise and receive a heartfelt applause from the audience. A mini-lecture then ensues; on this occasion, it is about the foolishness of removing statues. The announcer opines that history should not be erased, but rather, it should serve as a means for us to learn and grow. It is an inspiring message that resonates deeply with the primarily Republican crowd.

Suddenly, a lady standing on a horse, brandishing an impossibly large flag with fireworks emanating from its pole, charges into the arena at full speed over the freshly dragged red clay. The audience rises to its feet in sheer awe and remains standing for the national anthem.

The crowd is very much blue-collar and almost entirely white. If you were participating in a scavenger hunt, you would find it challenging to locate a mask-wearing Democrat of color among the ten-thousand-strong crowd.

The first two events are bareback and saddle bronc riding. In both competitions, the cowboy must lie flat on the horse's back with one arm raised in the air, displaying unwavering resolution to stay on for at least eight seconds. The unbroken horse, fitted with a flank strap, is equally determined to dislodge the rider. The horse's initial fury is reminiscent of a balloon in a cactus patch, and it takes several circuits around the arena to calm down post-dismount. The scoring system perplexes the amateur spectator, as unseen experts rate the rider's style and skill for maintaining their position on the horse.

Following that, several steer roping events then ensue. In team roping, the lead cowboy is tasked with lassoing the calf's head while the trailing cowboy ropes its two hind legs. Many attempts fail, as the young calf is swift and unpredictable. However, the most skilled riders immobilize the steer in approximately four seconds. Tie-down roping, on the other hand, appears more intense for both the calf and the rider. A lone cowboy chases the steer and lassoes its head. He then dismounts from his still-galloping horse, wrestles the calf to the ground, ties its legs together, and flips the young cow over. It's an explosively intense ten seconds, and the cowboys are immediately drenched in sweat from their exertions. This event demands a combination of technique and strength, and one can't help but think these cowboys might need a chiropractor on speed dial.

Are We There Yet?

Cowgirls also have their moments in the spotlight. They participate in formal events that involve galloping around barrels and roping breakaway calves. However, I often find their interlude performances even more captivating. One daring cowgirl races around the arena while carrying sponsors' flags on her horse, whereas another showcases a fiery spectacle. Her horse gracefully weaves and jumps through flames, and her pièce de résistance is straddling two horses, one for each leg, as her groin passes through a fire.

A cowboy dressed as a clown provides the entertainment. While I don't have coulrophobia, I do profoundly dislike clowns. However, I will make an exception for these brave fellows. With an accent so strong that he made Daughter #2 sound intelligible, he tells redneck jokes which she translates for me. Unfortunately, the audio system is so poor in the cavernous arena that you might as well invent your own punchlines, most of which involve Obamacare, Joe Biden, Hilary Clinton, or yoga.

As with all other American sports events, the music is eclectic and played in short bursts. It's the only place you will hear consecutive music from the Pink Panther, Thin Lizzy, Bubba Sparxxx, and John Mellencamp when he was still a Cougar.

Audience participation in the sport is restricted to children. The announcer invites all kids between six and ten to pull the artificial tail from the calves. Rodeo parents may be highly conservative but are liberal with their children's age qualifications. Some youngsters appear to be no older than three, and the young calves tower over these barely-toddling infants. Ignoring all health and safety guidelines, fifty children line up at one end of the arena while three steers eye them warily from the other end. When the compère gives the signal, the children sprint toward the calves, hoping to secure one of the $50 rewards. The calves might have found tie-down roping wild, but this is positively frenzied. The steers may be quicker and more agile than the children, but there are just too many children to escape from.

Our preferred position is just above where the competitors gather for the next event; I love to watch their evident camaraderie. Rather like S&M practitioners, they may want to beat each other but share the same dangerous lifestyle.

These wrangler-clad cowboys and cowgirls, ranging in age from fifteen to seventy-five, often don double denim attire complemented by Stetson hats. Daughter #1 adds yet another Stetson to her collection, a whopping

$709 from her hard-won earnings. This tightly-knit community transcends age and ethnicity, finding unity in a shared cultural code.

People-watching the crowd is equally rewarding. More round than slender and pervasively tattooed, various groups have chosen to watch rodeo today. The dominant group is the nuclear family unit, and this entertainment is designed for them—non-stop fun and never too risqué. Older couples like us have chosen this activity for their date night or, rather, date afternoon. While some young couples are on early dates, small groups of girls roam the stadium, flirting with similar groups of boys. In front of us sits a nearby children's group home. These 'discarded' boys may think they have seen everything, but they gape open-eyed and mouthed at their first rodeo.

The audience consumes vast amounts of Coke products, some in cups larger than the garbage containers in an English kitchen. While the usual junk food is readily available, the demand for healthy salads seems minimal. Meanwhile, Lorna is never happier than when she's the temporary owner of a funnel cake.

We all quickly do that thing you do when watching the Olympics. After observing for five minutes, we pretend to understand the rules and be able to distinguish between average and excellent performance. Even Lorna would critique a cowboy when he was unsuccessful at lassoing a calf. I point out that it is probably a bit more complicated than it looks, but she is having none of it.

The event ends with bull riding. This is for the bravest cowboys and the most bloodthirsty spectators. Bulls are naturally aggressive animals that dislike being ridden by humans. To encourage them to buck, the cowhands affix a strap near their genitalia. The bull will do anything to rid itself of its rider. However, once it has achieved its goal, it becomes vengeful. The dynamics change, and the bull will attempt to gore or trample over the fallen cowboy. Those quick to their feet seek refuge on or, preferably, behind the arena fence. Even-braver individuals are the bullfighters. Their job is to distract the bull from impaling the bull rider and encourage the bull to attack them instead. The clown has a role to play, as well. He attempts to attract the bull to the center of the arena and has only a barrel in which to take refuge. When the bull collides with the barrel, it rolls with the clown inside, fifty yards along the red clay floor.

Are We There Yet?

Now that we had a permanent residence, I could register to vote. Florida's registration process took under a minute online, with the only tricky decision being whether to align myself with a particular party. In many states, this affiliation is not crucial. However, Florida has something called a *closed primary*, meaning you can only vote in the primary election that chooses the party's official candidate if you are registered for that party. I couldn't bring myself to align with either the Democrats or Republicans, so I designated myself as an independent voter. Interestingly, the percentage of independent voters has surged over the past decade as the two main parties have become more polarized. Even in Florida, independent voters now comprise 37 percent of the electorate, compared to 36 percent Republicans and 27 percent Democrats.

Throughout human history, total consensus has likely always been challenging to achieve on any subject. Societies have traditionally resolved this issue through democratic compromise or by selecting a dictator to rule. In today's world, where there is an overwhelming amount of information, the media often resorts to creating conflicts to capture public interest (or, as they call it, 'eyeballs'). Unfortunately, this approach overemphasizes individuals with extreme views that deviate significantly from the general consensus. This, in turn, has rapidly led to the alarming polarization of society.

Unfortunately, it's unclear whether the latest generation will be able to resolve these issues. American teenagers appear to be facing unprecedented challenges in terms of their well-being. A striking 44 percent of high-school students report experiencing persistent sadness or hopelessness, which is twice the rate of a decade ago. Today's teenagers are also displaying a decline in traditional social activities; they are less likely to go out with friends, obtain driver's licenses, have sex, find employment, or engage in sports. Even more concerning, one in seven teenagers deliberately self-harm, often by cutting their arms or hands.

What is causing this change? Unfortunately, the number one suspect is (anti) social media, which delivers them 24/7 data points on everything they should be depressed about.

For many, politics has transformed into an all-out battle of 'us against them.' This confrontation appears to have occurred in tandem with the rapid ascent of social media, whose algorithms seem to prioritize and amplify illiberal opinions simply because they garner more reactions. Another flaw in social media is that it creates echo chambers amongst like-minded people, leading to extreme views seeming more normal.

Julian Bishop

As the world becomes more complex, problem-solving becomes increasingly challenging. Political parties, composed of individuals with diverse political views across a broad spectrum, increasingly struggle to find common ground on policies. Consequently, it becomes more expedient for them to vilify the policies and leaders of the opposing party to consolidate their own ranks and mobilize their supporters. The vilification of relatively moderate Republican presidential candidates, such as John McCain and Mitt Romney, backfired when a similar level of demonization was applied to a later candidate who arguably warranted more scrutiny.

This effect is well-known to social psychologists who have long recognized that dividing people into three groups, rather than just two, tends to reduce animosity. In a multi-party system, coalitions are more likely to form, creating an environment where it becomes less straightforward to demonize other political parties—especially those with whom you have recently been in an alliance or hope to form a coalition in the future.

Contrary to what you may see and hear, the average American tends to hold moderate views. According to pollsters, the center ground, which encompasses the 44 percent of registered independents, accounts for 56 percent of all adult voters. Nevertheless, the sensationalist nature of today's media results in a disproportionate share of attention being given to progressive activists and devoted conservatives, even though they collectively represent fewer than one-sixth of the US population.

Americans go to the polls a lot. They vote for the US President, US Senators, and US House of Representatives in federal elections. They select for statewide positions, including Governor, Secretary of State, Attorney General, State Auditor, Insurance Commissioner, Comptroller, State Senators, and State Representatives. County officials are elected, too: commissioners, judges, city attorneys, and their ilk. And because America is so decentralized, counties are further divided into cities and districts, where school boards, health boards, sheriffs, mayors, and more commissioners must also be chosen.

And you are not just voting once for these positions. Many of them have a primary to select the official Republican and Democratic candidate, and, in some states, there is often a run-off between the top two candidates if nobody gets more than half the vote the first time. Finally, there are an insane number of special referenda because elected officials cannot be trusted to make any substantive decisions.

Are We There Yet?

Accordingly, several times a year, there is some sort of election. My first opportunity to vote came a month after registering. There were two items on the ballot paper. The first asked whether "Sarasota County School District should continue the 1 mill per year ad valorem millage." These fourteen words included four words the average person, including me, may not initially understand. Nonetheless, from the yard signs, it seemed that we should vote 'yes' to save our schools or 'no' for no new taxes, both of which positions most people would likely agree with.

I decided to investigate further. The most accessible document I found was the four-page election article, which appeared to be a legal document full of 'whereases' and 'pursuant tos.' Eventually, I worked out what this referendum was about—the Sarasota School System asking for more money. In my old Georgia county, they added 0.5 percent to the sales tax on almost everything you purchased for improving school infrastructure. Here, they were proposing to impose an additional charge on property taxes. Voting in favor of this would slightly increase your tax bill but would provide Sarasota Schools with an extra $70 million a year for teachers, books, and facilities.

I have noticed they tend to schedule these special referenda at election times when fewer people typically vote, as they can count on teachers and parents turning out in large numbers to support better school funding. In any case, I was confident that this measure would be re-approved, as the Republican Party, the Democratic Party, and the League of Women Voters all supported the continuation of this measure in a rare sign of bipartisanship.

The second measure aimed to change how county commissioners were elected. In a 2018 referendum, 60 percent voted to allow only constituents in each district to vote for their district commissioner. However, the six commissioners, all Republicans, had subsequently voted to overturn this referendum, proposing that voters should be allowed to cast their ballots for any commissioner in the county, not just within their district.

After a brief analysis of voter registration in Sarasota County, I concluded that the motivation for this change was politically driven. Sarasota County had 150,000 registered Republicans, 104,000 Democrats, and 90,000 individuals without party affiliation. Upon examining district registrations, it became clear that one district had a slight majority of Democrats. I surmised that this election was held primarily to support the Republican representative of that one seemingly 'Democrat' district.

I looked at the election material. The Republicans asked me to 'Stop the Steal' and implored me not to 'let them steal our votes again.' They argued—feebly, I thought—that you should be able to vote for the best commissioner on offer. On the other hand, the League of Women Voters said I should vote against this proposal, while the Democrats—who hadn't seen election success as county commissioners here in over fifty years—claimed this was merely an attempt by the Republicans to fix election results and ensure that Democrats could never win.

These two special election referenda would incur a cost of around $630,000. However, after a few minutes of research, I found myself forming strong opinions on both measures. I relished the opportunity to have my say, and I believed that most reasonable people in Sarasota County would share my perspective.

The voting area in the local community center was nondescript, except for the occasional poster indicating its status as a legitimate polling place. I informed the volunteer checking my ID that it was my first time voting in the US.

With the ballot in hand, I proceeded to the booth to make my voice heard. The lawyers had worded the second ballot item so convolutedly that it took me a couple of read-throughs to discern which box I wanted to mark. Suddenly, I grasped both why the vote might not go as I had expected and why the campaign messaging was so straightforward: 'Vote Yes to stop the steal,' but 'Vote No to prevent the fixing of the election.'

Unlike in the UK, where you insert your vote into a ballot box, in Florida, you scan it via an optical scanner. It reminded me of Florida's 2000 election debacle when earlier technology had resulted in an inconclusive election and drawn worldwide ridicule. The hanging-chad scandal had captivated Americans for weeks, delaying the anointment of the forty-third US president.

The 2000 presidential election had been a closely contested campaign. As election day dawned, opinion polls were divided on the likely winner. Although Al Gore had secured a narrow majority of votes cast in the election, US presidents are elected via the electoral college. For the majority of states, this meant that the candidate who received the most votes in that state would win all of that state's electoral college votes. Whoever secured Florida's then-twenty-five electoral college votes was likely to win this presidential election.

One surprising feature of the narrow state of Florida is that it spans two time zones. Part, though not all, of the Republican stronghold known as

Are We There Yet?

The Panhandle sits in the Central Time Zone. Unfortunately, most TV networks 'called' Florida as having voted for Al Gore before voting had concluded in the Central Time Zone. Republicans later claimed that this premature projection may have affected last-minute turnout. Dan Rather, a prominent CBS news anchor, sanctimoniously declared, "If we call a state, you take it to the bank."

It initially appeared that Al Gore had won the election. However, from his home in Texas, George W. Bush believed that Florida was too close to call and announced that he would wait until all votes were counted. As the evening progressed, the TV networks started backtracking. Dan Rather red-facedly conceded that it looked as if Bush would win Florida. By 2 am, all the TV networks had changed their Florida prediction, thereby determining the next US president to be George W. Bush.

Believing that he had lost Florida and hence lost the election, Gore called Bush to congratulate him on becoming president and set off for a very early-morning Nashville Democratic rally to concede defeat. On arrival, however, he was informed that Bush's majority in Florida was fewer than six thousand votes and that thousands of further ballots remained uncounted. Gore phoned Bush back at 3:30 am and un-conceded. By 4 am, the TV networks reversed their projections again and said the vote was too tight to predict. NBC anchor Tom Brokaw famously acknowledged, "We don't just have egg on our face—we have an omelet all over our suit."

By this point, most Americans had sensibly retired to bed. Those who went to bed early believed Gore had won, and those who stayed up late thought Bush had won. It wasn't until Wednesday morning that everyone was finally aligned in not knowing who the victor was. At that juncture, Bush led Gore in Florida by a mere 1,784 votes out of over six million cast.

This is where the story gets complicated and somewhat surreal. While most readers may have some familiarity with this event, delving into the reasons and mechanisms behind it provides valuable insights into aspects of American culture.

With election processes being a state rather than a federal responsibility, each state must determine how an election is conducted. Due to the significant decentralization in the United States, states often delegate many of their responsibilities to individual counties.

In 1978, Democrat-leaning Palm Beach County led the way in voting technology by introducing the state-of-the-art Votomatic punchcard machines. Instead of marking their preferred candidate with an 'X,' voters punched out a hole next to their choice, and the Votomatic hardware automatically tallied the votes. However, by the 2000 election, most other Florida counties had upgraded their election technology to optiscan machines, leaving Palm Beach County one of many counties across America still utilizing the relatively old punchcard technology.

In Palm Beach County, local (Democratic) election officials had opted to use large print on the ballot to assist elderly voters in reading it. This decision resulted in the placement of the ten presidential candidates on the Florida ballot across two pages, creating what is commonly referred to as a 'butterfly ballot.'

It is likely that some two thousand Palm Beach voters were apparently confused and unintentionally voted for independent conservative Pat Buchanan instead of Al Gore or inadvertently spoiled their ballots by double-punching both names. Those who noticed the error could have requested a fresh ballot, but many did not realize their mistake.

Palm Beach was the best-performing Florida county for Buchanan, and nobody—including Pat himself—believed the Republican line that Palm Beach was a Buchanan stronghold. A better-designed Palm Beach ballot paper might have made Al Gore the US's forty-third president. Unfortunately for Gore, election officials cannot speculate about voters' intentions; they can only tally the votes.

An automatic recount is triggered under Florida state law if the margin of victory is less than 0.5 percent; in this election, the margin was much lower than this. Jeb Bush, Florida's Governor and younger brother of George, appropriately recused himself from involvement in the recount, placing the responsibility in the hands of the Secretary of State for Florida, Republican Katherine Harris. Thousands of lawyers from both political parties flocked to Florida that day, eager to secure victory for their respective parties.

By the end of the day after the election, a more careful machine recount of the votes had reduced Bush's margin of victory to fewer than one thousand. The Gore campaign requested that ballots in four historically democratic counties with punch-out machines be counted by hand. They were confident that this would crown Gore as Florida's winner.

In these punch-out counties, a small circular paper fragment, known as a 'chad,' is removed from the ballot by a device similar to a hole punch. In certain instances, this chad is not wholly detached from the paper, causing uncertainty regarding whether a vote was successfully cast.

Are We There Yet?

Unlike other states that used punchcard technology, Florida lacked a statewide definition of what exactly constituted a vote. Soon, America had a new vocabulary. A 'hanging-door chad' referred to one where only one corner remained attached to the ballot, while two corners secured a 'swinging-door chad.' 'Tri chads' had only one corner unattached, and 'dimpled chad' was indented but fully attached. Lastly, a 'pregnant chad' showed a slight indication of indentation. Suddenly, all of America developed strong opinions on what should be considered a valid vote and what should not.

Some individual counties ordered a manual examination of each ballot, and multiple partisan lawyers scrutinized each ballot paper as to the extent of its indentation. However, Florida courts shortly halted these examinations amid accuracy and consistency concerns.

The daily court battles between the two sides proved only that counting the votes in such a tight election race was impossible without an agreed standard of what exactly constituted a vote. Surprisingly, one month after the election, the Florida Supreme Court ordered a statewide manual recount of all 61,000 'undervotes.' The US Supreme Court then heard the case, with Bush Campaign lawyers arguing that only completely punched-out chads should be counted, while those representing Gore advocated for the inclusion of any indented ballot paper. Four days later, in a 5-4 party-line vote, the US Supreme Court declared the Florida Supreme Court's ruling unconstitutional and ordered a halt to the recount. This ruling effectively sealed the election—George Bush had won Florida by a mere 537 votes, just 0.009% of the total votes cast.

This decision did not quell the incriminations. Some Democrats questioned why Gore could not win his home state of Tennessee, while others attributed the outcome to non-mainstream candidates on the ballot. Both the Democratic and Republican parties have a vested interest in preserving the two-party system. In the 2000 election, the Green and Reform Parties had presidential candidates on the ballot in most states. Democrats argued that Ralph Nader's candidacy cost Gore the election, while Republicans believed Patrick Buchanan diverted votes from Bush.

The truth is that no party has the right to your vote—it's something each candidate should earn. We should not reduce our choice in each election to merely picking the lesser of two established evils. While it's true that an estimated 24,000 registered Florida Democrats voted for Nader (and about 60 percent of them might have preferred Gore to Bush), a much larger group of 308,000 Democrats preferred Bush to Gore. So, how does Nader become the villain in this scenario?

After the inauguration of President Bush, newspapers commissioned an accounting firm to review Florida ballots in April 2001. The outcomes of this review should make us question the competence of all specialists.

Using the Florida Supreme Court ruling of December 8, 2000 as their foundation, they examined all disputed 60,000 ballots from all sixty-seven Florida counties that had not registered a vote for the presidential election, commonly known as 'undervoted.' They assessed them according to four distinct standards. The *lenient standard* of accepting any indentation—and the one favored by Gore's attorneys—gave Bush his most significant margin of victory, 1,665 votes. The *Palm Beach* standard, which considered dimples as votes only if similar dimples were found elsewhere on the same ballot, also increased Bush's margin of victory. The *two-corner standard*, the criterion used in most other punchcard states to determine a cast vote, resulted in a 363-vote win for Bush. Strangely, the only scenario where Gore emerged victorious was the one advocated by Bush's Campaign lawyers; the *strict standard*, where only a clean punch counted as a legal vote, gave Gore a three-vote victory.

In May 2001, newspapers extended this analysis to include 110,000 who had voted for more than one candidate on top of those 60,000 who had undervoted. The Gore campaign never pursued this option, as these were technically spoiled ballot papers. However, it might show how voters intended to vote and help election officials provide better future instructions and ballot paper design. So, again, they applied the same four standards. Under these four scenarios, both Gore and Bush won twice each.

Finally, in November 2001, a media consortium and the University of Chicago analyzed the 175,010 overvote and undervote ballots rejected by the automatic vote-counting machines. According to their findings, if there had been a recount following the Gore proposal to review only the four problematic (Democratic) counties, Bush would have still emerged as the winner by a margin of 225 votes. Similarly, if the Florida Supreme Court's proposal for a hand recount of all disputed ballots had been implemented, Bush would have won by 493 votes. However, had a statewide recount with a uniform definition of what constituted a vote been conducted, Gore may have secured Florida by a margin ranging from 60 to 171 votes. Notably, this option was never pursued by Gore's legal team.

Are We There Yet?

The hanging-chad fiasco underscored the imperative need to enhance the conduct of elections in America. To his credit, President Bush established a task force to revamp election legislation, aiming to prevent a recurrence of this debacle. While the Federal Government isn't directly responsible for elections, it can allocate contingency funding to states to establish federal standards, working around the constraints of the Tenth Amendment. The Help America Vote Act of 2002 allocated funds to update vote-counting technology.

What can we glean from this debacle more than twenty years later? First and foremost, I don't believe the Republicans stole this election. It was simply an extremely close election marked by outdated equipment and a lack of well-defined rules. Secondly, it became increasingly clear that many judges based their rulings on their political affiliations. Thirdly, it was yet another example of partisans on each side cherry-picking various scenarios that (they thought) favored their candidate (even though, in most cases, it didn't). Few Americans trust politicians, and political people, in particular, definitely don't trust them.

While the 2000 election was indeed contentious and close, it may not hold the title of the most controversial or closest presidential election. That distinction belongs to the disputed election of 1876. The day after the election, Democrat Samuel Tilden led Republican Rutherford Hayes by 184 electoral votes to 165. However, 20 electoral votes remained undecided in Louisiana, South Carolina, and Florida, with their tallies neck and neck. The electoral bodies in these three states were controlled by Republicans who argued that fraud, violence, and intimidation had rendered enough Democrat votes invalid, paving the way for Hayes to claim victory.

Just as would happen one hundred and twenty-four years later, hundreds of partisan lawyers descended on these states to ensure their party would prevail.

A panel consisting of five senators, five representatives, and five Supreme Court justices—almost evenly split between Republicans and Democrats—was tasked with resolving the dispute. This resolution, later referred to as the Compromise of 1877, saw the Democrats agreeing to concede the election to Rutherford Hayes on the condition that the Republicans withdrew federal troops from the South. This concession effectively marked the end of the Reconstruction era and ushered in a period during which Democrats systematically disenfranchised Black voters through poll taxes, literacy tests, and intimidation for the next seventy years.

As I finished scanning my referenda vote, there was a round of applause from the three volunteers to celebrate my first vote in a US election. It was louder than the applause at me becoming a US citizen.

Incidentally, I shouldn't have doubted the wisdom of the Sarasota electorate. On both measures, they voted the way I did—which is to say correctly.

Amidst the widespread doubts many Americans harbored about their elections' trustworthiness, I volunteered as a temporary election official to form my own perspective. As an optimistic outsider, my natural inclination was to place my trust in the process. However, I have encountered numerous individuals from both ends of the political spectrum who do not share this sentiment.

As American friendship circles become more homogenized, many citizens isolate themselves from those who vote differently. In fact, they do know people with different views, but these individuals have learned to keep as quiet as a mouse with a guilty conscience about their political beliefs.

Over time, many Americans tend to assume that their social circles reflect a representative cross-section of the entire population. Consequently, when their preferred candidate fails to win, they question, "How is it possible that the other side emerged victorious when everyone I know is a Democrat/Republican?" For some, maybe it is easier to believe that the other side is stuffing the ballot boxes rather than acknowledging that you can only socialize with people who seem to agree with you.

I volunteered for one of the many election nights, then early voting, and finally, other aspects of the election process. The other volunteers were attorneys, teachers, and mothers who were playing their part to ensure a fair election.

After several weeks of work, I realized that I had been informally auditing the election process to conclude whether it was flawed or could be manipulated. I concluded that the process was fundamentally sound, at least in my county of my state. I saw absolutely no opportunity to stuff ballot boxes or remove inconvenient votes, as every ballot box was within arm's length of two independent people at every process stage.

The process, however, is deeply inefficient. Despite vote-scanning technology, many tasks are mind-numbingly manual, with the work often as captivating as a mime's podcast. Through conversations with the full-time election officials, I came to understand that we were meticulously adhering to thousands of detailed regulations.

Although many of the voters thanked us for our service, I was surprised by the number of curmudgeonly comments made by some when depositing their ballots. "I don't know if they will count my vote" was a sentiment I heard repeatedly, and it seemed to come from both sides of the political spectrum. Of course, we always reassured them that their votes would indeed be counted and suggested they could volunteer to audit the process themselves.

To an extent, I can understand the deeply ingrained distrust. Politicians of all convictions are deeply distrusted in America. "Ask not what your country can do for you, but what you can do for your country" seems a distant belief today. Reluctantly, as a trusting person, I concede that many politicians would fix election results if they could. Unfortunately, the ends seem to have triumphed over the means in the eyes of these political zealots. However, just because they would doesn't mean they could.

****

We attended a few spring-training baseball games. These occur before the baseball season begins and are akin to pre-season friendlies in soccer. The players use them to get match fit, while the clubs make decisions about their major league rosters. Half of the major league teams play in the Florida-based Grapefruit League and the other half in the Arizona-based Cactus League.

In Atlanta, we lived twenty minutes from the Braves stadium. Now we resided 550 miles away in Venice, we find ourselves, once again, just a twenty-minute drive from the Braves' spring-training stadium.

In 1997, the Braves relocated their Georgia stadium from the old Olympic track and field venue near Downtown Atlanta to a neighboring county. Cobb County had financed nearly 60 percent of the $672 million stadium through 30-year bonds, with the repayments funded by a new hotel and rental car tax. The rationale behind Cobb County's decision to fund a private company's new stadium was to create jobs and spur economic growth. The county argued that the investment would eventually pay for itself through increased tax revenues generated by the new stadium and the businesses surrounding it.

However, opponents of the move saw it as another instance of 'white flight' and lamented the loss of yet another amenity from Downtown Atlanta.

In Cobb County, many residents strongly objected to using public funds to support a private sports venue. Their discontent was evident in the subsequent election when they voted out the Chairman of the Board of Commissioners who had conducted these secretive negotiations.

The Braves used a similar trick to secure a new stadium in Florida by presenting an economic impact analysis that projected a $1.7 billion boost to the local economy if the Braves relocated to Sarasota County. This analysis persuaded other stakeholders to invest in the Braves' new spring-training stadium: Sarasota County agreed to contribute $21 million, the State of Florida stumped up $20 million, and a local developer, with plans to construct a new city around the stadium, provided $5 million and the land. Consequently, the Braves paid just $18 million for the new stadium, along with nominal annual lease payments for the next thirty years.

Ownership of sports franchises is a big business in the US, with most owners making billions from the American obsession with sports. In all US sports, the franchise owners fix the rules in their favor. This allows them to maintain a virtual monopoly within their respective professional sports without any system of relegation for underperforming teams.

Occasionally, a sports franchise will relocate to a different part of the country in search of a more favorable deal from their new host city. Take, for example, the heartbreak that befell a third of New York residents when the Dodgers and the Giants departed for California in 1958. This willingness to move has led to US cities funding most of the professional teams' capital costs. While there may be a short-term drop-off in fan support, the economic value of the franchise—which is what the owners care about—invariably increases.

The average NFL franchise is worth $4.5 billion, basketball $2.9 billion, baseball $2.3 billion, hockey $1.0 billion, with soccer $0.7 billion lagging but catching up fast. So, when you see an American-franchise owner buying an English Premier team, you can bet they are purchasing the club for economic reasons and will ultimately wish to stack the deck in their favor.

In the last fifty years, baseball has had many strikes. Players protested against owners in 1972, 1973, 1976, 1980, 1981, 1985, and 1990. Finally, the catastrophic strike of 1994-95 wiped out one and a half seasons of baseball and turned many fans away from the game forever.

Are We There Yet?

These strikes are invariably triggered by the owners who want to impose some change that serves their interests. However, these owners skillfully position the dispute as caused by greedy baseball players. With the mean salary of $4 million for a major league baseball player, it is unedifying to see people striking when they earn so much money. However, the reality is that all of these disputes are over money. The players want a bigger slice of the pie, while the owners want to preserve or increase their income.

The collective bargaining agreement between players and owners expired at the end of November 2021. Despite many years of negotiations, owners and players' representatives failed to reach a consensus on an updated deal. Consequently, on December 1, 2021, the owners declared a lockout, signaling that there would be no further baseball until an agreement could be reached. It was essentially the opposite of a strike; players were barred from using the clubs' facilities for training, and franchises could not enter into new contracts or utilize players' images.

Negotiations proceeded slowly. The two sides met only four times in December and January, and both declared they were no nearer to agreement than in November. Both sides were playing to the court of an increasingly disinterested public opinion. The owners professed that they wanted to continue the previous deal and insinuated that these millionaire players were greedily refusing arbitration. The players rebutted by saying that their respective positions were too distant and that the owners only offered arbitration to make the players look bad when they turned it down. Also, in any case, the salary negotiations were not about the millionaires but the bulk of the lower-earning players.

Baseball is an unequal sport, much more so than premiership soccer. The top one hundred players collectively earn more than half of total baseball earnings. The remaining sixteen hundred on major-league rosters typically make between half and one million dollars, still a lot of money. However, younger players usually sign six-year contracts at a relatively low salary, with the promise of more substantial paydays for the best later in their careers.

In March 2022, after a grueling ninety-nine days of lockout, the two sides finally reached an agreement. Consequently, the spring training baseball season for 2022 was significantly shorter, featuring only eighteen games. Although the first day of the regular season started a week later than the usual schedule, the teams completed the full 162 regular games by extending the end of the season and increasing the number of double-header matchups.

Predictably, both sides claimed victory. However, in reality, this was another massive victory for the owners. The owners voted 33-0 in favor of the agreement, while the players were split 26-12, with all eight members of the player executive committee voting against the offer.

The owners reasserted the 'unfair' collective bargaining agreement. They also agreed to increase the number of teams that qualify for the postseason to twelve, which should significantly boost some owners' income. In addition, some technical rule changes sped up the game for TV audiences, which in turn would increase media rights.

The players did not leave entirely empty-handed. The minimum MLB roster salary was increased from $575,000 to $700,000, and a $50 million pot was also formed to share amongst the most successful young players. These concessions meant that the players could claim victory. However, the reality is that the owners get to keep most of baseball's income for another decade.

****

While alligators are native to other southern states, they are most abundant in Florida. According to the Florida Fish and Wildlife Conservation Commission, their state is home to an estimated 1.3 million adult alligators, and they advise that any freshwater body of water should be assumed to be inhabited by at least one alligator. This recommendation is the most compelling reason why most swimming pools are caged, and lake vacations are much less common here.

Alligators are not known for their discerning palate. They will eat almost anything that moves, including fish, frogs, birds, snakes, small mammals, and other alligators. They disavow the advice from their grandmothers by not chewing each mouthful one hundred times before devouring, preferring to swallow their dinner whole and letting their stomach enzymes break down their meal. Where the prey is too large to be consumed in one go, alligators will wedge their meal underneath a tree root and allow nature to tenderize it for later enjoyment. They do this on the rare occasions when they catch a human. While Florida alligators bite humans six times a year on average, only twenty-nine human fatalities have been attributed to alligator attacks in Florida since World War II.

Are We There Yet?

Alligators are typically patient creatures who will wait opportunistically for their next meal to come to them. However, some alligators can be crafty. For example, naturalists have observed them placing branches on their heads to lure birds looking for nesting material.

In Spring, alligators will travel significant distances to find their mate. In April, I noticed an almost daily picture or video of an alligator wandering in a strip mall on my Facebook feed as it searched its former habitat for a mate. This temporary migration serves as a poignant reminder that we've infringed upon their home. On the plus side, seeing an older lady drop her purchases upon spotting a ten-foot alligator as she exited a pharmacy is enormous fun. She cleared the foyer faster than a tornado in a trailer park.

Once the male has identified a potential mate, he will perform a water dance. This courtship ritual involves the male displaying his prowess by slapping his head on the water's surface and releasing a deep rumbling bellow. Despite lacking vocal cords, alligators are skilled at producing various sounds by drawing air into their lungs and expelling it, much like a trumpet.

After mating—which typically takes about thirty seconds, ladies—the female will bury her eggs in mud. I would advise against alligator egg searching, as she usually stays around until September to protect her eggs from other animals. Similar to crocodiles, the gender of the baby alligator is determined by the temperature of their nest. If the temperature remains below 86°F, the hatchlings will be female; above 93°F, they will be males. For temperatures between these thresholds, a mix of both genders will emerge.

Someone once asked me if one could keep an alligator as a pet. The answer is that it is illegal to feed alligators and inadvisable to consider them as potential friends. They decidedly are not cuddly. There's a common myth that you should run in a zigzag manner if you encounter an alligator. Unfortunately, this tactic only gives the alligator more time to see you. With their eyes situated on the sides of their heads, they have limited frontal vision but excellent peripheral vision. Therefore, your best course of action is to run straight—and I can't stress this enough—<u>away</u> from the alligator.

If an alligator manages to catch you, the situation does not bode well. Alligators possess the third-hardest bite of any animal, ranking just behind the Nile and Saltwater crocodile. According to estimates by a professor at Florida State University, the average alligator exerts a staggering force of

13,172 Newtons, akin to the strength required to lift a pickup truck with your bare hands.

A second misconception is that alligators are incapable of climbing. In reality, they can use their claws and tails to scale barriers lower than five feet in height. In any case, I'm not sure fences are that effective at keeping alligators out, judging from the many videos I've seen of alligators slicing effortlessly through metal railings.

The bobcat is another species that has successfully adapted to its declining natural habitat. Some three hundred thousand of these large wild lynxes are estimated to live in Florida's swamps, forests, and urban areas. On our suburban island, while walking the dogs in the early evening, we regularly see a bobcat with some small mammal in its mouth returning to its young.

While alligators and bobcats continue to thrive in Florida, other animals have struggled to survive.

Like alligators and bobcats, the sea turtle must travel long distances to find mates. After doing what comes naturally, the female returns to the beach she came from to lay her eggs in the sand. Two months later, these hatchlings emerge and begin their journey to the sea. Regrettably, all seven species of sea turtles are currently endangered, primarily due to habitat disturbances, hunting, and marine debris. Volunteer groups diligently identify potential turtle-nesting sites, and most Florida beaches strictly enforce nighttime light restrictions between May and October to prevent recently hatched turtles from straying away from the ocean.

The Florida panther, a subspecies of the cougar, was among the first animals to be added to the US Endangered Species list in 1973. Their plight is primarily a result of ongoing-residential development in Southwestern Florida, leading to a staggering 95 percent reduction in their natural habitats. Just a few years ago, their population dwindled to a mere thirty adults. However, recent efforts by naturalists have expanded their territory to encompass other Central Florida regions outside the Everglades, resulting in a heartening increase to approximately two hundred adults today.

****

Florida has a hurricane preparedness week at the beginning of June every year. During this week, you can purchase certain hurricane-related goods without paying the Florida sales tax of 6 percent. It is the most cost effective time to buy generators, radios, reusable ice packs, and portable power packs.

Magazines are distributed to remind residents what they should do. All householders should ensure that hurricane shutters fit snugly within their window frames, that sandbags are adequately filled, and that they have a week's supply of food and water.

Florida hurricane season spans from June to the end of November. With the most destructive area of impact of hurricanes so small and the season so long, it is perhaps easy to see why experienced Floridians become blasé about the threat.

Wind buff Herb Saffir and meteorologist Bob Simpson were the first to categorize hurricanes, dividing them into five classifications based on their peak wind speeds. The first two categories do not concern most hardened Floridians—in fact, some may hold get-togethers with friends to celebrate the incoming storm. Category 1 hurricanes, with winds between 74 and 95 mph (120-153 km/h), might cause minor yard or roof damage, while a Category 2 hurricane (96-110 mph, or 154-177 km/h) can uproot trees and bring down power lines. However, residents understand that these storms usually lead to a relatively quick return to normalcy.

Category 3 (with winds ranging from 111-129 mph or 178-208 km/h, exemplified by Wilma in 2005) will lead to extended power outages, making it highly uncomfortable in the scorching 90°F heat without air conditioning or access to water.

Even the most resilient Floridians become concerned when faced with a Category 4 hurricane. With wind speeds of 130-156 mph or 209-251 km/h (and most recently exemplified by Irma in 2017), these storms have the potential to cause catastrophic damage, leading to the destruction of roofs and walls. The hardest-hit areas may remain uninhabitable for weeks.

Lastly, Category 5 hurricanes, such as Andrew in 1992, are exceptionally rare but can devastate a broader region. Often referred to as 'storms of the century,' they can obliterate most framed houses, and power outages could persist for a month or longer.

Hurricanes can only form when ocean temperatures exceed 79°F (26°C). In cooler waters, hurricanes either do not develop or weaken rapidly once they traverse areas with temperatures below this threshold. An increase in global temperatures appears to have both raised the oceans' temperature and prolonged the period during which they aid hurricanes.

Julian Bishop

With the Earth now 1.2°C warmer than during the pre-Industrial Revolution era, some argue that we may be witnessing an uptick in hurricane activity. While there isn't an overwhelming body of evidence supporting this claim, there is a notable trend of stronger and slower-moving hurricanes, which can significantly impact the areas they affect.

Hurricanes are named by the World Meteorological Organization, which constructs six years of names, one for each alphabet letter. After the sixth year, the list of names repeats. I am glad to report that 2021's Hurricane Julian spent all its time blowing harmlessly in the Atlantic. However, it will have another opportunity to be destructive in 2027. When a hurricane causes significant damage or loss of life, its name is retired from the list to avoid revisiting painful memories. For example, the name Andrew was retired and replaced with Alex.

As with most other Atlantic hurricanes, Ian had its origins as a wave near Cape Verde in 2022. A few weeks later, this wave had transformed into a tropical storm and passed over the western tip of Cuba, heading northward toward the Gulf. As it moved over the Gulf's warm waters, the storm gained strength, gradually intensifying into a hurricane.

Thirteen meteorological teams endeavored to forecast the hurricane's trajectory by analyzing data from various sources, including the International Space Station, ships, buoys, and reconnaissance aircraft intentionally flown into the cyclone. Their ensemble of 'spaghetti models' depicted a cone of uncertainty of where this hurricane might hit land, covering a vast distance from Louisiana to Eastern Florida.

Twelve models had projected Hurricane Ian to hit Florida's Panhandle or Alabama, with only the UK Met Office Model predicting it would make land in South-West Florida, seventy miles north of us in Tampa. It brought to mind the case of the UK weatherman, Michael Fish, who famously assured Britons in 1987 that no storm would hit the UK just before one of the country's most destructive hurricanes. However, it remained possible that the Met Office model could be accurate.

We finished our last-minute preparations over the weekend. We stocked up on gallons of water, filled the bathtub, purchased non-perishable food that could be prepared without power, and acquired more battery packs. I shoveled sand into bags at the local sandbagging facility—it was arduous work.

You cannot realistically evacuate for every storm but don't want to be around for the higher category hurricanes. Unfortunately, predicting exactly where it will hit or its wind speed is not always precise.

Are We There Yet?

We crafted two contingency plans. Plan A was the default plan, where the direct hit was somewhere other than Venice. It assumed we would lose mains water for a few days and power for a week. Plan B, on the other hand, was our strategy for evacuating if Venice faced a direct hit.

That weekend's weather was splendid, allowing us to make the most of our time at the beach, attend an outdoor theater performance, and catch up with friends. Then, late Sunday evening, all the other weather models converged toward the UK Met Office projections. They now all agreed that Tampa would get the direct hit, and communities south of Tampa might face a storm surge.

The most perilous position during a Northern Hemisphere hurricane is just south of the eye. The counterclockwise motion of the anticyclone draws ocean water into its vortex and pushes it outward, creating water surges. The meteorologists were forecasting surges of up to fifteen feet (5 m). Our house, positioned only thirteen feet above ground and situated just three blocks from the beach, was at risk.

By Monday, the models had shifted further southward, predicting an imminent direct hit on our town. We put Plan B into action and evacuated to Daughter #1's house in Atlanta, just a few hours before the authorities issued an evacuation order for the whole of Venice Island.

Our early departure enabled us to beat most of the traffic on the eight-hour journey northward. Meanwhile, on the other side of the highway, tens of thousands of linesmen trucks from nearby states were heading in the opposite direction. Like us, they didn't know where the hurricane would hit, but they knew it would land somewhere. The dogs enjoyed the long journey, but our Houdini cat frustrated me by prizing open the zip of her basket and finding refuge under my brake pedal.

We drove northward, our phones pinging with notifications ordering us to evacuate Venice Island and reminding us they would turn off the mains water before the hurricane hit.

Nearby communities were gripped by a heightened sense of alarm. The line for sandbags stretched for over a mile, gas stations had depleted their fuel reserves, schools and restaurants had shuttered their doors, and supermarkets had sold out of essential supplies such as water, flashlights, batteries, and snacks.

In these times of panic, the local meteorologists transform into local celebrities, and residents hang upon every word they utter. Social media posts from these messengers from the Gods received tens of thousands of comments within minutes of publication. In particular, everyone is anxious about the whereabouts of Jim Cantore from the Weather Channel. He is pretty likable, but nobody wants him to seek out their town.

On Wednesday, Category Four Hurricane Ian made landfall on the Florida mainland. In the last few hours, the hurricane eye had veered just southward of Venice. However, the northern edge of the eye struck Venice and lingered there for a relentless ten hours, subjecting the island to constant buffeting by one-hundred-mile-per-hour winds. Those who stayed told me that they spent their time regretting their intransigence.

Ian wreaked havoc on Venice, blowing down its theatre and the roofs of hundreds of houses. Our house lost its fence, two palm trees, and some siding, about average for our immediate neighborhood. One silver lining of having no swimming pool was that we weren't deprived of our pool cage, an expensive misfortune that befell almost every home nearby. The worst-affected areas were the older mobile home communities and neighborhoods near inland rivers, which had burst their banks.

The hurricane's impact was evident everywhere, with nearly every sign in the shopping areas destroyed by the powerful winds. Those street signs that remained were now misaligned, pointing in unintended directions.

The most devastating damage was concentrated just below the southern edge of the hurricane's eye in Fort Myers Beach. The storm surges had battered the nearby barrier islands, destroying bridges, homes, and roads. The images of the decimated communities were heart-wrenching as were the tragic loss of 149 lives, primarily due to drowning.

I was frankly impressed by the swift emergency response from the state of Florida. Within days, bridges to the outlying islands were reconstructed, emergency kitchens sprang into operation as soon as the storm had passed, and an army of fifty thousand linesmen, who had arrived in the state to restore power, worked tirelessly around the clock.

We returned to Venice on Friday, hopeful that our water and power would soon be restored. In the event, the palm trees in our garden had brought down our power lines. Fortunately, our neighbor Vincenzo graciously allowed us to cadge some electricity from his generator, enabling us to power our devices and fridges.

Over the weekend, almost every householder had diligently cleared their yard of debris, forming towering ten-foot piles along the roadside. Trees had been blown over everywhere, onto roofs, roads, and fences. The town's numerous parks had lost much of their arboretums and most of their squirrels, which had been blown out of the branches in the high winds to be splattered on the sidewalks—an unexpected delight for Dog #2.

Are We There Yet?

Remarkably, Venice authorities had removed almost all of this debris within a week.

By Monday, a linesman had arrived at our house to repair our electricity lines. He lived in Manchester, England, and had been flown over the previous week to deal with the inevitable chaos. He explained to me that this was a yearly routine for him. In the span of a three-month contract here, he would earn a remarkable 150 percent more than he would in a full-time job back in the UK.

Reportedly, 2.7 million people were left without electricity in Florida. Fortunately, most impacted would have their power restored within a week. However, the restoration process was more protracted in the hardest-hit areas, as it entailed rebuilding the entire grid from scratch.

A blitz spirit fell upon the town. Neighbors generously assisted older people, club members worked diligently to restore their facilities, and once electricity was back, local ice cream shops distributed complimentary treats to the community.

Life has a way of unfolding in unexpected ways. If someone had told us several decades ago that we would eventually call Venice our home, it would probably not have surprised us. Venice, Italy, was, at that time, our favorite place in the world. We were drawn to its unparalleled beauty, rich history, artistic treasures, delectable cuisine, enchanting canals, and, of course, the warm embrace of Italians.

However, at that point in our lives, we had never traveled to the United States. Once we did, we also discovered a deep affection for this country. While America, like any place, has its imperfections, we are drawn to the remarkable diversity of its people, the breathtaking beauty of its landscapes, and the rich tapestry of its cultures. Above all, what resonates with us most is America's unwavering spirit of optimism and a profound appreciation for its steadfast commitment to individual freedom.

While our passion for travel remains steadfast, I don't think either of us wants to do it full-time. For one thing, it is hard work to plan and travel simultaneously. I suspect our natural cadence is 'slomading' (slow nomading) for three months at a time. We've already embraced this approach during the last two summers (experiences not covered in this book), and we envision continuing this leisurely exploration of the world.

It felt good to be living in Venice, even if it was not the one we had envisaged all those years ago. Hurricanes notwithstanding, we cherished its 300-plus days of sunshine and the perpetual absence of seasons. While Florida's Venice may not possess the same levels of beauty, history, or artistic treasures as its European progenitor, it does share a common affinity for canals, a similar food palate, and, of course, a vibrant Italian presence.

We thought we would stay a while longer.

Are We There Yet?

Postscript – 2023 Updates

Determining the appropriate cutoff date for data for books with an element of current affairs is always problematic. For the book's main section, I have chosen to use data available to the end of 2022. This brief chapter is intended to offer thematic updates since that time.

January

Given the widespread closure of schools in many US districts and the shift to sparsely attended virtual classrooms during the Covid pandemic, it was unsurprising that standardized test scores for nine-year-olds saw a decline to record low levels. Math scores dropped by 7 percentage points and reading scores by 5.

These figures only account for children registered at schools. An analysis conducted by the Associated Press and Stanford University revealed that nearly a quarter of a million American children were still 'missing' from school rolls, in addition to a similar number who had recently transitioned to homeschooling.

One million fewer college students were enrolled than before the pandemic, as the allure of higher wages in low-skilled jobs drew young adults into the workforce. Community colleges suffered the most, with a 13 percent decline in enrollment. Many of these non-graduates may potentially have made a poor long-term decision, given that Americans with bachelor degrees earn nearly $3 million more in their lifetime compared to those with only high school diplomas.

Venice's duplicate bridge club closed its doors in its fiftieth year.

In 2022, Japan and Italy experienced record-low birth rates, with both countries falling below 800,000 and 400,000 births, respectively, for the first time. In both nations, deaths have been surpassing births for over a decade.

Things could be worse, however. Russia's demographics, which had started to pick up, have cratered again, with a combination of low birth rate, low life expectancy, war, and voluntary emigration. The exact number of Russian casualties in the Ukraine conflict remained disputed, with estimates reaching as high as a quarter of a million soldiers. Nevertheless, this figure was overshadowed by the exodus of one million young, educated Russians who had left the country to avoid conscription. Another estimate suggested that women in Russia now outnumbered men by some ten million, making a future baby boom problematic.

Three years after witnessing similar scenes in Washington DC, supporters of former Brazilian president Jair Bolsonaro stormed the Brazilian parliament and presidential palace.

After evading capture for over three decades, the alleged *Cosa Nostra* boss, Matteo Messina Denaro, was finally apprehended at a private cancer clinic in Palermo. A YouTube video depicts jubilant crowds of Sicilians applauding the Italian police as they took him into custody. In 2002, Messina Denaro was convicted in absentia for multiple murders, including the assassinations of anti-mafia prosecutors Falcone and Borsellino.

February

Italians again elected 86-year-old Silvio Berlusconi to the Italian Senate.

In a frankly bizarre story, the US shot down an alleged Chinese spy balloon in South Carolina. The Chinese claimed it was collecting weather information. This led to the downing of other high-altitude objects over US territory.

The South African Navy's participation in a military exercise in the Indian Ocean alongside Russia and China has raised eyebrows. Elsewhere, Russia declared it was suspending its participation in the START nuclear arms reduction treaty.

Florida's alligators claimed their thirtieth victim since World War II when one of their number killed an 85-year-old woman who was walking her dog. The alligator initially attacked the dog but turned its attention to the dog owner when she intervened. The dog survived.

March

Are We There Yet?

The National People's Congress unanimously re-elected Chinese President Xi Jinping to an unprecedented third term.

Bypassing the parliamentary vote he would not have won, President Macron forced through pension reforms that raised France's retirement age from 62 to 64. Demonstrations throughout France led to daily riots, uncollected garbage, and organized arson. The security concerns resulting from the unrest forced France to cancel King Charles III's planned visit to the country.

The number of prisoners who have died in Rikers Jail in 2022 reached nineteen, marking the highest death count in over a decade. With only four years remaining until the projected closure of the facility and the likelihood that replacement borough jails won't be ready until at least 2029, the new city administration has asked the City Council to reevaluate its plan to close Rikers.

Brazil and China reached an agreement to conduct trade using their respective currencies, bypassing the use of the US dollar as an intermediary currency.

A group of Texas lawmakers introduced a bill allowing their state to secede from the Union. Inevitably, this unapproved bill was nicknamed 'Texit.' This move came after US Representative Marjorie Taylor Greene's previous month's call for a 'national divorce' between red and blue states. Nonetheless, support for breaking up the Union remains minimal among Americans.

April

After successful deployments of modified mosquitos, which led to the suppression of up to 96 percent of harmful mosquito populations, Florida has initiated its third season of *Aedes aegypti* mosquito control. The Federal Environmental Protection Agency has approved releasing two billion Friendly^{TM} mosquitos in Florida and California. Oxitec plans to utilize similar technology to combat mosquito-borne diseases such as malaria, dengue fever, and other diseases worldwide.

India surpassed China to become the country with the largest population.

Pasquale Bonavota, who is alleged to be the head of *Ndrangheta*, was apprehended at Genoa Cathedral. On the run since 2018, he is now awaiting trial as part of the maxi-trial.

Rather than focus on building their own AI industry, the Italian regulator ordered ChatGPT to cease processing Italian data, effectively banning ChatGPT in Italy. Being Italy, it subsequently lifted the ban later in the month.

Joey Chestnut—who had clinched his fifteenth Nathan's Hot Dog Eating championship the previous year (despite a ruptured tendon in his leg)—emerged as the victor in the inaugural World Burrito Eating Championship held in Milwaukee. He devoured 14.5 burritos in just ten minutes.

May

My soccer team, Torquay United, was relegated to the sixth rung of English football.

One of the unintended consequences of Covid restrictions has been a concerning increase in isolation. Some scientists now project that loneliness may ultimately claim more lives than the virus itself. In a health advisory, the US Surgeon General confirmed, "Our epidemic of loneliness and isolation… harmed individual and societal health." The nation's top doctor further stated that isolation has significantly elevated the risk of heart disease, stroke, dementia, and mental health issues.

Naturally, the US is not the first developed country to address this epidemic of isolation, as both the UK and Japan have previously appointed Ministers of Loneliness.

According to the United Nations, the Afghan economy has collapsed, and its citizens are headed for near-universal poverty. Under the essentially unchanged Taliban regime, girls no longer have access to education, women must be covered from head to foot, and half of the population is starving.

Former French President Nicolas Sarkozy lost the appeal against his 2021 corruption conviction. Nevertheless, he can serve his one-year sentence at home while wearing an electronic bracelet instead of going to jail.

Most European countries have struggled to rebuild their military after benefiting from two decades of a peace dividend following the fall of the Berlin Wall. In response to the Russian invasion of Ukraine, Germany announced new military funding of $110 billion. However, over a year later, very little of this *Zeitenwende* budget has been spent. The funding could have been directed toward munitions, where Germany estimates it has only a two-day supply for high-intensity warfare. With most European NATO members (including Germany) still spending less than 2 percent of annual GDP on the military, Russia's Baltic neighbors, Greece, and the

Are We There Yet?

UK are the only European countries meeting their commitments. If President Trump is re-elected and fulfills his promises to end the war in Ukraine within twenty-four hours and leave NATO, European nations could be in a challenging and uncertain position.

Russia and their neighboring satellite state, Belarus, signed an agreement allowing tactical nuclear weapons to be placed on Belarusian territory.

The US avoided hitting the debt ceiling once more, as the Democratic President and the Republican Leader of the House reached a compromise that imposed limitations on future spending. As the saying goes, 'a good compromise is one where both parties are dissatisfied.' Judging from comments on Twitter, this was an exceptional compromise.

On his first day in office, Nigerian President Bola Tinubu made a sudden decision to eliminate government fuel subsidies worth billions of dollars. This abrupt move resulted in an overnight tripling of fuel costs and a significant increase in transport fares. As a result, the perennial miles-long traffic jams in Lagos dissipated, as many Nigerians chose to keep their vehicles off the roads. However, this led to economic challenges, as many workers could no longer afford their daily commute to work. Nigeria's path to superpowerdom will indeed be challenging.

June

Fueled by both Republicans and rival Democrats, rumors about the possibility of octogenarian Joe Biden stepping down as the Democratic presidential candidate in favor of a more dynamic leader continued to gain momentum. Every public appearance by Biden has faced scrutiny from online commentators, who haven't held back on highlighting instances of stumbling over words, navigating stairs, incoherent speech, or moments of confusion on how he should leave the stage. To be candid, these commentators have had no shortage of material to work with.

Silvio Berlusconi, another octogenarian and the third-wealthiest Italian, passed away, leaving behind an estate valued at $6.8 billion. Vladimir Putin described him as a 'dear person,' and Italian Prime Minister Georgia Meloni also offered kind words. Her eulogy might have been particularly generous because Forza Italia, the party he founded and still led, played a pivotal role in securing her majorities in both the Lower House and the Italian Senate.

Concerned about the long-term viability of their newspapers, Canada introduced legislation that compelled tech giants to compensate Canadian news providers for their content usage. In response, both Facebook's parent company, Meta, and Google opted to block all Canadian news content. This move triggered a tit-for-tat response from the Canadian federal government and some provincial governments, which decided to halt their advertising on Meta platforms. Ultimately, the departure of Google and Meta from the news market is expected to result in a significant decline in the readership of Canadian news content. This expectation was reinforced when Canadian politicians criticized Meta for impeding the timely dissemination of information on Canadian wildfires.

Juneteenth was celebrated by 39 percent of private employers (up a third from the previous year).

Meanwhile, the Florida Legislature passed a bill that allowed Manatee County to build a multi-story parking garage in Holmes Beach without the city's approval. Manatee County has announced it will begin construction in early 2024.

Sadly, *le Marché de la Buffa* in Nice has been permanently closed and sold to another company. This new company has pledged to develop senior housing, shops, and a four-star hotel by 2027.

As a result of implementing a shot clock that requires pitchers to throw within fifteen or twenty seconds, professional baseball games have been shortened by thirty minutes.

The Russian Government claimed they had uncovered an operation by American intelligence services in which staff from Russia's largest cyber company, Kaspersky, were sent malware to their iPhones. According to Russia, the American hackers then had access to all the phones' content, including cameras and microphones.

July

Speaking of Apple, it became the first company to reach a market capitalization of $3 trillion, about 50 percent more than the combined capitalization of the largest 100 UK companies.

While we were on an extended vacation in the Middle East, our dedicated Egyptian tour guide proudly shared the official letter confirming that he had recently won the 'green card lottery.' He was one of over half a million Egyptians who applied for the 2023 Diversity Visa, and his odds (1 in 928) paid off. When I asked him why he wished to come to the US, he explained that it was to provide a better life for his children.

On US Independence Day, China announced restrictions on the export of Gallium and Germanium, two metals crucial for manufacturing advanced military and telecommunications equipment. In the previous year, China was responsible for almost all of the world's output of these rare metals.

Indian refineries began making payments to Russia for oil in Chinese yuan instead of US dollars as a tactic to circumvent sanctions against Russia.

Finland and Sweden elected right-of-center governments, adding to the right-wing surge in the Netherlands, Greece, Germany, Spain, Italy, Poland, and Hungary.

August

In 2022, drug overdoses claimed the lives of over 100,000 Americans for the second consecutive year, over double the figure from a decade ago. Two-thirds of these fatalities were attributed to fentanyl, a synthetic opioid fifty times more potent than heroin.

In better news, the poverty rates for African Americans declined again to a new record low, although 17 percent of their number still live in poverty.

New York City Mayor Eric Adams has formally requested federal assistance to manage the unprecedented influx of new immigrants. In a display of protest against the immigration policies of the Biden administration, Republican governors from border states have organized buses to transport recently arrived migrants to northern sanctuary cities that have refused to cooperate with Immigration and Customs Enforcement. With only two-thirds of 2023 gone, 2.8 million illegal immigrants have crossed the US's southern border, more than in the whole of 2022, 1 million more than in 2021, and 2 million more than in 2020.

Meanwhile, rent for the average Manhattan apartment hit a new record of $5,588 per month.

New York City and Broadway have witnessed a triumphant return, with Broadway theaters reporting a doubling of revenue for the 2022-23 season. Nevertheless, one should note that this resurgence remains approximately 15 percent below pre-pandemic levels, reflecting the dip in New York City's tourist numbers for 2022. In contrast, the restaurant industry has seen a slower recovery, with reservations (a proxy for restaurant activity) still lagging one-third behind pre-pandemic levels.

It was a bustling month for lunar exploration. After a hiatus of successful missions beyond Earth's orbit since the fall of the Soviet Union, a Russian rocket unintentionally created a new crater as its Luna 25 mission crashed into the Moon's surface. Twelve days later, India proudly became the fourth country to successfully land a spacecraft on the Moon, with the Chandrayaan-3 executing a more controlled landing near the Moon's South Pole. Meanwhile, Japan postponed the launch of its moon lander due to a series of setbacks. The Moon is set to witness a surge in activity in the coming months, with additional missions in the pipeline from Japan, China, India, and the USA.

China's property crisis deepened, stemming from an oversupply of housing and a declining population. Chinese property prices have continuously declined for many years, and numerous housing developers are struggling to meet their debt obligations. Despite government efforts to bail out developers and lower interest rates, this crisis is expected to continue to exert pressure on the Chinese and global economies for an extended period. Since property constitutes about one-third of the Chinese economy, a prolonged downturn will likely result in economic slowdown, job losses, and financial instability.

Donald Trump faced his seventy-eighth felony charge when he was indicted for criminal conspiracy to unlawfully influence the election result in Georgia by pressuring officials to manipulate the vote count. Trump contends that the case is a politically motivated witch hunt by Democrats aimed at preventing his participation in the next presidential election. As of August 2023, the case is scheduled to be heard in 2024 in the same year as the next presidential election. His legal team is arguing for a delay until after the election and for a transfer to federal court, possibly with the intent of allowing a newly elected President Trump to pardon himself for federal crimes.

Joe Biden's son, Hunter, faced his own legal challenges. The Department of Justice continued investigating the president's son for drug use, tax fraud, and foreign business dealings. Much like Trump, Biden Jr denied any wrongdoing and asserted that he had never leveraged his father's position to advance his business interests.

Following a public ban on full-face veils in 2010, France implemented a new policy prohibiting female school students from wearing the *abaya*, a full-length robe worn by some Muslim women. The education ministry argued that wearing this attire violated secular laws, asserting that teachers should not be able to discern a student's religion merely by their appearance. The ban on the abaya adds to a growing list of other religious symbols also banned at schools, including crosses, headscarves, and kippas.

Are We There Yet?

Yevgeny Pirgozhin, the leader of the Russian mercenary firm Wagner, lost his life when the plane he was traveling in exploded mid-air. His passing followed a 'misunderstanding' in June when the Wagner Group seized the Russian city of Rostov and surrounding areas.

It had been an unlucky couple of years for influential Russians. In Russia, the former Deputy CEO of Gazprombank was found dead, shot in his Moscow apartment with bruises on his body and a bag over his head, alongside his wife and daughter. Previously, the founder of a Russian medical equipment company, MedStom, was also fatally shot twice in the head, along with his wife and two sons. Russian authorities ruled both incidents as murder-suicides.

In Western Europe, within just one month, three Russian oil executives met untimely ends: a former Gazprom vice president was strangled in his London apartment; a former owner of another Russian oil and gas company was found hanged in his Surrey garage; while the former top manager of Novatek was also discovered hanged in his home near Barcelona, with, tragically, his wife and daughter stabbed to death nearby. The police are currently investigating all of these deaths as potential homicides.

It's not only executives with unlucky health episodes. So far in 2023, Russian journalists Vladimir Kara-Murza, Yevgenia Chirikova, Dmitry Subbotin, Vitaly Shishov, Victoria Amelina, and Rostislav Zhuravlev have met untimely deaths in their homes. Rivaling Longboat Key's clear-up rate, I'm pleased to report that foul play has been ruled out in each case.

Russian opposition leader Alexei Navalny was sentenced to an additional nineteen years in prison (on top of his previous fifteen-year sentence), this time on extremism charges. He is currently incarcerated in a maximum-security prison.

Brazil's President, Luiz Inacio Lula da Silva, called for de-dollarization—reducing the US dollar's outsized influence in global trade, reserves, and currency exchange—of BRICS economies. He proposed that transactions between BRICS nations should be conducted in their local currencies. The last decade has seen America successfully defend the US dollar's share of International SWIFT payments (47 percent), the composition of official FX reserves (59 percent), and FX volume transactions (88 percent). However, this may be about to change.

The Bitcoin price has not been kind to Chris and Maddison, whom we met at the beginning of our journey. Assuming they held onto their long position (which, as Bitcoin maximalists, I think they would have), this amiable young couple saw their speculative investment rise by 75 percent in 2021 from the time of our meeting. Unfortunately, the Bitcoin price then plummeted by three-quarters from its all-time high in the subsequent year, leaving them substantially underwater. While Bitcoin has since made a partial recovery, as of the end of August, the value of their holdings remained significantly lower than when we first met.

In his continuing quest to fight misinformation with absurd misinformation, Peter McIndoe, the creator of the 'Birds Aren't Real' movement, announced that he was standing for president. The unproven conspiracy theories from other candidates should allow McIndoe to advance his own agenda.

Ukraine's much-vaunted summer offensive with new Western armaments has not lived up to expectations to date. According to an American think-tank (sic), as of the end of August 2023, Ukraine has taken back just 108 square kilometers of former Ukraine territory—roughly equivalent to 0.1 percent of the total territory occupied by Russia (including Crimea).

A year ago, half the Ukrainians believed that the war would be over within twelve months; now, only one-third think it will be over within a further year. This conflict continues to exhibit all the hallmarks of a long-drawn-out struggle.

It's said that an ill wind blows nobody any good. However, in this case, the share prices of Europe's defense companies have approximately doubled, driven by a 13 percent increase in Europe's defense budgets over the past year, with particular emphasis on the countries bordering Russia, which have significantly boosted their investments.

One-third of my six-person class at a month-long Italian school in Turin was a nun or friar. Fortunately, I had sufficient expertise in Catholic religious orders.

If you have enjoyed the book

Thank you for purchasing *Are We There Yet?* I understand that there are more than fifty million books that you could have picked, but you picked this book and, for that, I am extremely grateful.

All authors need the help of their readers to promote their books to others. I'm no different. If this book has improved the quality of your life in any way, I would be grateful further if you could share your enjoyment via your favorite social media site. Amazon reviews are particularly helpful to new authors.

You can stay in touch by following me on Facebook, Instagram, Twitter, or Amazon. You can also subscribe to my website, www.julian-bishop.com, where I will talk about future books.

Until next time.

Julian Bishop

About the author

Julian Bishop and his family have lived on three continents and traveled to over one hundred countries. For more than a decade, Julian has resided in the United States while continuing to explore the world extensively.

His first travel book, 'High, Wide, and Handsome,' was written to help new immigrants understand the United States better—or to engage others with a keen interest in the country. The second book—'Are We There Yet?'—delves into both America's future and its diverse communities.

Julian's passions span a wide range of eclectic interests, including how history affects culture, the foster care system, tennis, bridge, installation art, cricket, and fatherhood, to name but a few.

Julian Bishop

www.ingramcontent.com/pod-product-compliance
Lightning Source LLC
Chambersburg PA
CBHW071332080526
44587CB00017B/2805